Seeds of Victory

Defeat, Triumph, and the American Way of War

James Ellman

STACKPOLE
BOOKS

Essex, Connecticut
Blue Ridge Summit, Pennsylvania

STACKPOLE BOOKS
The Globe Pequot Publishing Group, Inc.
64 South Main Street
Essex, CT 06426
www.globepequot.com

Distributed by NATIONAL BOOK NETWORK

British Library Cataloguing in Publication Information available

Library of Congress Cataloging-in-Publication Data available

ISBN 978-0-8117-7677-6 (cloth : alk paper)
ISBN 978-0-8117-7678-3 (electronic)

∞™ The paper used in this publication meets the minimum requirements of American National Standard for Information Sciences—Permanence of Paper for Printed Library Materials, ANSI/NISO Z39.48-1992.

To my friend, Christian Wignall:

- Foolish enough to give me my first job in the asset management industry in 1994.
- Compounded that error by putting me in charge of a publicly traded mutual fund one year later.
- Acted as a mentor over the subsequent two decades in which we both managed hedge funds.
- Kind enough to proofread every one of my manuscripts in this, my second career.

Contents

Introduction

Both victory and defeat define the legacy of the U.S. military in equal measure. This may seem paradoxical for a nation that has achieved such triumph on the battlefield. However, a rarely considered feature of the American military experience is the significant list of painful strategic defeats suffered over the last 250 years. However, every time the United States has been beaten in a conflict that represented a crisis for our nation, the armed services have been able to react rapidly, recover, and move on to achieve ultimate victory. In each of these instances, the American people have also rallied behind the war effort and supported it with the treasure of their wealth and the blood of their sons.

Many historians have written that the American way of war has been characterized by utilizing overwhelming firepower and technological advances to destroy the enemy. Others emphasize the importance of our ability to field forces composed of free men committed to the cause of liberty. U.S. victory on the battlefield is certainly due to these factors, but another is the nation's impressive ability to bounce back repeatedly from major defeats and find a way to win. While counterintuitive, suffering significant reverses in war has often sowed the seeds of victory, which allowed the United States to prevail in the conflicts most important to its national interest.

To examine this aspect of our history, this book begins with battles fought on American soil against the British where relatively small opposing forces clashed to control vast areas of this great continent. It then shifts to the much larger and more deadly fratricidal conflict of the Civil War. After passing over an impressively long period of relentless American territorial and industrial expansion, the nation had to find a way to overcome the great challenge of fighting the Axis nations in which massive economies, entire populations, and new deadly technologies clashed. The next chapter follows the battlefield recovery in Korea to push back Mao Zedong's legions and extinguish the flame on a fast-burning fuse which threatened to ignite a global atomic war. A final chapter concerns the conflicts in Vietnam, Afghanistan, and Iraq where battlefield victories have seemingly yielded little but ruined lives, painful withdrawals, and political defeats. A concluding section evaluates lessons learned, and presents a discussion of how the United States can avoid the next defeat but still be ready to recover after a reverse to achieve ultimate victory.

Those hoping to find explanations here that contradict the "great man theory" of history will be disappointed. While each major U.S. battlefield defeat came about due to multiple reasons, poor military leadership turned difficult situations into disasters. The same goes for the U.S. military recoveries that led to victory. Of course, each triumph was the product of factors including the power of America's surging economy, the will of the population to persevere, luck, geography, and even the ravages of disease. However, decisions made by men such as George Washington, Nathanael Greene, Abraham Lincoln, Chester Nimitz, and Matthew Ridgway were primary drivers that led the forces under their command to prevail.

Each chapter in this book discusses a major battlefield reverse followed by eventual military triumph. Utilizing a narrative template that evaluates each defeat, recovery, and ultimate victory makes clear the similarities that help explain why the United States has so often lost in battle, but then been able to win the war:

1. Time and again, American commanders have failed to prepare effectively in advance of a clash of arms. Training was often less rigorous than that conducted by our opponents. The result was an inability to carry out plans with alacrity, unnecessary casualties, and loss of equipment and territory.
2. Military leaders have often succumbed to a mindset that focused on what they hoped an enemy would do rather than what he could do. This unfortunate tendency has cost the U.S. military dearly over the centuries.

3. When a defeat has seriously threatened American strategic interests, the nation has stood behind its fighting men and supplied the armies at the front with both the men and material needed to stabilize the line, and eventually go onto the offensive.

4. In the wake of a major military embarrassment, U.S. leaders have quickly learned not to repeat the mistake of underestimating their opponent. A better appreciation of enemy capabilities has often been a critical first step toward stabilizing a difficult situation and moving to an eventual triumph.

5. Our nation has often embraced Winston Churchill's quote that, "There is only one thing worse than fighting with allies, and that is fighting without them."[1] This doctrine has never been more true than after a defeat. At the very birth of the United States, after losing the new nation's largest cities of New York and Philadelphia, learning to fight side-by-side with the French was instrumental in achieving independence. Later, in the great conflicts of the twentieth century, coordination with the British, Australians, South Koreans, and other military allies was critical to overcoming initial reverses to achieve victory. It is difficult to see how the Cold War could have remained "cold" and eventually been won without a global network of alliances that contained, and eventually broke, the USSR.

6. The United States has often been willing to fire its commanders when necessary to shift the fortunes of war. Of course other nations have shown such a propensity from time to time. But in America, replacement at the top after defeat has been more the norm than the exception since 1776. Only Washington held onto his post after significant battlefield losses, achieved later success, and had his reputation as a wartime leader remain intact in the harsh light of historical scrutiny.

7. Whenever possible, the United States has found a way to achieve quantitative and qualitative advantages over its enemies so as to recover from defeats. This has taken the form of more and better

> manpower, intelligence, equipment, tactics, and technology. While not a prerequisite for victory, gaining such superiority has accelerated American military ascendency.

In addition to considering how these battles played out and why, each chapter evaluates the way history was impacted by our battlefield reverses and eventual victories. While the United States may have won its important wars, that in no way diminishes the influence and dangers of the defeats it suffered. By considering the potential larger disasters had we not been able to recover, the importance of later American military victories are brought into sharper focus.

Today the world appears a more dangerous place for the United States than at any time since the height of the Cold War. This is a paradox, as our military is stronger than ever and financial outlays to defense are in excess of a staggering $800 billion per year. This is well over 3 percent of the GDP of the world's largest economy despite the fact that we are technically not at war.[2] Our alliance system also seems robust with a recently enlarged NATO, and military ties that have been strengthening with dynamic partners along the Asian rim such as Japan, South Korea, the Philippines, Indonesia, Singapore, New Zealand, and Australia.

Yet, clearly all is not well. A geographically contiguous axis of nations run by totalitarian dictators has emerged across the Eurasian landmass, which stretches from the Pacific to the Baltic Sea and the Gulf of Oman. The Democratic People's Republic of Korea (North Korea), the Russian Federation, the People's Republic of China, and the Islamic Republic of Iran increasingly act in concert on the world stage and each is clearly committed to overthrowing democratic rule in at least one nation to which we are allied. Attempts by these states to militarily conquer the Republic of Korea (South Korea), the Republic of China (Taiwan), Ukraine, or the State of Israel could easily embroil the United States in a war that could quickly enlarge from a regional conflict into something much more ominous.

Technology has also been changing at an accelerating rate. For decades we have been repeatedly warned that our major weapons platforms such as the aircraft carrier, the fighter plane, and the main battle tank are threatened with obsolescence due to improving capabilities of inexpensive autonomous weapons that pose asymmetrical threats on the battlefield (for example see books such as *The Future of War*, 1996, *Never Quit the Fight*, 2006, or *Wired for War*, 2009).[3] Nevertheless, we continue to spend vast sums on legacy systems that may no longer be able to survive on the battlefield while our rivals perfect the killing of our allies using cheap drones and missiles to overwhelm traditional defenses.[4]

Is the United States prepared for the next major war? Certainly, our military is actively training to oppose likely threats posed by peer and near-peer rivals. But do we have the right weapons and the industrial base required to wage an extended conflict? Will cyber-attacks cripple our nation's infrastructure on the first day of a conflict? Why are we allowing our sworn enemies to engage in massive propaganda operations to undermine America's will to stand united? After all, each month they transmit millions, if not billions, of posts, emails, and deepfake videos that are delivered to the email inboxes and social media feeds of our citizens? There are no easy answers to these questions. However, by studying how the United States was defeated in the past, lessons can be learned to protect us from repeating earlier mistakes. Similarly, an analysis of previous reactions after a reverse that yielded recovery and ultimate battlefield triumph can provide us with a necessary guide for the resilience the future may demand.

A Note on Sources

A massive amount of scholarship exists regarding America's military history in general and its defeats and victories in particular. Thus, any analysis of more than two centuries of campaigns and battles reviewed in this book will certainly omit sources thought to be of primary importance by individual readers. Conclusions stated in this book rest on a foundation of several types of documents. First there are the writings, letters, and memoirs of the commanders themselves. Citations from the National Archives and other governmental agencies are called out when possible. *The New York Times* and other national news publications are also quoted to back up statements made, especially regarding how Americans perceived events as they were taking place. Secondary sources relied upon include those published by the U.S. Army's Center of Military History in Washington, DC, along with books from well-respected authors who are considered authoritative. When possible, internet addresses are listed in the endnotes to allow readers to quickly verify claims made, or delve deeper if there is interest.

Chapter One

From the Battle of Long Island to the Counterattack at Trenton and Princeton

Background of Defeat

More than a decade of increasing strife between London and its North American colonies burst into armed conflict in Massachusetts in 1775. Arguments over taxation, trade policy, geographic expansion, and local autonomy caused a rift that led many in the thirteen colonies to support independence. Fighting flared between local "Minuteman" militia and British Regulars in an extended fight that stretched between the towns of Lexington and Concord. After a subsequent brutal battle in Charleston, the "Patriots" bottled up the King's forces in Boston in what became a stalemate.

The Second Continental Congress meeting in Philadelphia appointed George Washington the commander of the new Continental Army and he proceeded north to personally oversee the besieging forces in Boston. He had cannons captured in upstate New York transported to Boston and emplaced on Dorchester Heights in early March 1776. From these positions the artillery dominated the city and the British were forced to withdraw. The Siege of Boston came to an end as the Royal Navy transported General William Howe and his forces out to sea. The first campaign of the American Revolutionary War had ended with a victory for the Patriots. However, the fighting soon migrated south to New York where Washington's attempt to hold the city almost cost the new nation its independence. Only a great deal of luck and the incompetence of the

British field commander allowed the newly born United States of America to survive the year.

The British had several military options to consider in the effort to suppress the American rebellion. Some in the Royal Navy wanted to adopt a strategy of blockade that would cripple the American economy and eventually force the Continental Congress to the negotiating table with a minimum of bloodshed. This was deemed unworkable as the coastline of the thirteen colonies was too long for even the world's largest navy to successfully interdict.[1] Some in the British military believed that the best course of action was to engage in a savage war of violence and terror—then known as *Shrecklichkeit* in German—similar to recent wars on the European continent: Towns would have been burned to the ground, the countryside plundered, and civilians ruthlessly attacked by British forces until Patriot will to resist collapsed. Such a strategy was dismissed by Howe who believed it would be counterproductive and only inflame the anger of the local population.[2]

The British commander also dismissed suggestions by his subordinate, General Henry Clinton, that the primary focus should be on the rebels' Continental Army, to pursue it relentlessly and bring it to battle until it was destroyed. Howe also discarded this option in the belief that Washington would not allow himself to be caught on open ground and would simply retreat to the continent's interior where the British could not follow.[3] The strategy Howe decided upon was to (1) seize the city of New York and its environs and use this as a primary base, (2) send contingents west into New Jersey and east to Rhode Island to pacify two additional colonies, and then (3) push up the Hudson to Albany and link up with a second British army moving south from Canada to cut off rebellious New England from the rest of the colonies.[4]

Even before the British ships departed Boston Harbor, Washington had begun to focus on the defense of the city of New York and he had been instructed by senior members of the Continental Congress to do everything possible to hold it.[5] The second largest population center in the colonies with around 25,000 residents, it was arguably the most strategically located. Washington correctly guessed that the British were indeed intent on seizing the area due to its large numbers of Loyalists (also known as "Tories"), its unsurpassed harbor, and location at the entrance to the Hudson River. As the U.S. Army's Center for Military History concluded: "If the British ever had a single strategic objective in the war, it was the Hudson-River-Lake Champlain line. The British believed that by taking and holding this line they would separate New England, considered to be the principal center of the rebellion, from colonies they considered more malleable in the south."[6] Had Howe immediately sailed south from Boston, it is likely that his force of more than 10,000 men would have taken New York quickly. Instead he headed to Canada so as to assemble reinforcements there first.

Washington, a Virginia planter whose previous military record was uneven at best, had been placed in command primarily for political reasons. His position was not only to lead the new Continental Army, but also to rally support from the Southern colonies to assist those in the North, which were in open revolt. He was intelligent, steadfast in his resolution that his side would prevail, and possessed a great deal of courage and perseverance. However, such positives could not entirely make up for his lack of experience commanding large formation of men in battle. Conventions of the day also required him to hold regular "councils of war" before embarking on most major military decisions. He initially placed the trusted General Charles Lee, a professional and veteran soldier, in charge of the defense of New York in January 1776. Lee relayed contradictory conclusions to his commander that, (1) strategically, the city was of such importance that it must not fall into British hands, but at the same time, (2) tactically, it could not be defended as the Royal Navy controlled the waterways in the region.[7]

As Lee pointed out, attempting to hold New York would be perilous for the Patriot army. Any of Washington's troops on Manhattan would find themselves cut off if the enemy were able to seize Harlem and the sole fixed egress point from the island (King's Bridge, the wooden span that stretched across to what is today part of the Bronx). In addition, if the Royal Navy was able to sail up the Hudson River, any Patriot force in New York would be unable to escape by boat, and likely forced to surrender. Even worse, the defenders needed to control the bluffs of Brooklyn Heights. Any artillery placed there would dominate the city of New York, which at the time only covered about a square mile along the southern tip of Manhattan.

The massive advantage the British had in sea power meant that Manhattan (or York Island as it was called at the time) should have been abandoned. However, Washington accepted that New York was too important to give up without a fight. He agreed with Lee that the British could be forced to pay a high price taking the city and reported to John Hancock, president of the Continental Congress, that his plan was to make the enemy, "wade through much blood & Slaughter before they can carry any part of our Works, If they carry 'em at all, and at best be in possession of a melancholy and mournful victory."[8] Throughout the 1776 campaign around New York, Washington and his subordinate generals hoped for a repeat of the June 1775 Battle of Bunker Hill where Patriot militia, defending a prepared position, were able to inflict lopsided casualties on British Regulars who engaged in a determined frontal attack.

Bunker Hill certainly provided a massive boost to the morale of America's Patriots. However, its most important impact may have been on the confidence of General Howe who led the attack in that battle and soon after became Britain's commander of all ground forces in America. Before Bunker Hill, the general's record was that of a dynamic and aggressive leader of men. Afterwards, he was invariably hesitant, chose delay rather than taking decisive action, and focused on seizing territory rather than defeating the Continental Army in the field. Not only did Howe shy away from frontal attacks for the rest of the war, many historians have criticized his subsequent command decisions in 1776–1777. Some, such as George Otto Trevelyan, went even further believing the battle was the point where the general's spirit was broken and his military skills began a rapid decline: "After Howe had succeeded to the supreme command, it [the Battle of Bunker Hill] exercised a permanent and most potent influence on the operations of the war. That joyous confidence, and that eagerness to bring matters to an immediate issue which had been his most valuable military endowments, thenceforward were apt to fail him at the very moment when they were especially wanted. Careless as ever of his personal safety, he was destined to lose more than one opportunity of decisive victory by unwillingness to risk his men's lives and his own fame, against an intrenchment with American riflemen behind it."[9]

While a member of Parliament in London in 1774, Howe had proclaimed that the entire British army could not conquer America.[10] In 1776 he took command of that army and, through his actions, found a way to prove his earlier assertion. While the King and his senior ministers in London deserve their share of the blame for the loss of the American colonies, Howe was the man in charge on the scene across the Atlantic. As will be discussed, he allowed Washington's army to escape defeat and surrender on multiple occasions in the campaign for New York. Howe's choice to march on Philadelphia the following year was instrumental in the Patriot capture of an entire British army at Saratoga—an event that led to France, Spain, and the Netherlands entering the armed conflict and ensuring the eventual independence of the United States of America. One can argue that Howe's generalship was nearly as important to Britain's military defeat as that of George Washington's.

Lee's plan to defend New York, which Washington agreed to implement, was centered on strengthening the defenses of the city by digging in around King's Bridge and constructing fortified artillery bastions to control the area's waterways. These included a set of forts on Brooklyn Heights and Governors Island, another at Horn's Hook (at a narrow point of the East River called the Hell Gate), and two more, which came to be known as Fort Washington (in Harlem) and Fort Lee (in New Jersey), situated across from each other on promontories dominating the Hudson.[11] Old ships were scuttled and other obstructions sunk in an attempt to deny the Royal Navy the ability to sail up either side of Manhattan. Reinforcements streamed into the area until Washington had in excess of 20,000 men to defend New York, which was significantly more than what he had under his command during the Siege of Boston.[12]

Unfortunately, the British also brought reinforcements when they began arriving off Staten Island on July 2. Ships continued to sail into the area until General Howe had more than 30,000 British soldiers and Hessian mercenaries at his disposal as well as a powerful fleet commanded by his brother, Admiral Richard Howe. In addition to overwhelming naval superiority, the larger British ground force was significantly better trained and equipped than the Continentals. While this was taking place, Congress adopted the final draft of the Declaration of Independence on July 4, and Washington read the document in an address to his troops five days later. A formal breach was now in effect between the American colonies and their imperial master.

On July 12, two Royal Navy warships, HMS *Rose* and *Phoenix*, sailed up the Hudson, past the Patriot forts and river obstructions, and arrived undamaged at Tarrytown in what is now Westchester County. At a stroke, the British demonstrated that they could move north of the City of New York, cut off supplies moving toward King's Bridge, and land a force in Harlem to trap Washington's army on Manhattan. The safe course of action for the Patriot commander after this was to abandon New York and place the survival of the Continental Army above that of securing any specific fixed point. Instead he decided to dig in and defend the city as well as Brooklyn Heights. The U.S. Army Center of Military History describes this decision as follows: "He therefore divided his army between the two places—a violation of the principle of mass and the first step toward disaster."[13]

The Defeat

Moving deliberately and carefully, Howe focused on minimizing casualties and seizing territory rather than destroying the Continental Army. The British general identified Brooklyn as his first target, and on August 22 landed 20,000 men on the southwestern tip of Long Island. This force moved inland while about a third of the 10,000 Patriot soldiers on the island sortied from their fortifications to take up positions along a wooded ridgeline that dominated the main north-south roads. Howe's men outnumbered this blocking force by more than six to one and made good use of the numerical advantage. A force under General James Grant launched a diversionary frontal attack to fix the Patriots in place. While the defenders fought resolutely and held their positions, a second British contingent marched around in an arc to the east, executed a wide flanking maneuver, and crumpled the American line. The Battle of Long Island, the largest engagement of the war in terms of

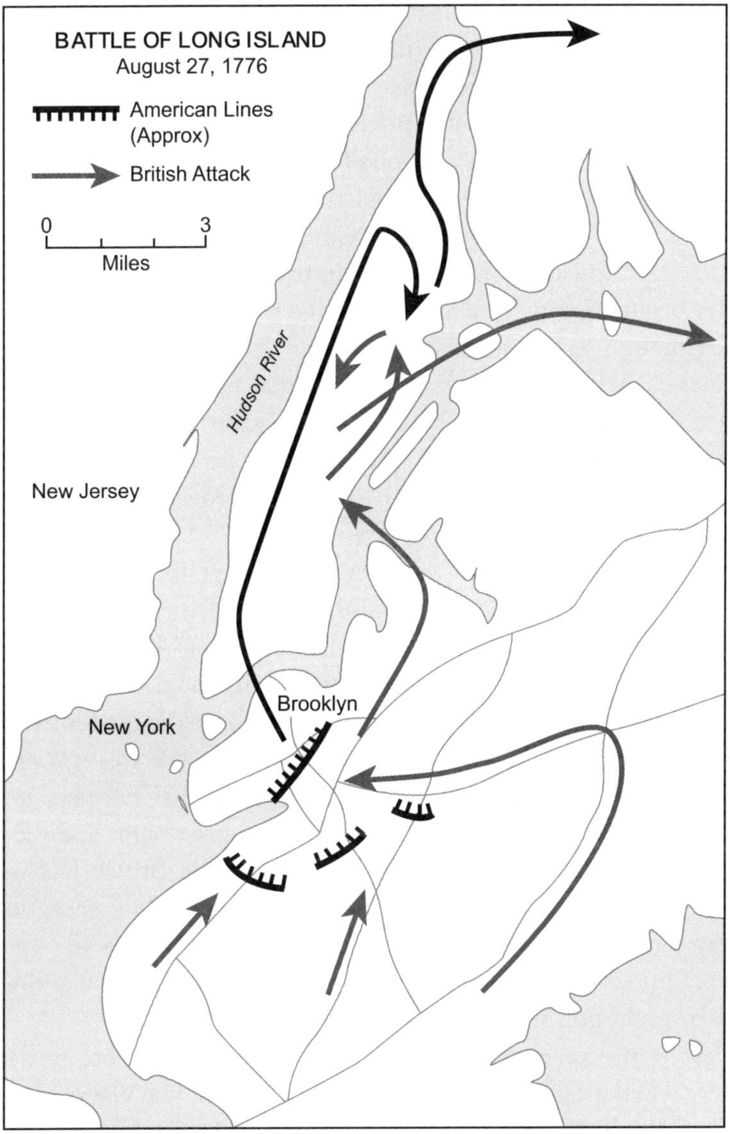

The Battle of Long Island, and Washington's subsequent escape from New York. WIKIPEDIA

total men engaged, degenerated into a rout in which more than 1,000 Patriot soldiers and three generals were killed or captured while Howe's force suffered only a few hundred casualties.

The dejected Americans withdrew into their fortifications along Brooklyn Heights, temporarily saved only by the wind that blew from the north. This precluded the British navy from sailing up the East River and surrounding Washington's force. Even without naval support Howe probably could have stormed the American forts immediately, capturing or killing much of the Continental Army as well as its commander.[14] Luckily for Washington, the wind held and the British infantry began digging trenches to besiege the rebel force. An axiom of military thought is to never reinforce failure, but that is exactly what the Continental Army commander chose to do as he ordered an additional 1,000 men cross from Manhattan to Brooklyn Heights. Those who rowed over included two regiments raised from the coastal seafaring towns north of Boston. Their maritime skills proved to be decisive in the survival of the Patriot force.

A storm then blew into the area, which kept the Royal Navy out of the East River and slowed the efforts of the British infantry as they labored to dig entrenchments toward the defenders' lines. Washington called a council of war that, after significant argument, led to an agreement to withdraw the Continental Army from Brooklyn under the cover of darkness that evening. Every small oared boat in the area was pressed into service and the recently arrived Massachusetts mariners quietly transported the Americans to Manhattan during the night and the fog-shrouded morning of August 30 that followed. The British had won a clear victory and the rebels had been forced to abandon a great deal of artillery and heavy equipment. However, Howe had missed an opportunity to capture Washington along with a large fraction of the Continental Army. It would not be his last.

Despite the near escape, Washington inexplicably chose to defend southern Manhattan with much of his force despite two key vulnerabilities: First, the British now controlled Brooklyn Heights and the artillery that dominated the area. Second, Royal Navy ships had arrived in the western part of Long Island Sound, meaning the British were now in a position to land troops on either side of King's Bridge. Instead of withdrawing safely while that was still an option, Washington relocated to a mansion in Harlem and divided his outnumbered force in an attempt to defend the entire 15-mile length of Manhattan.

Howe's subordinate, General Henry Clinton, urged an immediate advance to cut off the Patriots' northern escape. However, the British commander was hesitant and two weeks elapsed until he finally ordered Clinton to lead a landing of 4,000 men at Kip's Bay about a quarter of the way up Manhattan's east coast. While the operation was successful and American defenders in the area were scattered, Howe insisted on consolidating his position before authorizing a push west to the Hudson. During this pause, the 3,500 Patriot soldiers in the city successfully fled north to Harlem though much of their artillery and equipment was abandoned. While Howe had again outmaneuvered his opponent and captured territory, he missed another chance to inflict a major defeat on the Continental Army.

The next day a portion of both armies clashed in the inconclusive Battle of Harlem Heights in which British scouting troops were forced back by the rebels. Some sharp skirmishes took place over the next few weeks, but it was almost a month until Howe again bestirred himself to try to cut off the Continental Army. Landings took place on October 12 and 15 at Throgs Neck and Pelham Bay in what is now the Bronx. Once again, the British moved too slowly and the Patriots took their opportunity to withdraw, this time to the town of White Plains. In the resulting battle there on October 28, the Americans again showed that they could fight resolutely from prepared lines but British flanking maneuvers forced Washington's men to retreat. Rather than press his advantage, Howe waited two days to move by which time the Continentals had once more retreated under the cover of night. Howe, increasingly irritated by Clinton's recommendations and suggestions to speed up the pursuit, ordered the latter to prepare an amphibious contingent to seize Newport, Rhode Island, as a winter base for the Royal Navy.

The Patriots still held Fort Washington in Harlem Heights as well as Fort Lee across the Hudson in New Jersey. The U.S. commander considered abandoning this last position in Manhattan. However, his subordinate, General Nathanael Greene, argued that the fort was a strategic asset and the post's commander, Colonel Robert Magaw, claimed he could hold the position through a lengthy siege. Washington agreed and the garrison was reinforced in size to 3,000 men. This proved to be a disastrous decision.

When Howe finally attacked Fort Washington on November 16, Royal Navy ships took up positions in the Hudson to prevent any chance of escape. Upwards of 8,000 British and Hessian soldiers pressed home their attacks and overwhelmed the Patriot's outer defenses. Magaw surrendered later that day after only 150 of his men had become casualties. Howe took possession of 2,800 prisoners of war along with great numbers of weapons and supplies. While barely remembered today, this was Washington's largest defeat of the war. It was also arguably the deadliest. More than half of these POWs would die over the next year and a half crammed into miserable, filthy conditions aboard prison ships in New York Harbor, where they succumbed to disease and starvation.[15] A few days later, Howe sent General Charles Cornwallis across the Hudson where his men ascended a narrow path up an unguarded section of the local steep cliffs known as the Palisades. This triggered a hasty and panicked withdrawal of the defenders holding Fort Lee who left behind most of the supplies and cannon stationed at that post as well.

While Howe had failed to take advantage of multiple opportunities to capture the Patriot commander and the bulk of the Continental Army, he had accomplished his declared mission: seizing Manhattan and the region around it while capturing thousands of rebels who the empire hoped would eventually revert to being loyal citizens. Losses among Britain's armed forces employed to achieve these goals were relatively low. Howe's reputation soared and he was knighted and awarded the Order of the Bath by King George III.

Recovery

The Patriot force had lost more than 20 percent of its men in the New York area as well as precious stores of weapons and supplies at a string of abandoned or surrendered fortifications. Washington accepted that his army had been terribly weakened and did not know if the British would next push north, south, or east. He split his remaining forces into three groups with his New Englanders remaining on the east bank of the Hudson to block any enemy move into Connecticut, a contingent holding the high ground farther north on the river to defend Albany, and personally retaining around 3,000 men in New Jersey. Cornwallis waited only one day after the capture of Fort Lee to begin a pursuit of Washington's shrunken command. Clinton urged that his task force be landed along the New Jersey coast so as to cut off the Continental Army's escape. Howe again overruled his subordinate and sent him off to seize Newport.

Outnumbered three to one, Washington began a cold and bitter withdrawal to the south. As the Continental Army pulled back behind one New Jersey river after another, the Revolutionary cause was arguably at its lowest ebb. Participating in the retreat, the ardent Patriot and writer Thomas Paine composed his famous pamphlet, *The American Crisis*. Designed to restore morale, it begins famously, "These are the times that try men's souls: The summer soldier and the sunshine patriot will, in this crisis, shrink from the service of their country; but he that stands it now, deserves the love and thanks of man and woman. Tyranny, like Hell, is not easily conquered; yet we have this consolation with us, that the harder the conflict, the more glorious the triumph."[16]

Washington noticed that the British were also dividing their forces into smaller contingents that could potentially be defeated in detail. Not only had Howe sent Clinton to Newport, but he retained a large force in New York to defend the city and its approaches. Rather than move northwest as many of his officers urged, into the hilly defensible country around Morristown, the Patriot commander chose to march southward, keeping his army between his pursuers and the seat of the Continental Congress in Philadelphia. This extended British supply line and Cornwallis had to shrink his striking force as he was forced to leave garrisons in his rear.

While enlistments for many of his soldiers would soon expire, Washington noted that his force was growing as reinforcements arrived, and other sizeable units were not too many days march away along the Hudson. Also, as he neared Philadelphia, he could hope a large number of Pennsylvania militia would turn out to help him defend that city. As the front moved south, there was a real chance the Patriot forces would soon outnumber their pursuers. In addition, as Cornwallis drew closer, the Congress became increasingly alarmed and took extreme financial measures to secure proper supplies for the Continental Army. It also approved cash bonuses to soldiers whose enlistments were expiring to incent them to remain in the service. Then on December 12, it voted to give up much of its power over the administration of the armed forces and transferred it to Washington for the following six months. At the same time, it granted him the authority to arrest Tories and confiscate their property.[17] Congress then fled Philadelphia and decamped to Baltimore.

Even as Washington retreated with the remains of his bedraggled force, he believed an opportunity would soon offer itself to strike back at the British pursuers. As early as December 1 he wrote to his subordinate General Lee, "The advantages they have gained over us in the past have made them so proud and sure of success that they are determined to go to Philadelphia this winter. I have positive information that this is a fact and because the term of service of the light troops of Jersey and Maryland are ended they anticipate the weakness of our army. Should they now really risk this undertaking then there is a great probability that they will pay dearly for it for I shall continue to retreat before them so as to lull them into security."[18]

The retreating Revolutionaries crossed the Delaware River at Trenton and took up positions on the Pennsylvania side. Howe arrived at the front and decided to suspend the advance and postpone taking Philadelphia until 1777. With snow falling and temperatures dropping, it was time to settle down into winter quarters. Cornwallis's army was broken down into several garrison units stretching across New Jersey from Brunswick (now New Brunswick) to the town of Trenton on the Delaware. Ending operations in the field for the season was a customary practice among European warring parties in the eighteenth century. However, the British colonists' genocidal wars against the American Indians were not conducted in such a manner, and they had become accustomed to fighting throughout the colder months of the year. In addition, the Patriot commander believed the Revolutionary cause needed a victory or it was doomed. As historian John Ferling explained:

While Howe may have been ready to suspend the fight for the next several months, Washington was not. A proud man, he had chafed miserably under his string of defeats. He thought a retreat—any retreat—was mortifying. As a young soldier in Virginia, he had craved being on the offensive. Now, more than ever, he burned with desire to lash out at an enemy that had acutely humiliated him and brought him to the threshold of ruin. But more than revenge gnawed at him. Washington knew that the war, and American independence, hung in the balance. Flagging spirits must be revivified. Recruitment of another army for 1777 was likely to be linked indissolubly to achieving some immediate success.[19]

Victory

Washington's force along the south bank of the Delaware surged in size in late December 1776. While General Lee was captured by the British, his brigades arrived safely at the commander-in-chief's encampment on December 20. Two days later, General Horatio Gates also arrived with a sizable contingent from northern New York. These reinforcements brought the total number of Continentals to more than 6,000 men who were supported by significant numbers of local militia. On December 22, Washington held a council of war in which it was agreed that an attack would be staged at first light on December 26 against the 1,500 Hessian soldiers stationed in Trenton.

The plan was daring: Three contingents would strike across the ice-choked Delaware River during the long winter night at different points and then converge on Trenton at daybreak. The main strike force of 2,400 Continentals under Washington would cross at McConkey's Tavern 10 miles to the north and then march on Trenton. Eighteen hundred Continentals and militia under General John Cadwalader would land 12 miles south of the town to block any movement north from the garrison posted at Bordentown. Finally, a smaller force of militia was to row to the east bank across from Trenton and take up a blocking position to stop any Hessians' attempt at escape.

Colonel Johann Rall in command of his 1,500 Germanic troops was a seasoned professional, had a poor opinion of the bedraggled American rebels, and did not expect a major attack so late in the season. However, realizing that he was outnumbered in the region, Rall sent a request for reinforcements that was turned down by his superiors. His men also suffered from what is today called "alert fatigue" as New Jersey militia regularly harried the garrison's dispatch riders and cavalry reconnaissance in what were effectively anti-patrol operations. Most importantly, Trenton had no walls or major defensive fortification and Rall ignored recommendations to build them.

Christmas Night was cold and a storm of sleet and snow descended on the area. The weather hindered operations by both sides. It slowed down Washington's crossing north of Trenton and his other two detachments failed to even attempt to get to the other side of the Delaware. However, the storm also kept the Hessians from sending out patrols. Washington's 2,400 men pushed ahead through the snow and did not reach Trenton until well after sunrise. However, the attack still achieved almost complete surprise. The Hessians were quickly driven back in disarray and Rall was killed in the fighting.

In a sharp battle that lasted less than an hour, 400 of the mercenaries were able to flee, but the remainder, almost 1,000 in total, surrendered along with all their arms and equipment. Over the next few hours, Washington withdrew his force, prisoners, and booty back to the other side of the Delaware.

While a small engagement compared to many in the conflict, the Battle of Trenton had a dramatic impact on the American Revolution. The rebels had proven that they were far from a spent miliary force and that they could defeat professional Hessian mercenaries in battle. Multi-year enlistments to the Continental Army increased, and morale among the Patriot cause surged. Washington's reputation also rose after what had been a string of defeats stretching back several months.

However, the Patriot commander-in-chief was not yet done fighting for the season as he gathered together his 6,000 men and again crossed the Delaware to confront Cornwallis who was marching south. Washington had his men dig in along the south bank of Assunpink Creek, which flows generally southwest through New Jersey before emptying into the Delaware River at Trenton. Skirmishers were then sent northward under

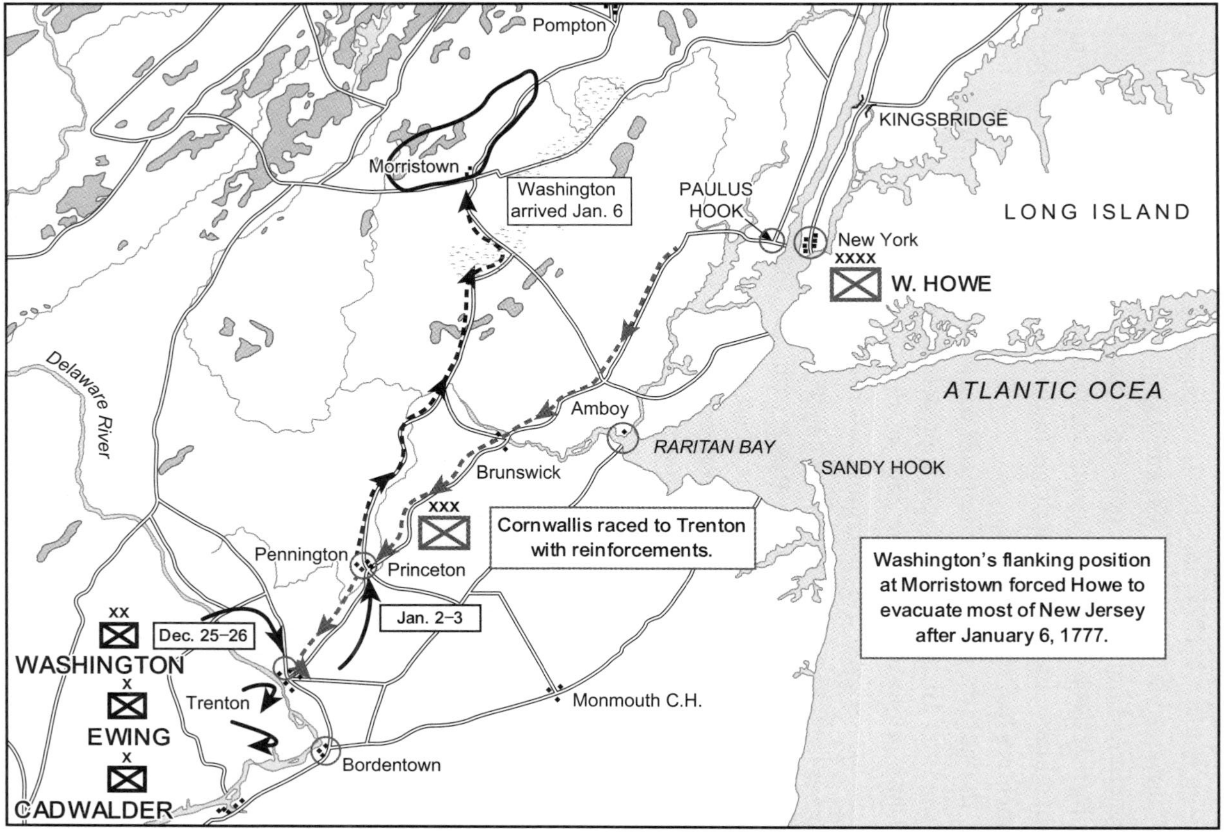

The Long Retreat to the Delaware, and Washington's counteroffensive. UNITED STATES MILITARY ACADEMY

Colonel Edward Hand toward the British base at Princeton. Leaving a garrison at that town, Cornwallis headed south with more than 5,000 men on January 2, 1777, and almost immediately came under fire. Fighting "Indian style" and taking just a few shots from behind trees and walls before retreating to the next position, Hand's men significantly delayed the British force. Again and again, Cornwallis's columns formed up into a firing line to break the Americans to their front, only to find that their tormentors had melted away.

The sun was nearing the horizon when the British vanguard finally finished the 10-mile march and approached Trenton. The temperature had been above freezing for days so that the roads were generally a morass of mud, and the Assunpink was running fast with snowmelt and only fordable in a few places. Eager to avenge the recent defeat, Cornwallis decided to immediately attack with the troops he had at hand. Hessians, supported by field guns, charged across the sole stone bridge over the creek, which was the strongest point of the Patriot battle line. This was exactly what Washington had hoped for and his artillery and massed musketry drove back the attackers. Additional attempts by British Redcoats met with the same fate and darkness halted the fighting except for some desultory artillery exchanges.

The Battle of Assunpink Creek, also known as the Second Battle of Trenton, was a triumph for Washington. He had used his men brilliantly and played to their strengths: Many had fought against the Indians in the past and were more used to fighting from cover than in tight formations on an open field. As at Lexington to Concord at the start of the war, such tactics against the slow-moving columns of the British could inflict unbalanced casualties on the enemy. In more formal battles, the Continentals tended to fight with greater resolution when confronting the King's soldiers from behind entrenchments no matter how hastily constructed. As at Bunker Hill and White Plains, the Patriots held their fortified lines against determined British attacks. Exact casualty figures for the day are uncertain due to the running nature of the fight from Princeton to Trenton with its crescendo at sunset. However, losses on the British side may have been greater than 400 compared to only around 100 for the Americans.[20]

Cornwallis wished to continue the battle but postponed his attack to daybreak despite warnings that the Patriots might retreat before then. However, the British general had little choice as battlefield communications in the eighteenth century were little different from those of two thousand years before, and night attacks often became undisciplined affairs. Attempting to storm across the fast-flowing creek full of snowmelt in the dark could have resulted in a disaster. In addition, his men were tired after an entire day of marching and fighting. Cornwallis hoped that Washington would stay and fight and reportedly boasted: "We've got the old fox safe now. We'll go over and bag him in the morning."[21] Of course, the American general had no intention of remaining in place to be "bagged." In a council of war, the Patriots chose the aggressive option of an immediate forced march to attack the garrison at Princeton. Soon after midnight, the bulk of the Continentals were on the move, utilizing the little-traveled Quaker Bridge Road, which wound northeast around the left flank of Cornwallis's forces.

While the bulk of Washington's army marched through the night, a small contingent was left behind with a few cannon to keep large fires burning, make entrenching noises with picks and shovels, and continue firing the occasional shell at the British encampment. As dawn approached, these men abandoned the front lines, and at daybreak the British found only an empty camp on the south bank of the Assunpink.

Washington's forces were unable to achieve complete surprise approaching Princeton, as the Patriot columns encountered Lieutenant Colonel Mawhood with two British regiments marching south from the town to join Cornwallis. In a running, confused battle, the Patriots pushed the defenders out of Princeton and captured a couple hundred prisoners along with significant weaponry and wagons full of supplies. Casualties were similarly uneven to those of the prior day and again represented a victory for Washington.

Meanwhile, alerted by the sound of cannon fire from the north, Cornwallis assembled his army and began the march back up the road to Princeton. With the British main force approaching, and his men exhausted from their night march, Washington chose to withdraw. The

Americans retreated to the northwest into the defensible hill country around Morristown where they settled down into winter quarters.

In little more than a week the Patriot cause had recovered from near utter defeat to electrifying victory. In three consecutive engagements Washington successfully used surprise, maneuver, and concentration of force to inflict dramatically lopsided casualties on the professional soldiers of the British military. Desperately needed weapons and supplies also fell into Washington's hands. Those in favor of independence were heartened while Britain's enemies across the Atlantic, especially the French, watched events unfold and prepared to enter the conflict.

Causes of Defeat

Washington suffered five major defeats in the second half of 1776 in which the British drove him from New York at the Battles of Long Island, Kip's Bay, White Plains, Fort Washington, and Fort Lee. In each case he overestimated the capabilities of his force and underestimated those of the British. The American Patriots enjoyed a righteous belief in their cause, but almost none of them were professional soldiers. In an era when many land battles were determined by the rapidity a formation of men could reload and fire their muskets in unison, training trumped morale. In addition, the British enjoyed a significant advantage in number of cannon and skilled artillerymen to use them. Washington should have concluded before the campaign began that he had to do everything possible to avoid pitched battle against the combined might of General Howe's army except when able to defend prepared positions where his flanks were secure and there existed a plausible line of retreat.

In addition, and perhaps even more important, the rebels had almost no warships and were up against the world's strongest navy. Defending the city of New York on the southern tip of a long, thin island surrounded by navigable waterways was folly when confronted with the overwhelming number of ships the British anchored off Staten Island in the summer of 1776. Any force Washington exposed on Manhattan or Long Island would effectively be positioned in a salient, which could be surrounded and then forced to surrender or destroyed. Only fortuitous weather and an unimaginative, fearful British commander would allow such forward-deployed Patriot contingents to retreat in good order.

Thus, Washington was living dangerously when he divided his army in the face of a much more numerous foe and tried to defend New York after the British demonstrated their ability to sail up the Hudson and cut off his escape route. Nevertheless, the American general gambled that rather than seize the narrow northern stem of the Manhattan geographic bottle in Harlem, Howe would choose to land his men in Brooklyn. There they could be tempted to attack prepared positions in a replay of the Battle of Bunker Hill from the previous year. Luckily for the cause of American liberty, the British came ashore on Long Island rather than Manhattan. In the resulting battle, Howe refused to engage in a bloody direct advance. Instead he took advantage of his greater numbers to overlap the end of the Patriot lines and took advantage of poor generalship by the rebels who had failed to guard their left flank.

After the miraculous escape of Washington and his men from Brooklyn Heights, the U.S. commander still seemed unwilling to accept that British control of the sea and a superior ground force made holding the island of Manhattan untenable. It was only Howe's indecisiveness that allowed much of the Continental Army to slip away once again after the landing at Kips Bay two weeks later. Then, entrenched across Harlem Heights and in what is now the Bronx, Washington yet again was exposed to an amphibious landing in his rear, which could have led to his army becoming surrounded and destroyed. Luckily, the British commander continued his plodding pace of operations and did not order such a landing until late October. After retreating farther north, Washington had his men dig in along a line of hills hoping again that the British would attack him at his strongest point. In the subsequent Battle of White Plains the Americans fought well for a time against a determined attack, but Howe made good use of his numbers and superior artillery and rolled up Washington's flank (this time on the right) forcing a general retreat.

The British pursuit was again dilatory and the Continental Army was able to make its escape. After Howe marched south toward Fort Washington, the American commander considered abandoning that post, but eventually chose not to as he was again overconfident in his Patriots' ability to fight well on the defensive. In the short battle that followed, the garrison surrendered, handing Washington his greatest defeat of the war. Rather than accept that British naval supremacy meant that Fort Lee was now in imminent danger, he failed to order that bastion be abandoned in an orderly manner. The result was that the garrison was forced to flee, leaving behind much of its supplies and heavy weaponry.

The similarities in these defeats are clear: Washington was willing to bet that the British would do what he hoped they would do rather than what they obviously could do by utilizing their command of the sea and more numerous and professionally trained ground forces. The Patriot general was repeatedly forced to execute hasty retreats in reaction to enemy movements—twice due to amphibious landings in his rear, and twice due to Howe's forces turning his flank and collapsing his defensive line. As the rebels fled, they invariably suffered greater casualties and abandoned critical supplies, equipment, and weaponry.

In addition to ignoring British capabilities, Washington failed to focus on what was most important in an insurrection against a stronger opponent: the necessity of maintaining a viable military force in the field rather than holding any individual physical location. While the loss of New York (or Philadelphia) would represent a painful setback for the Revolutionary cause, no individual city represented the center of gravity of the insurrection against King George III. The farther from a major port Washington fought the British, the better the chance he would win engagements or at least extract the bulk of his army from disaster. While Congress may have emphasized the importance of holding New York, it had not provided its armed forces with the means of holding that city. As General Lee pointed out well before the campaign began, "it is so encircle'd with deep navigable water, that whoever commands the Sea must command the Town."[22] With no navy of size, the Patriots could not hold the city of New York. Washington could have embarked on a similar strategy to the one that led to success in Boston: cede the port to the British, entrench defendable positions from which retreat was possible, and hope to draw the enemy into an attack by contingents on which outsized losses could be inflicted.

In contrast to the loss of New York, had the Continental Army and its top commanders been surrounded and forced to surrender, it is much more likely that Patriot morale would have plummeted, and Britain's rivals, France, Spain, and the Netherlands, would have stayed out of the conflict. In other words, when Washington saw the size of the military force that sailed into New York Harbor in 1776, he should have focused on the fact that he was engaged in a long war against a more powerful foe. His primary task was to ensure that his army avoided large, decisive battles where he would be at a disadvantage, and instead strike against smaller detachments of the enemy when given the opportunity to achieve victories that were as much political as military in nature. The longer the Patriot cause could demonstrate to the world that it was actively opposing Britain's might, the better the chance London's enemies would enter the fight. It was always unlikely that the Patriots could have thrown off British rule on their own. Leaders in Congress understood this and knew their cause was dramatically more likely to succeed if they received the support of major European continental powers.

In retrospect, what is miraculous is not that Washington was repeatedly defeated, but that the bulk of the Continental Army was not surrounded and forced to surrender. Only in the assault on Fort Washington did the British truly make full use of their military advantages: Admiral Howe's naval forces cut off any chance of retreat in that battle, and General Howe's overwhelming manpower pressed home a concerted attack to effect a complete victory. Had such tactics been utilized in Brooklyn or Manhattan, the American Revolution could have ended in defeat in 1776.

Causes of Victory

After the fall of Fort Lee, Washington retreated into New Jersey. While he certainly made many mistakes from August to November, he deserved credit for finding a way (often by the thinnest of margins) to successfully maintain his army in the field and remain one step ahead of his opponent. His men were also learning their grim craft and continued to show bravery and an ability to go toe-to-toe with the British on the battlefield when fighting from prepared positions. This tenacity showed itself in the fighting in both Brooklyn and White Plains. As

Cornwallis pursued him, Washington began to formulate the tactics that would allow his side to win the Revolutionary War and ensure his nation's independence. Many have described this as a "Fabian strategy" after the Roman general of that name who successfully harassed and wore down Hannibal's army while refusing pitched battles in southern Italy during the Second Punic War (218–201 BC).

While dividing one's force in the face of a superior enemy is a dangerous choice in a conventional war, Washington realized there were times it played to the Patriots' advantages in the insurgency they were fighting against the British. By splitting his army into separate contingents, the enemy was forced to do the same to ensure control of territories recently recaptured. When pursued, Washington retreated away from the coast, which resulted in the British having to maintain a longer supply line protected by garrisons at key posts. As the Patriots fell back, they marched into regions where friendly militia forces rallied to the flag while others harassed the British rear. The farther he retreated, the closer Washington's force approached parity in numbers with his pursuers.

While colonial militia had little chance of prevailing in a prolonged battle on level ground, retreating also allowed the Patriots to engage in tactics in which they excelled. For more than a century, the colonists had been engaged in intermittent war against the Indigenous peoples of the continent. This fighting looked very different from the set-piece battles common in Europe in that era. Instead, small, light contingents fired from behind trees, fences, or stone walls and then fell back after inflicting casualties on a stronger opponent. While no such attack of this kind could defeat a large and professional armed force, each one served to wear down the British as men were killed, others were wounded who needed to be cared for, and battle fatigue increased.

Another American weakness in having limited supplies and artillery was turned into a strength as the lighter rebel columns generally moved faster than those of the British. This allowed Washington to order dispersed contingents under subordinate commanders Lee and Gates to engage in forced marches and concentrate on his position along the Delaware to gain a temporary relative manpower advantage versus

Cornwallis. When the Patriot army took up positions behind that river, Howe arrived on the scene and decided to give up the chase and settle into winter quarters.

This was Washington's moment to attack. He targeted the garrison at Trenton and risked his army in a night operation. While only his main force made it across the Delaware, Washington still achieved surprise and numerical superiority in the battle that followed. As previously mentioned, while the victory was relatively small in terms of the total of General Howe's opposing force, the American success had an outsized positive political impact on the outcome of the Patriot cause and provided Washington's force with sorely needed supplies and cannon.

Refusing to defend urban coastal areas and retreating also gave the American general more options in the selection of the ground on which he would fight. Defending prepared positions offered the Continental Army the greatest chance of victory in a pitched battle against the professional Redcoats and their Hessian mercenaries. Earlier in 1776, in Brooklyn and White Plains, Washington's men were well sited on ridgelines and hills dominating the enemy approach, but on both occasions the British prevailed when they were able to turn one of the American flanks. In contrast, at the end of that year, assembling along the far bank of the major obstacle of the Delaware River, any attack staged by Cornwallis would have placed the leading elements of his army at risk as contingents rowed into a potential ambush by the waiting rebels.

Then in early 1777, after the Battle of Trenton, Washington crossed back to the east bank of the Delaware and sent skirmishers north to Princeton to harry Cornwallis as he approached. The resulting "Indian tactics" utilized by the Patriots inflicted casualties, wore down the British, and, most importantly, delayed their arrival in Trenton until the end of the day. Washington had formed up his army behind the fast-running Assunpink Creek where he was able to concentrate his force in front of the only obvious crossing points. His right was protected by unfordable sections of the creek and his left flank was anchored along the Delaware. Cornwallis took the bait and attacked, resulting in a battle in which his forces suffered unequal losses.

Finally, Washington made use of the Americans' less encumbered force and better knowledge of the local terrain. In a forced night march, his army arrived at Princeton before Cornwallis and his army had even had a chance to break camp the next morning. Again, as at Trenton, the American commander was able to concentrate force to attack a smaller garrison of the British, inflict uneven casualties, and capture weapons and supplies. He then fled northwest into more defendable territory to wait out the winter.

In less than a week of fighting, Washington demonstrated the integrated tactics that could be used to defeat the stronger professional British forces:

1. refuse to defend coastal port areas dominated by the Royal Navy,
2. separate into disparate contingents while utilizing mobility to retreat into the interior so as to accumulate local militia strength and extend British supply lines that needed to be defended,
3. employ guerrilla hit-and-run tactics to wear down the enemy,
4. choose defendable positions where flanks were secure and retreat was possible, and
5. whenever possible, attack smaller British outposts with overwhelming force so as to secure victories that had not only important military but also political benefits.

Similar tactics were utilized with great success later in 1777 in upstate New York when multiple Patriot contingents initially retreated in the face of a determined southern thrust by a British army under General John Burgoyne before making a stand near the town of Saratoga. In a series of battles, the Americans employed Indian tactics to wear down the British before taking up a blocking position on Bemis Heights where General Horatio Gates's line was anchored on the right by the Hudson River and on the left by strong entrenchments. The subsequent surrender of Burgoyne and his entire army was a turning point in the conflict that brought the French into the war and ended any attempt by the British to cut off New England from the rest of the American states.

As will be explored in the next chapter, as the fighting wore on and moved to the south, Patriot generals slipped back into making the same errors committed by Washington in the summer of 1776. However, when the suite of tactics used with such success at Trenton and Princeton were once again employed, they paved the way to eventual victory for the new United States.

Impact of Defeat

Washington's setbacks in the second half of 1776 had major reverberations. Many today believe that the United States was destined to win its independence in the Revolutionary War. However, the success of the revolt of the American colonies was not preordained. Certainly, the defeats in New York extended the war and made winning independence for the United States that much more difficult.

The morale of Loyalist Americans and that of the British army was mightily lifted by the victories on Long Island, Kip's Bay, White Plains, and Fort Washington. In contrast, for those favoring independence, as Thomas Paine wrote of the result of the campaign around New York, "these are the times that try men's souls." While Washington, his chief subordinates, and the Continental Congress wished to defend New York in 1776, the chances of doing so successfully were very small due to the overwhelming strength of the British expeditionary force that arrived in the area that summer. Even defending posts on Manhattan and Long Island and hoping to exact outsized casualties on Howe's army was unlikely and could have easily led to disaster with rebel forces surrounded, defeated, and forced to capitulate.

While a painful decision, the correct military choice for Washington would have been to abandon the city and hope to lure the British into a battle on unequal terms on the mainland of the continent. Such an ignominious retreat would have been viewed as a setback to the Revolutionary cause, but it would have represented a lesser one than what historically took place: a string of defeats, wholesale abandonment of precious cannon and supplies, along with thousands of rebels surrendering and marched off to slow deaths by starvation and disease.

Had Washington accepted that his position was untenable and pulled out of New York after the British navy forced its way up the Hudson to Tarrytown, he could have chosen a time and place to fight. Consider just one counterfactual example for a few paragraphs: Had the American commander retreated and transferred his artillery from Brooklyn Heights and Manhattan to Fort Lee, such a concentration of firepower acting as an impediment to navigation along the Hudson would have surely required Howe's attention. The commanding heights of the Palisades on the New Jersey side of the river would have made any British landing there in the face of serious opposition improbable. Thus, Howe most likely would have landed much of his army to the south near Jersey City and moved north.

As the British marched toward Fort Lee, they would have been funneled for several miles between the Hudson to the east and the marshes and wetlands of the Hackensack River to the west. This would have represented an excellent opportunity for Patriot light forces to engage from cover and inflict casualties before retreating in stages. From Washington's other battles, it is extremely likely that he would have anchored his lines on the wide Overpeck Creek in the west to Fort Lee on the high ground along the Hudson in the east. American cannon from the fort would have dominated the field. With no obvious way to outflank the defender's lines would Howe have ordered a frontal attack along the flatter land along the Overpeck? Would the British then have suffered terrible losses or been thrown back in the attempt? We will never know, but the results of such a Battle of Fort Lee likely would have been far better for the Continental Army than the historical clashes that took place in Brooklyn, Kip's Bay, and Fort Washington.

Even in the best of circumstances, it is difficult to see how Washington could have held New York in 1776. However, a better showing by the American army, which pulled back and then stoutly held its ground north, east, and west of the city, and inflicted serious casualties on Howe's force, could have had a major impact on history. Such a scenario could have easily led to an earlier French intervention, an acceptance in London that an attempt to crush the rebels would fail, and a faster resolution of the Revolutionary War.

However, Washington did not withdraw from the area and it is surprising that his defeats were not worse than what took place in the historical record. Consider Washington being captured in Brooklyn Heights along with several thousand of his men when a favorable wind allowed the Royal Navy to sail up the East River cutting off the Americans' chance of escape? Or imagine the results if the tall Virginian general, representing an obvious target, had been shot off his horse when he rode within a hundred yards of the rapidly advancing British after their landing at Kip's Bay? The campaign for New York offered the British several opportunities to capture or kill the American commander as well as force the surrender of a large portion of the Continental Army. After such a defeat and the removal of Washington from the field, would the rebellion against King George III have fizzled in the face of historic offers of clemency? We will never know for sure, but many respected historians certainly believe this to be the case.[23] Certainly prominent contemporary leaders of the Patriot cause considered Washington to be the "indispensable man" of the Revolution. The Marquis de Lafayette wrote to the Continental Army's commander in 1777 that, "if you were lost for America, there is no Body who Could keep the army and the Revolution for Six months."[24]

Impact of Victory

If avoiding capture or death represented an accomplishment for Washington, it certainly was not enough to sustain the Revolutionary cause. By the end of 1776, the Continental Army had shrunk considerably due to casualties suffered in the field, desertion from flagging morale, and expiring enlistments. By the end of their retreat, the Patriot soldiers along the Delaware were hungry, poorly armed, irregularly paid, underdressed, and often without shoes. In contrast, the British were everywhere ascendent on the battlefield, well supplied and confident in snuffing out the rebellion. Many Patriot leaders, Washington included, harbored reasonable concern that the cause of American independence would soon collapse.

As already discussed, Washington's counteroffensive was brilliantly executed but was a risky endeavor. There were many obvious ways it could have gone terribly wrong: The night crossing of the Delaware and the subsequent forced march on Trenton could have been disrupted by a snowstorm that became fiercer than it was historically. The Hessians could have been better prepared or Colonel Rall could have listened to advice and fortified the town in advance. When Cornwallis marched south days later, colder weather could have made the Assunpink fordable along most of its length allowing the British to push south and pen the Patriots in along the Delaware River where they might have been forced to surrender. Or, more aggressive patrols sent out by Cornwallis that night might have discovered that the Americans had broken camp and were marching north toward Princeton. Had the British general acted quickly, Washington might have been trapped between Colonel Mawhood to his north and the main British contingent attacking his rear.

Also the lack of a counteroffensive would have had a massive impact on history. Consider if Washington, instead of attacking Trenton, had settled into winter quarters on the Pennsylvania side of the Delaware River at the end of 1776. Certainly in this counterfactual, the Revolutionary cause, if it did not wither away entirely, would have entered 1777 in a much weaker state and the British in a stronger one. Patriot enlistments rose significantly on the back of the victories at Trenton and Princeton and weapons captured in those battles were put in the hands of new recruits. Washington's reputation, and that of his army, were both enhanced by these victories and this change certainly aided Congress's agents in France in their efforts to recruit professional soldiers from across Europe. Those who boarded ships in 1777 to join the Revolutionary cause included, but were not limited to, the Marquis de Lafayette, Casimir Pulaski, and Friedrich Wilhelm von Steuben. The flow of military supplies and financial assistance from France to the new United States also increased.

As with all counterfactual questions, we can never know for sure if the cause of American independence in the eighteenth century would have failed in the absence of Washington's successful counteroffensive in New Jersey. However, many at the time, as well as historians today, believe that the events around Trenton and Princeton directly saved the Revolutionary cause. How important was such a turn of history? Consider the following:

An absence of Washington's counteroffensive (or a failed one) would have led to a weaker response to both the British invasion from Canada and the move to capture Philadelphia in 1777. Had Burgoyne been able to make it to Albany and Howe encountered less resistance as he moved into Pennsylvania, the French (along with the Spanish and the Dutch) might have stayed out of the conflict. The subjugation of the nation's capital and control of the Hudson River–Lake George–Lake Champlain line would have split the United States in two with New England cut off. In such a scenario the rebellion likely would have been doomed.

The impact on the course of the nineteenth and twentieth centuries of such a scenario would have been dramatic. No French intervention in the American Revolution means no build-up of French debt and, thus, no French Revolution (at least not as it took place). Would an obscure Corsican military officer have come to dominate much of Europe in such a world? How much faster would the economy of a British North America have developed if slavery had been abolished there along with the rest of the empire in 1834? No American Civil War would have spared more than 600,000 young men from an early death and another million from often debilitating wounds.

Consider all of North America being either a crown colony or a self-governing Dominion of the British Empire in 1914. Why would men from New York, Virginia, California, and Texas not have rallied to London's side at the start of the First World War as did those from Canada, South Africa, Australia, and New Zealand? Would Germany have even taken the chance to go to war under such circumstances? And if it had, would the Kaiser's armies and those of Austria-Hungary have been crushed more quickly by such a strengthened British military allied with that of France, Russia, and Japan?

While it is merely conjecture to imagine repercussions in the twentieth century of the failure of an American rebellion in the late eighteenth, it is clear that the impact would have been dramatic and could have changed the path of world history in ways few of us can fully appreciate today. What can be said with assurance is that Washington's successful recovery from his initial defeats in 1776 to stage a miraculous counterattack at the end of the year had a major impact on world history.

Chapter Two

The Fall of Savannah and Charles Town to the Battle of Guilford Courthouse[1]

Background of Defeat

After failing to snuff out the rebellion in America in 1776 by capturing or killing the leaders and the mass of the Continental Army around New York, the British had a second excellent opportunity to achieve a smashing victory in 1777. The plan was to cut off New England from the rest of the thirteen colonies. General John Burgoyne, commanding the main British army in Canada, was to lead his men southward down Lake Champlain in late June. He hoped that within a few months he would link up around Albany with General Howe's separate command moving up the Hudson from the city of New York. A final smaller column led by General Barry St. Leger would also march on Albany after proceeding south from Ontario and then east along the Mohawk River Valley.

Such a multipronged attack would not only cut the new United States of America in two, but also force General Washington to give battle to protect this from taking place. The pincer movement of the British ground and naval forces from New York and Burgoyne's army supported by large numbers of American Indian allies represented a dramatically greater strength than what the Continental Congress could muster to oppose the operation. However, despite this being an excellent and feasible plan, it resulted in a great Patriot victory due primarily to fatal decisions made by General Howe.

In the north, Burgoyne's advance began well as he sailed down Lake Champlain. However, as he began to march south through the rugged forests and ridges of central New York, his progress bogged down due to an increasingly lengthy line of supply, harassing rebel attacks, and American forces who worked tirelessly to impede roads by felling trees, diverting waterways to create swaths of deep mud, and destroying bridges. To the west, St. Leger's force was turned back by a contingent under General Benedict Arnold. Of greater consequence, Howe refused to move north.

Rather than proceed up the Hudson toward Albany and force Washington to fight, the British general wasted months of good campaigning weather at his base in New York. Finally, in late July, rather than attempt to link up with Burgoyne, Howe decided to target Philadelphia and leave a garrison force in New York under Clinton. While he could have traveled overland (the march from the British outpost at New Brunswick, New Jersey, to the rebel capital was only around 60 miles), Howe assembled his army on transports and embarked on a voyage that eventually required more than a month to first sail south and then turn north to reach the head of the Chesapeake.

While the rebel capital was indeed an attractive target and one that Washington would likely need to defend, this move left Burgoyne alone in his drive on Albany. While Howe slowly moved on Philadelphia, some of the best contingents of the Continental Army were sent to augment the force assembling to block Burgoyne. Washington took the rest of his men south to challenge the main British force. Howe was victorious in the resulting Battle of Brandywine Creek on September 11, but Washington was again able to execute a successful retreat. The Congress fled Philadelphia and the city was captured by the British on September 26 in what soon became clear was a Pyrrhic victory. As in the previous year, the loss of any one urban area did not have a major impact on the Patriot cause as long as the Continental Army survived in the field. Even more importantly, Howe's decision to move south instead of north had a dramatic impact on the fighting in upstate New York, the outcome of the war, and the course of history.

Burgoyne found himself in increasingly desperate straits as he advanced to the town of Saratoga and confronted Patriot forces under Generals Horatio Gates, Benjamin Lincoln, Benedict Arnold, and Enoch Poor. Not only was the British army outnumbered, but its opponent fought on the same terms practiced by Washington after he was forced out of New York the previous year: The rebels fought "Indian style" before falling back with riflemen hiding behind trees, rocks, and fences targeting British officers. Rather than trying to hold territory, the Patriots retreated and only made decisive stands defending fortified positions.

British supply lines leading back up to Canada were severed and contingents sent out to obtain supplies were ambushed and forced back. At the Battle of Freeman's Farm on September 19, Burgoyne's army defeated the Patriot army blocking the way south and won the field, but only after suffering much higher casualties. The rebels fell back to prepared fortifications on the high ground of Bemis Heights. Unable to receive assistance from British forces farther south on the Hudson, Burgoyne's army was effectively surrounded. A major battle then failed to break the American lines. Outnumbered and low on provisions, Burgoyne surrendered his entire army.

The British still held the cities of New York and Philadelphia, which were the largest in the colonies, but morale among the Americans soared following the victory at the Battle of Saratoga. Of even greater significance, concluding that the rebellion would not collapse, the French entered the war as full allies of the new United States. The Netherlands and Spain eventually followed (though technically, not as American allies, but still as belligerents against Britain). What had begun as a poorly organized rebellion based in Britain's New England colonies had expanded into a world war waged from India to Africa to the English Channel. Chances that all thirteen American colonies attempting to gain their independence could be defeated became increasingly unlikely.

The disastrous loss of Burgoyne's army and the entry of France into the war led to a change in both strategy and senior personnel for the British in America. Howe returned home to his seat in Parliament and General Henry Clinton was placed in overall command, later writing of his former superior: "Had Sir William Howe fortified the Hills round Boston, he could not have been disgracefully driven from it: had he pursued his Victory at Long Island, he had ended the Rebellion: Had he landed above the lines at New York, not a Man could have escaped him: Had he fought the Americans at the Brunx, he was sure of Victory: had he cooperated with the N. Army, he had saved it, or had he gone to Philadelphia by land, he had ruined Mr. Washington and his Forces. . . ."[2]

Clinton was ordered to withdraw from Philadelphia and protect his New York base from any potential attack by the French fleet. Frederick Howard, the Earl of Carlisle, led a peace commission that sailed from London to negotiate with the Continental Congress. The thirteen colonies were offered a form of self-rule within the Empire (the basis of which was incorporated into the "Dominion" status later adopted by Canada, Australia, New Zealand, South Africa, and Ireland).[3] Had such a proposal been made a few years earlier, the Revolutionary War could have been avoided entirely. However, too much blood had been spilled and the Congress demanded immediate full independence for the United States. This was a step the government in London was not ready to take, and hostilities continued.

Forced to shift men and ships to protect their valuable sugar-producing islands in the Caribbean from the French, the British decided that the best option to combat the American rebellion was to switch to what became known as the "Southern Strategy." Simply put, the rambunctious colonies of New England would be abandoned, the area around the city of New York would be defended, and a force would be landed in Georgia. After securing that colony, the British would work their way north, potentially as far as Virginia, to bring these territories back under King George's rule. With London needing to deploy its Redcoats to protect its far flung Empire, Clinton was to place a greater emphasis on recruiting Loyalist colonists to fight their neighbors and suppress the North American rebellion.

Such a policy made a great deal of sense. Recall that from 1763 until the end of the Revolutionary War, the British Empire in America stretched from Newfoundland to the southern tip of Florida and from there to a collection of Caribbean islands. Inland, at least on paper, it reached from Hudson Bay, south to the western end of the Great Lakes and from there all the way down the Mississippi to the Gulf of Mexico. Great power European conflicts of the eighteenth century were not wars of state annihilation and generally ended in a peace treaty where combatants got to keep what they held at the time hostilities were halted. If the British could reconquer the Southern American colonies, an independent United States emerging from the war that was confined to New England and a few Mid-Atlantic states would likely become a weak dependency of the British crown with the Royal Navy patrolling the sea lanes of the Atlantic in the east and the Ohio River remaining under British military control in the west.[4]

The Southern colonies were also potentially ripe to be seized. Georgia and the Carolinas had relatively smaller populations rumored to be full of Loyalists willing to flock to the royal banner if a British army of size could be landed in the region. The Royal Navy could also sortie from its bases in New York, Florida, Bermuda, and the West Indies to help suppress the rebellion in these Southern colonies. Finally, it was more advantageous economically to retain the Southern colonies as they produced cash crops such as sugar, rice, indigo, and sea island cotton, which could not be grown in Britain.

The breakdown of population by American state/colony in 1780 bears out this logic:[5]

Estimated Population 1780[6]

State	Population	Black	% Black	White	% White
New Hampshire	87,802	541	0.6	87,261	99.4
Massachusetts	268,627	4,822	1.8	263,805	98.2
Rhode Island	52,946	2,671	5	50,275	95
Connecticut	206,701	5,885	2.8	200,816	97.2
New York	210,701	21,054	10	189,647	90
New Jersey	139,627	10,460	7.5	129,167	92.5
Pennsylvania	327,805	7,855	2.4	319,950	97.6
Delaware	45,385	2,996	6.6	42,389	93.4
Maryland	245,474	80,515	32.8	164,959	67.2
Virginia	538,004	220,582	41	317,422	59
North Carolina	270,138	91,000	33.7	179,138	66.3
South Carolina	180,000	97,000	53.9	83,000	46.1
Georgia	56,071	20,831	37.2	35,240	62.8
Total	2,629,281	566,212	21.5	2,063,069	78.5

Not only was the South more sparsely inhabited than the Northern region of the infant United States, its percentage of Black slaves in the local population was dramatically larger. Many colonial militiamen of the South who might otherwise join the rebellion would be compelled to remain neutral and at home to ensure their valuable human property did not flee. This sapping of Patriot strength could be accentuated if Britain offered freedom to escaped slaves who enlisted in Loyalist regiments. General Clinton did just this when he issued the Philipsburg Proclamation in June 1779, which effectively freed all slaves owned by rebels who successfully escaped to British lines.[7] While such a directive would have little impact in the North, it would, of course, be of great significance in the South.

The Defeat

From December 1778 to August 1780, the British enjoyed a series of victories in which multiple American armies were crushed and the colonies of Georgia and the Carolinas effectively returned to King George's rule. Again and again, Patriot commanders, many of whom had participated in earlier battles in the North, forgot the tactics demonstrated by Washington in how to defeat London's numerically superior, professional armed forces. The result was that the United States nearly emerged from the Revolutionary War shorn of the Deep South—a scenario that would have had a dramatic impact on history.

The character of the campaign also changed as most of these engagements were waged by smaller contingents than those that had taken place in the North. Due to the entry of France into the war, which triggered manpower demands to protect its global possessions, the British began to utilize large numbers of colonial Loyalists in the effort to suppress the American rebellion. Earlier in the war only a very small number of men in the thirteen colonies had been recruited to fight against the Patriot cause. However, by the end of 1778, the head count in provincial units of the British army in America and Loyalist militia raised in occupied areas of New York and New Jersey approached the entire total of 18,700 at that time in the Continental Army.[8] Those recently arrived from Scotland and Ireland were most likely to rally to the King's standard along with Black slaves who were willing to serve in return for a chance at gaining their freedom. While Loyalist sentiment in the South never matched British overoptimistic hopes, recruitment also gathered pace there, especially after much of Georgia and South Carolina were occupied by Clinton's forces.

Success in raising local levies likely helps explain why the fighting also became more vicious in the South as it took on more the dimensions of a civil war. This period of the conflict saw greater intentional destruction of property and many Americans being killed on the spot when attempting to surrender. Both sides in the conflict were guilty of such conduct and these events were most prevalent in smaller engagements in the backcountry where Loyalist units were matched up against Patriot militia.

The shift to the Southern Strategy began in December when Clinton dispatched Lieutenant Colonel Archibald Campbell from New York with a force of more than 3,000 Redcoats, Hessians, and Loyalist volunteers to the coast of Georgia. After coming ashore near Savannah, the British were confronted by Patriot General Robert Howe commanding a small force of fewer than 1,000 who were primarily green troops and local militiamen. The Patriots were outnumbered four to one and could have retreated, defended the town from within its fortifications, or seized and entrenched along the bluffs above where the British were landing. However, Howe chose to arrange his small army a mile from Savannah in a single line across open ground anchored by swampy forest on either side.

This was likely the worst of Howe's options. However, his decision only became truly disastrous when a local slave showed the advancing British a footpath through the swamp to the east. Five hundred British and Loyalists followed the slave and were able to move unopposed into the American rear as Howe had neglected to post scouts on his flanks. Just as the Patriots began to hear the sound of gunfire behind them, Campbell ordered his artillery to fire and the main British force charged the wavering defenders.

The result was a rout in which most of Howe's force was killed or taken captive. Over the following months small engagements at Kettle and Brier Creek took place across Georgia in which Patriot and British contingents fought for control of the interior of the state. Campbell wrote back to England that, "I am not without the hope of being the first officer to take a stripe and star from the rebel flag of Congress."[9]

General Benjamin Lincoln was appointed as the replacement commander of the Southern Department by the Congress. In September of 1779, he left his base in Charles Town with around 2,000 men and marched on Savannah.

There he joined up as a junior partner with Charles Henri Hector, the Comte d'Estaing, who had arrived with his French fleet along with a significant contingent of infantry. While the defenders of Savannah had been reinforced from British East Florida, they were still outnumbered more than two to one. However, the resulting month-long siege ended in a disaster for the allied force. The French commander, generally unlucky in his efforts throughout the war, eventually ordered a night assault on the British fortified lines that was poorly organized and failed miserably. Almost a thousand of the besiegers were killed or wounded compared to only about a tenth of that number on the British side. The Comte d'Estaing, twice wounded in the final attack, called off the campaign and departed with his men to sail back to France.

To regain the offensive, General Clinton departed New York to besiege Charles Town in March of 1780. Lincoln's force of Continentals, militia, and sailors around the city totaled more than 4,500 men. However, the British force of Redcoats, Hessians, and Loyalists was more than twice that size. They were also supported by a significant fleet that was dramatically more powerful than the small flotilla the Patriots had on hand. The previously mentioned success in recruiting Loyalists into both local militia and provincial army units allowed Clinton to leave sufficient defensive strength in New York while embarking a major amphibious force to take the South's largest and most important city.

Despite having participated in the 1776 New York campaign, Lincoln seemed to have forgotten the folly of attempting to defend an island or peninsula when the Royal Navy could provide transportation to a larger landing force, supplies, and artillery support. Lincoln proved to be an accomplished military administrator during and after the war, but was a poor general in independent command, racking up one defeat after another.[10] His confrontation with the British at Charles Town proved to be one of the worst reverses experienced in U.S. history.

Clinton had repeatedly urged General William Howe to act quickly to surround, cut off, and destroy or force a surrender of Washington's army around New York in 1776. Now in charge, the British commander planned to engage in just such aggressive tactics against the American army if it was foolish enough to remain in the city. Unfortunately for the Patriot cause, that is exactly what Lincoln chose to do. The Patriot general's logic for remaining in Charles Town was flawed: First, he expected a stream of reinforcements to arrive from the north. Of course, the Revolutionary cause was always short of funds and men to spare. Even if that had not been the case in 1780, lacking what Washington referred to as the Royal Navy's "canvas wings" meant that moving significant supplies and bodies of men north and south was difficult and time consuming.[11] Without command of the sea, men of the Continental Army would have to march over hundreds of miles on poor roads to reach South Carolina. While more than 1,000 reinforcing Patriot soldiers did arrive during the siege, their numbers were not large enough to tip the balance.[12]

Secondly, Lincoln was heavily influenced by local leaders who insisted that Charles Town be defended at all costs. While the loss of the city would represent a setback to the Patriot cause, it was in no way more important than Philadelphia or New York, which had fallen to the British without triggering a collapse in the rebellion. Lincoln's primary mission was to maintain his army as a force in the field. Were it to be surrounded and then destroyed or compelled to surrender, there would be hardly any organized armed resistance to British rule remaining in the United States south of Virginia. Nevertheless, he deployed his men behind the fortifications defending the southern tip of the peninsula on which Charles Town is located between the Ashley and Cooper Rivers where they merge and empty into the Atlantic.

Clinton moved quickly, and sent men upriver to force a crossing of the Ashley. Patriot scouting units detected the movement and Lincoln had an excellent opportunity to attack the British when they only had a small beachhead on the far bank.[13] However, the American general chose not to oppose the crossing and ordered his men to fall back. Clinton quickly secured the neck of the peninsula above Charles Town and began constructing trench lines several hundred yards north of the city. The British fleet also successfully sailed past the guns of Fort Moultrie on Sullivan's Island and anchored in Charles Town's harbor while the small U.S. flotilla retreated up the Cooper River.

Lincoln's force engaged in furious but generally ineffectual cannonades of the besieging lines as they approached the city but did little else except consume the garrison's shrinking food supplies. Clinton then sent a column of around 1,400 men under Colonel James Webster inland to defeat a force of 500 militia and cavalry that was protecting Lincoln's supply lines to the interior. The vanguard of this advance was led by Lieutenant Colonel Banastre Tarleton, who commanded the light infantry and dragoons of the Loyalist British Legion. Moving with the speed and boldness for which he was soon to become famous, Tarleton completely surprised the Patriots at Monck's Corner on April 14, 1780, killing or capturing many and scattering the rest. The northern escape routes for the American army in Charles Town were increasingly coming under control of the British.

There was still time for Lincoln to attempt a retreat, and the day before the rout at Monck's Corner he called a council of war to discuss options. His senior officers all urged an immediate evacuation while such a movement was still possible.[14] Senior civilian leaders opposed such a move as they argued that the British would overrun and sack the city if they detected that the Continentals were attempting to flee. While his primary mission was to preserve his army, Lincoln hesitated and soon the noose was pulled tight as thousands of British under General Cornwallis crossed to the east bank of the Cooper to cut off any chance of escape.

Over the next few weeks, British reinforcements arrived from New York and trenches were dug ever closer to the American fortifications. The garrison did little more than fire off its cannons and one small sortie was sent out to interfere with the construction of the siegeworks. Finally on May 11, Clinton ordered the use of heated shot by his artillerymen, which ignited fires that burned several buildings in Charles Town to the ground. The civilian leadership of the city urged Lincoln to give up, and on the May 12 he formally surrendered. The defeat represented the only

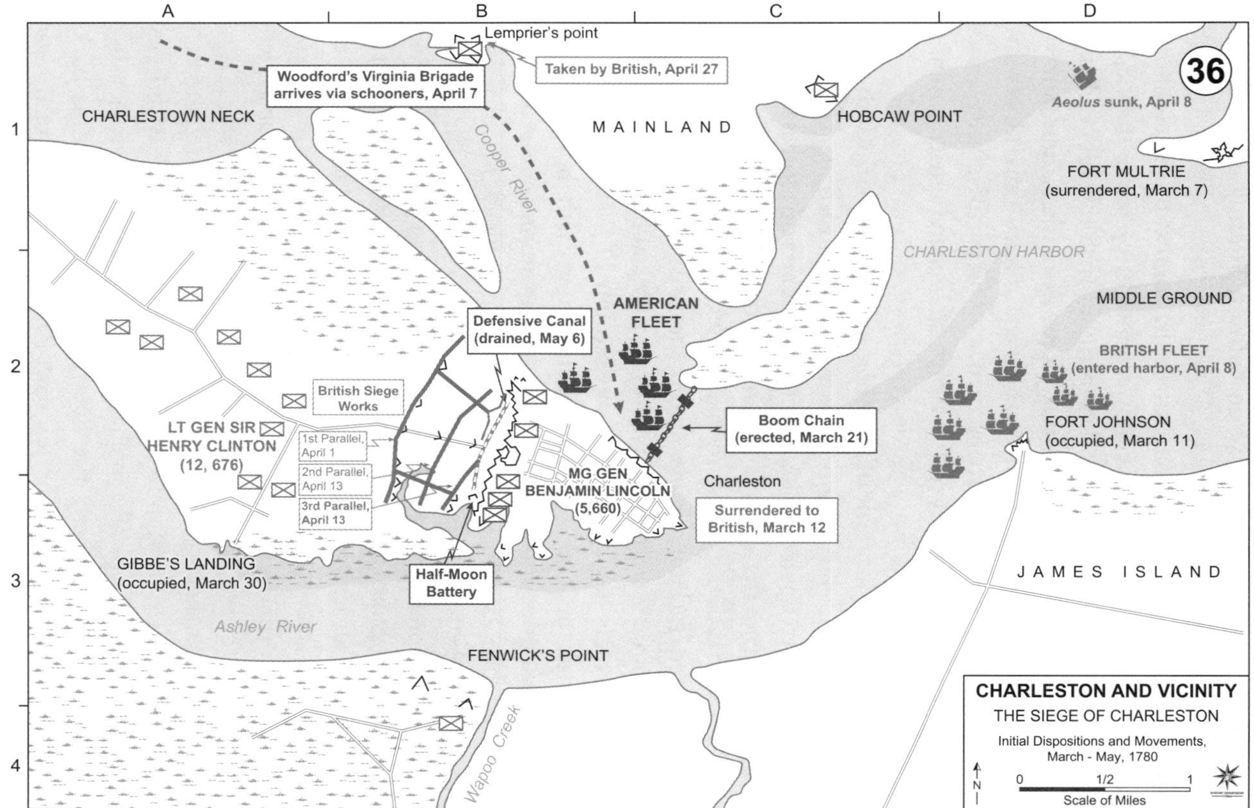

Clinton traps Lincoln and wins the greatest British victory of the war. UNITED STATES MILITARY ACADEMY

time in the Revolutionary War that an entire field army of the Patriot cause was surrounded and captured.

The size of the defeat was dramatic in the context of the conflict in the South where many engagements were fought by fewer than 2,000 soldiers per side. 5,466 men were taken prisoner with the fall of Charles Town along with 390 cannon and vast stores of muskets, ammunition, and powder. That Lincoln's losses in the siege totaled only ninety-two killed, or less than 2 percent of his men, compared to seventy-six on the British side is a testament to the American general's utter failure to mount a vigorous defense.[15]

There was yet one last unit of Continentals left in South Carolina: a contingent of around 400 Virginians who had been rushing to Charles Town before it surrendered. When the news reached this force, it turned around and began to march back toward North Carolina. However, the Patriots never made it. Clinton received intelligence about their presence and ordered Tarleton to give chase. The British lieutenant colonel drove his legion extremely hard over almost 150 miles and caught up to the Continentals just before they crossed out of South Carolina on May 29. Though he had only around 150 men with him when he overtook the Continentals, Tarleton ordered an immediate attack and quickly overwhelmed the much larger, but unseasoned, force of Virginians in what became known as the Battle of Waxhaws. The Patriots attempted to surrender but the Loyalist dragoons cut many down with their sabers and more than half of the Continentals were killed or wounded before order was restored. The event became known as the "Waxhaws Massacre" among Patriots across the South and many took revenge for what they referred to as "Tarleton's Quarter" in subsequent engagements of the war in the South.

Believing that the Southern Strategy was working out quite well indeed, Clinton sailed back to his headquarters in New York with much of his army. He left Cornwallis in charge with orders to recruit Loyalists into armed formations, pacify the South Carolina and Georgia backcountry, protect his base at Charles Town, and move when ready into North Carolina to suppress the rebellion in yet one more wayward province of the Empire.[16] On the first point of Clinton's orders, Cornwallis had some success. More than 1,500 men stepped forward to join local Loyalist militias, but overall recruitment was still less than what senior British officers had hoped to achieve. The effects of the Philipsburg Proclamation had mixed results. More than a thousand Black slaves escaped from servitude and made their way to British-held areas where they were employed as both soldiers and laborers for the King's army.[17]

However, this latter recruitment effort interfered with efforts to pacify the backcountry. Many slaveholders who might otherwise have wanted to remain neutral in the conflict were incensed by what they saw as the British authorities threatening their property rights over human chattel. The strength of Patriot fervor in the backcountry was also inflamed as General Clinton began demanding the local citizenry take loyalty oaths. This forced men to side with the Patriots who otherwise would have stayed out of the fighting. The result was that several small bands began a campaign of hit-and-run guerrilla warfare behind the British front lines over the course of the summer of 1780. Like any good insurgent force, they struck quickly against smaller enemy detachments or supply trains and then either hid in rugged terrain (swamps and deep woods) or melted back into the general population.

While Cornwallis chose to wait out the hot summer months before marching north, Congress appointed Horatio Gates as Lincoln's replacement in charge of the Southern Department. The "Hero of Saratoga," as Gates had come to be known, was yet another able administrator with an uneven record on the battlefield. After learning of his appointment, he rushed to North Carolina and took command of his recently organized army. Despite this force being poorly armed and clothed and short on food, he immediately ordered it to march south without even getting an accurate count of its size. His goal was to attack the British supply depot at Camden, 100 miles away in South Carolina. Many of Gates's new field officers suggested caution, or at least taking a less direct route to instead move through a region known to have many Patriot sympathizers and that would be more likely to yield provisions for the army. Unfortunately, the general refused this advice, and chose the direct road toward Camden.[18]

Twenty days later, the third Continental commander of the Southern Department in twenty months was thrashed by the British. Gates's force of fewer than 4,000 mostly green militia was suffering through terrible summer heat and low on supplies as they approached the British garrison at Camden. Unfortunately for the Patriot cause, Cornwallis had been alerted to Gates's movement and marched north from Charles Town with reinforcements. On the night of August 15, the vanguard of the two armies blundered into each other and a confused skirmish took place. Prisoners taken in the fighting informed Gates that he was up against Cornwallis who had a significantly larger cavalry force. The Patriot general concluded that as he had few supplies and the British horsemen were capable of cutting off his escape routes, he could not retreat and had to stand and fight.[19]

At dawn both armies formed up for battle with the Patriots significantly outnumbering Cornwallis. However, Gates made a terrible blunder: He adhered to tradition and placed his most experienced troops on the right side of his line. This meant his militia were on the left where they would be confronted by Hessians and Redcoats, while the Continentals faced formations of Carolina Loyalists. As at many other battles throughout the war, Patriot militiamen could not be counted upon to stand and fight in the open against Britain's professional soldiers. Even worse, instead of defending from behind hastily dug defensive works, Gates ordered his militia to charge the enemy line. The unsurprising result was a rout as the militia fled and left the Continentals alone on the battlefield. The remaining Patriots put up a stout and extended defense until overwhelmed on their now-unguarded flank at which point they broke and fled into the woods.[20]

Gates bolted from the field even while much of his army was still fighting bravely, and the general did not stop riding hard until he reached Hillsboro three days and 180 miles later. It was yet another defeat for the Patriot cause in the South. More than 600 men of Gates's army were killed and another 1,000 captured as they attempted to flee back into North Carolina. In contrast, the British only suffered 324 total killed and wounded in the battle.[21]

In addition, Cornwallis soon learned that a small detachment of 100 Continentals had been sent north with several hundred militia under General Thomas Sumter to raid British supply lines. Tarleton again set out on the hunt and pursued the rebels with his usual alacrity. Despite being vastly outnumbered, he attacked immediately when he caught up with the Patriot force along Fishing Creek near the North Carolina border. Sumter was literally caught napping and while he escaped, more than half his force was killed or captured. As at Waxhaws, many Patriots attempting to surrender were cut down with sabers or shot out of hand.[22]

Once again there were no organized formations of Continental troops at large in the two recovered British colonies of Georgia and South Carolina. Three rebel armies had been defeated in quick succession and Clinton's forces had amassed a huge haul of prisoners, cannon, horses, supplies, and muskets. In the South, some of those Thomas Paine called "sunshine patriots" began to waver and consider taking the loyalty oath to the King. Had a peace conference been convened in late 1780 in Europe, it is likely the Continental Congress would have had to accept the loss of its two most Southern states.

Recovery

Of course, the war continued and the Patriot cause had not been extinguished in the Deep South. Even after the Battle of Camden, a large percentage (if not the majority) of the population in the South Carolina and Georgia backcountry remained committed to the Patriot cause. Aided by the residents of the region, partisan bands under men such as Sumter, Francis Marion, Andrew Pickens, and Elijah Clarke operated behind enemy lines and intensified their attacks on supply trains and small contingents of British and Loyalist formations. In many areas, the British were unable to successfully establish control with locally raised forces, and backcountry garrisons such as those at the towns of Augusta and Ninety-Six were often in danger of being cut off from the coast due to Patriot interdiction efforts.

The British also overplayed their hand. As already mentioned, freeing of slaves, insistence on loyalty oaths, and membership in Loyalist militia from all local residents forced many to choose the Patriot cause. In addition, rather than focusing on subduing South Carolina and Georgia, Cornwallis convinced himself that he could only hold these two Southern colonies if he moved north into North Carolina. A few days before the Battle of Camden, he wrote his commander, "It may be doubted by some whether the Invasion of North Carolina may be a prudent measure, but I am convinced it is a necessary one; and that if we do not Attack that Province, we must give up both South Carolina, and Georgia, & retire within the Walls of Charles town. . . ."[23] He moved into North Carolina and established a base at the town of Charlotte. However, far from the coast and deep in territory generally more disposed to the Patriot cause, Cornwallis's line of supply now reached more than 200 road miles back to Charles Town. It was the high water mark of Britain's strategy in the South.

The British general also sent the Scottish officer Patrick Ferguson and a force of 350 Loyalists west with instructions to recruit more to the King's banner. At first all went well as several hundred additional men joined up, and a marauding Patriot partisan band under Isaac Shelby was forced to turn tail and withdraw over the Blue Ridge Mountains into what is now Tennessee. The settlers there were known as "Overmountain Men" who, according to the Proclamation of 1763, had emigrated to the area illegally. While most identified with the Patriot cause, they were generally most concerned with being left alone and defending their land from Cherokee attack. However, Ferguson went too far when he issued a confrontational edict to the Overmountain Men: "If you do not desist your opposition to the British Arms, I shall march this army over the mountains, hang your leaders, and lay waste your country with fire and sword."[24]

Such a challenge was taken up with gusto by these frontiersmen who grabbed their rifles, mustered a "posse," and marched over the mountains. Patriot militia from the Carolinas, Georgia, and Virginia joined the force as it moved east. Ferguson, learning he was being pursued, chose to abandon his base at Gilbert Town and marched toward the safety of Cornwallis and his army. However, for reasons that are not entirely clear, the Loyalist force chose to halt and camp on top of a forested hill known locally as Kings Mountain. The pursuing Patriots surprised Ferguson and his 1,100 Loyalists on the afternoon of October 7, and killed, wounded, or captured the entire force. It was the largest American versus American battle of the war. As the Loyalists attempted to surrender, many of the attackers continued firing as they yelled, "Tarleton's Quarter!" The only British soldier involved was Ferguson himself, and Patriot militia urinated on his bullet-riddled corpse before dumping it into a hastily dug grave.

Many years later Clinton wrote that the Battle of Kings Mountain was, "an Event which was immediately productive of the worst Consequences to the King's affairs in South Carolina, and unhappily proved the first Link of a Chain of Evils that followed each other in regular Succession until they at last ended in the total loss of America."[25] Over the next two years the backcountry of the Carolinas and Georgia increasingly came to be controlled by Patriot bands. Many who supported the King's rule were forced to switch allegiance or flee. British hopes of recruiting significant Loyalist militia formations in the region were dashed. Cornwallis, after hearing of the loss of Ferguson's force, retreated back to South Carolina.[26] But small groups of Patriot partisans could not defeat a professional British army. To redeem South Carolina and Georgia, aid would have to come from the north.

After Gates's defeat, Congress finally let George Washington choose the leader he wanted in Nathanael Greene, who was appointed commander of the Southern Department in October of 1780.[27] Colonel (soon to be General) Daniel Morgan, a tough frontiersman from western Virginia, was ordered to join him. Both men were veterans of many battles in the North since the start of the war and understood the superiority the professional British soldiers had over Patriot militia. They accepted that they could only stand and fight Cornwallis on chosen ground and even then they would have difficulty defeating the enemy. The best course was along the lines of the attritional campaign Washington had demonstrated at the end of 1776: fall back and weaken the British as they were forced to extend their supply lines, inflict casualties when possible, and be prepared to retreat when necessary. As Greene wrote to Washington in 1781, "We fight, get beat and fight again."[28]

America's new Southern commander traveled to Charlotte, North Carolina, where the survivors of the Battle of Camden had assembled. Along the way he sent out men to investigate and scout the fords and crossing points along the major rivers of the state. Greene was already considering the potential of falling back in front of an advancing British force and utilizing watercourses as barriers to slow down his pursuers. He also discussed using flatboats, similar to the ones Washington employed on the Delaware in December 1776, to cross rivers and leave the British trapped on the far bank.[29]

When Greene arrived in Charlotte, he found that he only had around 2,000 men, and 1,200 of them were not properly clothed, armed, and equipped. In contrast, Cornwallis had 4,000 men with him at his headquarters in Winnsboro, South Carolina, and another 5,000 in garrisons in Charles Town, Savannah, and in backcountry posts such as Augusta, Ninety-Six, and Camden. Clearly the odds were not in Greene's favor. Nevertheless, he soon ordered an advance specifically designed to lure the British into giving chase in which he could emulate Washington's winter campaign across New Jersey at the end of 1776.

Victory

Greene chose to divide his army in the face of the enemy despite being qualitatively and quantitatively outclassed by his opponent. He turned over his most seasoned and best equipped men, along with all his cavalry, to Morgan in what was termed the "Flying Army." He ordered his subordinate to head southwest and cross into South Carolina, find a good place for winter quarters, and be ready to retreat if Cornwallis sent a stronger force against him. Greene then took the other half of his army south and made camp near the town of Cheraw on the Pee Dee River.

While a violation of the norms of military strategy, there was logic behind the Patriot leader's decisions. First, the region around Charlotte had been picked clean of provisions and he needed to move so as to be able to feed his men over the winter. Dividing his force would allow his army to forage across a larger area. Secondly, spreading his men across more of the map would allow for greater recruitment of local militia and improve morale among Patriots in the countryside. Finally, Greene believed that if he divided his army, Cornwallis would quickly be informed of this and be forced to do the same. If the British general did not do so, one of the two Patriot forces would be able to march south to attack isolated British garrisons. With luck, after dividing, one of Cornwallis's two formations would try to close with a Patriot force that could then withdraw, collecting reinforcements along the way and pulling the British farther from their lines of supply to a place where battle could be held on more even terms.[30]

The Flying Army crossed to the south shore of the Pacolet River, and collected local militia reinforcements as he marched. His cavalry ranged ahead and quickly surprised and overwhelmed two Loyalist contingents. This faster force of light infantry and horsemen could strike more quickly into the Carolina backcountry and was deemed a greater threat by Cornwallis. Tarleton with a similarly unencumbered command was dispatched from the main British army to intercept Morgan. Cornwallis also began marching the slower remainder of his army on a parallel route northwest to keep the two Patriot forces from linking back together, and in the hopes of catching the Flying Army in a vice.[31]

Morgan retreated and kept ahead of Tarleton's pursuit, but he did not push his men to exhaustion as did the British commander. To ensure he would not be surprised, the Patriot leader stationed small groups of horsemen at river fords to slow his pursuers and identify their location. While Tarleton woke his men at 2 A.M. every morning to close on his prey, Morgan kept his force reasonably well rested and fed as he searched for the right location to make a stand. He chose a place known as Hannah's Cowpens in the very northwest corner of South Carolina. Riders had gone out calling on Patriot militia to assemble there and local residents were familiar with the site as they had historically brought their animals there for pasture.

Morgan understood the weaknesses of the non-professional Patriot soldiers who made up much of his fighting force. He had chosen a battlefield devoid of deep woods or swamps on the flanks that would appear as attractive havens to militia prone to panic and communicated an unorthodox plan to his men. The first battle line would be composed of local riflemen lined up across the open, grazed-over meadow and hiding behind trees along its sides. Morgan asked these men to wait until the British got close and then fire just two or three shots before pulling back 150 yards. These men would then form up with the second line made up of militia in a shallow swale, which would not be immediately visible to the British. Together this combined militia force would fire three times before pulling back in an orderly manner to pass through the final battle line to safety.

This last infantry formation would be made up of the Flying Army's seasoned Continentals who would make their stand along a low ridge. By the time they reached this third line, the British would be fatigued, have taken casualties, and lost some of their unit cohesion. The cavalry would be stationed in the rear where it could be deployed as needed. Behind them flowed the Broad River where, it was hoped, the militia would rally as further retreat would be impossible. Morgan carefully explained the details of the plan to his men the night before the battle, insisting on the need for making controlled retreats, and that such withdrawals were to be expected and not interpreted as the start of a panicked rout.

The Patriot force got a reasonable amount of sleep the night of January 16, 1781, and were awakened before dawn to have a quick breakfast before assembling to await the arrival of their British pursuers who were already on the march. Tarleton arrived with his 1,100 men soon before sunrise, and, in character, immediately ordered an attack. The exact size of the opposing Patriot force was likely a bit larger due to recent arrivals of militia. Morgan's plan worked almost exactly as planned with the militia lines inflicting losses on the British before retreating in reasonably good order and passing through the third line of Patriots. Mistaking the militia's retreat for the start of a rout, Tarleton's men broke ranks in pursuit only to be staggered by volleys of musket fire from the Continentals. Morgan sent his cavalry around to strike the British right flank, and much of the militia re-formed and returned to the fight by hitting the enemy on their left flank. It was a double envelopment many compared to Hannibal's famous victory at Cannae in the Second Punic War.

An hour after it began, the battle was over with almost the entire British force killed or captured. It was one of only a handful of significant engagements in the Revolutionary War where the Patriots held the field at the end of the day. A wounded Tarleton escaped with a small number of cavalrymen, but Cornwallis had lost several of the best units in his field army. Despite the number of combatants on either side being relatively

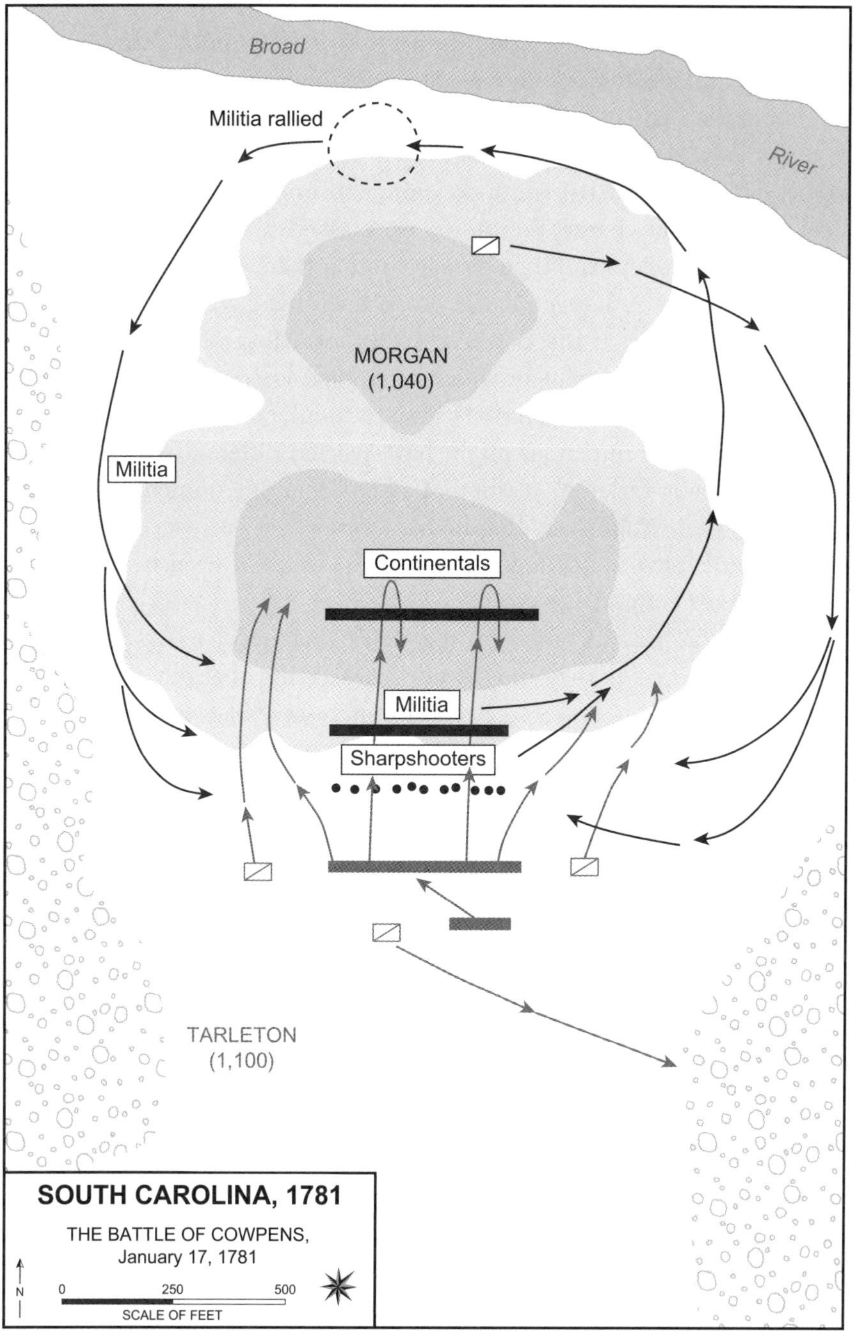

Morgan's innovative tactical deployment defeats Tarleton at Cowpens.

UNITED STATES MILITARY ACADEMY

small, the battle had an outsized impact on Patriot morale throughout the South and a commensurate negative one on local Loyalists.

More than any other Patriot commander, Morgan had found a way to turn the weakness of the militia into a strength. Unable to reload and fire as quickly as the British opposition, and unlikely to resist the cold steel of a bayonet charge, the militia were asked to do what they could do—fire a few volleys and then retreat—rather than what they couldn't—stand and fight a prolonged battle on an open field against professional soldiers. Effectively, at the Battle of Cowpens, Morgan found a way to compress a lengthy retreat in which attritional losses were imposed on the pursuer into a fight that lasted only a portion of one morning. A more cautious British commander might have reacted differently to the rebel deployment, but Tarleton's method of a hard-charging immediate frontal attack was well established. That he had everywhere been successful previously made it that much more likely that he would react as he did when he arrived at Hannah's Cowpens.

Cornwallis was incensed by the defeat and resolved to catch the two Patriot forces as they moved north. Realizing that what remained of his army was too slow and hauling unnecessary baggage, the British general chose to burn almost anything that would retard his advance. Wagons, rum barrels, books, beds, tents, and other goods went up in a giant bonfire. Now unencumbered, Cornwallis accelerated his pursuit and closed the distance on Morgan who was fleeing to the northeast into North Carolina. However, the Flying Army forded the Catawba River just before a winter storm brought heavy rain to the area and made the watercourse impassable for days.[32]

Once across the Catawba, Cornwallis pushed his men hard, intent on bringing his opponent to battle to make up for the defeat at Cowpens. The British commander's second-in-command, General Charles O'Hara, later wrote, "In this situation without Baggage, necessaries, or Provisions of any sort for Officer or Soldier . . . with zeal and Bayonets only, it was resolv'd to follow Green's Army to the end of the World."[33] What followed became known as "the race to the Dan" as the Patriot army pushed north, in an attempt to cross the Dan River into Virginia before being caught by the British pursuers.

Greene was almost overtaken during this race, but earlier planning saved his army. At the Yadkin River, all boats in the area had been assembled to bring the Patriots across and Cornwallis arrived just as Greene's rear guard was floated to the far bank. The British were forced to march 40 miles upstream to find a passable ford by which point the Patriots had moved farther north. Even so, the race continued, and it was only in the middle of February that Greene's army crossed the Dan. Again the Patriots finished crossing to the north bank of a river using all boats in the vicinity just as Cornwallis and his army arrived. The British general had lost 250 men to desertion, malaria, and other illness out of his force of 2,500 during the six weeks on the march and his soldiers were worn out from the long chase. But at least he could claim to have ejected the rebel army from a third colony and there was now no Continental force of size south of Virginia. Cornwallis chose to declare victory via a proclamation and retire southward with his force to Hillsborough to recuperate.

Historian John Ferling summarized the reasons for Patriot success to this point in the campaign as follows: "Greene's actions had replicated those of Washington in the autumn of 1776. Like the commander in chief, Greene had divided his army, pursued a Fabian strategy, and sought an opportunity to make a sudden strike."[34] Of course the Patriot general still had a mission to reclaim South Carolina and Georgia. As soon as Cornwallis began his withdrawal, Greene's army, now reinforced with several hundred fresh Virginian militia, crossed the Dan River and began to follow with the cavalry ranging ahead to harass the British. Morgan, suffering from sciatica, hemorrhoids, and rheumatism, was unable to participate and returned to his home on sick leave.

After Greene's forces wiped out a force of a few hundred Loyalist militia in late February 1781 in what is now Alamance County, North Carolina, Cornwallis felt compelled to emerge from Hillsborough and once again try to crush the Patriots. For the next two weeks Greene avoided battle though he became increasingly confident as reinforcements, both local militia and seasoned Continentals, arrived. By the middle of March he had 4,500 men compared to Cornwallis who had less than half as many. Finally, the rebel commander was ready to stand and fight, though only on ground of his own choosing.

At Guilford Courthouse in central North Carolina, Greene borrowed much from Morgan's tactics and deployed his force in three lines of battle. The first composed of 1,500 militia, riflemen, and 150 dragoons were drawn up behind a split-rail fence. The second, 350 yards back in a wooded area, was composed of 1,200 well-seasoned Virginia militia. On a low hill, 500 yards farther to the rear, was the third line of 1,400 Continentals.

As the British force approached in the early afternoon, they initially only saw the first line of militia, formed up, and attacked. The Patriots followed their orders and fired a few concentrated volleys before falling back through the second line. The Virginians, some of whom had been routed at Camden, stood their ground and fired their two volleys before they too began a fighting retreat through the woods. Advancing through the trees made it impossible for the British to maintain the proper order of their advancing infantry formations and the battle, for a time, became a contest between smaller groups of men.

Cornwallis led his men out of the woods and dressed their ranks to attack Greene's third and final line. The advantage in the fighting swung back and forth with both cavalry and infantry charges leading to an intermingling of the opposing forces. Cornwallis's army seemed close to breaking and he ordered his artillery to fire grapeshot (a short-range anti-personnel ammunition of small lead balls, which effectively turns a cannon into a giant shotgun) into the mass of men, killing Redcoat and Continental alike. This cruel order allowed the British to re-form their battle line while Greene ordered a retreat and his men withdrew in good order.

Cornwallis held the field in a Pyrrhic victory in which around a quarter of his force was killed or wounded. Since he began the pursuit from Winnsboro months earlier, the British general had lost more than half his army while his opponent's had nearly doubled in size. While the Patriots lost a similar number at Guilford Courthouse, their Southern force was twice as large and could more easily make up the deficiency. As Greene correctly put it in a letter sent north, "the Enemy got the ground the other Day, but we the victory. They had the splendor, we the advantage."[35] In another he wrote, "they have met with a defeat in victory."[36] Cornwallis's men, tired, sick, hungry, and worn out, began a march to the port of Wilmington, North Carolina, where they could be resupplied by the Royal Navy.

Greene then chose a radical course as he sent many of his militia home and began to move south with around 1,300 men toward South Carolina. He decided that even though he would be leaving an enemy force in his rear, his mission to free the Southern states would be best served if he could move to attack isolated British garrisons throughout the region utilizing local Patriot forces in the effort.[37] Cornwallis, in contravention of his orders, decided that continuing to fight in the Carolinas was folly, and the only way to win the South was to march into Virginia, merge with the British army already operating there under General William Phillips, cut off the flow of supplies to Patriot insurgents operating in his rear, and find a way to win a decisive victory.[38]

As the two opposing armies moved in opposite directions, Greene's subordinate commander, General Richard Henry Lee, compared his commander's action to that of the Roman Scipio Africanus in the Second Punic War who ignored Hannibal's army in his rear and pushed on to conquer enemy-held territory.[39] That Cornwallis chose not to pursue Greene was the beginning of the end of the British Southern Strategy. Over the course of the next six months, one enemy-held post after another across Georgia and South Carolina was liberated by Greene's forces. After the Battle of Eutaw Springs in September 1781, the British withdrew to their two coastal bases at Savannah and Charles Town leaving the rest of the two states under Patriot control.

Cornwallis moved to Virginia and was eventually ordered to entrench his army at Yorktown. Clinton was concerned that a combined American-French assault under Washington's command was imminent on his base in New York. By having Cornwallis move to a fortified position on the coast, some of his army could be shipped north if necessary. Of course, Clinton's decision led Washington and the French general Comte de Rochambeau to change their plans: Instead of attacking New York, they began to march the bulk of their forces south in August. Clinton equivocated and missed the opportunity to either extricate Cornwallis's army by sea or come to its aid before a French fleet arrived to blockade the Chesapeake.

Finally, after years of being outnumbered and playing defense, Washington had an outright advantage on a battlefield. With a large professional French army at his side and temporary command of the sea, the siege of Yorktown began on September 28. After a desultory defense, the British were forced to surrender three weeks later. Cornwallis feigned illness and sent his subordinate to hand over his sword and the army to Washington. Following tradition, the American general refused and had his second in command, Benjamin Lincoln (who had returned to the battlefield after a prisoner exchange), accept the sword instead. The hard fighting of the war was over, and the thirteen United States legally obtained their independence when the Treaty of Paris was signed two years later.

Cause of Defeat

The battlefield reverses suffered by multiple Patriot military leaders in 1780–1781 had several causes. The most important was that the Royal Navy could give the British an ability to move and supply large masses of men along the eastern seaboard to overwhelm a stationary garrison. When coupled with an amphibious force led by an aggressive commander, a rebel army needed to retreat or it could quickly find itself surrounded and defeated. Ignoring this lesson learned in the 1776 New York campaign cost Benjamin Lincoln his entire army in the largest defeat the Patriot cause suffered in the war.

In addition, mixed Patriot forces of militia and Continentals could not successfully defeat similarly sized professional British and Hessian formations in a battle of dressed ranks exchanging volleys of musket fire on open ground. The contest became almost suicidal when Patriots chose to stand and fight a superior force as at Savannah in December 1778. Even when they significantly outnumbered the British at Camden in August 1780, unless militia were handled correctly on an open battlefield the result could be a disaster. Finally, in a theater such as the Deep South with a lower population density, a small and fast-moving British force employed aggressively could wreak havoc against bodies of citizen soldiers new to war. The Patriots found this out the hard way at Waxhaws and Fishing Creek.

The overarching issue was that the rebels could not win when they allowed the British to utilize their strengths of sea power, massed fire, and tactical movement in traditional set piece battles. The rebels needed to make use of the size of their nation to draw enemy forces far from their supply bases into territory teeming with those who supported the cause of independence. The best course of action was forcing the British to divide their forces and inflict attritional losses on them in an attempt to wear down their strength and negate their general superiority on the battlefield. As these lessons seemed to have been forgotten by Patriot leaders Howe, Lincoln, and Gates, it would not be until generals who understood the asymmetric nature of the war for America arrived on the scene that the British Southern Strategy could be successfully contested.

Cause of Victory

Morgan had fought the British at Saratoga, and Greene in the retreat from New York to Trenton. From their surviving letters it is clear that both had thought deeply about how best to fight the war, utilizing distance, attrition, and subterfuge to wear down their more powerful opponent. They also understood the importance of ensuring that the rebel army not be destroyed or forced to surrender, as a force in the field could be regenerated using new recruits after battlefield losses. This did not mean aggressive actions were off the table. In fact, Greene started the campaign by splitting his meager contingent in two and advancing on the enemy. This movement was to be followed by a retreat after enticing Cornwallis into also breaking up his force and attempting to bring one or both Patriot columns to battle.

Of the divided rebel command, Morgan's was the first to have to fight. He set an extremely well-conceived trap for Tarleton in which the British arrived exhausted and hungry at a prepared battlefield to confront relatively fresh Patriots drawn up in an unorthodox battle formation. Another of the King's officers might have considered calling a halt and letting his men recover from their grueling forced march before fighting. But Tarleton was not that sort of commander. Instead the British advanced headlong into what was effectively an innovative trap.

Morgan realized that American militia armed with hunting rifles and muskets produced a slower rate of fire than professional soldiers and could not stand and fight when confronted by British regulars charging with fixed bayonets. This weakness had led to Patriot defeats in many battles earlier in the war. So, instead of demanding that these citizen soldiers fight in a manner in which they would lose, he devised a plan where he best utilized their accuracy with the rifle and proclivity to retreat to inflict maximum casualties on Tarleton's attacking formations. British armies had often engaged in practiced outflanking maneuvers when confronted with large masses of Patriots. But at Cowpens, the rebels presented only a relatively thin line of skirmishers inviting a frontal attack. As the British advanced, suffered casualties from the first line, and then followed up the retreating militiamen, they suddenly came into view of the second line of militia, which also fired only a few shots before retiring. Finally, when Tarleton's men began to charge after the retreating rebels, they were confronted with Morgan's Continentals. The British still might have broken through this third line, but they were soon attacked on both flanks by Patriot cavalry on one side, and the re-formed militia on the other.

After this first victory, Greene made use of prior reconnaissance to fall back before the pursuing Cornwallis. The long chase took the British ever farther away from their supply lines even as the Patriot army grew larger as it attracted more men to the colors from the hinterland through which it moved. By the time Greene had assembled enough strength to risk a battle, his opponent was exasperated from pursuit and was willing to fight on ground of the rebel general's choosing. As previously related, he emulated Morgan's tactics in the use of militia and the result at the Battle of Guilford Courthouse was a vicious fight in which Greene effectively emerged victorious due to losses imposed on the enemy.

The innovative use of movement, battlefield formations, and attritional tactics resulted in much of Georgia and the Carolinas being freed of British rule prior to the peace negotiations that ended the war. Greene understood that the key to Patriot success was to trade casualties, wear down his opponent's professional soldiers, rely on his large reservoir of militia manpower to make up his losses, and keep the British from recruiting Loyalists from the same population. An officer in the opposing camp wrote of the Patriot general, "the more he is beaten, the farther he advances in the end."[40] Utilizing these tactics, Greene fought long odds to achieve victory against a larger and better trained and supplied foe. While most Americans consider Saratoga and Yorktown to have been the great decisive battles of the war, the engagements in the Carolinas in 1781 deserve their due as they likely saved two states for the nation with great consequences over time.

Impact of Defeat

Imagine if, rather than being defeated, Patriot leaders Howe and Lincoln had successfully held Savannah and Charles Town in the face of British attack. Or consider a more likely scenario where they retreated to the interior and maintained control of much of the Georgia and Carolina backcountry. Faced with a failure of the Southern Strategy from the outset, and a Continental Army that did not need to rush a stream of reinforcements from around New York to North Carolina, would the British have accepted an earlier end to the war? It certainly seems likely as the government in London had already come to terms with the idea that many of the American colonies were to be granted at least a certain level of independence as evidenced by the proposals brought across the Atlantic by the Carlisle Commission in 1778. Had London offered to withdraw from all thirteen former colonies at the end of 1780, Congress undoubtedly would have accepted regardless of French desires. An earlier end to the War of the American Revolution would have resulted in France running up much smaller debts during the conflict, and eliminated the precipitating catalyst of the French Revolution in 1789.

Of course, the British were initially successful in the Southern Strategy. Patriot loss of control of South Carolina and Georgia could have had immense impact on the future history of the United States in particular and the world in general. While the leaders of the Continental Congress and Army had no intention of giving up two states, they could not continue the war alone. Aid from France (and to a lesser extent, the Netherlands and Spain) had been instrumental in keeping the rebellion alive after 1776 and those European powers were tiring of the economic impacts of the conflict. By early 1781, many of Washington's soldiers were forced to suffer through yet another winter with poor clothing and limited food and had not been paid for more than a year. Disgruntlement was rife at West Point, and an outright mutiny broke out among Continental Army troops garrisoned in Morristown, New Jersey, who marched on the Congress in Philadelphia to present their demands. The rebel cause was hanging by a thread that could break at any time and it was desperately dependent on French financial and military support.

In general, eighteenth-century conflicts ended with a treaty emerging from a peace conference that generally followed the Roman legal concept of *uti possidetis* with each party retaining territory it militarily controlled at the time of the conclusion of hostilities. Four calls to hold a conference to end the war were proposed by neutral European powers between late 1778 and early 1781 including a final invitation for mediation by Russia and Austria. France had not been ready to stop fighting previously, but the lack of action around New York and the string of British battlefield victories in the American South forced the Comte de Vergennes, the French foreign minister, to consider if it was time to end the financial drain of the war.[41]

Vergennes decided to fight on for one more year, but it was a close decision. Had the French decided the war was too expensive to continue, the Continental Congress would have had little choice but to accept the decision of its ally even if that meant the permanent loss of South Carolina and Georgia. Even worse, with Cornwallis driving Greene into Virginia, Britain could have argued that North Carolina remained in their possession as well in early 1781 based on *uti possidetis*.

IMPACT OF VICTORY

Imagine a scenario where the armies commanded by Greene and Morgan were defeated rather than achieving their unlikely victories. The British would have marched north victoriously into Virginia while concurrently cutting off supplies flowing south to bands of Patriot insurgents in the backcountry of Georgia and the Carolinas. Cornwallis would then have had a much stronger army to resist Washington and his French allies had they arrived to confront him along the Chesapeake. Even if the British still suffered a great defeat at Yorktown, the Deep South would have remained in their hands with their significant garrison forces backed with large formations of Loyalist militia. Congress might have wanted to continue fighting, but the French were financially exhausted by the end of 1781 with its remaining efforts focused on the unsuccessful siege of Gibraltar.

The United States that emerged from the Treaty of Paris would then have been one that lacked Georgia, South Carolina, and perhaps North Carolina as well. Had Britain retained these colonies, it is also likely to have had a claim to the territory to the immediate west, which now constitutes the states of Tennessee, Alabama, and Mississippi. A scenario resulting in a smaller United States polity would have had dramatic impacts on history. With large British territories remaining in North America in both Canada and the Southeast, the War of 1812 would have played out differently. Unless the Deep South was recaptured in that conflict, it is difficult to imagine how (1) Spanish Florida would have become U.S. territory in 1821, (2) waves of American slaveholding settlers would have flowed into Texas and mounted a rebellion to separate that territory from Mexican control in 1836, and (3) a smaller Confederacy declaring independence in 1861 would not have been defeated quickly by the greater resulting comparative strength of Abraham Lincoln's Union forces.

The current borders of the United States of America may seem preordained today. After all, the policy of "manifest destiny" required that the vast center of the continental landmass be conquered, resulting in the United States reaching from sea to shining sea. However, had Daniel Morgan and Nathanael Greene not been as successful in recovering from defeat and adopting tactics that wore down and then defeated the British army in the Carolinas, the map of North America could look significantly different today. Furthermore, had the British retained the Deep South indefinitely in a status similar to what prevailed in Canada, significantly greater Loyalist manpower would have supported the Empire's forces in wars against Napoleon, the Kaiser, and perhaps even Hitler. Such additional British strength on the battlefields of Europe could have had a major impact on the arms of the scale of history.

Chapter Three

From the Failed Invasion of Canada to the Battles of Lake Erie and the Thames

Background of Defeat

After the conclusion of the American Revolution, the U.S. economy expanded rapidly. Its population more than doubled to seven million over the following thirty years due to a high birthrate, significant voluntary migration from Europe, and importation of African slaves.[1] The new nation and its former colonial master remained at peace over this time period, though relations were often strained to the breaking point. There were several areas of friction with Britain including restrictions on trade, impressment of American sailors into the Royal Navy, and relations with the Indians in the "Old Northwest" (today's states of Ohio, Indiana, Illinois, Michigan, and Wisconsin).

These disputes likely could have been settled peacefully. However, the outbreak of a series of wars in Continental Europe in the wake of the French Revolution of 1789 acted as a catalyst that resulted in armed conflict between the United States and Britain in 1812. The Royal Navy often refused to respect the sovereignty of the American flag on the high seas and the King's troops also remained at several forts on U.S. soil in the Old Northwest. From these posts, the British traded with the Indian tribes in the regions and supplied them with guns and ammunition that were used to hold back American settlers pushing into the region.

Of the nascent two-party system in America, the Jeffersonians (later the Democratic-Republicans) agitated for war, but the Federalists, who controlled the White House at the time, were more inclined to maintain the peace. This was accomplished with the ratification of the Jay Treaty in 1794, which resulted in the British evacuating the contested forts and paying $11 million in restitution for seized American shipping. In the west, American forces decisively defeated a group of Indian tribes at the Battle of Fallen Timbers in Ohio Territory allowing for a greater influx of white settlers to the region. For a time, war with Britain was averted.

While fighting raged across Europe, America was granted breathing room to expand and grow. Kentucky's population surged and it was admitted as a state of the union in 1792. Similarly, Tennessee joined in 1796, and Ohio in 1803. In that latter year, the United States effectively doubled in size with the Louisiana Purchase from Napoleon's France. This agreement codified the purchase of the entire western watershed of the Mississippi for the bargain price of $15 million, or less than three cents per acre. While the United States may have obtained an enormous empire on paper, its western lands were still inhabited by hundreds of thousands of Indigenous peoples who had no interest in relinquishing the territories they had claimed as their own for centuries.

Relations with Britain then began to deteriorate. The London government's Orders in Council in 1807 again disrupted neutral trade in the North Atlantic and resulted in the seizing of 400 U.S. merchant ships and their cargos.[2] The Royal Navy's need for personnel also increased impressment of sailors from vessels flying the American flag. Later that year, HMS *Leopard* fired on the USS *Chesapeake*, killed some of its crew and impressed others. This sparked outrage in Washington. However, America was so militarily unprepared for war that President Jefferson instead chose to support the passage of the Embargo Act of 1807, which disallowed trade with all foreign nations in the hopes of injuring the British economy. The result was primarily to financially damage the American economy in general, and northeastern states controlled by the president's political rivals, the Federalists, in particular.

The British also continued to support the independence of Indian nations in the Old Northwest and traded weapons and ammunition to the natives in return for furs and skins. Many of these tribes were being organized by military and political leader Tecumseh and his brother, the religious prophet Tenskwatawa, into a confederation with the mission of mounting armed resistance to American westward settlement toward the Mississippi. The British negotiated a military alliance in 1810 with Tecumseh, which was a major incitement to the United States.

As tensions and small-scale violence increased along the frontier in 1811, William Henry Harrison, the governor of the Indiana Territory, decided on a preemptive attack and marched with around 1,000 men on Tenskwatawa's settlement of Prophetstown. Tecumseh was away at the time and his brother led an attack on the American army, which was repulsed in the Battle of Tippecanoe. While the American Indians likely suffered fewer casualties, they withdrew westward and Harrison's men were able to loot, despoil, and burn the town. The Indians soon returned to rebuild, increased their attacks on white settlers, and cemented their new alliance with the British. Tecumseh also traveled south to rally additional tribes to his cause. While many chose not to join the war against the United States, others, such as the "Red Stick" faction of the Creeks in what is now Alabama, began to raid American settlements along the frontier.

Neither the British, occupied with waging a massive war in Europe, nor the administration of President James Madison wanted war in 1812. However, a faction in the United States known as the War Hawks, led by congressmen Henry Clay of Kentucky and John Calhoun of South Carolina, pushed for an armed conflict. While most in maritime New England were strongly opposed to a war with the world's largest naval power, many in the rest of the country believed that American honor was at stake after repeated infringements of the nation's sovereignty on the high seas. Westerners also desired a conquest of Canada so as to eliminate British efforts to arm the Indians and slow American expansion into the lands of the Old Northwest and the Louisiana Purchase. The War Hawks expected that there would be no need to raise and equip a significant army, conquest of Canada would be easy, and all that was required to seize Britain's territories to the north was a bit of marching.

Negotiations almost maintained the peace between the two English-speaking nations, and the British were prepared to compromise. However, on June 18, 1812, the United States declared war. In London, the Orders in Council were repealed just a few days later, which likely would have prevented the conflict, but the news did not reach America until weeks later. A young nation with almost no military had decided to challenge the much more powerful Britain at a time when its attention and resources were focused on defeating Napoleon. While the resulting War of 1812 is barely remembered today, except perhaps for inspiring our national anthem, the conflict was of significant consequence.

Had Washington prosecuted the war effectively, much or all of Canada could have been conquered before Britain was able to marshal the required resources to react. Of course, the War Hawks' expectations of an easy campaign to the north proved incorrect and the conflict resulted in significant U.S. human and economic losses. While American historians often spin the conflict as a heroic victory due to the young nation standing up to the bullying of the British Empire, facts tell a more nuanced story. The small U.S. Navy did score some heroic but strategically unimportant single-ship naval victories in the Atlantic, but Washington, DC was burned to the ground, and much of the Chesapeake region was plundered by the British. More importantly, the United States nearly lost its then-fragile sovereignty over what is now the state of Michigan and points west, and control of the southern terminus of the Mississippi was placed at great risk. The war also fomented a secession movement in New England that could have split the nation in two. Had the American military not recovered rapidly from an embarrassing run of early defeats along the northwestern frontier, the War of 1812 could have resulted in a national calamity with major reverberations.

The Defeat

With a population greater than seven million, exceeding Canada's by an order of magnitude, the United States had a reasonable expectation that it could conquer Britain's colony to the north while the Napoleonic Wars forced London to concentrate its forces in Europe. Lower Canada (now the province of Quebec) hosted the majority of Britain's forces in the cities of Montreal and Quebec, which could be directly resupplied by Royal Navy ships sailing up the St. Lawrence River. In contrast, sparsely settled Upper Canada (now the province of Ontario) represented an easy potential prize for the United States. Then, as today, most residents in that region made their home in the Ontario Peninsula, which is bordered by Lakes Ontario, Erie, and Huron. This water-girdled territory is actually south of several modern U.S. states and now has the highest population density in Canada, containing both its largest city (Toronto) and much of its industrial base. Even in the early nineteenth century, its rich agricultural lands, forests, relatively mild continental climate, and potential water route to the Atlantic (via canals connecting to the St. Lawrence or the Hudson) made the area attractive to European settlement.

Seizing Upper Canada, while attractive in its own right, would also sever the flow of arms and supplies from the British to the Indians living in the U.S. territories of the Old Northwest and the northern portion of the Louisiana Purchase. On their own, the Indigenous tribes had little chance of holding back the wave of American settlers moving west. The Indian population was declining as diseases and alcoholism brought by Europeans caused massive suffering. In a pitched battle, tomahawks and arrows were no match against Americans armed with rifles and cannon. However, Indians supplied with modern weapons and supported diplomatically by the United Kingdom hoping to carve out an independent state for the natives in the middle of the continent could dash the dreams of many Americans who believed the United States was destined to become a great empire.

The War Hawks believed that the conquest of Canada would be exceedingly simple. There were few natural barriers to invasion, and the majority of the Canadian population was composed of recent American settlers and descendants of French colonists. In 1810, Speaker of the House Henry Clay stated in Congress that, "the conquest of Canada is in your power. I trust that I shall not be deemed presumptuous when I state that I verily believe that the militia of Kentucky are alone competent to place Montreal and Upper Canada at your feet."[3] The former president Thomas Jefferson concurred when he wrote soon after the declaration of war: "The acquisition of Canada this year, as far as the neighborhood of Quebec, will be a mere matter of marching, & will give us experience for the attack on Halifax the next, & the final expulsion of England from the American continent."[4] The War Hawks and the Madison Administration were so confident, they hardly felt the need to prepare a professional military. When the president asked the Congress to declare war, the U.S. Army totaled fewer than 12,000 men even though it had an authorized strength twice that size. The Navy had only six frigates and a collection of smaller gunboats, none of which were on the Great Lakes.[5]

While total British armed forces in 1812 were an impressive 391,000 men (145,000 in the Royal Navy and 246,000 in the Royal Army), out of a population of close to twenty million, only a small contingent of 7,000 professional soldiers were stationed in Canada under Governor General George Prevost along with a few small armed vessels on the Great Lakes.[6] Most of these Redcoats were in Lower Canada where the British planned to focus their defense. Further west, General Isaac Brock in Upper Canada was allocated only 1,600 regulars to support 800 local militiamen to defend an enormous territory.

Militarily, the Ontario Peninsula would be difficult for Brock to defend as the United States could attack from multiple directions. In the east, the Niagara Peninsula offered an obvious invasion route, as did the Detroit River farther west. In addition, the Americans could build ships to launch amphibious attacks across both Lake Erie and Lake Ontario to strike at will against British lines of supply. The U.S. War Department's plan for the invasion of Canada was, on paper, well designed. It envisioned a two-pronged attack on Upper Canada, as well as a thrust up Lake Champlain to seize Montreal.

The first force to invade was led by the governor of the Michigan Territory, William Hull, a corpulent, elderly veteran of the Revolutionary War. He presided over a region dominated by Indians except for the trading posts that had grown up around Forts Detroit, Dearborn (now Chicago), and Mackinac (which controlled the straits between Lakes Michigan and Huron). Even among the small white population, most were ethnic French Canadians, who could not be counted on to back the American cause. The governor had never led an army in the field and at first refused an offer to assume the rank of brigadier general and lead operations against the British. After the second choice candidate fell ill, Hull reluctantly accepted the commission.[7] Gathering a mixed force of one regiment of regulars and three of Ohio militia, he crossed the Detroit

The northwestern theater of the War of 1812. NATIONAL PARK SERVICE

River into Canada in mid-July. Arriving at the town of Sandwich (now Windsor), he issued a proclamation to the local inhabitants that included the following:

> *You will be emancipated from Tyranny and oppression and restored to the dignified station of freemen. Had I any doubt of eventual success, I might ask you assistance, but I do not. I come prepared for every contingency. I have a force which will look down all opposition, & that force is but the vanguard of a much greater. If contrary to your own interest, and the just expectation of my Country, you should take part in the approaching contest, you will be considered & treated as enemies, & the horrors & calamities of war will stalk before you. If the barbarous & savage policy of Great Britain be pursued, and the savages are let loose to murder our citizens, & butcher our women and children, the war, will be a war of extermination. The first stroke of the Tomahawk, the first attempt with the scalping knife, will be the signal for one indiscriminate scene of desolation. No white man found fighting by the side of an Indian, will be taken prisoner. Instant destruction will be his lot.*[8]

This high-handed announcement served to strengthen the resolve of many Canadians to resist. The British were also formally aligned with Tecumseh's federation of Indian tribes and were not about to abandon them due to Hull's empty threat to ignore the rules of war. The American general acted with great timidity and did little except send out parties that engaged in some small skirmishes with the region's defenders. Prevost had been able to negotiate a temporary truce with the American forces to the east, which allowed British reinforcements to be rushed to Fort Malden at Amherstburg 20 miles south of Detroit. The quiet prevailing along the Niagara front also gave Brock the opportunity to travel west to take personal command of his forces in the area. After the British general arrived at Fort Malden, he proved himself to be an aggressive leader and strengthened ties with the Indians by formally committing his government to supporting the creation of an independent nation stretching from the Ohio River to the Mississippi. Such a state controlled by Indigenous peoples would not only threaten U.S. control of the Louisiana Territory, but also much of the Old Northwest including the entirety of the state of Ohio.

In early August, Tecumseh's Indians and elements of the 41st Welch Regiment of Foot crossed the river to the U.S. side of the border, fought two engagements with American detachments, and cut Hull's land-based supply line. Panicking, and believing the small American civilian population left in his rear was in peril, Hull retreated back to the fort at Detroit. Brock quickly followed up on his enemy's withdrawal and emplaced cannon across the river that began to bombard the U.S. base. He engaged in multiple subterfuges that led Hull to believe that his 2,200 men were dramatically outnumbered when the opposite was the actual case. Brock demanded an immediate surrender and threatened that he could not protect the inhabitants of the fort from Indian savagery if there was any fighting.[9] The American general capitulated, and the British captured a huge quantity of arms and ammunition. Hull was later condemned to death at a court-martial for his cowardice though his sentence was commuted by President Madison.

The Americans also quickly lost control of their other two posts in the Michigan Territory. Soon before his capitulation at Detroit, Hull had ordered the evacuation of Fort Dearborn as he believed it could not receive supplies traveling through enemy Indian territory. Captain Nathan Heald led a group of 150 soldiers and civilians from the post in an attempt to march east to safety. They were almost immediately ambushed by an Indian force that massacred more than half the Americans, took the rest prisoner, and set fire to the empty fort. At Mackinac, a small garrison of sixty American soldiers was besieged by a force several times its size composed primarily of Canadian volunteers and Indians. Fearing a massacre if they resisted, the men in the fort immediately surrendered.

Rather than gain Upper Canada, the three American defeats left all of Michigan Territory under control of the British and their Indian allies. Many tribes in the region that had remained neutral to this point now joined the fight against the United States. This resulted in the loss of several forts farther west in the Territory of Illinois, raids on settlements in Ohio, and a strengthening of Tecumseh's movement to build an independent state east of the Mississippi supported by the British.

The second invasion of Canada along the Niagara Peninsula was only slightly less embarrassing for the United States. General Stephen Van Rensselaer, in charge in this theater, was a rich landowner and New York politician who had almost no military experience. He had about 3,000 men, mostly militia, under his command at Lewiston. Nominally he also had authority over General Alexander Smyth with 2,000 additional men at Buffalo, but the latter was a regular army officer who refused to accept orders from Van Rensselaer who was "merely" a general of the New York militia. The American commander accepted a temporary truce for a set period of time proposed by the British who argued that a letter should first go to Washington to find out if the arrival of news that the Orders in Council had been repealed would lead to an immediate diplomatic conclusion of the war. This process took several weeks and the reply from the Madison War Department was that hostilities were to continue.

After the expiration of the truce, Van Rensselaer finally decided that an attack should take place in the middle of October to take control of the heights above the town of Queenston on the Canadian side of the Niagara River. Smyth refused to participate, but Van Rensselaer's men still significantly outnumbered the British forces in the area. However, the American general failed to obtain or build enough boats to bring most of his army across at one time and did not successfully disguise the time or place of his planned amphibious assault. The result was a disaster.

The first wave was composed of U.S. regular army troops who crossed the river and were initially pinned down in Queenston by fire coming from the heights above. The 13th Infantry Regiment found an unguarded path that allowed them to gain the heights and eject the British there. General Brock had recently arrived in the region from Detroit and rashly led a charge to regain the position. He was shot multiple times and died on the field, but the mixed force of Redcoats and Canadian militia retook the heights. The Americans counterattacked, and once again forced the British to retreat.

Van Rensselaer should have achieved a victory on the day, but when he ordered his New York militia to cross the river, they refused to leave the state.[10] The exasperated American general ordered a withdrawal back across the river, but the U.S. regulars, under command of Lieutenant Colonel Winfield Scott, were trapped on the Canadian side as the militia would not even row to the far bank to save their fellow countrymen. Scott and his entire force of nearly 1,000 men were compelled to surrender. The British suffered few casualties and won the day, but Brock's death had a major impact on the fighting along the frontier as his replacements proved less competent throughout the remainder of the war.

The refusal of eastern state militias to cross into Canada was not an isolated incident. When General Smyth finally attempted to lead his men across the Niagara, it was the Pennsylvania militia in his force that refused to follow him. Finally, after an overly lengthy sojourn in New England recruiting, the overall American commander in the theater, General Henry Dearborn (known as "Granny" to his men due to his age and bearing) was finally ready to launch what was supposed to be the largest invasion thrust into Canada via Lake Champlain to seize Montreal. However, militiamen from New York and the New England states refused to cross the border arguing that due to the terms of their enlistments, they were not legally required to fight on foreign soil. Eventually, the operation was cancelled.

Back in the West, the Americans suffered a final brutal defeat. In January 1813, General James Winchester with about 1,000 men had pushed across the Ohio border and seized the fortified post of Frenchtown along the Raisin River in Michigan Territory. Hearing of this, Colonel (later General) Henry Proctor, who had assumed command in the area after Brock's departure, immediately marched south from Fort Malden with a mixed force of Redcoats, Canadian militia, and Indian allies. He attacked before sunrise and achieved complete surprise on the January 22. The Americans were routed with a large number killed and scalped before surrendering. Despite Proctor promising fair treatment to the prisoners, many were massacred by the Indians who left mutilated bodies along the river's banks to be gnawed upon by local dogs and packs of wolves. "Remember the River Raisin" became an effective recruiting slogan and battle cry in the western United States for the rest of the conflict.

The defeat of the War Hawks' plan was total. American forces had performed poorly in combat and the leadership was sorely deficient. Not only had the United States failed to conquer Canada, it had lost control of much of its western territories in the Old Northwest. Residents of the British colony, rather than embrace joining the republic to the south, had shown they were ready to resist an invasion and were led by competent professional officers. Reacting to failures on the battlefield, Indian tribes who had remained neutral early in the conflict were now taking up arms all along the American frontier in an effort to push back settlers who had moved onto their lands. Back east, dissent in New England against the war was rising so as to sap U.S. military strength, and an aroused government in London was sending reinforcements and supplies to its colony's aid.

Recovery

The War Hawks realized to their chagrin that taking Canada was not going to be a mere matter of marching. To avoid a catastrophic defeat, more soldiers would be needed led by effective commanders. In addition, a fleet would somehow have to be procured to challenge the naval squadrons the British were constructing on Lakes Erie, Ontario, and Champlain. The struggle of the War of 1812 was no longer only over American rights at sea and control of Canada. Victories by the Indians and British meant that the war would now determine if the United States would lose sovereignty over what we now call the American Midwest.

Of course, all was not lost and a kind of victory was still possible. Dreams of an easy conquest of Quebec and march on Halifax had become wildly unrealistic, but a recovery along the western frontier was achievable. After all, British control over Upper Canada and aid flowing to its Indian allies in the Michigan and Illinois Territories was dependent upon supply lines flowing along Lakes Ontario and Erie. Cut that artery and the larger local American population in the region could reestablish U.S. territorial claims.

Despite a series of reverses on the battlefield, President Madison was reelected in November 1812 with a narrow 50.4 percent of the popular vote but a lopsided Electoral College victory of 128 to 89 due to the three-fifths clause of the Constitution that boosted the voting power of slave states. He carried the Mid-Atlantic, the West, and the South but lost almost everywhere in the Northeast. With the safety of four additional years in office, Madison hoped that major changes in the personnel carrying out the war with Britain would lead to better results. Secretary of War William was replaced by John Armstrong, Secretary of the Navy Paul Hamilton gave way to William Jones, and new commanders were soon installed along the Canadian border.[11]

The British and Indian allies were increasingly outnumbered in 1813 as American men and material streamed northward toward the frontier. While many U.S. commanders remained subpar and its soldiers were not professionally trained, its outsized population advantage would be brought to bear against Canada while Britain remained focused on the war in Europe against Napoleon. Hardened American frontiersmen, fearful of an emboldened Indian offensive against their settlements, rallied to the flag and several young aggressive officers got the opportunity to lead from the front. While many of the actions along the Canadian frontier through the rest of the War of 1812 resulted in lopsided U.S. casualties, it was a campaign of attrition that favored the young nation against its former imperial master.

After Hull's embarrassing defeat, William Henry Harrison had been made commander of the Army of the Northwest. He was tasked with retaking Detroit, and placed in charge of a wave of new recruits being armed to defend the frontier. Initially greatly outnumbered, he took up a defensive position and ordered the construction of Fort Meigs in Ohio on the Maumee River near where it empties into the far western end of Lake Erie. There Harrison directed a rising number of soldiers and militia into a force that could go onto the offensive.

In the center of the Canadian front, Commodore Isaac Chauncey was tasked with overseeing the construction of warships or conversion of merchant vessels to compose fleets intended to seize control of Lakes Erie and Ontario. He delegated the former flotilla to Master Commandant Oliver Hazard Perry who was not yet thirty years of age, while directing the bulk of arriving naval resources to his efforts on Lake Ontario. As the size of the armies in the region increased, command of these two bodies of water became increasingly critical to both sides. The road network around the lakes was generally composed of dirt paths through the woods that became morasses of mud after rains. Thus, large bodies of men, weapons, and supplies could only be transported effectively by ship. However, the British could not sail their ocean-going vessels through the rapids on the St. Lawrence west of Montreal. A shortage of materials, tools, craftsmen, and sailors along Lakes Erie and Ontario hindered the construction and operation of warships by both nations. It was clear that whoever's fleet came to dominate these freshwater seas would also have a marked advantage in the land combat to follow.

Victory

As the spring campaigning season opened in 1813, the United States achieved its first victory in Canada. General Dearborn had been ordered by Armstrong to attack the British base and shipyard at Kingston on Lake Ontario where it empties into the St. Lawrence River. However, the U.S. theater commander chose a target that seemed to be less well defended. Chauncey's small flotilla of armed lake schooners and a couple of purpose-built warships crammed more than 1,500 men of Dearborn's army aboard and sailed them across to the north shore of Lake Ontario. Their target was the town of York (now Toronto), the provincial capital of Ontario.

The Americans brushed aside resistance on the shoreline as they landed and forced the smaller defending force of Redcoats and Canadian militia to retreat from the town. Dearborn's men seized warships under construction along the waterfront and captured naval stores destined for the British fleet being built on Lake Erie. However, close to 20 percent of the invasion force became casualties by the end of the operation, primarily due to a massive detonation of the garrison's munition stores triggered by the Redcoats who escaped overland to the east. Dearborn ordered the burning of all government buildings, and a good deal of looting took place. As a result, local Canadian opinion across the region hardened against the invaders, and the British swore revenge for the destruction of the provincial assembly building. The American amphibious force sailed back to the Niagara Peninsula having at least compromised enemy naval strength on Lakes Ontario and Erie.

Soon after the attack on York, the United States won another small, though costly, victory in northwest Ohio. A joint British and Indian force under General Proctor and Tecumseh besieged Fort Meigs. The post's commander, General Green Clay, received reinforcements so that the garrison swelled to almost 3,000 and soon outnumbered the attackers. A sortie across the Maumee River captured British cannon and drove off the besiegers. The fort remained in American hands and the Ohio frontier was protected. However Kentucky militia under Colonel William Dudley rashly pressed their pursuit into the woods where they were ambushed. Dudley was killed early in the fight and most of his 850 men were killed or taken prisoner with many massacred by the Indians after their surrender.[12]

Over the next few months both sides worked feverishly to build serviceable fleets to gain control of the two Great Lakes while raiding the other side's shipyards. Another minor American victory was achieved in late May when Dearborn and 4,000 men embarked on Chauncey's growing flotilla to seize Fort George at the terminus of the Niagara River where it empties into Lake Ontario. The commander of the British garrison, General John Vincent, was outnumbered more than three to one but chose to oppose the first wave of the amphibious landing. As the vanguard of the American force, led by the young and aggressive Colonel Winfield Scott, was disembarking from small boats, the Redcoats attacked and a brisk fight took place along the shore. The British were driven back with the aid of cannon fire from Chauncey's ships and additional waves of U.S. soldiers were able to land. Rather than allow himself to be surrounded and besieged, Vincent chose to withdraw from Fort George, which was captured mostly intact.

The British commander then decided to concentrate his outnumbered forces and ordered that Fort Erie be abandoned and its garrison merge with the rest of his men along the northern shore of the Niagara Peninsula where they dug in along defensive heights. When Dearborn followed up his victory by sending a column in pursuit, Vincent staged a nighttime counterattack at Stoney Creek, captured two American generals, and forced the invaders to pull back. Once again, Dearborn was derided for allowing a large British force to escape. He was subsequently relieved of his post and soon chose to retire from the Army. While certainly not the greatest of American generals, Dearborn deserves more credit than he has received by most historians. After his poor showing in the first campaign of the war, he did become more aggressive and successful in the second, and his accomplishments had a major impact later in the conflict.

While not a decisive victory, the abandonment of Fort Erie resulted in a critical enlargement in the size of the U.S. fleet on the lakes. Without the Redcoats manning the cannon at the western end of the Niagara Peninsula, the blockade of the American naval station of Black Rock downriver from Buffalo was lifted. This allowed four converted merchantmen, the USS *Somers*, *Trippe*, *Ohio*, and *Caledonia* to be towed up the Niagara River into Lake Erie. They then sailed west to join the rest of Perry's growing fleet at the port of Presque Isle (now Erie, Pennsylvania).[13] At the same time, while Chauncey's fleet was off Fort George, the British attempted to seize the American naval yard at Sackett's Harbor and the corvette USS *General Pike*, which was nearing completion there. The garrison held off the attack, and Chauncey subsequently sailed the completed ship to an engagement against the British squadron on Lake Ontario off York in September. In the resulting battle, the enemy flagship, HMS *Wolfe*, was badly damaged and the Americans gained control of the lake for the remainder of the year.

To the west, Commander Robert Heriot Barclay was in charge of the British flotilla of seven ships docked at Fort Malden. As with those of the Americans, his ships were composed of converted merchant schooners along with a few purpose-built warships that had been hastily constructed of green wood and often held together with wooden pegs due to a shortage of iron nails. Cannon and ammunition had to be hauled overland by both sides; the naval commanders had only a few trained sailors each and were forced to use soldiers and militiamen to fill out their crews. In August of 1813, Barclay had Fort Malden's cannon stripped so as to arm his largest ship, the HMS *Detroit*. Perry and his nine ships had effective control of the rest of Lake Erie and blocked waterborne shipments of food for the Redcoats and Indian allies concentrated around

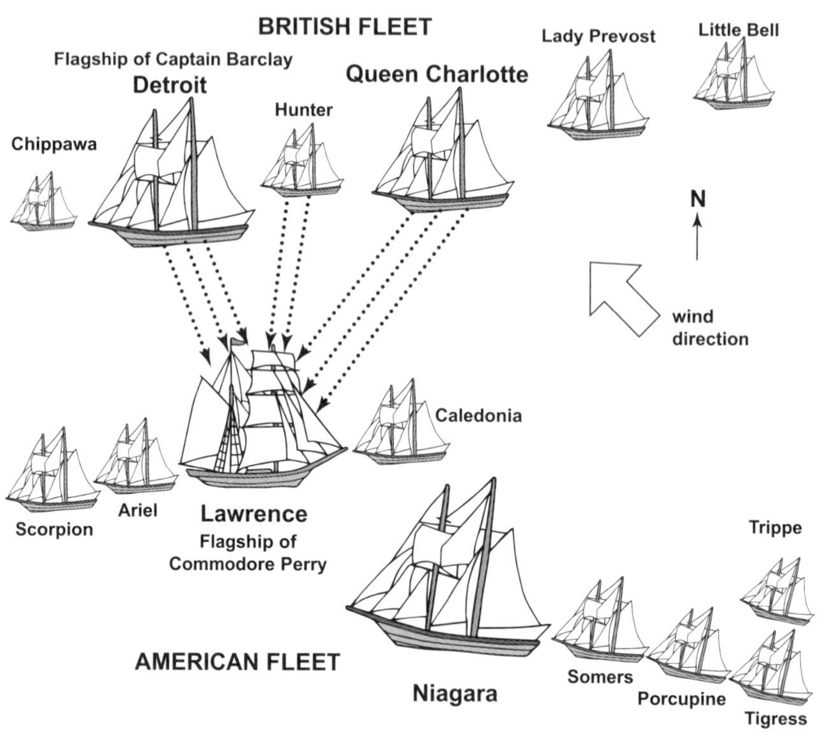

The opposing fleets in the Battle of Lake Erie. NATIONAL PARK SERVICE

Fort Malden. With supplies running low and winter approaching, Barclay needed to sortie and fight. Perry was ready and waiting for him when their two fleets clashed in the late morning of September 10.

While the British flotilla had fewer ships, it boasted a larger total number of cannon. However, Perry had a greater complement of men aboard his fleet and the throw weight of his guns was almost double that of Barclay's command.[14] In the resulting Battle of Lake Erie, the two fleets slugged it out with the American commander flying his pennant adorned with "Don't give up the ship," which remains the unofficial motto of the U.S. Navy to this day. Perry started the fight on the USS *Lawrence* but it was eventually shot to pieces by the British, most of its crew became casualties, and its cannon were disabled. Under constant fire, he was then rowed in a small boat to the USS *Niagara* where he took command and continued the battle. After more than three hours of gunfire, Barclay and most of his officers had been wounded and the largest British ships, HMS *Detroit* and *Queen Charlotte*, were forced to strike their colors. The rest of Barclay's flotilla surrendered soon after. Perry penned a short note to General Harrison, "We have met the enemy and they are ours. Two ships, two brigs, one schooner and one sloop."

While only around 1,000 men participated in the naval battle, the American victory was decisive and dramatically shifted the fortunes of war against the British and their Indian allies in the region. The United States retained control of Lake Erie, which had a major impact on the ground campaign in the Ontario Peninsula in the remainder of 1813. While Dearborn may have been replaced for perceived deficiencies of generalship, it can be argued that his victories were of the greatest import for the Battle of Lake Erie and the subsequent Battle of the Thames. Dearborn's capture of cannon at York that were on their way to British ships on Lake Erie reduced Barclay's firepower in the resulting battle. Also, Dearborn's operation against the Niagara Peninsula forced the British to retreat from Forts George and Erie, with the latter's abandonment leading directly to Perry having a larger fleet when he confronted the British. As the future president Theodore Roosevelt wrote of the Battle of Lake Erie in 1883, "The important fact was that though we had nine guns less, yet, at a broadside, they threw half as much metal again as those of our antagonist. With such odds in our favor it would have been a disgrace to have been beaten."[15]

Cut off from supplies, low on food, and with Fort Malden stripped of its heavy guns, General Proctor decided to retreat. Tecumseh and the rest of the Indian allies were shocked that the British would not stand and fight. To convince the native warriors to move north farther into Canada with him, a compromise was reached in which Proctor agreed he would only march his Redcoats a short distance up the Thames River to Moraviatown where appropriate defendable ground would be fortified to hold off any pursuing force.

The Americans took quick advantage of the situation with Perry's fleet transporting Harrison and 2,500 men to seize Fort Malden on September 27, while a separate force of 1,000 mounted Kentuckians regained Detroit. This time, state militia had no compunction against crossing the border into Canada after passing American remains rotting at the sites of earlier massacres near Frenchtown and Fort Meigs. The Kentuckians moved to the east side of the river to link up with Harrison's main army. The Americans then began a pursuit of Proctor and soon closed the distance between the two forces. The British, with about 800 Redcoats and a similar number of allied Indian warriors, were low on food, and morale was poor. Concerned that they would be overtaken before they reached Moraviatown, Proctor had his men form up in line of battle on the morning of October 5. They assembled in a forested area along the banks of the Thames with the Indians on their flank. This was a poor choice as fighting in the woods from an unreinforced position negated the British ability to mass their fire, communicate, and maneuver while also not providing any significant barrier to the mounted Kentuckians.

Upon arriving on the scene with his much larger force, Harrison ordered an attack and the horsemen raced forward yelling "Remember the Raisin!" The Redcoats were overrun and routed with most being captured. The Indians fought on for a time but they too were forced to retreat and fled the field. They left behind the corpse of Tecumseh who had been shot in the chest. His body was mutilated by the Americans: It was scalped, remaining tufts of hair were yanked out, and strips of skin were cut off from the legs and back to make into razor straps.[16] With the British armed forces in the area defeated, and his militiamen's term of enlistment coming to an end, Harrison withdrew back to the U.S. side of the Detroit River.

The Battle of the Thames is one of the least known decisive engagements in American military history. After the loss of naval control of Lake Erie, the abandonment of Fort Malden resulted in Britain losing any claim to control of the Michigan Territory in a peace conference. In addition, its ability to exert diplomatic and military influence into the Ohio and Mississippi River valleys was greatly diminished. The death of Tecumseh also led to a shattering of his confederation of Indian tribes that he and his brother had spent over a decade assembling. The following year, General Andrew Jackson led a militia force to decisively defeat the Red Stick Creek Indians at the Battle of Horseshoe Bend in what is now Alabama. Never again was there a concerted effort by the Indians to hold back the advancing wave of Americans in their quest to fulfill their "manifest destiny" of conquering westward to the Pacific. While individual tribes or tribal grouping such as the Seminole, Nez Perce, or Sioux may have successfully opposed the U.S. Army for a time, their eventual defeat was inevitable due to their smaller relative numbers and lack of a western patron nation that could furnish a steady supply of modern arms and ammunition.

The war continued, and 1814 saw the United States progressively forced onto the defensive. With Napoleon's defeat at Leipzig and his subsequent abdication, Britain was able to shift large military resources to North America. The Royal Navy either sunk the ships of America's Atlantic fleet or bottled them up in port, while reinforcements exceeding 15,000 Redcoats poured into North America. Luckily for the United States, rather than formulating a single strategy, British leaders could not agree on a unified plan. Some simply wanted to exact vengeance and humiliate the Americans. Others had a larger vision and wished to seize northern territories from the United States or gain control of the Mississippi delta.[17] Had the government in London focused on one of these geographic goals, it likely could have achieved it. However, it split its resources and ended up gaining none.

Along the Atlantic in 1814, rather than move quickly to seize New Orleans and control the exit of the Mississippi, Admiral George Cockburn of the Royal Navy chose to focus on a punitive campaign in the Chesapeake, which had already been successfully raided the year before. He landed an amphibious force of 1,500 Redcoats that easily scattered a much larger American force, primarily of militia, defending Washington at the Battle of Bladensburg. Madison and his government fled and the U.S. Capitol was sacked and burned by the British on August 24 as revenge for the destruction of the provincial legislature at York. Cockburn then targeted Baltimore. This effort was stymied by the courage of the defenders of Fort McHenry (which gave birth to the U.S. national anthem). Believing the American government had received sufficient chastisement, the British then sailed to Bermuda and began preparations for a campaign against New Orleans. This latter effort was defeated after a peace treaty was signed but prior to the news reaching North America. While the sack of Washington, DC was embarrassing for U.S. military forces, Cockburn's incursion secured no territory for the British and did not have a strategic impact on the outcome of the war.

In Canada, Britain made use of reinforcements to go on the offensive. In the Northwest, new ships were launched that outclassed the American fleet on Lake Ontario, and the British made an attempt to regain control of the Niagara Peninsula before pushing across Lake Erie. U.S. Generals Jacob Brown and Winfield Scott conducted themselves well against the British regulars but were eventually forced onto the defensive and withdrew to Fort Erie after the Battles of Chippawa and Lundy's Lane. However, the British were repulsed in a series of assaults in August and September during the siege of the fort and were unable to regain control of Lake Erie. Finally, in Montreal, yet another army under Prevost marched south along Lake Champlain with the hazy goal of detaching Vermont and other restive parts of New England from the United States. However, the fleet engagement on September 11, known today as the Battle of Plattsburg, resulted in an overwhelming American victory. Without control of the lake, Prevost concluded that he could not supply his large army and ordered a retreat back to Canada.

Both sides were tired of the conflict by the end of 1814. With the end of the Napoleonic Wars in Europe, Britain no longer needed to impress American sailors to crew its ships nor interfere with neutral U.S. shipping sailing to Europe. The Warhawks' dream of seizing Canada had been proven to be infeasible and the British ceded any claim to the creation of an independent Indian nation in the lands south of the Great Lakes. Thus, the two English-speaking belligerents agreed to a peace treaty at Ghent that affirmed the status quo ante.

The United States and Britain both declared victory. The British, always primarily focused on Napoleon's defeat, believed they had prevailed as Canada had been successfully defended and the upstart United States had been taught a lesson as the government buildings in Washington were burned to the ground. The Americans could also claim to have won as they had successfully stood up for their rights on the high seas, ensured U.S. sovereignty over the lands of the Old Northwest, and defended the city of New Orleans. The subsequent Rush-Bagot Treaty of 1817 demilitarized the Great Lakes and laid the foundation for a peaceful border with Canada, which stands to this day. What was clear is that the Indians were the losers of the War of 1812. Tecumseh's confederation was shattered, and native tribes east of the Mississippi would increasingly find themselves exterminated or ejected westward from their ancestral homelands in subsequent years. The American victories at the Battles of Lake Erie and the Thames ensured that the United States would be left alone to develop its rapidly growing continental empire.

Causes of Defeat

There were several specific reasons for the series of defeats suffered by U.S. forces early in the conflict along the Canadian frontier. The overarching problem was that the young republic was unprepared to fight. The Madison Administration chose to start a war without taking the proper steps to win it: It failed to raise an army large enough for the task, ignored advice to procure sufficient shipping to transport forces and supplies along the Great Lakes, and entrusted command to older, tentative officers unfit for the mission.

The initial invasion of Canada resulted in a string of embarrassments for the Americans. The most blatant failure was from General Hull who did not want the command offered to him, but after accepting it, chose to cross the border without securing his supply lines. Then he failed to move with alacrity to besiege Fort Malden, which allowed a detachment of enemy forces to operate in his rear. A panicked Hull beat a hasty retreat back to Detroit rather than attempting to seize the British base of power in the region. In addition, he failed to maximize his striking power versus that of his opponents. While there is little chance he could have kept Tecumseh and his confederation out of the war, he certainly could have done more to create alliances with other Indian tribes in the region and bring in some of their warriors as auxiliaries to enlarge his force's strength. Similarly, Hull made little effort to win favor and recruits at the many settlements populated by frontiersmen who had recently moved from the United States into Upper Canada. Instead, his high-handed proclamation helped push the locals into supporting the British. Finally, rather than defend his well-fortified and supplied position at Fort Detroit and wait for reinforcements to arrive, he precipitously surrendered after suffering almost no casualties.

Van Rensselaer and Smyth did little better with their two armies along the Niagara. While they heavily outnumbered the British in the area, Smyth refused to coordinate with his militia officer counterpart in what can only be viewed as a criminal dereliction of duty. This allowed the British to shift forces to counter the American attack on Queenston. Van Rensselaer's generalship, while more aggressive than that of Smyth's, was almost as deficient as the preparation of his amphibious operation and management of the morale of his men was atrocious. The result was the surrender of a large body of U.S. troops and a victory for the British marred only by the loss of their commander, General Brock, on the field of battle.

Finally, General Dearborn, in charge of American forces along the northern front, also performed poorly. After frittering away much of the campaigning season focused on recruitment, the men he rallied to the flag simply refused to cross the border with him into Canada even though an invasion of the British colony was the specific task for which they had been recruited. While his leadership was somewhat more energetic in 1813, his stillborn invasion of the prior year placed Dearborn in a precarious position with his superiors in the Madison Administration.

The United States expected an easy victory in Canada. President Madison could have achieved it had he instructed his War Department to focus on the basics prior to asking Congress for a declaration of war. Attempting to invade a hostile nation with poorly supplied troops led by timorous, amateur generals lacking naval support was a recipe for disaster. And a series of disasters was indeed the result. It was the first time the United States failed to prepare for an armed conflict that was clearly going to take place. It would not be the last.

Causes of Victory

The United States reacted and looked to find a way to recover from its initial setbacks along the Northwest frontier. The first important step was to install aggressive, capable commanders and accept the necessity of building a navy on the Great Lakes. The latter was required to contest British control of those waters, ferry ground forces from point to point, and transport supplies. Commodore Chauncey rapidly assembled a flotilla on Lake Ontario that achieved significant success. It carried General Dearborn's troops to York and then Fort George in what resulted in U.S. victories and defeat of the British fleet in September. After retreating to harbor, the Americans gained control of the lake for a year. It was only in late 1814 when the HMS *St. Lawrence* was launched that a now outgunned Chauncey retreated to Sackett's Harbor where he and his flotilla were forced to wait out the final few months of the war.

While General Dearborn retained his position after his poor showing in 1812, and recorded some victories the following year, he was seen as overly indecisive in nature and was replaced by General Jacob Brown who was a much more aggressive commander with a reputation for attention to detail. He was ably assisted by Winfield Scott who rose through the ranks to command a brigade by the end of the war. In a series of battles in 1814, the American armies performed well against British regulars and successfully defended Fort Erie on the Niagara Peninsula.

The 1813 victories at York and Fort George were small in of themselves, but they reduced British naval power on Lake Erie and increased that of the United States. The result was that Oliver Hazard Perry gained a critical advantage that he put to great use when he captured the entire opposing British fleet. This triumph gave the United States control of Lake Erie, which in turn forced enemy forces to abandon Fort Malden. American General William Henry Harrison immediately took advantage of this and his aggressive pursuit paid off in the Battle of the Thames in which most of the British regulars surrendered, Tecumseh was killed, and his Indian warriors scattered. Lake Erie remained in U.S. control for the rest of the war and while fighting continued with Indian tribes across the Old Northwest, American sovereignty over the lands south of the Great Lakes was assured.

How the United States reacted to its initial defeats, recovered, and ultimately triumphed was quite clear: Better commanders were placed in key roles, and a larger population and industrial base in the region was mobilized. Without the rapid building of two fleets and aggressive naval commanders, American forces would not have gained the ability to take control of the lines of supply on Lakes Ontario and Erie. General Harrison took advantage of this change in relative strength to defeat the British and their Indian allies and regained control over Michigan and adjacent U.S. territories.

However, America's military recovery and victory was not solely due to the nation's own efforts. Luck and events in Europe were critical. The War of 1812 was precipitated by Britain's efforts to defeat Napoleon's France. The Royal Navy was focused on blockading European ports while the Duke of Wellington was leading a British army of more than 50,000 men in Spain and Portugal. It was only after Napoleon's abdication in 1814 that significant reinforcements could be sent to Canada in an attempt to roll back American gains there. Had France been defeated sooner, large formations of veteran British troops transported earlier across the Atlantic could have tipped the balance resulting in defeats for the United States. Such a scenario could have yielded a very different set of borders along the Great Lakes than those that prevail today. Conversely, had Napoleon remained in power through 1815 or later, for example in a scenario where he chose not to invade Russia, local preponderance of U.S. military strength could have resulted in Upper Canada falling into American hands.

Impact of Defeat

As previously discussed, the failure of American arms along the Canadian frontier in 1812 resulted in the British/Indian alliance taking control of much of the land west of Lakes Erie and Huron. Had the United States not been able to recover and successfully go over to the offensive, a peace treaty likely would have resulted in the territory now composing the states of Michigan and Wisconsin (and perhaps Indiana and Illinois as well) being ceded to either British Canada or a new Indian republic under London's protection. While we now generally accept the current borders of the United States to have been preordained, it is important to recall that territories across the Caribbean and North America regularly changed hands as the result of wars in the period 1615–1815.

It is difficult to believe that the rapidly expanding population of the United States would have accepted the loss of lands south of the Great Lakes with equanimity. Leaders in Washington might have launched another war in an attempt to regain this lost territory. Or perhaps peace could have prevailed in the "Old Northwest" due to British strength, with Yankee expansion instead focused on the much larger region of the Louisiana Purchase. Either way, such a defeat in the War of 1812 could have dramatically bent the course of history. After the loss of lands that historically became prosperous states in the upper Midwest, would America have compensated by seizing even more land from Mexico in 1848 in the Treaty of Guadalupe Hidalgo? Would the border agreed upon between what is now Washington State and British Columbia in 1846 be farther north . . . or farther south? Without the men of Michigan and Wisconsin, could the Union have prevailed over the Confederacy in the 1860s? Would an Indian nation south of the Great Lakes have provided military aid to native tribes such as the Sioux, Pawnee, Crow, and Cheyenne, retarding the pace of American westward expansion? Asking such counterfactual questions reveals the importance of the United States finding a way to recover militarily in 1813, gain naval control of Lakes Erie and Ontario, push into Upper Canada, and regain Detroit and the Michigan Territory.

Impact of Victory

Of the conflicts fought by the United States in the first 170 years of its existence, the War of 1812 was the only one that did not result in a decisive victory that satisfied all the goals for which the nation had fought. The Revolutionary War won America its independence, and the Civil War ensured its overall integrity. Fighting with Mexico, Spain, and Indian nations resulted in the United States gaining the geographic expansion it coveted, and Washington dictated the terms of the peace at the conclusion of both world wars. The War of 1812 stands apart in that America failed to achieve its goals in a military conflict. None of Canada was conquered, and while the Royal Navy ceased seizing American merchant ships and impressing members of their crews on the Atlantic, Britain did not repudiate its right to engage in either action in the future.

However, this does not mean that the war did not result in a significant victory for the United States. While American forces may have been repulsed from marching deep into Canada, and the White House was reduced to ash by British troops, there is no doubt that Tecumseh's Indian federation suffered a crushing defeat. While other native tribes had come together previously in certain regions to resist American expansion, the Shawnee chief's effort was the one that came close to creating a functioning alliance stretching from the Great Lakes to the Gulf Coast presenting a united military front against the white frontiersmen surging west from the Atlantic. With the death of its charismatic leader, the Indian movement collapsed. And without a steady supply of arms and ammunition from a European patron such as Britain, subsequent Indigenous resistance to American expansion was foreordained to fail.

Thus the victories along the Canadian frontier in 1813 were much more consequential than most Americans understand them to have been. In their absence, the peaceful northern border of the continental United States could have remained a contentious frontier. By the end of the war Britain accepted that the interior of the North American continent south and southwest of the Ontario Peninsula was going to be settled and controlled by Yankees. That also meant the United States would be left to conquer the Indian tribes within its borders as it saw fit. The end of British influence over events on the southern shores of the Great Lakes also resulted in American acceptance that Canada was not going to be conquered to become part of the United States. Thus, both Washington and London agreed that the freshwater inland seas separating British Canada and the United States should be demilitarized and jointly developed. The opening of the Erie, Lachine, and Welland Canals in the 1820s connected the Great Lakes to the Hudson and the St. Lawrence Rivers, and the Atlantic beyond. Peace, canals, and the later construction of railroads triggered the dramatic rapid agricultural and industrial economic growth that took place in the region over the following century on both sides of the U.S.-Canada border.

Chapter Four

The Rout at First Bull Run to the Critical Victory at Antietam

Background of Defeat

After the conclusion of the War of 1812, the United States grew remarkably quickly. By 1820 the nation's population had expanded to almost 10 million, rose to 12.8 million in 1830, and surged to over 17 million in 1840.[1] As the population pushed west, the states of Louisiana, Indiana, Mississippi, Illinois, Alabama, Maine, Missouri, Arkansas, Michigan, Florida, and Texas were admitted to the Union. The last was not part of the Old Northwest or the Louisiana Territory but broke away from Mexico in 1836 after around 15,000 Americans streamed into the sparsely settled territory and then successfully rose in revolt.

That such a small population could defeat the weak Mexican army made it clear that the United States could effectively seize as much of its neighbor's northern territory as it so desired. This was accomplished in a short war from 1846 to 1848 that forced the Mexican government to cede all its lands west and north of Texas. The dream of Manifest Destiny and a republic that stretched from the Atlantic to the Pacific had been fulfilled. However, this expansion only temporarily papered over the cracks that were slowly ripping the young nation apart.

The American Civil War of 1861 to 1865 is known by several names, which reflect the differing mindsets of those who survived it. The dictum is that history is written by the victors. Thus, as the Federal government arguably won the military conflict in the field, it is surprising that it is not generally known by the title used by the official history issued in the late nineteenth century by the U.S. War Department: "The War of the Rebellion."[2] As a rebellion is a violent uprising, and it was one that took place against a government defending the U.S. Constitution and its Bill of Rights, the name implies that the Confederates were engaged in treason and a fight against liberty.

Of course, many in the South reject such a characterization of their forefathers and refer to the conflict as the "War of Northern Aggression." This implies that the Union states were the unjust belligerents who suppressed the Confederacy when it was only attempting to protect the freedoms enshrined in the American Constitution. One can reasonably argue today as to whether or not the result of the conflict, whichever name it is given, ended in a Union victory in 1865, concluded in a draw in 1877, or even that it still has not yet been decided.

No matter how we reflect back on the Civil War today, it was clearly a military conflict that the Federal government could have lost. Had the Confederacy been successful in its attempt at secession, the impact on world events would have been enormous. The fighting from 1861 to 1865 was a terrible bloodletting, which shaped the nation's history. Many historians point out that the Civil War resulted in more U.S. dead than World War II due to the soldiers on both sides being American. While true, this does not really convey the magnitude of the losses that took place among the population of Americans, which totaled thirty-one million at the start of the war. The number of *just* Union military dead in the Civil War was close to that suffered by the *entire* United States from 1941 to 1945 (364,511 vs. 405,399). The fatality rate among those who served on the Federal side under Lincoln was greater than 15 percent, and the figure for the Confederates was similar. In contrast, this ratio was only around 3 percent for Americans who fought in World War II.[3] In no other American war did the rate of those serving who never returned home even begin to approach that which occurred from 1861 to 1865.

Today we still argue about why the Civil War took place. Many embrace the "lost cause myth" claiming that the tragically outnumbered

Rebels were honorable and heroic men who fought not to preserve slavery, but to promote the freedoms and states' rights promised to all Americans in the Constitution. Others argue that the conflict was due to tariffs imposed on the South by a tyrannical Federal government.[4] When Nikki Haley, a GOP candidate for president, was asked why the South seceded in 2023, the former South Carolina governor and U.S. ambassador to the United Nations (UN) replied: "I think the cause of the civil war was basically how government was going to run, the freedoms and what people could and couldn't do."[5] This was a shocking statement from someone campaigning to lead the Republican Party, which was founded in 1854 by antislavery activists who wished to restrict the spread of human bondage in the United States. Its first presidential candidate was John C. Frémont who in 1856 ran under the slogan, "Free men, free soil, and Frémont!" Its second nominee, famously, was Abraham Lincoln: a man who was publicly opposed to the expansion of slavery in the United States, expressed great antipathy for the "peculiar institution," and who is best remembered for the Emancipation Proclamation that made millions of Black men and women "forever free" as the Union advanced steadily toward victory.[6]

After her initial answer was broadly criticized, Ms. Haley soon shifted her stance and stated, "of course the Civil War was about slavery, we know that, that's the easy part of it. I'm from the South. Of course you know it's about slavery."[7] While states' rights and tariffs were certainly contributing factors to the Confederacy's secession, protection of slavery was the driver of the conflict and had a vast impact on how the war played out over time. The point is not that we have divisive politics in the nation today, but rather that the Civil War was an ideological struggle in which, increasingly, neither side believed it could compromise or give quarter. As historian James McPherson put it, "the Civil War was pre-eminently a political war, a war of peoples rather than of professional armies."[8] This helps to explain why the conflict was so bloody and the reasons it was fought remain controversial to this day.

In the South in 1860, a Union invasion was seen as one that would trigger a social revolution: An end to slavery would decimate the capital investments of the wealthy oligarchs who controlled the Confederacy, and freeing of the slaves was feared by working class whites as an event that would reduce their wages and their status in society. To Unionists, a successful secession of the Confederacy would not only allow the abomination of human servitude to continue, but also undermine the stability of the dramatically successful democratic enterprise on which the republic had been launched with the ratification of the Constitution in 1788.

Many on both sides believed that the conflict would be a quick one. In the South, there was hope that the North would accept the secession or come to agree to it after some performative bloodshed made clear that the men of the Confederacy would fight to the end rather than yield. In the North, many believed that the rebellion would collapse quickly in the face of overwhelming Federal armed might. Of course, neither scenario played out, and instead the result was a long fratricidal war.

In this, the North had a great advantage. It is a core fact that slavery retarded economic growth in the South. In 1848, Alexis de Tocqueville traveled the nation and explicitly detailed how slavery resulted in less industrialization and a weaker economy wherever it was legal. He described the stark difference between the south bank of the Ohio River in Kentucky, which had slavery, compared to the more productive enterprise on the north bank in the "free" state of Ohio.[9] In 1857, the "proud Southerner" and extreme racist Hinton Rowan Helper published *The Impending Crisis of the South: How to Meet It*, which had a great impact across the nation. The book cited detailed statistics to argue that slavery was economically crippling wherever it was allowed and that the institution needed to be abolished.

By the time eleven states in the South seceded to form the Confederate States of America in 1861, the negative impact of slavery on economic growth and desirability of where immigrants to the United States wished to settle had created great regional imbalances in the nation. The North had twenty-two million residents in 1860 compared to only nine million in the Confederacy of which three and a half million were slaves. Only 18,000 of the nation's 128,000 industrial firms were in the South and the

Confederacy's industrial output was only 7.5 percent of the U.S. total. The states remaining in the Union dominated the nation's shipbuilding and had 22,000 miles of railroad compared to only 9,000 in the Confederacy.[10] These disparities led many to hope that the rebellion would be quickly suppressed after Lincoln ascended to the presidency.

However, the South had many advantages. First, it controlled a vast territory (comparable in size to Western Europe), and thus had some strategic depth. It was also defended by men who were ready to fight and believed that any potential loss of perceived honor must be resisted by force of arms. The South had a military tradition, and its white men were better trained to fight due to the potential need to suppress slave revolts. The region also had strong ties to Britain due to trade and family connections. The Union would have to tread carefully in its effort to conquer the South without bringing London into the conflict on the side of the Confederacy.

The South was also a haven for the Anopheles mosquito, which transmitted malaria. Many in the Confederacy had built up a level of natural immunity to the disease while soldiers from the North had not. Thus, Union armies regularly suffered from outbreaks of malaria when they marched into the South. Finally, technological changes on the battlefield (as will be discussed) shifted the advantage to a force defending fixed positions. Nevertheless, there was hope in Washington that the secession movement was poorly organized, and Lincoln received advice from many who called for an immediate march south to subdue the rebellion.

General Winfield Scott, commanding general of the U.S. Army, understood that the war was likely to be a lengthy, bloody, disease-ridden affair. Rather than recommending a rapid invasion of the South, he proposed what became known as the "Anaconda Plan": The rebellious states would be slowly squeezed into submission in a campaign that would minimize loss of life and property. First, large volunteer armies would need upwards of a year to be raised and trained while suitable equipment was procured for them.[11] While this took place, Southern ports were to be blockaded by the U.S. Navy, prior to sending an expedition down the Mississippi River to cut the Confederacy in two. Finally, columns would march into the heartland of the rebellion to reduce remaining centers of resistance. Such a gradual victory would be achieved with less bloodshed than a campaign of frontal assaults. When Scott's plan was leaked to the press, it created a great deal of derision as the mood in the North was one that called for an immediate effort to crush the Rebels.[12]

Lincoln had little military experience previous to entering the White House, and eagerly took advice from a variety of sources as he slowly came to form his own strategy for winning the war. He was an astute politician in what was very much a political war and his major decisions regarding the conflict are generally now considered to be the correct ones. Lincoln did not initially adopt Scott's Anaconda Plan realizing that public sentiment demanded an attempt to quickly extinguish the rebellion.[13] After initial attempts to end the rebellion failed, the president realized that to achieve victory, the Union would have to engage in something akin to lengthy "total war" requiring a massive

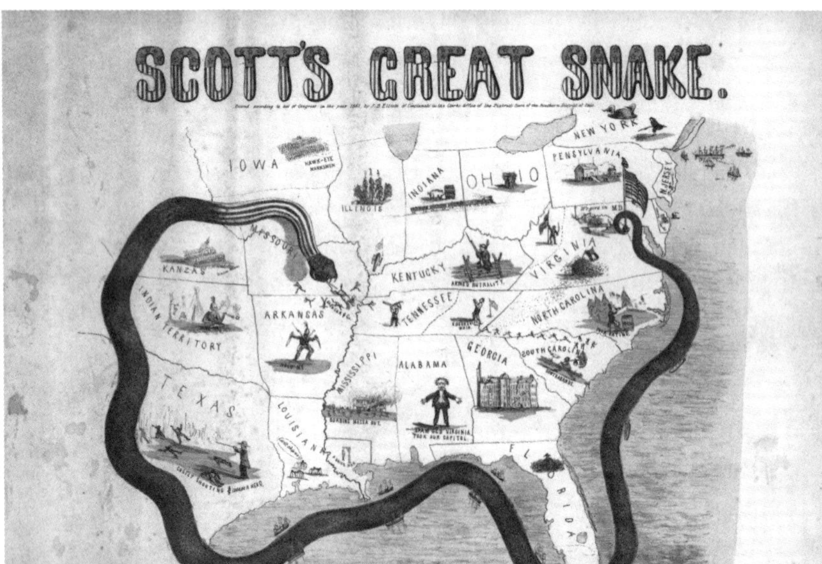

Many in the North initially disparaged the Anaconda Plan to defeat the Confederacy. LIBRARY OF CONGRESS

mobilization of the North's resources, a campaign to convert slaves from assisting the South to free men who would assist the Federal military, and a willingness to engage in brutal attritional fighting to wear down the Confederacy. Such a policy also exploited a contradiction at the heart of the rebellion in that it was a rejection of a strong centralized government. Fighting a long conflict that mobilized all the potential of the state required the Confederate government to become just such an overbearing force leading many in the South to question if they were simply swapping one tyrannical regime based in Washington for another in Richmond.

Lincoln's greatest challenge in carrying out this policy of a long, "total war" was not so much maintaining public support for the effort but getting his generals to carry out his military and political policies even when they opposed strategies that resulted in high casualties and emancipation. Many of his field commanders were pro-slavery political appointees whose competence was uneven. Others shied away from throwing their young men into frontal attacks that yielded such terrible losses. Only over time was Lincoln able to identify and elevate leaders who were bloody-minded enough to inflict defeats on the South severe enough to preserve the Union.

The Defeat

Soon after the start of the war with the April 1861 attack on Fort Sumter, the Confederacy moved its capital from Montgomery, Alabama, to Richmond, Virginia. This change shaped much of the fighting over the course of the following years. While the Virginia city would have been of great importance to the Rebels due to its industrial production of munitions and locomotives, the siting of the two opposing government capitals only 100 miles apart defined the major military dispositions that continued throughout the war. Each side deployed their primary armies near the Potomac River to protect the seats of their respective governments. Secondary forces faced off slightly to the west to block north-south movement through the Shenandoah Valley, which could be used as a secondary path for the Confederates to attack Washington. Thus, a concentration of battles and casualties throughout the war were clustered within a narrow band of geography ranging from slightly north of Washington to slightly south of Richmond. Finally, additional armies assembled in the West along the Ohio, Cumberland, and Mississippi Rivers where finally, over time, the war was decided in the Union's favor.

General Scott, at seventy-five years of age, was too old to take the field, so command of the main Union army protecting Washington was given to Brigadier General Irvin McDowell. He was opposed by the Confederate P. G. T. Beauregard whose force was camped 40 miles to the south along the railway junction at the town of Manassas. McDowell's 35,000 men of the Army of Northeastern Virginia were untrained, poorly prepared, and composed mostly of ninety-day volunteers leavened by a small number of regular army professionals. While McDowell wished to spend time preparing his force for battle, many in the North pushed for an immediate march on Richmond. They believed that morale in the South was weak and the rebellion would collapse after being struck an early blow that led to the capture of the Confederate capital. When the Union general resisted an early offensive, Lincoln urged him to march south and commented of McDowell's army: "You are green, it is true, but they are green also; you are all green alike."[14]

As the Federal troops prepared for their first offensive, the outdated tactics to be employed by the professional West Point–trained soldiers on both sides would result in a gruesome level of casualties on battlefields throughout the war. Many commanding generals and colonels throughout the conflict had fought in the Mexican-American War of 1846–1848 where they achieved a decisive U.S. victory in combat where relatively small armies faced off employing smoothbore muskets and artillery pieces. By 1861, decisive technological differences in the art of war resulted in a dramatic increase in the casualty rate for men employed in battle.

Most importantly, the smoothbore musket, firing round lead balls, was rapidly being replaced with a rifled barrel firing a bullet with a conical pointed top and a hollow base. This newer technology resulted in soldiers having a significantly faster rate of fire and improved aim and range while inflicting more devastating wounds per hit on a target.[15] In the past, to concentrate fire, a commander needed to mass his men in dense lines on the battlefield. By 1861, such tactics resulted in appalling loss of life. A defending force firing from entrenchments gained that much more of an advantage in 1861 compared to those doing so in 1776, 1812, or 1846.[16]

The longer range, faster reloading time, and more accurate rifled musket barrel also had the effect of negating much of the mobility and shock value of cavalry on the battlefield. A man on a horse now represented such a large target that it could not survive a lengthy charge on open ground toward enemy lines. Commanders of such units soon learned the necessity of using the speed of their mounts only to get their men close to the action and then dismounting to close with the enemy. The newly improved infantry weapon generally imparted a greater advantage to the defender. In the Revolutionary War or that of 1812, a larger force could often win the day by firing a volley and then charging with the bayonet to close with an opponent. By 1861, the increased range, accuracy, and rate of fire of the rifled musket often made such an effort suicidal.

Similarly, a formation of advancing cavalry would suffer much greater losses before it could reach an enemy line. The power of the new primary infantry weapon was also effective in slowing pursuit. Time and again, defeated armies in the Civil War were able to successfully retreat behind a rearguard screen. In addition, victorious forces generally suffered such significant losses seizing the battlefield that organizing an effective pursuit was not feasible.[17] Even at Robert E. Lee's great victory of maneuver at Chancellorsville in which a much larger Union army was forced into a general retreat, it was the Rebels who suffered a higher percentage of casualties among men engaged.

Artillery also became more effective in the Civil War. Similar to the musket, cannon became rifled, more accurate, and longer ranged. "While a smoothbore Napoleon cannon could hit a barn at just under a mile, a rifled Parrott gun firing from the same distance could hit the barn door."[18] The rise of railroads also meant that more heavy guns and ammunition could be transported to near the front than in previous conflicts. A higher rate of artillery fire with greater accuracy at a longer range helped to devastate many massed infantry charges throughout the war.

While the weapons on the battlefield had changed, the means to communicate orders under fire had not. While the new technology of the telegraph and the railroad could, and did, relay information quickly between the front and cities in the rear, once the fighting began, generals still had to rely on letters carried by runners and horsemen to convey orders along with bugle calls, drumbeats, and banners to coordinate advances and retreats. Particularly in the early years of the war, commanders on both sides had difficulty synchronizing their forces to conform to a plan of action, which often led to entire divisions of armies unscathed on the day while others were decimated. The Confederates almost always went into major battles with fewer modern weapons than their Union foes, but usually suffered fewer casualties. This was a result of generally superior Southern generalship, the Rebels operating on their home terrain, and utilization of interior lines to shift forces to confront Union offensives. The combination of these factors resulted in Federal troops more often than not being ordered to charge defensive positions in an era when technological changes on the battlefield placed the attackers at a significant disadvantage.

The road to the Battle of First Bull Run (named after a narrow river running near Manassas) began on July 16, 1861, when McDowell and his 36,000 men marched south from Washington to engage Beauregard's opposing force of 22,000. As historian Bruce Catton wrote, "There is nothing in American military history quite like the story of Bull Run. It was the momentous fight of the amateurs, the battle where everything went wrong, the great day of awakening for the whole nation, North and South together. It marked the end of the ninety-day militia, and it also ended the rosy time in which men could dream that the war would be short, glorious, and bloodless. After Bull Run the nation got down to business."[19]

Several other battles took place in the vicinity over the next three years (including a second major clash on the same ground in 1862), and in many particulars First Bull Run was a template for much of the fighting that followed: The Union almost always had greater manpower and equipment but struggled to make use of these advantages. Confederate leadership was generally superior especially as the Rebels were usually able to position themselves to fight from defensive positions while utilizing interior lines. When the Rebels did pivot to the attack, their leaders were better at making decisions and taking initiative in the heat of battle. In most cases, Federal losses were significantly higher at the end of the day. Time and again, Lincoln's generals found reasons to be hesitant to advance, often convinced themselves that they were outnumbered, and shied away from making use of tactics designed to wear down the weaker Confederacy. It was only later in the war that leaders willing to engage in bloody attritional campaigns such as Grant, Sherman, Hancock, Thomas, and Sheridan were promoted to command that the tide turned conclusively in favor of Union arms.

While wary of committing his green troops to battle, McDowell hoped to utilize the bulk of his army to confront the enemy entrenched along Bull Run while another column shifted south and east to threaten Beauregard's rear and hopefully compel the Confederates to retreat. At the same time, the Union force at the northern end of the Shenandoah, under the command of sixty-nine-year-old Major General Robert Patterson, was to tie down the opposing Rebel commander Joseph Johnston and his 9,000 men in the vicinity so that they could not come to the assistance of the main Confederate force. However, when the battle began on July 21, little went McDowell's way.

First of all, he frittered away his manpower advantage as 5,000 men were stationed to guard the supply lines back to Washington. At the same time, Johnston successfully slipped away unnoticed from Patterson in the Shenandoah and his Rebel army was transported by rail to Manassas Junction in time to turn the tide of the battle. With the two sides evenly matched in numbers, McDowell still could have won the day as his men were better equipped with more muskets and cannon that were rifled than those possessed by the Rebels. However, his plan only called for a portion of his army to push across the water barrier of the Bull Run while the rest remained on the far bank and through demonstrations tied down much of Beauregard's force.

When the right wing of McDowell's command advanced to attack in the morning of the July 21, it was initially quite successful and began to roll up the Confederate flank. However, General Thomas J. Jackson (forever after known as "Stonewall") positioned his arriving brigade in the Union troops' path, and while the Rebel unit suffered crippling casualties, the advance was halted.[20] Much of the fighting was confused as units often held their fire as a panoply of different colored uniforms led them to

Johnston's ability to shift his forces southeast to Bearegard at Manasas was decisive in the Battle of Bull Run. MAP BY HAL JESPERSEN, WWW.CWMAPS.COM

think approaching formations were on their side. The early Confederate "Stars and Bars" flag was also similar enough to the one carried by Federal forces that additional confusion ensued in the heat of battle. Orders were often not delivered on time, or commanders ignored those they received.

Beauregard was able to feed in reinforcements, which stabilized the line. With the raging battle in the balance, the Union commander made multiple critical errors. He failed to properly protect his artillery that had been advanced too close to enemy lines, and did not bring up additional units to exploit the success his divisions had made after pushing across Bull Run.[21] The Union left wing was also ineffective in holding in place the Confederates opposing them. This allowed Rebel formations to march to the sound of the fighting in the afternoon to confront the tiring Federal units that were engaged. Without reinforcements, and the Southern front thickening as the day wore on, the Union forces broke and began to retreat. This movement soon became a disorganized rout, which infected even units that had not fired a shot in anger. McDowell's men streamed back northward toward Washington.

During the course of the battle, both inexperienced armies were only able to engage about 18,000 men each in the fighting. Of course, the Union generals came off looking worse. Had McDowell successfully deployed more than half his force into the contest, his better-armed men could have produced a victory. In addition, upwards of an additional 15,000 Federal soldiers remained inactive in the Shenandoah who could have marched south into the void left by Johnston's redeployment. On the Confederate side, Beauregard was similarly unable to bring many of his units into the battle, but this was less important at the end of the day as the Federal troops failed in their attempt to break through the Rebels' defensive lines. Many in Washington were initially in a panic that fresh Confederate troops would soon march on the capital. Luckily, no such pursuit took place. In wake of the debacle, Patterson retired from the army, and McDowell was forced to assume a subordinate command role until he was eventually removed from a front-line position in 1864.

Despite the relatively small percentage of men from both sides participating in the fighting, the casualty count was still shocking in size and represented the largest loss of men in a battle in U.S. history up to that point: 1,500 Federals were killed or wounded with the Confederates suffering close to 2,000 in these categories. A 10 percent casualty rate in men engaged was a cruel wakeup call to both sides that the nature of this new war would be bloody, expensive, and long. While the Rebels mourned their losses at Bull Run, at least they could count upwards of 1,000 Union prisoners and claimed victory as they held the field after the battle.

In the North, all hope that the rebellion could be crushed with little in the way of expense and casualties was snuffed out by Bull Run. The situation for the Union appeared bleak as Beauregard seemed poised to attack Washington, the blockade of Confederate ports declared by Lincoln in April was untenable due to the small size of the U.S. Navy, and major European powers were moving toward recognition of the Confederacy. Even if the people of the North remained committed to the cause of defeating the rebellion, was it even possible? Would the cost in blood and treasure be insurmountable after the abject defeat suffered outside Manassas? Despite what appeared to be long odds in late July 1861, the people of the North rallied to the great military challenge that loomed ahead. Some were willing to fight and die to preserve the Union. Others fought to abolish slavery. Some had economic reasons to fight, and others worried the United States would crack apart into several small nations if the South was allowed to break away. For a variety of reasons, the people of the nation rallied around Lincoln after Bull Run and chose to bear the awful burden of crushing the Confederacy.

Recovery

In the wake of the defeat, President Lincoln begrudgingly came to adopt much of General Scott's Anaconda Plan, though it resulted in much greater loss of life and property than the old general had envisioned. The president pushed his generals to advance more quickly and come to grips with the Confederate armies. These Union battlefield leaders often wished to minimize casualties and thus failed to focus on destroying the rebellion's armies, which were the core of its strength. Instead, many of these generals fixated on outmaneuvering their Rebel opponents and such tactics rarely led to victory. This significantly slowed the U.S. recovery from the initial defeat. Over time, Lincoln accepted that victory would be achieved only if the rebellion was destroyed economically and its armies bled away through attrition. In the end, a policy of blockade slowly cut the Confederacy off from the rest of the world, the Mississippi was seized to slice the rebellion in two, upwards of 100,000 former slaves were recruited to fight for the Union, and a series of bloody battles destroyed enemy strength leading to eventual triumph.

Compared to other examples in U.S. military history where strategic defeats triggered reactions and recoveries that led to resulting victory, the timetable was significantly extended in the Civil War. This was due to several reasons, including the ideological nature of the conflict, the fact that the war was fought between fellow Americans, and the time it took the North to assemble a preponderance of strength to wear down its rebellious opponent. However, the greatest impediment to shifting usefully to a total war of conquest was the resistance within the upper ranks of the U.S. Army itself. Commanders on both sides were predominantly drawn from one source: "Out of the approximately 560 Union generals to serve during the war, about 220 were West Point graduates (in the Confederacy, the ratio was a little lower but still significant, 140 out of 400)."[22] These men had studied the Napoleonic Wars in detail and many read the writings of Antoine-Henri Jomini in depth, which inculcated a focus on limited war, maneuver to gain control of an opponent's territory, and limiting the level of casualties.

In contrast, the key to winning the Civil War was not taking enemy cities or outmaneuvering opposing armies. While seizing territory in the American South was certainly important, the center of Confederate power was its armies and the will of the Southern population to fight for secession. To achieve victory, the United States needed to raise a large well-trained military and wear down the Rebels on the battlefield. Soon after the defeat at Bull Run, Lincoln signed a bill on July 22 that authorized the enlistment of 500,000 men for up to three years of service. A few days later, he appointed Major General George McClellan commander of the armed forces around Washington. This young, energetic officer was exactly the man to organize the rapid expansion of the new Army of the Potomac, even though he would prove not to be the one to win the war. McClellan, a graduate of West Point and former successful railroad executive, proved to be an excellent administrator who oversaw the training, development, and improvement in morale of the Union army in the East. It grew in size from around 50,000 in July 1861 to close to 200,000 by the end of the year. By early 1862, it was ready to go on the offensive.

At the same time, while a blockade of the Rebel states had been proclaimed in April, the U.S. Navy had only forty-two ships in commission at the start of the war. The service expanded dramatically in size so that it could execute on a campaign to seize Southern ports or block access to them. By the end of July 1861 the Navy had almost doubled to eighty-two ships. This number surged to 467 at the end of the year, had increased again to 588 in December 1863, and topped out at more than 670 ships by the end of the war, becoming the largest navy in the world.[23] Early in the conflict, very few ships were intercepted, but over time an increasing number of Rebel ports were captured or blockaded. The squeeze of the snake was initially barely noticeable, but over time it became constricting to the Confederacy. While large number of blockade runners continued to evade the U.S. Navy even into 1864, these ships were generally fast, smaller vessels that carried lighter cargos that focused on military supplies. The result was that the South collected little in the way of customs revenues to fund its war effort, export volumes collapsed, and imports of consumer items were severely restricted, which increased a sense of hardship and international isolation among the citizens of the Confederacy.

Many in the South were confident at the start of the war that their men would make better soldiers and they were not surprised by the victory in the first major clash of arms at Bull Run. Any hopes that the Yankees would give up easily soon faded, and Confederate President Jefferson Davis called for 400,000 volunteers to serve. He also supervised the development of armaments industries and divided his nation into a series of command regions that would attempt to hold every mile of territory of the nation. For the next six months there were few major battles as both sides focused on recruiting, equipping, and training their new armies.

As the North ramped up preparations to launch a major offensive, Lincoln and his Cabinet began to put in motion what was effectively a three-pronged strategy to destroy the rebellion: (1) Along the Potomac, the Union's major army would attempt to defend Washington while defeating the Rebel force screening Richmond. (2) In the West, advances would push south from Ohio to break through enemy resistance there while at the same time efforts would be made to secure the Mississippi and cut the Confederacy in half. (3) The Navy would land troops to seize strategic ports or coastal forts and cut the Rebels off from the wider world. Smaller engagements took place along the Confederate borders in the remainder of 1861 with the Federal Army pushing Rebel units out of Union-leaning areas of Kentucky and western Virginia (which later became incorporated as the State of West Virginia), as well as launching its first combined operation under General Ambrose Burnside in conjunction with the U.S. Navy to seize the strategic point of Cape Hatteras, North Carolina.

McClellan, basking in the glow from successfully building up the army, was able to force Scott into retirement. This allowed him to become general-in-chief of all U.S. forces as well as head of the Army of the Potomac and he proclaimed that, "I can do it all."[24] However, there were signs that trouble with Lincoln was brewing as McClellan did not believe in the Anaconda Plan and instead believed he could defeat the Confederacy in a single great campaign without ending slavery and imposing little pain on the South's civilian population. While the Army of the Potomac appeared to be ready for action in early 1862 and outnumbered the Confederate army in northern Virginia by more than two to one, Lincoln was unable to get McClellan to move in what became an increasing point of friction between the two men.

In the West, Union Generals Henry Halleck and Don Carlos Buell were also cautious and resisted calls from Washington to advance. However, the pugnacious General Ulysses S. Grant pushed south and won the first two major victories for the Union in the war. In the Battles of Fort Henry and Fort Donelson in the first half of February, Grant's larger force, assisted by a Navy flotilla under Andrew Foote, drove deep into Tennessee and captured the primary Confederate forts on the Tennessee and Cumberland Rivers. The latter garrison surrendered, which netted the Union more than 12,000 Rebel soldiers who became POWs and were shipped north for the duration of the conflict.

At the same time, Burnside's amphibious force landed on Roanoke Island, capturing multiple forts and 2,500 Confederates. He took control of the Outer Banks, which dominate the North Carolina coast, effectively sealing off several ports' access to the Atlantic. These victories were soon followed by General John Pope's descent into Missouri at the start of March to besiege the battlements on Island Number Ten guarding a bend in the Mississippi River. The fort finally surrendered in early April yielding several thousand additional Confederate POWs. While the siege was taking place, two other major Union victories took place: Just south of the Missouri border, a Rebel army was defeated at Pea Ridge and on April 6–7, Grant was able to repulse a surprise attack at Shiloh in a bloody battle that yielded more than 10,000 casualties per side. Kentucky and West Virginia, along with much of Missouri and Tennessee, were now in Union hands. While the struggle waxed and waned in the West, the Union progressively gained the upper hand.

The process of wearing down the Confederacy was progressing except in Virginia where McClellan had continued to resist deploying his splendid army for battle and complained that Rebel strength in front of Richmond significantly outnumbered his force. Lincoln issued an order in late January 1862 that all Union armies should begin offensive operations by February 22 and a few days later ordered that the Army of the Potomac should advance south to confront the Confederate army that was now under the command of General Joseph E. Johnston. Relations with McClellan deteriorated with the general privately referring to his commander-in-chief as "nothing more than a well-meaning baboon" or a "gorilla." In response to the Army of the Potomac's lack of action, Lincoln sardonically quipped, "If General McClellan does not want to use the army, I would like to borrow it for a time."[25]

McClellan finally relented and offered a plan of attack: He would embark his army and sail it by ship down to Fort Monroe at the end of the Virginia peninsula, which was "only" 80 miles from Richmond and then march on the Rebel capital receiving supplies via the U.S. Navy operating up the York and James Rivers. The movement by ship finally began on March 17 with more than 120,000 men transported along with huge numbers of guns, wagons, and horses. The greatest problem with this plan is that it forced the Union to fritter away much of its numerical advantage as large garrisons needed to be left behind to guard Washington and the northern end of the Shenandoah. The Confederates could then shift forces as necessary to the peninsula to oppose McClellan. The main Union force would also have to be supplied by ship, which would distract the Navy from its efforts to bottle up Southern ports as well as negating the North's advantages utilizing its larger railroad network flowing into Washington, which could facilitate the supply of a force moving overland directly from there toward Richmond.

The Army of the Potomac's advance up the peninsula was almost immediately halted by a much smaller force under Confederate General John Magruder who had fortified the port of Yorktown and made constant demonstrations to make McClellan believe he was opposed by a much larger force than the 13,000 or so men actually there. As the Union general hesitated, Southern reinforcements flowed into the area. Finally, in the middle of April, McClellan ordered an attack with only a small portion of his army. After this failed, he settled down to implement a formal siege. He finally began a general bombardment of enemy lines in early May and the Rebels promptly retreated from Yorktown leaving the Army of the Potomac still a full 60 miles from Richmond.

Out west, things progressed somewhat better for the Union cause as an amphibious operation from the Gulf of Mexico seized New Orleans, the South's largest port, and Baton Rouge was secured soon after. Forces pushing south also captured Memphis, leaving all of the Mississippi River in Union hands except for the fortifications around the city of Vicksburg. The strategic point of Corinth, Mississippi, also fell to forces under Halleck's command, which opened up future operations against Chattanooga and Vicksburg. While the Confederates had staged several successful counteroffensives and raids in the Western Theater, the Union position in the region steadily improved in 1862. The goals of cutting the rebellion in two by taking control of the Mississippi and pushing into Georgia seemed to be within reach.

The balance of the month of May saw the Confederates engage in a fighting retreat as the Army of the Potomac closed in on Richmond as it reached the Chickahominy River. More than 100,000 Union men faced off against Johnston with about 60,000, but McClellan continued to believe faulty intelligence that he was heavily outnumbered. In the inconclusive Battle of Seven Pines, both sides suffered more than 5,000 casualties and General Johnston was badly wounded, which resulted in General Robert E. Lee being sent to command the Confederate army. The Army of the Potomac halted, redeployed over the next month along the approaches to Richmond, and gave up the strategic initiative as

McClellan begged for reinforcements. Lee, revered today by many as one of the great field commanders of history, played off McClellan's fears and caution and moved to take the offensive.

Stonewall Jackson had thrashed the Union generals arrayed against him in the Shenandoah and then redeployed south to aid the main force defending the Rebel capital while large Union forces remained near Washington. This allowed Lee to confront McClellan on roughly equal terms in total manpower at the same time that the Union general convinced himself that he was outnumbered two to one. In a series of attacks launched by Lee over the last week of June known as the Seven Days Battles, the Rebels suffered staggering casualties of 20,000 versus 16,000 for the Union but were able to force McClellan to retreat. Despite the Confederates being badly defeated in a final set of frontal attacks on fortified positions at Malvern Hill on July 1, McClellan gave up on his attempt to take Richmond and pulled his army back to Harrison's Landing on the James River under the guns of the U.S. Navy. Later that month, having lost faith in his lead general, Lincoln offered the command of the Army of the Potomac to Burnside, but the latter declined the position and claimed he was unqualified to lead such a large force. Thus, McClellan remained in his post.[26]

While the war waged, it continued to be not just a military, but also a political conflict with slavery its most contentious issue. To understand how the United States recovered from its initial defeats and advanced to victory in the Civil War, one must step aside from the battlefield briefly to consider Lincoln's policy on the matter. In August 1861, General John Frémont issued a proclamation in Missouri placing the state under martial law and freeing all slaves of Confederate sympathizers there. With the status of slave-owning border state areas such as Kentucky, Missouri, eastern Tennessee, western Virginia, and Maryland potentially in flux, and many in Northern states focused on preserving the Union rather than slavery, Lincoln ordered Frémont to retract his edict. The president wanted to maximize support for the war effort and worried that if Kentucky sided with the Confederacy, the rebellion would prevail. The Congress generally agreed with Lincoln's policy at that point and enacted a resolution that declared the war was being fought to preserve the Union and not abolish slavery.

However, Lincoln certainly wanted to end slavery and General Benjamin Butler offered him a partial solution in the summer of 1861. The general, in charge of the coastal post of Fort Monroe in Virginia, allowed slaves of a Confederate officer to pass through his lines. He then declared them "contraband property" and refused to return them to the Rebels. The president blessed this policy and from that point forward, slaves who made it to Union positions were free, at least for the duration of the conflict, and could be employed by the Federal Army. The Congress agreed with this and passed the Confiscation Act, which formally stripped Rebels of their ownership rights of such escaped slaves.

This policy was also a positive in the effort to maintain Britain and France's neutrality in the conflict. Those two nations had ended slavery in their empires in 1834 and 1848, respectively, and their citizens generally abhorred the "peculiar institution" that survived in the United States. The suspension of exports of cotton from the Confederacy to Europe presented a major challenge to the fabric and clothing manufacturing centers in England and forced many workers into unemployment. This, ties between British aristocratic families and those of oligarchic planters in the American South, and geopolitical desires in London that the United States be weakened by supporting a policy that resulted in it being divided into multiple republics increased a movement to recognize the Confederacy and intervene in the war. Through 1862, however, abolitionist sentiment, the appearance of Union momentum toward victory, and economic activity from sales of war-related materials of all kinds from British firms to the U.S. Federal government kept London from allying itself with the South.[27] Of course, without a clear policy to end slavery throughout the American South, a shift in the tides of war in favor of the Rebels could tilt London into recognizing the Confederacy, and France would likely follow such a move.

As the war progressed into the summer of 1862 with casualties mounting, and the status of border states in the Union generally resolved, Lincoln decided that the time had come when he must shift his policy toward abolishing slavery if the Confederacy was to be defeated. Not only would this be moral and motivate many Northerners, it would undermine the rebellion's economy and military might. Of course, many pro-Union Democrats disagreed with this policy including prominent military officers such as Buell and McClellan. The latter general even personally delivered a letter to the president that included the following: "Neither confiscation of property, political executions of persons, territorial organization of states or forcible abolition of slavery should be contemplated for a moment. . . . A declaration of radical views, especially upon slavery, will rapidly disintegrate our present Armies."[28]

Nevertheless, Lincoln pressed ahead and prepared the public for a major change in policy on the issue. In a letter meant for newspaper publication, he wrote, "If there be those who would not save the Union unless they could at the same time destroy slavery, I do not agree with them. My paramount object in this struggle is to save the Union, and is not either to save or to destroy slavery. If I could save the Union without freeing any slave I would do it, and if I could save it by freeing all the slaves I would do it; and if I could save it by freeing some and leaving others alone, I would also do that. What I do about slavery and the colored race, I do because I believe it helps to save this Union. . . ."[29] In other words, the president meant to satisfy all Unionists: If the slaves belonging to the Rebels were to be freed, it would only be out of military necessity to speed victory on the battlefield.

A month earlier, when Lincoln's Cabinet met soon after the Seven Days Battles, its members agreed with the president that the time had come to issue an Emancipation Proclamation. However, Secretary of State William Seward argued that it should only be released on the occasion of a Union victory so that it was not perceived as a policy born of weakness so soon after McClellan had been driven back from Richmond. Lincoln agreed with this advice and waited for a victory. Sadly, it proved to be a long wait.

Victory

The North had recovered from its initial defeat at Bull Run, mobilized greater resources, and retaken large swaths of Rebel territory. Confederate generalship in the late summer of 1862 outclassed that of their opponents, especially in the East, and undermined Union efforts. Units along the Potomac had been formed into the Army of Virginia under

General John Pope, and ordered to move south. Lee correctly guessed that McClellan was beaten and that he could safely send Jackson to attack Pope near Manassas. While Halleck ordered McClellan to ship his men northward to reinforce the Army of Virginia, the latter general sullenly proceeded with his characteristic sluggishness, which allowed the Confederates to mass against Pope's force. Lee sent General James Longstreet north with an additional 25,000 men who caught Pope's left flank unawares at the end of August. In the Second Battle of Bull Run, the Union forces were badly defeated, suffered significantly greater casualties, and were forced to retreat back toward Washington.

Lee, sensing an opportunity to fight the war on enemy ground and raid enemy supplies of food, weapons, and ammunition, invaded Union Maryland. Fear gripped Washington with worries that the Confederate general would strike at the capital, Baltimore, or Harrisburg. While Lincoln and his Cabinet were extremely wary of McClellan's abilities at this point, the president believed he had no choice but to put the general in charge of all forces around Washington while Pope was relieved of command. Lee first hoped to capture the Union garrison at Harpers Ferry before moving into Pennsylvania. While significantly outnumbered, the Confederate general divided his force into separate foraging columns as he was confident that McClellan was simply too timid a commander and his army too demoralized to go on the offensive and cut him off from a path of retreat to Virginia.

Suddenly the Union cause seemed to be in jeopardy everywhere as the Confederates were also staging a counteroffensive out of Tennessee and in the Mississippi Valley. Two Rebel armies marched north into Kentucky in which they scored major victories at Munfordville and Richmond in which more than 8,000 Union soldiers were captured and much of the center of the state fell into Rebel hands. The Confederates also repulsed an attack on Vicksburg and then dispatched a force down the Mississippi to retake Baton Rouge. The attempt to retake that city was unsuccessful, but Union forces soon abandoned their posts there and retreated to New Orleans, while the Rebels entrenched on the bluffs overlooking the river at Port Hudson. At the same time, a Confederate force pushed westward out of Alabama attempting to regain the strategic rail hub of Corinth, Mississippi.

The outlook was dimming rapidly for Lincoln's cause, with Rebel armies on the attack and Britain rumored to be preparing to recognize the Confederacy. It was at this point that the Union cause suddenly received a great piece of luck. On September 9, 1862, an Indiana corporal discovered an envelope in a Maryland camp recently vacated by Lee's army. Inside was a copy of the Rebel general's movement orders laying out where his divided columns would advance over the following days. The paperwork was verified and quickly passed along to McClellan who ecstatically telegraphed Lincoln, "I have the whole rebel force in front of me, but I am confident, and no time shall be lost . . . I think Lee has made a gross mistake, and that he will be severely punished for it . . . I hope for a great success if the plans of the Rebels remain unchanged . . . I have all the plans of the rebels, and will catch them in their own trap if my men are equal to the emergency."[30]

Knowing Lee's target of Harpers Ferry and that his opponent's forces were dispersed, McClellan began to move with a bit more alacrity than usual and was soon able to disrupt the Confederates' plans. He pushed his men through the passes of South Mountain and defeated detachments of Lee's force there while much of the Confederate army under Jackson was farther south attacking the Union garrison at Harpers Ferry. Realizing he was heavily outnumbered and unable to concentrate his forces, Lee ordered a retreat toward the town of Sharpsburg, and on September 15 took up positions on a row of low hills above Antietam Creek with his lines anchored on either end by the banks of a bend of the Potomac. McClellan's forces began to arrive along the Confederate front that afternoon with the rest arriving throughout the evening.

While Jackson and his contingent arrived just in time after scoring a significant victory and forcing the Federal troops at Harpers Ferry to surrender, Lee's army with a force of only around 30,000 was pinned against the Maryland side of the Potomac and confronted by more than 72,000 soldiers under McClellan.[31] As usual, the Union general was deliberate, hesitant to act, and spent the entire day of September 16 evaluating the terrain in front of him. It was not until dawn on September 17 that an assault was launched along Lee's left flank. Instead of ordering a general advance, McClellan had four of his Army Corps attack sequentially from north to south along the Rebel line over several hours. This allowed Lee to slowly feed reinforcements into one threatened section of his front after another. In multiple instances, the outnumbered Confederates were close to breaking, but McClellan decided not to send supporting thrusts against weakened defensive positions and instead chose to hold back two fresh corps with more than 20,000 men as a strategic reserve and clung to his usual belief that his Union army was strongly outnumbered.

The intense fighting died down at sundown and both sides took stock. It was the bloodiest day in American history with the Federals suffering 12,000 casualties to 10,000 for the Rebels. While McClellan's force had larger losses, he could better afford to absorb them as his force was larger, he had unused reserves, and Federal reinforcements were arriving in the area. In contrast, the Confederates had lost upwards of a third of the army that invaded Maryland. Lee prepared to hold off another assault on September 18, but McClellan was inert. Under cover of darkness, that evening the Rebel commander and his force slipped over a ford in the Potomac and retreated into Virginia. Northern newspapers announced a great victory had been won as the Union army held the field and the Confederate invasion of Maryland had been repulsed.

Of course, McClellan's victory could have been much greater had he chosen to give chase. By September 22, Lee was at Martinsburg 10 miles from Antietam with 36,000 men, compared to the Union force around Sharpsburg, which had swelled to 93,000 with the arrival of reinforcements.[32] Despite repeated entreaties from Lincoln, and the War Department, McClellan refused to pursue the enemy claiming that the Army of the Potomac was worn out and needed time to rest and refit. With the Rebel army having suffered such great losses, and the Federal force having so many fresh units to utilize in the attack, additional Union victories would have been likely had Lee been pressed as he retired toward Richmond. In disgust, the president relieved McClellan of his duties in early October, and the general would never hold another command.

At almost the same time, the Confederate offensives in the West were broken. At the Battles of Iuka and Corinth, a Rebel attempt to

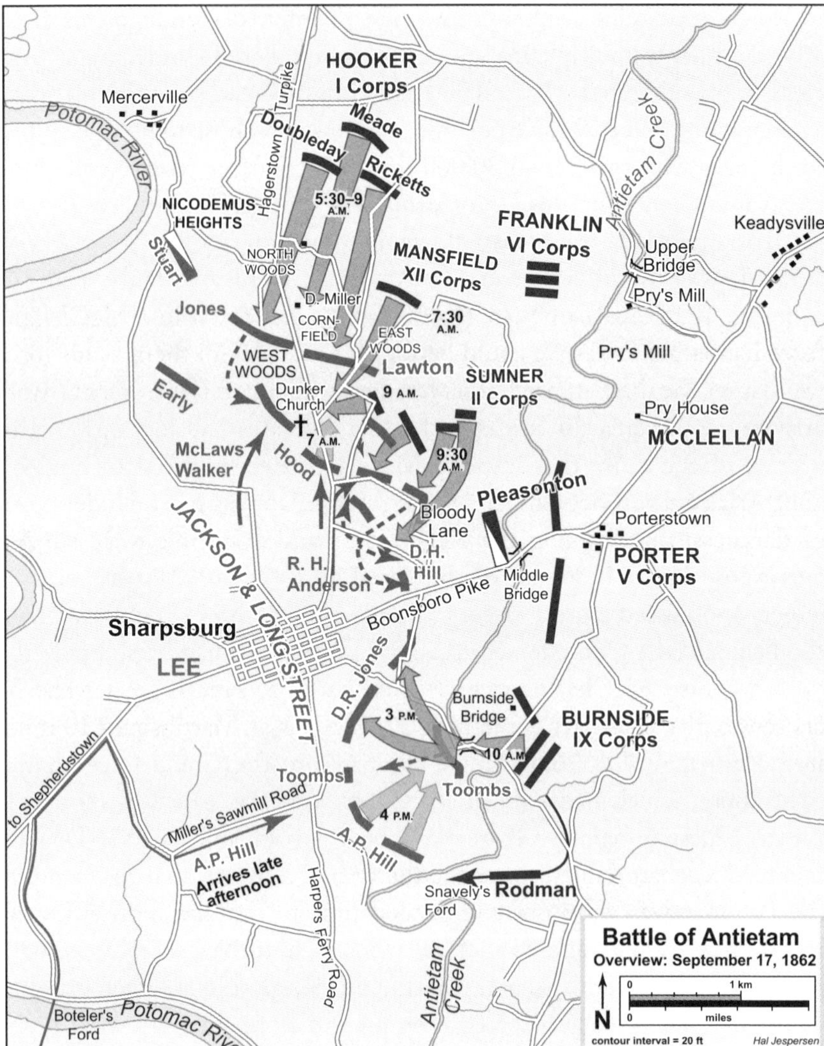

McClellan's choice to stage sequential attacks at Antietam likely saved Lee's army from destruction. WIKIPEDIA

push back toward the Mississippi River was thwarted. Then at the Battle of Perryville on October 8, the Confederate offensive into Kentucky was halted and the Rebels retreated back into Tennessee. The progress of the war and particularly the victory at Antietam was the window Lincoln needed. Finally, he was able to issue his previously written Emancipation Proclamation, which utilized presidential war authority to seize the property of Rebels and framed the measure as a military expediency to weaken the Confederacy. Of course, the wording of this executive order did not in fact immediately emancipate America's slaves as it did not go into effect until the first day of 1863. Furthermore, it only promised permanent freedom for any enslaved person in territory then in rebellion who either escaped to Union lines or found themselves under Federal control due to the advance of Washington's armed forces.

The proclamation had several immediate positive impacts on Lincoln's war effort. Abolitionists were heartened, while those in the North, and even border state slaveowners who cared mostly about preserving the Union, generally accepted that a measure depriving the Confederates of their human property would help end the conflict. Also, by broadening the struggle of the Civil War and making it one that would end slavery in the South, Britain and France turned away from their consideration of recognizing the Confederacy.[33] Siding with the South would now explicitly be a policy of supporting slavery, which was at violent odds with general public opinion in those two western European nations. Finally, the Emancipation Proclamation was a force multiplier for the Union war effort as a swelling number of former slaves, rather than toiling for the South, were soon employed in a variety of roles in the Federal armed forces. After the proclamation went into effect, Black men were also allowed to join the U.S. Army and the Navy and the odds stacked against the Confederacy became even more one-sided.

Cause of Defeat

In many ways the primary causes of the Union defeat at Bull Run (and other battles in the first year of the war) were both political and military. Northerners wished to prevail and suppress the rebellion, but not as badly as many Confederates were motivated to gain independence for their new nation. However, the North had the advantage in manpower, as historian Richard Stewart points out that when "Lincoln asked Union governors for 75,000 militiamen, the northern states sent him 100,000."[34] Clearly, had the Congress and the president acted with greater purpose, a much larger and more committed force could have been mobilized more quickly in time to fight at Bull Run. Had Lincoln called for 150,000 or 200,000 volunteers, perhaps McDowell would have had that many more men under his command in his first offensive and the weight of their numbers could have tilted the balance in what was a close-fought engagement.

In contrast to the men of the North, those joining the Confederate military in 1861 were bound to serve for a full year. Many Unionists believed fervently that slavery should be abolished, but Lincoln's policies in 1861 seemed to indicate that legalized human bondage might well survive the war—both in the South if the rebellion was crushed, and even in loyal border states such as Kentucky and Maryland if the Confederacy survived. Finally, the Union advantage in population and industry was dramatic, but it was not successfully brought to bear until later in the war.

While McDowell's army was larger than Beauregard's in 1861, that so many leaders on both sides had been trained at the same military institute at West Point often allowed the Confederate leaders to guess correctly what their opponents were likely to do. The Rebels were fighting on their own ground, which raised their morale, and the new weapons of war being introduced to the battlefield tilted the advantage to the defenders. Confederate soldiers at Bull Run were fighting on Southern land that had been thoroughly scouted in advance. While the Union troops believed the nation to be a legal whole and that their cause was just, they were still advancing into hostile territory. In contrast, the Confederates could see with their own eyes that McDowell's Northern men were marching as invaders into a Southern state.

The Union army that moved south from Washington was composed almost entirely of ninety-day volunteers. While these men were willing to fight and perhaps die for the Union, their enlistment periods were short and inculcated a mindset that the rebellion would be quickly suppressed with a minimum of bloodshed. In fact, thousands of enlistments expired on the eve of the battle and despite McDowell's entreaties, an entire regiment and an artillery battery headed back toward Washington just before the fighting got under way. As McPherson put it, "The longer enlistments of Confederate soldiers gave them a psychological advantage, for the recruit whose time was almost up seemed less motivated to fight."[35]

Thus, several factors aided the Rebels in the first great battle of the war: They were better motivated, their leaders did a superior job of utilizing interior lines to concentrate forces at the point of attack and direct reinforcements to where they were needed the most, and new military technology gave an advantage to those fighting on the defensive. The result was not foreordained, but in the end, it was the Union troops who retreated before panic set in and the invaders began to stream back toward Washington in disarray.

Cause of Victory

By the time the Battle of Antietam was fought more than a year later, both sides had learned much about the brutal reality of the war being waged. Pitched battles resulted in enormous casualties, attacked positions could only be overrun with great effort, and even when defenders were forced to flee, the force on the offensive often suffered much greater losses in the effort. While the North had better equipment and greater manpower, its generals were often hesitant and outmaneuvered by their adversaries leading to battlefield reverses. Despite this, the weight of the Union's numerical advantages had yielded significant victories in the West, along the East Coast, and at the mouth of the Mississippi that resulted in important territorial gains including much of Kentucky, West Virginia, North Carolina, Missouri, Tennessee, and Louisiana. Even in some of the engagements of the Seven Days Battles, which broke McClellan's spirit to push on against Richmond, the Rebels were the ones who came off the worse for the fighting.

At Antietam, General Lee took too many risks and his assessment of his opponent's abilities were overly negative. To invade the North with a seriously outnumbered army and win a series of victories would require almost everything to go the Confederate general's way. Lee was an extremely lucky leader at many points throughout the Civil War, but in the Maryland campaign the fates handed out their gifts in equal measure. While Lee was fortunate to be up against a hesitant General McClellan, the loss of a copy of the Confederates' operational orders gave the Union leader the confidence to move faster and more aggressively than his norm. While the Rebels seized a great haul of armaments and supplies when they captured Harpers Ferry, the victory left Lee's army spread out and exposed to defeat in detail when McClellan's forces attacked his columns and surged through the gaps at South Mountain. This left the Confederate army pinned on the wrong side of the Potomac.

Despite these setbacks, Lee's luck returned as McClellan's attack on September 17 was poorly planned and executed. Unfortunately, more than a quarter of the Union force was held in reserve when its deployment could have forced Lee to surrender. What should have been a disaster for the Confederates resulted instead in a similar number of casualties on both sides and the Rebel army being able to retreat unmolested back into Virginia. Thus, the Union victory was not so much military as political. McPherson concluded:

> *The victory at Antietam could have been more decisive. The same was true of two lesser victories that followed at Corinth and Perryville. But Union armies had stymied the supreme Confederate efforts. Foreign powers backed away from intervention and recognition, and never again came so close to considering them. Lincoln issued his Emancipation Proclamation . . . Here indeed was a pivotal moment. No other campaign and battle in the war had such momentous, multiple consequences as Antietam. In July 1863 the dual Union triumphs at Gettysburg and Vicksburg struck another blow that blunted a renewed Confederate offensive in the East and cut off the western third of the Confederacy from the rest. In September, 1864 Sherman's capture of Atlanta reversed another decline in northern morale and set the stage for the final drive to Union victory. These also were pivotal moments. But they would never have happened if the triple Confederate offensives in Mississippi, Kentucky, and most of all Maryland had not been defeated in the fall of 1862.*[36]

The strategy that would lead to the defeat of the Confederacy had been found by late 1862. Union forces did not have to crush the Rebel armies in any single battle or campaign. Instead, they needed to wear them down through attritional combat and avoid abject defeats in the process. Even if this process resulted in somewhat higher nominal levels of Northern casualties, the cruel math of the relative size and strength of the two opponents meant the Confederacy could not stand toe to toe with the Union indefinitely. This became especially true as tens of thousands of escaped slaves came to serve in the front lines fighting to defeat their former masters. The key was for Lincoln to maintain support for a long war among the population in the North while finding generals willing to carry out his strategy.

Impact of Defeat

The Union defeat at the First Battle of Bull Run had major consequences that shaped the development of the United States in the second half of the nineteenth century. Imagine a scenario where McDowell had done a slightly better job of shifting his forces so more than half of his army was committed to the fight on July 21, 1861. Or what if Rebel forces from the Shenandoah did not arrive just in time to tilt the balance in the fighting? Such a change in history could have meant that it was the Confederates who broke and were routed rather than the Union army. Would such a defeated force have been able to rally and make a stand before Richmond? Perhaps, but the odds would have been against the Rebels. After winning at Bull Run, McDowell, supported by Patterson's troops, would have been able to advance south with more than 50,000 effectives against fewer than 30,000 for Beauregard. Union forces also had a significant advantage in rifled artillery, which would have been of great use in a siege.

Even if Richmond itself was not captured in the summer of 1861, it is difficult to see how the Confederacy would have lasted through 1865 after losing much of northern Virginia with its food production, industry, and mining. And holding the battle lines in front of the capital city against a Union army constantly receiving reinforcements via rail and sea (up the York River) would have diverted much of the rebellion's forces away from points farther west leading to a faster advance by Federal troops into Tennessee and down the Mississippi. While there is no way to know for sure if a Union victory at First Bull Run would have led to an earlier end to the Civil War, the likelihood of such a result is high.

If the Confederates were defeated in the first great battle in Virginia, they could have been forced onto the defensive and lost Richmond, Nashville, and New Orleans by the end of 1861. There would have been little likelihood of British intervention in the conflict, no invasion of Maryland in 1862, and Union troops would have been poised to strike deep into the South by the end of that year. Would Lincoln have issued an Emancipation Proclamation in such a scenario and might the Confederacy have collapsed sooner than 1865?

While it is probable that slavery would have ended in the United States with an earlier end to the Civil War, the 14th and 15th Amendments to the Constitution might not have been ratified with significant impacts on future jurisprudence across the nation. After a shorter, less contentious Civil War, Lincoln could have escaped assassination in 1865 and served out his second term. Perhaps most importantly, a shorter conflict might have precluded upwards of one and a half million American casualties that historically took place. Hundreds of thousands of additional men (with their wives and children) participating in the rapid industrialization of the nation and settling of the West would have resulted in a stronger United States, which emerged as a world power by the end of the century.

IMPACT OF VICTORY

The Union defeat of the Confederate offensives in Maryland, Kentucky, and Mississippi in late 1862 had great impacts on history. Consider what would have happened if McClellan moved with his usual sluggishness in his pursuit of the Army of Northern Virginia that September? Lee had planned to have his men provision themselves off the rich farmland of western Maryland and strike for the Susquehanna River. Had he been allowed to do so, the Confederates could have moved on the Pennsylvania capital at Harrisburg, or cut the strategic railroads connecting Baltimore and Washington with the rest of the North. News of such Rebel triumphs could have had a major impact on the Union's November midterm elections and also convinced the British to recognize the Confederacy.

Of course, a McClellan who moved more slowly would not have ensured a Confederate victory north of the Potomac in 1862. Had Lee been able to march farther into Northern territory, it is possible that he would have been defeated much more severely in a later battle than what historically occurred at Antietam. However, the farther the Rebels pushed into the North, the more damage they would have done to the economy and the morale of the Union. While fears of a successful assault on Baltimore or Washington were likely overblown, McClellan would have come under ever more strident demands to defeat the Confederate army. Lee was a talented commander who would have encouraged a battle on defensive ground of the Virginian's choosing in an attempt to achieve just the sort of victory he won at Fredericksburg a few months later.

In the 1862 midterm elections, frustration with a lack of progress to crush the rebellion led to the opposition Democratic Party gaining a net twenty-seven seats in the Congress at the expense of Lincoln's Republicans and their allies in the Unionist Party.[37] Democratic gains were concentrated in southern Ohio and Pennsylvania, which were the areas most at risk of Confederate invasion. The Republican Speaker of the House, Galusha Grow, lost his seat. So did Philip Fouke, a Republican from Lincoln's hometown of Springfield, Illinois, who was defeated by the Democrat John Stuart who was one of the president's former law partners. Despite these losses, the Republican/Unionist coalition maintained control of the House with 116 seats to 72 held by the Democrats, and the president's pro-war policies remained in the ascendency in the Congress. However, had Lee been more successful in his invasion of the North or at least avoided a defeat such as the one that took place at Antietam, antiwar sentiment at the ballot box could have been much more significant. In such a scenario, Republican election losses in the House could have impacted the direction of the war.

Many historians believe that British recognition of the Confederacy would have ensured the rebellion's success. Certainly for decades, London feared that a United States that dominated North America would eventually build a fleet that could challenge the Royal Navy and worked to block this from taking place. Prior to the Civil War, Britain made efforts to impede the western growth of the United States by supporting the establishment of an Indian buffer state along the southern shores of the Great Lakes in 1812, and attempted to keep the Republic of Texas from being annexed by the United States in the 1840s.[38] In the furtherance of the goal of a North America divided into multiple, less powerful states, the successful secession of the Confederate States of America would represent a significant diplomatic victory for London.

By September of 1862, the Civil War was causing economic hardship in parts of England, and the war looked like it was becoming a stalemate. This led the British government to consider recognition of the South, or at least offering to mediate an end to the conflict, which could lead to the same result. France, involved in an imperialist venture in Mexico that was in violation of the U.S. Monroe Doctrine, was expected to follow London's lead. While British recognition of the Confederacy would not automatically have triggered armed conflict with the United States, many on both sides of the Atlantic believed that would have been the result. Had open warfare broken out between British and Union forces, the odds of a Confederate victory would have risen dramatically.

Of course, there is no guarantee that Lee avoiding a defeat in Maryland in 1862 and the absence of the issuance of the Emancipation Proclamation would have crippled Washington's pro-war governing coalition in the midterm elections of that year. Neither would they have guaranteed a change in the British diplomatic position toward the two warring parties. However, had McClellan not won his (admittedly narrow) victory at the Battle of Antietam, which gave Lincoln the political opportunity to issue the Emancipation Proclamation, the odds of the Confederacy achieving independence would have grown dramatically.

What would have been the result of the United States being split in two on the course of world history? The impacts could not have been anything but momentous. It is difficult to believe that the border between the Union and the Confederacy would have been devoid of friction, and both nations would have required large standing armies to guard its length. The South had clear intentions of conquering Cuba and parts of Mexico to expand slavery, and Madrid and Mexico City would have had a difficult time resisting such an armed intervention. Instead of slavery ending in North America, it could have spread. The rapid industrialization of the United States that occurred in the back half of the nineteenth century would have taken place more slowly due to a more fragmented market for consumer goods. The politics of building the Panama Canal would certainly have become more complicated with the United States wanting to control the path between the seas to knit together the Atlantic and Pacific coasts. However, the Confederacy, potentially in control of Cuba and representing the largest naval presence in the region, would have been wary of threats to free navigation from New Orleans, Galveston, and Mobile to the rest of the world. We can also ask whether or not a United States that lost the South would have gone on to purchase Alaska or seize Hawaii?

A Confederate States of America that emerged as an independent nation after 1865 would have likely defeated Spain to seize Cuba and Puerto Rico prior to 1898, but such a scenario would have removed the catalyst for the United States to gain control of the Philippines. A South closely aligned with Britain through exports of cotton, petroleum, and tobacco might have joined the Triple Entente in 1914 to help defeat the Central Powers in World War I. Or, in contrast, due to a continuation of slavery, the South could have had particularly cold relations with the nations of Western Europe and refrained from entering the conflict. A truncated United States that declared war on Germany in 1917 would have had that many fewer men to surge to France to halt the Ludendorff Offensive in 1918. Later, in the 1930s, how would a slave-owning Confederate ruling class have responded to diplomatic entreaties from Hitler and his racist regime? Obviously, conjecture can only take us so far. What is clear is that the victory at Antietam and the issuance of the Emancipation Proclamation made the defeat of the Confederacy much more likely. In the absence of these events, the history of the next hundred years could have been dramatically altered.

Chapter Five

Disaster at Pearl Harbor to Victory at Midway

Background to Defeat

An amazing feature of America's rise to great power status is that from the end of the Civil War until its entry into the Second World War, the nation suffered no major defeat on the battlefield. In 1865 much of the United States lay in ashes and more than one and a half million of its prewar population of thirty-one million had been killed, succumbed to disease, or wounded in the conflict that extinguished the Confederacy. Yet, over the next seventy-five years, the nation conquered the American West, acquired Alaska, and seized Hawaii, Puerto Rico, Guam, Samoa, Wake, and the Philippines. It politically dominated, and often militarily intervened in much of Latin America and the Caribbean, most notably in Panama, Cuba, and Nicaragua. Then, it surged an army of almost two million men to Europe, shifting the balance in the First World War in 1918 and converting what would have been a decisive German victory over exhausted French and British forces into a successful counteroffensive that triggered the collapse of the Central Powers.

Of course there were minor setbacks along the way, but the U.S. military never suffered a major defeat. The Battle of the Little Bighorn is understandably famous, but the loss of 275 members of the 7th Cavalry Regiment hardly qualifies as more than a skirmish in the context of a rapidly growing nation with a population in the tens of millions.[1] While small contingents of U.S. troopers were beaten by American Indian forces in the 1870s, the Sioux, Cheyenne, Arapaho, Nez Perce, and other tribes were militarily crushed, their women and children often massacred and the pitiful survivors forced onto reservations.

Similarly, the U.S. forces suffered small reverses in the Spanish-American War such as at Las Guasimas and Tayacoba in Cuba, but the Spanish were rapidly defeated and ejected from what remained of their overseas empire. That conflict, and suppressing the Philippine Insurrection that grew out of it, saw greater U.S. losses caused by tropical diseases rather than enemy action. Almost two decades later, the U.S. military incurred more than 50,000 battlefield deaths in the terrifically bloody fighting of World War I. However, the Americans emerged victorious in every major action fought in that conflict including those at Cantigny, Belleau Wood, Chateau Thierry, St. Quentin, St. Mihiel, and the final Meuse-Argonne Offensive, which helped trigger the final collapse of the German war effort.

What is most impressive is not that the United States prevailed in its major foreign policy goals and desired strategic territorial expansion over the long period of 1865–1918, but that it did so without suffering even one major defeat in the process. It would not be until an additional two decades had passed until the American military once again had to prove that it could react, and recover after a strategic battlefield setback and go on to achieve ultimate victory.

After the carnage of the "Great War," America chose to retreat into isolationism. It refused to join the League of Nations, raised tariffs, enacted the Neutrality Act of 1935, and generally attempted to remain aloof from conflicts that increasingly raged around the world as the Axis powers of Italy, Germany, and Japan grasped for territorial aggrandizement. After war broke out in 1937 in Asia with Japan's invasion of China, and in 1939 with Germany and the Soviet Union's invasion of Poland, the U.S. president, Franklin Delano Roosevelt, began to move the country toward war.

In the Pacific, diplomatic complaints led the United States (in concert with the British and Dutch) to issue threats to impose an embargo on exports of oil, steel, and other critical supplies to the Japanese. This lack of industrial inputs threatened Tokyo's ability to continue its war in China. In Europe, arms and ammunition were sold in ever larger volumes to Britain to be used against Germany. The U.S. Navy protected ships carrying such supplies in the Western Atlantic from packs of marauding U-boats, which triggered an undeclared naval war with Germany. American relations with the Axis powers deteriorated even more rapidly with the defeat of the Netherlands and France by Germany in 1940. In Europe, Britain appeared on the brink of disaster unless it received dramatically greater assistance from the United States. At the same time, across the Pacific, Japan looked to conquer British Malaya, French Indochina, and the Dutch East Indies to seize these colonies' production of raw materials, especially petroleum. Such an offensive to the south would likely necessitate an attack on the U.S. colony of the Philippines.

FDR, and a rising number of Americans, realized that military triumphs by the Axis powers represented a dire crisis for all remaining democracies in the world. In an attempt to deter Japanese aggression against the European colonies in Southeast Asia, FDR ordered that the U.S. Pacific Fleet sail from its home port in California to the Hawaiian Island of Oahu in 1940. This move made possible the most infamous defeat in American military history: the December 1941 attack on Pearl Harbor.

Relations between Washington and the Axis powers continued to sink. In September, Japan invaded the northern half of French Indochina and the United States retaliated with an embargo on exports of steel and other metals. Then in March of 1941, the Lend-Lease Act was signed, which effectively allowed for unlimited arms shipments to Britain. When Germany invaded the USSR in June, Washington began sending military aid to Moscow as well. Finally, when Tokyo seized the southern portion of French Indochina in July, FDR froze Japanese assets in the United States and ordered what became a complete embargo of sales of petroleum. Despite having built up stockpiles, the Japanese war machine would grind to a halt in under a year unless oil imports were reestablished.

In Tokyo, the military-dominated government settled on a two-track policy. It hoped that a diplomatic understanding could be secured with America accepting Japanese control or outright conquest of East Asia. If such an agreement could not be negotiated, then prior to running down its oil supplies, Japan would go to war and seize the Philippines, the Dutch East Indies, Malaya, and Burma. A fortified perimeter would then be established around this new "Greater East Asian Co-Prosperity Sphere." The western powers would be unwilling to suffer the vast number of casualties required to reclaim their former colonies in a long campaign of attritional fighting and a negotiated peace would codify Japan's new southern empire. To pursue this plan, Tokyo dispatched a new set of diplomats to Washington while at the same time the military prepared to fight. Army minister General Hideki Tojo was appointed prime minister in October 1941. He favored a "preventive war" against the United States and opposed a compromise solution.

Admiral Isoroku Yamamoto, commander-in-chief of the Imperial Japanese Navy (IJN), believed that going to war against the western democracies was folly. He had studied and traveled in the United States and did not believe his nation could prevail in a long military conflict with America due to the great disparity in economic output: In 1938 the United States had a GDP of $1.928 trillion (in 2024 U.S. dollars) compared to $554 billion for Japan and its colonies, which included Korea, Manchuria, and Formosa (the island now known as Taiwan).[2] In addition, while Japan's economy was running at full capacity to prosecute the ongoing war of conquest in China, America's had a great deal of slack. The United States was only finally recovering from the Great Depression and still had an unemployment rate north of 12 percent at the end of 1940 indicating that America's peak output could rise significantly higher in a military conflict.[3] In the industries most important to wage modern warfare in the first half of the twentieth century, the disparity between the two economies was stark. The Imperial Japanese Army (IJA) estimated that the specific ratios in relevant areas were as follows: "steel production, 20:1, coal, 10:1, aircraft, 5:1, labour, 5:1, shipping, 2:1, oil, 100:1."[4] Of course Yamamoto planned to do his duty, and stated his outlook for a war with the colossus of the Western Hemisphere: "If I am told to fight regardless of the consequences, I shall run wild considerably for the first six months or a year; but I have utterly no confidence for the second and third years."[5]

If Japan was going to go to war with the western democracies, the timing in late 1941 might maximize the nation's chances of success. The USSR, Tokyo's most powerful regional rival, was on the brink of collapse.

The French and Dutch militaries had been eviscerated. Much of coastal China had been conquered and its government forced to flee to the western city of Chungking. A combination of Tokyo's military procurement program in the late 1930s and Britain and the U.S. navies focusing on confronting Nazi Germany in the Atlantic resulted in the IJN having a major naval advantage in the Pacific.

The 1941 Naval Balance in the Pacific[6]

	Japanese Fleet	Soviet Pacific Fleet	U.S. Pacific Fleet	U.S. Asian Fleet	Britain and Commonwealth	Dutch East Indies
Battleships	10		9		2	
Aircraft Carriers	10		3			
Cruisers	38		20	2	8	3
Destroyers	112	9	50	13	5	7
Submarines	65	48	33	17		15
Totals	**235**	**57**	**115**	**32**	**15**	**25**

This imbalance was unlikely to last long. American shipbuilding capacity was dramatically greater than that of Japan, and the United States had initiated a massive rearmament program. Under the Two-Ocean Navy Act in July 1940, the U.S. Congress authorized a doubling in the tonnage of the nation's warships. By the end of the following year, the United States had begun construction on much of a new fleet of more than 210 ships including seven battleships, twelve aircraft carriers, and thirty-five cruisers.[7] Japan's limited industrial base could not hope to compete with such a shipbuilding program. Within a few short years, the IJN would no longer have the ability to prevail militarily in the Pacific.

Japan's goal of going to war with the western allies was to seize Malaya and the Dutch East Indies to gain control of a steady supply of petroleum for the empire, along with other commodities such as rubber, rice, sugar, tungsten, tin, iron ore, copper, zinc, chromium, nickel, and coal.[8] Waging war on the United States was also seen as necessary as the Philippines needed to be conquered or American aircraft and naval vessels operating from the island colony could cut sea lanes leading back to Tokyo. The weak British naval squadron at Singapore and the even less powerful U.S. Asiatic Fleet based in Luzon would either have to retreat in haste or be quickly overwhelmed by the bulk of the IJN's battleships, cruisers, and destroyers that would support the invasions of both Malaya and the Philippines. These strikes to the south would be supported by ground-based aircraft flying from occupied Indochina, which could reach much of northern Malaya, as well as those from Formosa, which could reach Manila. Air bases seized in Malaya and the Philippines would then be used to support an invasion of the Dutch East Indies.

The Defeat

The weakness of the British and American fleets based at Singapore and Manila, respectively, and the location of Japanese airfields in the region meant that Yamamoto could utilize his carrier fleet to attack a completely different target at the initiation of hostilities. The admiral was aware that on November 11, 1940, twenty-one British Swordfish biplanes launched from the HMS *Illustrious* had successfully attacked the Italian fleet at its Taranto naval base. Despite heavy antiaircraft fire, barrage balloons, and torpedo nets, the Swordfish successfully carried out their attack with torpedoes and bombs to sink or seriously damage three battleships, one heavy cruiser, and two destroyers. If a small force of slow (top speed of 143 mph), fabric-covered biplanes could do that much damage to a fleet at anchor, what could a massed attack of hundreds of Japanese carrier aircraft accomplish? The IJN studied the British raid closely, sent representatives to Taranto to investigate the harbor, and held discussions there with counterparts from the Italian navy.[9]

Two months later Yamamoto devised a plan to destroy much of the U.S. Pacific Fleet on the first day of the war with a surprise carrier-launched air attack on the naval base at Pearl Harbor. Believing Japan would lose an extended conflict against the United States, he hoped that a devastating battlefield victory might break the spirit of the American people and its military. In early 1941, he wrote to navy minister Admiral Koshiro Oikawa: "The most important thing we have to do first of all in a war with the U.S., I firmly believe, is to fiercely attack and destroy the U.S. main fleet at the outset of the war so that the morale of the U.S. Navy and her people goes down to such an extent that it cannot be recovered."[10]

In the second half of 1941, compared to three American carriers in the Pacific, and Britain having none, Yamamoto oversaw a flotilla of ten aircraft carriers that operated what was arguably the world's best naval aviators flying some of its most advanced aircraft.[11] He realized that this force could be used similarly to the Japanese destroyers that launched the Russo-Japanese War in 1904 with a devastating surprise torpedo attack on the Russian Fleet docked at Port Arthur (now Dalian, China). If planes from Yamamoto's floating air bases could successfully sink much of the U.S. Navy's capital ships concentrated at Pearl Harbor at the very outset of a conflict, the IJN would overwhelmingly dominate the Western Pacific. Such control of the sea would facilitate the conquest of Japan's new southern empire and give it time to fortify a defensive perimeter before the U.S. Navy's massive building program could impact the military balance of power. Admiral Chuichi Nagumo was assigned command of the planned strike force, which eventually totaled a fleet of sixty-seven ships, with six Japanese fleet carriers at its core.

Such an attack on Oahu was not a new idea—at least not to the U.S. military. Army Air Force General William "Billy" Mitchell predicted with uncanny precision how Japan would begin a war with the United States with a Sunday morning surprise attack. His 1925 book, *Winged Defense*, included the following: "Attack will be launched as follows: Bombardment, attack to be made on Ford Island (in Pearl Harbor) at 7:30 a.m. . . . Attack to be made on Clark Field (Philippines) at 10:40 a.m."[12] In 1932 the U.S. Navy also took up the issue in its annual wargame known as Fleet Problem XV when a squadron with two U.S. carriers posing as a "Blue" force launched a surprise attack on the "Black" force on Oahu. The "Blue" commander, Admiral Harry Yarnell, chose Sunday, February 7, for the strike on the theory that many "Black" military personnel would be off-duty and thus unable to oppose the air raid. The carrier planes achieved complete surprise and the wargame judges adjudicated that the entire fleet in Pearl Harbor was sunk and all army air aviation on Oahu had been destroyed.[13]

Fleet Problem XIX in 1938 also highlighted a carrier air attack against Pearl Harbor, and again the "defenders" were surprised and suffered significant simulated damage.[14] Finally, Fleet Problem XXI in 1940 showed that while Oahu-based PBY Catalina reconnaissance planes with their impressive 2,500-mile range were very effective in finding and tracking ships from high altitudes, coordination between the Army and Navy in their defense efforts for Hawaii was lacking.[15] Thus, the potential for the staging of a carrier-launched attack on Pearl Harbor had been studied by senior ranks of the U.S. military for a decade prior to 1941. The success of the surprise British air raid on the Italian navy at its base at Taranto was also well known in the United States and should have alerted senior members of its military to Oahu's danger.[16]

While the IJN had to actually carry out the daring raid, it would have been much less effective or even resulted in a Japanese disaster without a number of poor decisions made on the American side in the months, weeks, and days leading up to the attack. First of all, Yamamoto's plan only became possible due to FDR repositioning the U.S. Pacific fleet to Pearl Harbor in 1940. Had the American ships remained at their home base in southern California, it would have been almost impossible for an IJN task force to sortie more than 8,000 kilometers across the ocean undetected to reach them. After the United States, Britain, and the Netherlands cut off sales of petroleum to Japan, the latter nation was confronted with a choice of going to war or acceding to American demands of removing its military forces from both China and Indochina.

A voluntary withdrawal from China was anathema to the Japanese, so the American embargo and demands to end it could only result in armed conflict. Thus, moving the U.S. Pacific Fleet westward to Pearl Harbor in no way acted as a deterrent to Japan. Admiral James Richardson, the Fleet's commander, realized this, believed his ships could be better prepared for war back in California, and traveled to Washington where he expressed his views frankly to FDR. The president did not appreciate this advice, and Richardson was soon relieved from his post and replaced by Admiral Husband Kimmel.[17]

Then, a year after the fleet was moved to Oahu, it was reduced by a quarter in the summer of 1941 as ships were redeployed to the Atlantic to confront Germany. Three battleships (USS *New Mexico*, *Idaho*, and *Mississippi*), one carrier (USS *Yorktown*), four cruisers, and seventeen destroyers were detached and headed through the Panama Canal.[18] While this meant there were fewer American ships in Pearl Harbor that could have been sunk by the Japanese on December 7, the redeployment also significantly reduced the number of reconnaissance planes that could have been used to spot an enemy strike force approaching Hawaii. Not only did the Pacific Fleet lose the use of a quarter of its carrier aircraft with the departure of the *Yorktown*, but each of the detached battleships and cruisers operated multiple long-range Kingfisher or Seagull reconnaissance floatplanes that could no longer be employed in the region.

Next, while the army garrison on Oahu was strengthened and reached more than 42,000 men by December 1941, the strident calls for reinforcements from General Douglas MacArthur (see next chapter) resulted in a large number of men and equipment being shifted to the Philippines. This was most evident in aircraft as there were thirty-five B-17s (America's most modern bomber) and more than ninety P-40s (its newest fighter plane) in the Philippines at the outbreak of war. In total, MacArthur's FEAF (Far Eastern Air Force) had more than 175 total aircraft when the war began.[19] This meant that the U.S. Army Air Force had a less effective local collection of planes to protect the strategically critical U.S. Pacific Fleet berthed at Pearl Harbor. Shockingly, there were fewer B-17s and P-40s on Oahu than in the Philippines when the Japanese attacked. While the Army Air Force had 234 planes on Oahu on December 7, many were older or even obsolescent aircraft with 109 not operational on the day due to a lack of replacement parts.

Finally, a catastrophic series of failures by Kimmel, and the U.S. Army commander in Hawaii, General Walter Short, led to American forces being almost completely unprepared to detect or defend themselves when Yamamoto's planes appeared over Oahu. While the Pacific Fleet needed to bring squadrons of its ships into harbor on a regular basis for resupply, maintenance, and crew leave, such port visits could not be hidden from agents operating out of the Japanese consulate in Honolulu. Unfortunately, Kimmel tended to have most of his ships return from sea to Pearl Harbor by Saturday each week and many crewmen would be out on shore leave that evening and the following morning. Establishing such a routine, a prime error of operational security, allowed Tokyo's consulate to communicate to the IJN that it was highly likely that most of the Pacific Fleet would be at anchor in Pearl Harbor and manned with incomplete crews on Sunday, December 7.[20] In addition, even as increasingly urgent warnings arrived from Washington that war in the Pacific was imminent, Kimmel was guilty of not taking reasonable precautions to make sure his fleet was ready to react in a scenario where it was attacked by carrier-launched aircraft while in port. This is particularly surprising in light of his knowledge of how Japan had begun its war against Russia in 1904, as well as the success of the British raid on the capital ships of the Italian navy in Taranto that had taken place just one year earlier.

The U.S. Army commander for Hawaii, for his part, was just as culpable. As historian Gordon Prange wrote in his classic, *At Dawn We Slept*: "Short did not understand his basic mission on Oahu, despite all his instructions and despite his own lip service to the concept. We seek in vain . . . for the slightest indication of a drill aimed at protecting Kimmel's ships . . . Almost equally disturbing is Short's obvious failure to understand or trust air power . . . Combine these two blind spots in Short's mentality, and one understands why he simply could not conceive of the type of attack the Japanese actually launched: an air strike complete in itself aimed at the destruction of the U.S. Pacific Fleet with no intention of planting one Japanese boot, let alone the Rising Sun banner, on Hawaiian soil."[21]

The U.S. military in the territory also was amazingly lax in its curiosity regarding the actions of the Japanese around Hawaii. To achieve surprise, Yamamoto needed to sail his strike force to Oahu without it being detected. As tensions mounted in the Pacific, the civilian ocean liner *Taiyo Maru* departed from Yokohama for Honolulu in late October carrying 300 of the few western foreign nationals remaining in Japan. The ship was under direct Japanese government control, maintained strict radio silence, and proceeded on an unusual course that took it outside of regular shipping lanes so that it approached Hawaii from the north and then turned almost due south to reach its destination. IJN personnel on board wearing civilian attire paced the deck around the clock with binoculars and noted a complete absence of sightings of planes or ships during the voyage. Finally, an American reconnaissance plane flew overhead when the *Taiyu Maru* was 200 miles north of Oahu.

The ship docked in Honolulu on November 1, and departed a few days later via a more traditional route having taken on board 400 Japanese nationals evacuating back to their home islands. None of the Americans disembarking in Hawaii seemed to have noted the ship's unusual course, nor the presence of men continuously pacing the deck and scanning the horizon of an empty ocean during the entire voyage. Somehow, even though Army military intelligence and the FBI had agents keeping a close eye on the *Taiyo Maru* while it was in port, no one bothered to note that a 14,000-ton ship had approached America's main military fortress in the Pacific undetected from a novel direction and was not spotted until it was well within the range of carrier-launched strike aircraft.[22]

As negotiations came to an impasse in Washington, deciphered Japanese diplomatic cables were being read by American intelligence agencies, and a massing of the IJN's invasion fleet for its strike south was detected. Increasingly dire "war warnings" were transmitted to U.S. military commands across the Pacific. On November 27 the Department of the Army transmitted a cable that included the following: "Japanese future action unpredictable, but hostile action possible at any moment. If hostilities cannot, repeat, cannot be avoided, the United States desires that Japan commit the first overt act. The policy should not be construed as restricting you to a course of action that might jeopardize your defense. Prior to hostile Japanese action you are directed to undertake such reconnaissance and other measures as you deem necessary. . . ." [23] In a second message sent December 3, the chief of naval operations informed bases across the Pacific that, "categoric and urgent instructions were sent yesterday to Japanese Consular posts . . . to destroy most of their codes and ciphers at once and burn . . . confidential secret documents."[24]

It is difficult to understand why the U.S. military in Hawaii failed so spectacularly to operate sufficient long-range air reconnaissance in the days immediately prior to the Japanese attack. By early December, the Army Air Force in Hawaii had thirteen (six operational) reconnaissance planes to patrol the seas around Oahu along with seventy-two bombers (thirty-nine operational), which could have been used in such a role. In addition, the Navy had sixty-nine PBY Catalina flying boats, which had been designed specifically to patrol open ocean and attack enemy shipping.[25] Finally, the U.S. Pacific Fleet's cruisers and battleships each operated multiple long-range reconnaissance float planes. Thus, the more ships at Pearl Harbor on December 7, the greater the number of reconnaissance aircraft on hand to patrol around Oahu.

In the aftermath of the attack, Kimmel and Short's defenders argue that the lack of reconnaissance flights in the days leading up to the attack was due to a shortage of trained crews and spare parts for the aircraft that made a proper search of the 360 degrees around Oahu impossible. The commanders also wished to minimize wear and tear on a limited supply of mission-ready aircraft until war actually began. Of course, the greater danger was a surprise attack at the very start of any war, which would dramatically reduce U.S. combat power in the Pacific more severely than any loss due to wear and tear on patrol aircraft in the remaining days of peace. Also, any attack would almost certainly emanate from the north or west of Oahu so that 360-degree air reconnaissance was not required. Clearly maximum airborne search efforts did not take place and could have had a major impact on the results of the raid on Pearl Harbor even if the Japanese were not spotted until after their strike force had been launched. A radio warning from an American patrol plane sighting either a fleet with six carriers 250 miles north of Oahu, or a large mass of incoming attack aircraft could have been the difference between a surprise attack and one confronted by squadrons of U.S. fighters in the air and antiaircraft batteries manned and ready to fire.

Even in the absence of effective air reconnaissance, U.S. military forces on Oahu were still provided with multiple opportunities to sound the alarm in time to mitigate the damage of the imminent disaster. Five Japanese midget submarines were assigned the mission of infiltrating the waters of Pearl Harbor the morning of the attack. The periscope of one of these small boats was spotted at 3:20 a.m. on December 7 heading for the harbor entrance.[26] The destroyer USS *Ward* assigned to patrol the area was unable to locate and attack it. Then, another of these submarines developed mechanical difficulties and could not remain completely submerged. It was spotted at 6:30 a.m., and the *Ward* sank it with gunfire and depth charges before promptly sending multiple warning messages of the event by radio.[27] Sadly, this report did not lead to any change in the readiness status of the rest of the U.S. Pacific Fleet, and neither was the Army Air Force informed of the incident.

Around 6:45 a.m., two reconnaissance float planes launched by the Japanese cruisers *Chikuma* and *Tone* were picked up on radar by the U.S. Army technicians manning the station at Opana on the north shore of Oahu, but no fighters were scrambled to intercept these unidentified aircraft.[28] *Tone*'s plane scouted the anchorage off Lahaina on Maui while *Chikuma*'s plane circled Pearl Harbor and reported back via radio the exact number of capital ships docked in the harbor and their locations. While these planes were emblazoned with the bold red disks of the rising sun, their appearance over the area triggered no alarm.[29] Then at 7:02 a.m., the radar station technicians noted, "the largest blip they had ever seen," which they believed represented more than fifty incoming aircraft. The contact was promptly reported to the Air Information Center at Fort Shafter. However, it was dismissed as likely being an expected flight of B-17s arriving from California even though the U.S. bombers would have generated a much smaller radar contact.[30] Again, a chance to alert the Pacific Fleet and the American defenders of Oahu was missed.

Finally, at a few minutes before 8 a.m., the first of two waves of more than 350 Japanese aircraft arrived over Oahu and began the attack that brought the United States into World War II. The force that winged in over the island consisted primarily of bomber aircraft along with forty torpedo planes protected by almost eighty fighters. Most famously, the enemy aircraft bore down on "battleship row" moorings at Pearl Harbor to target the capital ships of the U.S. Pacific Fleet. In many instances, antiaircraft batteries had not been supplied with ammunition, or were not manned until well into the course of the battle. Of the eight battleships present, two were sunk beyond repair and another six were heavily damaged with two settling to the bottom of the shallow harbor with only their superstructures remaining visible. Three cruisers, three destroyers, and five auxiliary ships were also hit.[31] While the American carriers in the region were not at Pearl Harbor, Kimmel's fleet suffered a devastating

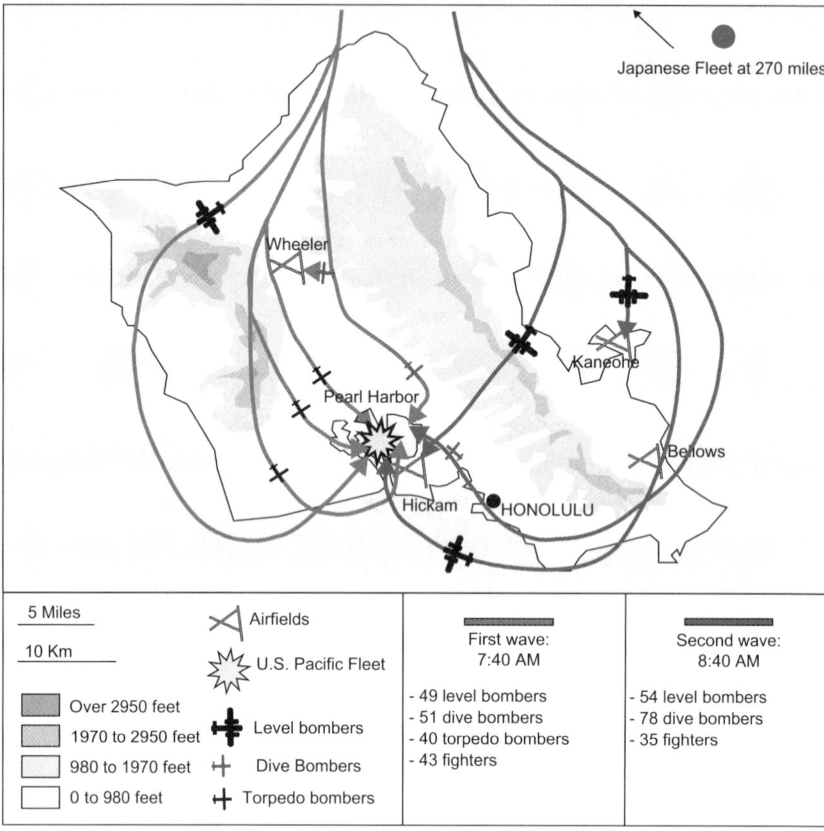

The Japanese air attack on Oahu. WIKIPEDIA

blow, which, at a stroke, gave the IJN a dominant naval superiority across the breadth of the Pacific.

While the prime targets of the Japanese attack were U.S. capital ships, the incoming planes also had the mission of attacking air bases on the island to gain control of the skies above the battlefield and ensure that no counterstrike could be launched against Japan's carrier force. Thus, Wheeler, Bellows, and Ewa fields were all bombed and strafed along with the naval air stations at Kaneohe and Ford Island. Only a few of the more than 150 P-40 and P-36 fighters on Oahu were able to take off to oppose the Japanese; 169 American military planes were destroyed and another 159 damaged, almost all while on the ground lined up in neat rows on the tarmac.[32] This was an overwhelming loss that granted the enemy air superiority over Oahu.

As his planes returned to the carriers, Admiral Nagumo contemplated ordering a third attack wave to target the dry-docks and petroleum tank farm at Pearl Harbor. He decided against this for a variety of reasons: His destroyers were running low on fuel, he had already accomplished his primary mission of neutralizing the U.S. Pacific Fleet, the volume of antiaircraft fire had become increasingly fierce as the attack wore on, and by the time his fliers finished such a mission, some would be returning after dark and had been lost attempting to land. Most importantly, he knew there were American carriers somewhere in the vicinity and already they might be launching a strike against his task force.

So Nagumo turned his ships around and headed back to Japan after having savaged the U.S. military force on Oahu. Over the hour and a half of his airborne attack, more than 2,400 Americans were killed and another 1,000 wounded. The Japanese had twenty-nine of their planes shot down, or only 8 percent of those involved. Five IJN midget submarines were also destroyed in and around Pearl Harbor resulting in the Japanese suffering sixty-five total casualties on the day. It was one of the most lopsided victories in military history. World War II had truly become a global conflict.

Recovery

The devastating raid on Oahu and the destruction of much of the U.S. Pacific Fleet was followed rapidly by several additional Japanese victories. Despite hours of warning, enemy planes destroyed much of MacArthur's air force in the Philippines on the ground on December 8 (see next chapter). Further east, the IJA invaded Malaya and rapidly forced the British defenders into a long retreat back toward their fortress bastion of Singapore. On December 10, the HMS *Prince of Wales* was sunk by ground-based Japanese aircraft, which eliminated the last operational Allied battleship in the Pacific. That same day, Japanese forces stormed ashore on the U.S. territory of Guam and seized the island. On

December 11, an attempt was made to land on Wake, but was rebuffed by the U.S. Marine Corps garrison, which sank two enemy destroyers. However, a second larger attack overwhelmed the island's defenders later in the month. Luzon was invaded by the Japanese Fourteenth Army on December 22, which quickly drove MacArthur's forces back into the peninsula of Bataan.

Everywhere the Japanese were victorious. By the end of the year it was obvious that Philippines and Malaya would soon be in enemy hands, Singapore was besieged, Burma had been invaded, and landings were taking place in the Dutch East Indies. In Washington, the FDR Administration had chosen to adopt a "Germany First" strategy focusing the bulk of available military resources on the earliest possible defeat of the Nazis and sending only limited reinforcements to the Pacific. The outlook was bleak for U.S. military forces in Hawaii.

The president chose Admiral Chester Nimitz from more than a score of more senior officers to take over in the Pacific and told him to, "get the hell out to Pearl Harbor and don't come back until the war is won."[33] He arrived in Hawaii on December 24 and viewed the destruction by boat the next day. A Navy helmsman asked the admiral his opinion of the Japanese raid and all on board were shocked when Nimitz replied that the enemy had made three major mistakes: (1) that the Sunday attack saved the lives of thousands of trained seamen as they were on shore leave rather than on ships sunk in the open ocean, (2) the attacking aircraft had failed to bomb the port's maintenance facilities, which would be used to repair the damaged ships sunk in the shallow water of the harbor, and finally (3) the 4.5 million gallons of petroleum in the nearby tank farm had not been targeted.[34]

In addition, it can be argued that an even greater error of the raid on Pearl Harbor is that it did not specifically target the three aircraft carriers of the U.S. Pacific Fleet. After all, when Yamamoto ordered Nagumo to attack Pearl Harbor utilizing solely a carrier-launched strike force, he was making the point that the heavy artillery gun of the battleship was no longer the preeminent naval weapon system. While the U.S. carriers could have been in port on December 7, that they were not represented a major oversight in Japanese planning, which left the most critical determinant of success in the surprise attack to . . . luck. If the Japanese proved anything when they struck, it was that in the Pacific the carrier was the most important naval asset and each one was strategically important.

Had Nagumo closed in on Oahu and sent out large numbers of scout planes on December 8 and 9 they likely would have found the USS *Lexington* and *Enterprise*, which were returning to Oahu after delivering aircraft to the U.S. base on Midway Island (USS *Saratoga* was at San Diego on the day of the attack).[35] With six Japanese carriers to take on only two American ones, had Nagumo remained in the area he would have been able to maintain sufficient combat air patrol fighters above his fleet, bomb the oil tank farm and ship repair facilities on Oahu, and still have overwhelming numbers of attack aircraft to strike the *Enterprise* and *Lexington* when spotted.

The consensus view today is that the United States was lucky that Nagumo decided to accept a partial victory and head back to port rather than remaining off Oahu to potentially achieve a complete one. Of course, while many historians blame the admiral for this decision, logistics and a failure of planning were the true errors. The hard truth was that the Japanese ships, especially the destroyers, were running low on fuel by the end of December 7. The IJN had learned to refuel its ships at sea specifically for the mission of attacking Pearl Harbor, but many of its warships still had a relatively short cruising range especially when engaging in continuous high-speed movement. Four tankers refueled Nagumo's ships at sea on December 4, and then again on December 6. Then, while these tankers remained far to the northwest of Hawaii, the admiral and the rest of his force began the high-speed run toward Oahu to launch the attack the following morning.

Perhaps, Yamamoto could have planned an even more aggressive operation where the tankers remained with the fleet, and Nagumo remained on station to laboriously refuel his ships on December 8. In such a scenario, he could have bombed the fuel tanks, submarine pens, and ship repair facilities at Pearl Harbor, and the *Lexington* and *Enterprise* could have been sunk. Such an outcome requires posing that a lot of things went right for the Japanese rather than starting to go wrong. After all, the Americans knew approximately where Nagumo's fleet was from the direction his aircraft took as they flew away from Oahu. In contrast, the Japanese had no idea as to where they might find the U.S. carriers. Had Nagumo's slow-moving fleet engaged in at-sea refueling on December 8, it would have made an attractive target for the aircraft from the two U.S. carriers arriving in the area as well as remaining planes striking from bases on Oahu. Thus, had the Japanese carriers remained in the area, December 8 could have easily become a day when the Americans at least partially settled the score for losses suffered the day before.

In any event, on the final day of 1941, Nimitz assumed command of what was left of the U.S. Pacific Fleet from Kimmel on the deck of the submarine USS *Grayling* as a way to indicate that boats such as that one would immediately be sent out to attack the Japanese. There would be no period of reaction, retraining, and recovery. Despite grievous losses, and an enemy with massive numerical superiority, the fleet's new leader demanded that the Navy regain its offensive spirit with what it had on hand. In addition to submarine sorties, while the United States no longer had any operational battleships in the Pacific, its three aircraft carriers would be used as the kernel of task forces and directed to strike back at the Japanese. Calculated risks with these flattops would be taken to wear down the enemy while salvageable battleships were repaired at Pearl Harbor and shipyards on the American mainland completed an entirely new fleet that would carry the fight across the Pacific.

This strategy was almost immediately put into effect. Only one month later on February 1, planes from the carriers USS *Enterprise* and *Yorktown* attacked Japanese installations in the Marshall and Gilbert Islands while surface vessels engaged in shore bombardments. This was followed by a task force centered on the carrier USS *Lexington* threatening the major Japanese base at Rabaul on February 20. Carriers then hit Wake and Marcus Islands on February 24 and March 4. While only moderate damage was inflicted, and the enemy continued its successful ongoing invasion of the Dutch East Indies, valuable operational experience was gained by the U.S. Navy and morale in the fleet improved. Finally, on March 10, the *Lexington* and *Yorktown* sailed into the Coral Sea south of New Guinea and launched raids that struck Japanese forces landing on the north shore of the island at Lae and Salamaua.[36] This resulted in the sinking of several Japanese ships including multiple cruisers. While enemy naval forces were still dramatically stronger, the U.S. Pacific Fleet was clearly in the fight and remained a greater threat to Tokyo's territorial ambitions than the enemy believed after the success of the attack on Pearl Harbor.

Nimitz was rewarded for his aggressiveness by being put in charge of the newly created Pacific Ocean Areas (POA) military command on March 24. This theater of operations controlled all air, sea, and land units across much of the world's largest ocean except for the Southwest Pacific Area (SWPA), which consisted of the area around Australia, New Guinea, the Dutch East Indies, and the Philippines that was to be controlled by General Douglas MacArthur. The following month, Nimitz's forces executed the tactically inconsequential but strategically momentous Doolittle Raid. The idea of the operation was formulated in late December 1941 when FDR met with the Joint Chiefs and urged the earliest possible bombing mission against Japan's Home Islands to avenge the attack on Pearl Harbor. A member of the staff of the new head of the U.S. Navy, Admiral Ernest King, suggested to him that long range Army Air Force bombers could be launched from a carrier, and a "crazy" idea was born.

The famous aviator Lieutenant Colonel James Doolittle was placed in command of the mission. He chose B-25 Mitchell medium bombers for the daring operation, which would consist of having these planes take off from a U.S. carrier in the North Pacific, bombing Tokyo, and then landing at airfields in China outside the zone of Japanese control. The USS *Hornet* practiced launching some of these bombers in Virginia and then transited the Panama Canal to California. Doolittle's crews trained in planes that had been stripped of all non-essential equipment to reduce their weight, and extra fuel tanks were installed for the long flight. These planes then flew to the West Coast where sixteen of the modified B-25s were loaded onto the *Hornet*. As the carrier would not be able to launch other aircraft with her deck packed with long-range bombers, Nimitz was forced to allocate the *Enterprise*, one of the three flattops he had in the Pacific, to provide fighter cover to the operation. The POA commander knew the raid would likely do very little real damage to the

Japanese military, but he was in favor of the morale-boosting potential of the operation, and as soon as the B-25s took off, he would also gain another carrier for use in his area.

On April 18, Doolittle's sixteen bombers lumbered off the deck of the USS *Hornet* and headed for Japan. Six hours later the first of the planes began to arrive over Tokyo and dropped their payloads. Other B-25s struck Kobe, Nagoya, Osaka, Yokohama, and Yokosuka. One of the U.S. bombers landed at Vladivostok in the USSR and its crew was interned. The others all made it to China but were unable to locate friendly airfields and when they ran out of fuel their crews either crash-landed or bailed out by parachute. The mission's commander stated that, "I felt lower than a frog's posterior," due to the loss of his planes and thought he would be court-martialed.[37] Instead, Doolittle was ordered to rush back to the United States and was awarded the Medal of Honor by the president.

Of course, such a small number of bombers attacking a nation the size of Japan did little serious damage on the ground. However, just a few months after the supposed destruction of the U.S. Pacific Fleet at Pearl Harbor, it was clear that American naval power remained robust in the region and could strike into the very heart of the so-called Greater Asian Co-prosperity Sphere. News of the raid had an electric effect on American morale at a time that the Axis powers were in the ascendency from the Atlantic, to Stalingrad, to Burma, to New Guinea. The effect in Japan was even greater. Historian John Keegan writes that, "Doolittle's Tokyo raid caused an agony of shame among Japan's admirals and generals, to whom protection of the emperor's person and residence was a sacred trust; and it would subsequently influence with disastrous effect, Japanese strategic decisions over the future of the Pacific War."[38]

Victory

Prior to appearance of the U.S. bombers over Tokyo in April, the war for the Japanese had been proceeding even better than planned. Against the British, Malaya had been overrun, the defenders of Singapore surrendered on February 15, 1942, and the IJA had recently captured Rangoon in Burma. Dutch forces in the Netherlands East Indies surrendered on March 9. Manila had fallen in the Philippines, and the

American garrison in Bataan was weakening. The Japanese succumbed to what they later referred to as "victory disease," and discussions began at the highest levels in Tokyo to expand the previously planned perimeter of the empire, push farther into the Indian Ocean, resume attacks on Hawaii, and perhaps even invade Australia. The IJA balked at the final option due to a lack of resources but agreed to support Operations MO and FS, which called for the conquest of a chain of islands (New Guinea, the Solomons, Fiji, Samoa, and New Caledonia) so as to cut Australia off from U.S. aid transiting Hawaii.

This plan was counterproductive in retrospect as it required the Japanese to push a salient out eastward into Allied territory that extended more than 2,000 miles at the very end of an already tenuous supply line. The success of the Doolittle Raid also focused the Japanese military's attention on neutralizing the threat of U.S. forces in the Pacific. Interest in pushing into the Indian Ocean waned, and Yamamoto began planning an operation for June in which he would attack the American base on Midway Island northwest of Oahu to lure the U.S. Pacific Fleet out to sea where it would be decisively defeated. At the same time in Washington, Admiral King, while supporting FDR's "Germany First" policy, was determined to put up more of a fight against the Japanese. With the British balking at an early invasion of France across the English Channel, King lobbied to shift a larger percentage of America's growing military forces to the Pacific. This would allow a switch from retreat to what he called the "Offensive-Defensive," and an attempt to hold the sea lanes connecting Hawaii and Australia.[39] Of course, Nimitz was heartily in favor of taking the fight to the enemy, incorporating reinforcements as they were fed into his theater, and eager to engage in significant calculated risks to inflict losses on the Japanese and thwart their plans.

In early May, the IJN launched convoys from its major base of Rabaul on New Britain Island to seize the first two targets of Operation MO: Tulagi in the Solomon Islands and the Australian base of Port Moresby on the south shore of Papua New Guinea. This pair of amphibious assaults was supported by two fleet carriers, the *Zuikaku* and the *Shokaku*, along with the light carrier *Shoho*. Japanese military intelligence discerned correctly from radio intercepts that two carriers were returning to Pearl Harbor after the Doolittle Raid but were unaware of the arrival of the *Hornet* in the region and were thus mistaken in the belief that only one American carrier was still at large somewhere else in the Pacific. At the same time, American "Ultra" signals intelligence had begun to break the IJN's main code and had guessed correctly that an invasion force to take Port Moresby would be imminently sailing south from Rabaul with two fleet carriers. Nimitz sent a task force centered on his two available carriers *Yorktown* and *Lexington* to the Coral Sea to block the enemy operation. He also ordered the *Enterprise* and *Hornet* to the area immediately after they resupplied at Pearl Harbor, but they were unable to reach the area in time to participate in the imminent naval clash.

The Battle of the Coral Sea was the first in which neither navy's ships sighted the other and attacks were made solely by carrier-launched aircraft. As historian Samuel Eliot Morison describes it, "the ensuring action was full of mistakes, both humorous and tragic, wrong estimates and assumptions, bombing the wrong ships, missing great opportunities and cashing in accidentally on minor ones."[40] The United States lost the carrier *Lexington*, a destroyer, an oiler, and scores of aircraft. The *Yorktown* was also heavily damaged. Japanese casualties were somewhat lighter with the light carrier *Shoho* sunk along with several smaller vessels. The *Shokaku* was also damaged, and the IJN lost a similar number of carrier aircraft. However, while technically a tactical defeat, the battle turned into a strategic victory for the United States as the invasion force destined for Port Moresby turned around and returned to Rabaul. American fliers also grossly exaggerated their efforts and the engagement was reported as a lopsided victory to the U.S. public. Nevertheless, Nimitz had taken a calculated gamble based on his superior military intelligence and prevailed.

The stage was now set for the decisive carrier battle Yamamoto wished to trigger. In early June he once again sent a major Japanese fleet toward Hawaii. The bait to draw out Nimitz's carriers was an air attack and then amphibious landing to seize the airbase on Midway, a small atoll that represents the farthest northwest point in the Hawaiian archipelago. Yamamoto believed reports from his fliers that two American carriers had been sunk in the Coral Sea, which left only two remaining to be destroyed in the battle to come. Aircraft based at the newly captured airbase on Midway would then pound Oahu and effectively push U.S. naval power back to the North American West Coast. With the *Shokaku* damaged and the *Zuikako* having lost so many planes and needing to assimilate new squadrons, Admiral Nagumo's carrier force would only approach Hawaii this time with four flattops. However, with the United States only having two carriers that could possibly sortie from Pearl Harbor after Midway was attacked, and the Japanese force sailing with seven battleships, the odds seemed stacked very much against the Americans.

Of course, Yamamoto's view of the overall situation in the Central Pacific was critically incomplete. First of all, the *Yorktown* was indeed severely damaged, but very much not sunk in the Coral Sea. It was sufficiently patched up in Pearl Harbor and took on new aircraft squadrons in time to participate in the coming battle. In addition, the airbase on Midway had been reinforced and its aircraft complement included Army Air Force B-17s, armed PBY scout planes, Navy torpedo and dive bombers, and around twenty-five fighters operated by Marine pilots. Thus, the relative effective carrier strength for both sides was roughly even at four versus four.

Ultra intelligence then gave the Americans a critical advantage with the ability to read much of the IJN's radio code. Cryptographers believed the enemy would engage in a three-pronged attack in early June against the Aleutians, Midway, and a renewed push in the South Pacific. Through a creative subterfuge they were able to confirm that Midway Island was indeed one of the Japanese targets. Thus, rather than the Japanese laying a trap for the U.S. Pacific Fleet, Nimitz was able to turn the tables and prepare what was, in effect, a giant naval ambush. Choosing to concentrate his forces, the admiral had his three carriers sail with two task forces that deployed northeast of Midway at "Point Luck" where it was unlikely the enemy would expect them to be.[41]

In the early hours of June 4, around half of the Japanese carrier aircraft took off to strike Midway, with the rest held in reserve to attack any American flattops that might be discovered. An hour later, the enemy invasion force was sighted by a PBY operating from the island

and announced its findings via radio. Midway's bombers took off to find the Japanese ships and, alerted by the island's radar station, its fighters rose to challenge the incoming air attack. The initial bombing raid did serious damage, but the island's airfield remained operational. The initial counterstrike from Midway was repelled but made clear that the island and its planes remained a threat to the Japanese fleet.

Rather than follow Yamamoto's instructions to retain a contingent of attack planes for an antiship mission, Nagumo ordered his reserve aircraft readied for a second strike on Midway and rearmed with contact-fused bombs used for land targets. However, about half an hour later, a Japanese scout plane reported sighting a large naval squadron with a carrier to the east, which led to a scramble to once again load the proper ordnance for an attack on the recently discovered American ships. However, taking evasive action against additional B-17 bomber attacks from Midway and then recovering the Japanese aircraft returning from the initial strike on the island precluded the enemy carriers from launching the reserve force of attack aircraft. By 9:25 A.M. it was too late as waves of American planes from the *Hornet*, *Enterprise*, and *Yorktown* arrived over the Japanese carriers. The *Akagi*, *Kaga*, and *Soryu* were all hit by dive bombers, which set off secondary explosions among the fully fueled and armed Japanese planes aboard. The three enemy carriers were mortally wounded leaving only the *Hiryu* operational and able to launch a counterstrike against the U.S. fleet.

In a series of further combat actions during the day both the *Yorktown* and the *Hiryu* were hit and eventually sank to the bottom of the Pacific. The Japanese, having lost their entire complement of carriers, retreated after suffering a defeat from which they never recovered. While Yamamoto still retained a marked advantage in battleships, cruisers, and destroyers, the Americans had achieved relative parity with the Japanese in terms of aircraft carriers, which had clearly become the dominant weapon in the vast expanses of the Pacific. Even worse, the IJN had lost a majority of its best-trained naval aviators who would take significant time to replace. And this was time the Japanese did not have due to the rapid and dramatic expansion taking place in the size of the U.S. Navy.

While the Battle of Midway was decided by a relatively small number of men in the context of the enormous resources dedicated to fighting World War II, it was nevertheless a strategic victory. The great military base of Oahu was never again seriously threatened and the United States used it to stage increasingly offensive operations. Tokyo's hopes that the Americans would be unwilling to suffer large casualties breaking through the fortified perimeter of the newly conquered oceanic empire were misplaced. Throughout the next two years the Japanese were forced into increasingly unequal attritional battles that played against their smaller population and industrial base. The successful American landings to seize the Marianas Islands in mid-1944 led many senior Japanese officials to accept that the war was lost and triggered the collapse of the government of Prime Minister Hideki Tojo. Sadly, too many members of the IJA and IJN refused to accept defeat, and the fighting continued with increasing savagery until the dropping of two atomic bombs on Hiroshima and Nagasaki finally led to an end of the conflict.

Causes of Defeat

There were several factors that contributed to the disaster that took place at Pearl Harbor on December 7, 1941, but the greatest was the failure of Admiral Kimmel and General Short to be ready for war itself. While many of the defeats suffered by the U.S. military in its history were caused by reasonably plausible decisions that turned out to be overly optimistic such as General Washington trying to hold New York, or McDowell pushing south to take Richmond, how the Pacific Fleet was caught completely by surprise at its base in Oahu is still difficult to fathom. A common theme running through this book is that American commanders have failed most spectacularly when they focused on what they thought an enemy would do rather than what it could do. But the U.S. military establishment had made a habit of contemplating how a surprise Japanese carrier attack on Pearl Harbor would inflict tremendous damage. In fact some of its commanders had staged this exact operation in wargame exercises in the decade before the fighting began. That the Japanese had attacked Russia in 1904 without a prior declaration of war and done such damage in the initial hours of that conflict made the scenario of a surprise raid on Oahu that much more likely.

Kimmel and Short's political and military superiors in Washington certainly deserve blame for the success the IJN achieved at Pearl Harbor. FDR's policies diplomatically backed the Japanese into a corner and effectively forced them to go to war. He then ordered the Pacific fleet to reposition to Oahu where they would be within range of a Japanese surprise attack. Marshall and Stimson directed significant reinforcements, especially in aircraft, to the Philippines even though that colony had little chance of resisting any sustained Japanese assault. In contrast, those planes sent to Luzon could have made a real difference had they been based in Hawaii instead on December 7. But in the final analysis, it was the Army and Navy commanders on Oahu who deserved to take the fall for the level of success the Japanese achieved when they launched their carrier aircraft at the U.S. Pacific Fleet that Sunday morning.

Kimmel and Short were instructed to do everything in their power to prepare and protect the military assets and installations under their command. They received regular updates from Washington that Japan was likely moving toward war, and starting in late November they were given explicit warnings that a military attack was likely imminent. Nevertheless, there was no combat air patrol established above the harbor, barrage balloons were not installed, antiaircraft batteries were not armed and manned, and there were no torpedo nets protecting the Navy's battleships. When Nagumo neared Oahu, scores of long-range American military aircraft were sitting on the tarmac rather than out on reconnaissance missions to the north and west of Oahu in the areas from which any attack was most likely to emanate.

Furthermore, the battleships of the Pacific Fleet could not move out to sea immediately to take evasive action once the raid began as none of their boilers were fired up, and even if they had been, the vessels had only a small percentage of their crew complements on board. There were actually as many military U.S. aircraft on Oahu on December 7 as the Japanese were able to launch to carry out the raid, but most were not fueled and armed that morning. Even worse, too many were parked wingtip-to-wingtip to protect against fears of possible sabotage. This made them perfect targets for a surprise attack from carrier aircraft, which the U.S. military had previously identified as a likely way any war with Japan would begin.

In addition to this multitude of failures of preparation, Short and Kimmel failed to establish an effective coordinated tactical alert system that would track unusual activity that might presage the incoming attack Washington had repeatedly warned was likely imminent. Multiple submarine sightings at the entrance to Pearl Harbor, multiple unidentified inbound radar contacts, and actual Japanese scout planes flying over Oahu and Maui failed to trigger an alarm. Though the situation was not as bad in Hawaii as in the Philippines (as addressed in the next chapter), there was insufficient coordination between the Army and the Navy even though previous wargames had identified that this was a deficiency in the territory that needed to be addressed. A central command center for the two military branches staffed with a senior officer with authority to sound an alert on the morning of December 7 could have made a huge difference. That Japanese strike aircraft arrived to find empty skies over Pearl Harbor and achieved complete surprise is one of the great failures of U.S. military history.

Causes of Victory

The most important factor leading to strategic victory at Midway was, to a great extent, luck. Had the three American carriers of the Pacific Fleet been in Pearl Harbor on December 7, 1941, they would have surely received the brunt of the Japanese aerial attack. Had those ships been sunk, there would have been a pressing need to redeploy from the Atlantic one or more of the remaining four carriers in the U.S. Navy. However, the Germany First strategy of the FDR Administration would have likely required that some of the American flattops remained off the East Coast escorting convoys and hunting U-boats.

Without a few carriers in his fleet to deploy, it did not matter how aggressive Nimitz wanted to be in the first half of 1942, he would not have been able to carry out the missions that historically took place. Of course, three of the four American fleet carriers in the Atlantic at the start of the war were eventually transferred over time to fight in the

Pacific with only the relatively slow and small USS *Ranger* participating in the European Theater of Operations for the duration of the conflict. This included the USS *Wasp*, which was also undersized and underpowered compared to the Yorktown class of ships.

Had Nimitz only had submarines, destroyers, and cruisers to attack the Japanese in early 1942, it is highly likely he would have utilized them in a variety of aggressive roles. However, without at least two carriers he could not have overseen the Doolittle Raid on Tokyo, which forced Yamamoto to order the attack on Midway. In a scenario where Nimitz did in fact have only two carriers to carry out the mission to bomb Tokyo, there would have been no others to wage the Battle of the Coral Sea with the Japanese amphibious force likely succeeding in landing at Port Moresby and completing the conquest of New Guinea. No engagement in the Coral Sea would have allowed Nagumo to sail for Midway in June with six rather than four fleet carriers giving the Japanese an overwhelming advantage in the subsequent engagement.

As always in war, luck was a great determinant of victory and in this case, it favored the United States in that the Pacific Fleet's carriers were not at Pearl Harbor on December 7. Their survival gave Nimitz the naval assets required to engage in multiple offensive operations over the six months following the outbreak of war. Certainly, a different commander could have chosen a defensive stance more in accordance with the "Germany First" strategy of the FDR Administration, but that would have been out of character for the aggressive doctrine of the U.S. Navy in the 1930s. Of course, Nimitz was not alone in that he was clearly supported in his efforts by his direct superior, Admiral King, in trying to wrest back a measure of the initiative from the Japanese despite being heavily outnumbered at sea. The POA commander was also aided by those he put in charge of his carrier-centered task forces (Admirals Wilson Brown, Frank Fletcher, and William Halsey), as well as all the personnel of the Pacific Fleet that quickly regained their fighting spirit after Pearl Harbor to turn the tide of the war by the following June.

Undoubtedly the pilots of the U.S. Navy's dive bombers would have demanded the lion's share of the credit for America's victories in the Pacific in the first half of 1942 due to the hits they scored on *Shokaku*,

Akagi, *Kaga*, *Shoho*, *Soryu*, and *Hiryu*. However, it can be argued that the men most responsible for defeating the Japanese were the cryptologists who cracked the IJN communication codes. They informed Nimitz of the need to deploy his scarce resources to the Coral Sea in May, and Midway in June. Without such an advantage in the field of signals intelligence, the tide of the war in the Pacific would likely have not turned until significantly later in the conflict no matter how brave and skilled were the pilots Nimitz sent into the fight.

Impact of Defeat

While the debacle at Pearl Harbor is the best known U.S. military defeat, many historians have done their best to tease out a silver lining from the event. It is the consensus opinion that only the perfidy of the Japanese attack overcame American isolationist sentiment, brought America into World War II, and guaranteed the defeat of the Axis powers. Certainly, national opinion was strongly against getting involved early in the conflict. Soon after fighting broke out in Poland in September 1939, a Gallup poll registered 84 percent opposition to sending the U.S. Army and Navy to fight in Europe and only 8 percent were in favor of declaring war on Germany. However, is it really true that without the defeat at Pearl Harbor, the United States might have continued to watch the fighting play out from the sidelines?

Polls show that national opinion followed FDR as his policies increasingly steered the country right into the conflict. By September 1940 the number of Americans who were willing to aid Britain even if that risked war with Germany had risen to 52 percent. In March 1941 the Lend-Lease Act was passed and the United States began shipping rapidly increasing volumes of military aid to Britain and soon thereafter, the USSR. This triggered an undeclared naval war in the Western Atlantic with U.S. warships protecting convoys of foreign merchant ships and exchanging fire with U-boats. By April, 68 percent of Americans polled were in favor of war with the Axis nations if that is what it took to ensure their defeat.[42]

Then, on the last day of October, the destroyer USS *Reuben James* was sunk by a U-boat off Iceland while escorting a convoy bound for England. Scores of American sailors died, the news occasioned a banner front page headline in the *New York Times*, and public opinion in favor of going to war assuredly rose in response.[43] In response, Congress granted FDR's request two weeks later and repealed the 1939 Neutrality Act. This meant that the U.S. Navy would now be allowed to escort American merchant ships right into the ports of Liverpool and Murmansk. Clearly such a change in policy ensured hostilities between the United States and Germany in the immediate future and moved the two nations into an open state of war. Even immediately after the surprise raid on the U.S. Pacific Fleet, most Americans believed Germany represented a much greater threat to the country than did Japan, and a Gallup poll indicated 91 percent supported FDR declaring war on Germany as well as Japan.[44]

Thus, if an "infamous" attack on Pearl Harbor was not required to pull the United States officially into World War II by early 1942, was there indeed any silver lining to the American defeat? The answer is uncertain. Certainly, opposition to war evaporated as more than 1,000 sailors died with the sinking of the battleship USS *Arizona*. In addition, as previously discussed, Admiral Nimitz believed that had the Japanese not attacked Hawaii, the U.S. Pacific Fleet would have sortied to fight the Japanese in the open sea and would have been sunk in deep water with most of its personnel killed. Certainly this is possible, even likely, as the IJN had significant advantages in terms of numbers of capital ships, quality of weapons (especially in fighter planes and torpedoes), and tactics (particularly in night engagements) in 1941. However, as this volume has highlighted many times, Lady Luck has a say in how battles play out and the American battleships and carriers could have prevailed. Perhaps Admiral Husband Kimmel would have emerged from World War II as a hero rather than a goat. We will never know for sure.

So what can be concluded regarding the impact of the Japanese attack on Pearl Harbor? First of all, it certainly solidified U.S. public support behind the war effort and accelerated America's entry into the conflict, though perhaps by less than the accepted historical consensus. It also shaped the early years of fighting in the Pacific as the U.S. Navy focused on carrier operations. The loss of so many ships on the first day of the war also ensured that the Philippines garrison would be overwhelmed before relief could arrive. Finally, the abject failure of the U.S. military on

December 7 remains an object lesson to those in our armed services that preparation and a certain level of paranoia in advance of hostilities is of paramount importance.

Impact of Victory

Yamamoto famously stated that he and his navy would be able to "run wild" for six months to a year after attacking the United States. That the Battle of Midway took place almost exactly six months after the attack on Pearl Harbor is often cited as showing the predictive power of the Japanese admiral. However, without Nimitz's leadership, the bravery of the men of the U.S. Navy, and being on the receiving end of a little luck, the Japanese might have continued to "run wild" for a full year until the end of 1942. Had Nimitz been a commander willing to move onto the defensive until his fleet grew in size, had the IJN signals codes not been deciphered so quickly, and had combat aviators not been so willing to press their attacks on Japanese ships regardless of the odds, the Battles at Coral Sea and Midway might have resulted in significantly different results.

In these two engagements the Japanese lost five carriers with another heavily damaged compared to only two lost on the American side. This led to the cancellation of amphibious operations to seize Port Moresby and Midway. History could have easily played out much more in Japan's favor. Had Ultra intelligence not alerted Nimitz to the threat to Papua New Guinea, he would not have had his carriers in position in the Coral Sea, Port Moresby would have fallen to the enemy, and MacArthur and the SWPA command would have been forced onto the defensive guarding northern Australia. Then Nagumo would have sailed toward Hawaii in June with six or seven carriers versus three or four on the American side. In such a scenario, in the absence of intelligence warnings of the Japanese attack, Nimitz's fleet could have suffered grievous losses, with Midway being overwhelmed by the enemy amphibious force.

In such a scenario, the United States would have started its successful counteroffensive later than historically took place, and from farther away from Tokyo. Would the United States still have pushed ahead with a two-pronged offensive after suffering additional military reverses? Could the Japanese have used their extra time fortifying their armed perimeter to slow the Allied advance? Would the Marianas still have been seized by Nimitz's forces and had suitable airfields built in time to launch atomic bombing missions in August of 1945? Or perhaps, would the United States have had its B-29s fly from the Aleutian Islands of Attu and Kiska that same month and still have been able to shock the Japanese into surrender with the unworldly power of Little Boy and Fat Man destroying the cities of Sapporo and Sendai?

An extended war would have in no way been of benefit for Japan. As the noose tightened around the Japanese government in the late summer of 1945, the USSR entered the war and rapidly seized great swaths of Manchuria and Korea. The southern half of Sakhalin Island and the Kuriles were occupied and the Soviets prepared to launch an August 24th amphibious attack on the northern Japanese home island of Hokkaido, which was relatively undefended. Luckily, the Japanese surrendered before this took place and the United States objected strenuously to the Red Army advancing any farther. Had Nimitz and his Pacific Fleet not been able to turn the tide quite so quickly in 1942, the northern third, or even the northern half, of Japan might have fallen under Soviet rule similarly to what took place in Germany at the end of the war. Forty-five years of Japan being divided would have undoubtedly have had a major impact on the progression of the Cold War, the Korean War, and of course, Japan's remarkable recovery as a peaceful, democratic nation in the second half of the twentieth century.

What we can conclude with confidence is that the United States recovered remarkably quickly from its defeat at Pearl Harbor to regain the strategic initiative in the war. Errors made in underestimating the Japanese were rapidly rectified with a set of engagements where a military intelligence advantage allowed for calculated risks that favored American victory. Any hope in Tokyo that the United States would be unwilling to fight a painful, attritional war to advance across the Pacific was quickly dashed in one vicious tropical island battle after another.

Patriot forces flee during the Battle of Long Island. NATIONAL ARCHIVES

The man who lost America: General Sir William Howe NEW YORK PUBLIC LIBRARY/ WIKIMEDIA COMMONS

Washington inspects captured Hessians after the Battle of Trenton. NATIONAL ARCHIVES

The British bombard Charles Town during the siege of the city.
BROWN UNIVERSITY/WIKIMEDIA COMMONS

After three brutal defeats in the South, Washington sent General Nathanael Greene to stabilize the situation. NATIONAL ARCHIVES

Greene's Continentals hold the line at the Battle of Guilford Courthouse. WIKIMEDIA COMMONS

Mortal enemies: Chief Tecumseh and William Henry Harrison
NEW YORK PUBLIC LIBRARY/WIKIMEDIA COMMONS

Perry gives up the ship but wins the Battle of Lake Erie. NATIONAL ARCHIVES

The Battle of the Thames secures Michigan and Ohio for the United States.
LIBRARY OF CONGRESS

Union soldiers flee in panic from the First Battle of Bull Run.
NEW YORK PUBLIC LIBRARY/WIKIMEDIA COMMONS

Lincoln and McClellan in 1862. One man saved the Union. The other almost destroyed it. LIBRARY OF CONGRESS/WIKIMEDIA COMMONS

Union soldiers advance on Confederate lines in the Battle of Antietam. LIBRARY OF CONGRESS

The U.S. Pacific Fleet burns on December 7, 1941. LIBRARY OF CONGRESS

Admirals King (left) and Nimitz (right) pose against a backdrop of the Pacific. NATIONAL ARCHIVES

The USS *Yorktown* takes a fatal hit during the Battle of Midway. NATIONAL ARCHIVES

A besieged General Douglas MacArthur and his chief of staff, General Richard Sutherland, in Corregidor's Malinta Tunnel U.S. ARMY

U.S. POWs during the Bataan Death March NATIONAL ARCHIVES

Australians with a U.S. M-3 light tank advance on Buna in early 1943.
AUSTRALIAN WAR MEMORIAL

U.S. General Robert Eichelberger and Australian General Thomas Blamey inspect a captured Japanese bunker. AUSTRALIAN WAR MEMORIAL

October 14, 1943: Schweinfurt's ball-bearing plants under bombardment at a cost of sixty B-17s NATIONAL ARCHIVES

Generals Eisenhower, Spaatz, and Doolittle (left to right) oversaw the defeat of the Luftwaffe before D-Day. NATIONAL ARCHIVES

The arrival of large numbers of P-51 Mustangs was instrumental in achieving air superiority over Western Europe in 1944. U.S. ARMY AIR FORCE/WIKIMEDIA COMMONS

Chinese People's Volunteer Army soldiers assaulting UN positions in the Second Phase Offensive in late 1950 CHINESE MILITARY SCIENCE ACADEMY/WIKIMEDIA COMMONS

Architect of two of America's greatest military defeats: MacArthur inspecting U.S. troops in Korea in February 1951 NATIONAL ARCHIVES

General Ridgway (second from right) engineered one of the great military recoveries in U.S. history. U.S. ARMY

The U.S. massive advantage in armor, artillery, and airpower did not translate into victory in Vietnam. U.S. MARINE CORPS/WIKIMEDIA COMMONS

Most Americans forget that by the time the final helicopter evacuations from Saigon took place in 1975, the U.S. military had long since withdrawn from Vietnam.
U.S. MARINE CORPS/NATIONAL ARCHIVES

U.S. Special Forces and Air Force Combat Controllers advance on Kabul with local allies during the invasion of Afghanistan in 2001.
U.S. SPECIAL OPERATIONS COMMAND/WIKIMEDIA COMMONS

As in Vietnam, overwhelming military power allowed the United States to seize territory in Iraq in 2003. Suppressing a local insurgency was much more difficult. U.S. AIR FORCE/ WIKIMEDIA COMMONS

After withdrawng from Iraq, U.S. troops had to return in 2014 to fight Islamic State. U.S. ARMY/DEFENSE VISUAL INFORMATION DISTRIBUTION SERVICE

Images from the fall of Kabul in 2021 were unpleasantly similar to those from Vietnam forty-five years earlier. U.S. MARINE CORPS/DEFENSE VISUAL INFORMATION DISTRIBUTION SERVICE

Instruments of victory or expensive outdated targets? USS *John C. Stennis* and *Abraham Lincoln* sail from Pearl Harbor into an uncertain future. U.S. NAVY/INTERNET ARCHIVE

Chapter Six

The Fall of Luzon to the Siege of Buna-Gona

Background of Defeat

As the Japanese fleet recovered its final strike aircraft off Oahu on December 7, 1941, the phone rang in downtown Manila. Commander of U.S. Army Forces in the Far East, General Douglas MacArthur, was informed that Pearl Harbor had been attacked and the nation was at war. Thus began a very different and much more brutal defeat for American arms.

If anyone was going to deliver a victory for the forces holding the Philippines it should have been Douglas MacArthur. He was the son of General Arthur MacArthur Jr., who had overseen the conquest of the islands for the United States from 1899 to 1902 and served as the colony's military governor. Douglas, after graduation from West Point, spent significant time in the Philippines as well as being assigned as his father's aide on extended official trips across East Asia, which included two visits to Japan. The young MacArthur proved his mettle on the battlefield in World War I in which he was awarded a bevy of medals and rapidly promoted to become the youngest general in the U.S. Army. In the interwar period he continued his rapid advancement through the ranks and, after serving once more in Manila, assumed the Army's highest position as chief of staff in Washington.

While in DC, he argued against the military's long-established War Plan Orange (WPO) for a conflict against Japan. As Tokyo's armed forces grew rapidly in size, it seemed increasingly unlikely that in case of conflict between the two nations that the United States could successfully hold the Philippines: The islands were simply too close to the potential enemy and much too far away from relief sailing from the U.S. West Coast, or even the territory of Hawaii. WPO called for the colony's garrison to hold out for as long as possible on the bastion peninsula of Bataan and the small offshore island of Corregidor that together dominated the entrance to Manila Bay. Reinforcements would be assembled on the U.S. West Coast, but it was assumed that the defending force in the Philippines would be forced to capitulate before aid could arrive.

MacArthur believed this plan was "defeatist" and that the colony, which he had come to love as a second home, must be defended. As his term as chief of staff came to an end, still vigorous and only in his mid-fifties, he was appointed in 1935 to the rank of field marshal in command of the military forces of the newly created Philippine Commonwealth, which was to be granted its full independence in 1946. He arrived in Manila confident that a force could be built to defend the islands. The Philippine Army (PA) was established on December 21, 1935, and ten divisions were formed that comprised a formidable force on paper of more than 100,000 men.

After 1935 and the establishment of the PA, significant weapons and supplies began to arrive from the United States. While the force was never well equipped, it did have 75mm artillery guns, an assortment of other older field pieces, M2 Browning machine guns, and its soldiers were given the outdated but still accurate Enfield rifle. The latter weapon was used by various American units throughout World War II and would still be quite effective in the hands of Chinese Communist troops in the Korean War.[1]

Sadly, while MacArthur had proven his abilities on the battlefield in 1918, by 1941 he was no longer the detail-oriented front-line leader he had been. Increasingly, he spent his time in downtown Manila in his headquarters and lavish apartment rather than focusing on the training of the under-equipped and under-paid conscript force he commanded. He claimed to know "the oriental mind" and that the government in Tokyo would not attack prior to the middle of 1942.

In July of 1941, he lobbied for and was reinstated into the U.S. Army and placed in command of both the colony's garrison as well as the Philippine Army. His requests for additional forces and plan to deviate from WPO and defend all of the Philippines were soon approved by his superiors in Washington.

During this period, actions taken by the Japanese inevitably led to conflict with the western democracies. The invasion of China that began in the 1930s was damaging to British and American business interests, and atrocities committed against civilians in cities such as Nanking and Shanghai appalled the U.S. public. The nationalist Chinese military was forced to retreat west into the interior of the nation as it lost huge swaths of territory. Relations between Tokyo and the FDR Administration in Washington deteriorated and became increasingly hostile after Japan signed the Tripartite Pact with the other Axis powers of Nazi Germany and Fascist Italy in 1940.

With the defeat of France and occupation of the Low Countries by Germany in that same year, the government of Prime Minister Hideki Tojo began making preparations to seize the colonial possessions of French Indochina (now Vietnam, Laos, and Cambodia), British Malaya (now Malaysia and Singapore), and the Dutch East Indies (now Indonesia). Such a move would isolate the beleaguered Nationalist Chinese government from western aid flowing in through Indochina as well as provide the Japanese with reliable supplies of rice, rubber, iron ore, and petroleum, which they imported from the western powers. After Tojo pressured the French to grant military basing rights in northern Indochina in late 1940, FDR began to tighten exports of oil and steel to Japan with the British and Dutch following suit. After the Japanese seized the rest of Indochina, the United States and the other western powers banned exports on August 1, 1941. With only a year's supply of oil stockpiled, the government in Tokyo was confronted with a painful choice: accede to American demands to withdraw from Indochina and China or go to war to seize the resources in the Dutch and British colonial possessions.

As war in the Pacific became increasingly likely, additional weapons and men were being shipped to the Philippines as per MacArthur's demands. The American garrison grew in size to more than 20,000 men including the arrival of the veteran 4th Marine Regiment. Chief of Staff General Marshall suggested sending an additional U.S. infantry division, but MacArthur turned down the offer as being unnecessary. The garrison also received modern armor in early September with the arrival of seventy-five self-propelled guns and two battalions operating 108 M-3 tanks. In addition, large numbers of new aircraft arrived in the colony. These included more than one hundred P-40 fighter planes and thirty-five B-17 heavy bombers. In fact, by the end of November, there were more of these two most modern U.S. aircraft types in Luzon than anywhere else in the world. MacArthur declared to Marshall that the combination of the U.S. garrison and the PA would be able to repel a Japanese invasion force of up to 100,000 men.

Negotiations between the Tojo and FDR governments ground to an impasse and expectations of war grew throughout the Pacific. However, MacArthur continued to argue that war would not break out in 1941, and that Japanese forces were also dramatically inferior to those of western nations. Admiral Thomas Hart, the head of the U.S. Navy's Asiatic Squadron based in Manila, disagreed and confided to his wife and his superiors that he believed the general was no longer sane. Coordination between the two military branches was poor and deteriorated as MacArthur belittled Hart with quips such as, "small fleet, big admiral."[2] The general also refused to harmonize reconnaissance flights of the Army Air Force and those of the U.S. Navy. MacArthur argued that, "The Navy has its plans, the Army has its plans and we each have our own fields."[3]

MacArthur kept his men on a peacetime training regimen due to his belief that hostilities were not imminent. His new U.S. Army Air Force commander, General Lewis Brereton, arrived in November 1941 and was shocked that the squadrons were engaged in a lax routine, revetments had not been built to protect newly arrived aircraft, and most of his planes were concentrated and positioned within range of attack from Japanese bases on Formosa. While Brereton urged his boss to disperse the most modern aircraft and shift many of them farther south, this did not take place. Even repeated specific war warnings sent to MacArthur from Washington did not convince him that the Japanese would soon attack.

The Defeat

When the bombing of Pearl Harbor commenced, the Japanese had planned to strike Luzon at daybreak from airfields in Formosa. However, as the sun rose over the Far East on December 8, a heavy fog covered the Japanese airstrips. Thus, MacArthur was given time to decide what to do before the blow fell. Brereton asked repeatedly for permission to send his B-17s north to bomb Japanese installations. MacArthur temporized and only authorized a couple of planes to sortie on a reconnaissance mission over Formosa near the middle of the day. Sadly by then it was too late: The fog had burned off and the Japanese planes arrived over the Luzon airstrips. In the debacle that followed most of the P-40s and B-17s were caught on the ground and more than half the U.S. air fleet was destroyed. Thus, on the first day of the war, the Japanese had achieved air superiority over the Philippines.

After December 8, enemy aircraft arrived over Luzon daily. Their raids destroyed much of what remained of MacArthur's air force as well as hitting important Army and Navy installations. Shorn of protective aircover, Admiral Hart withdrew his squadron south to the Dutch East Indies. One would have assumed that with the loss of control of the air, and the destruction of much of the Pacific fleet, the commander of the Philippine garrison would adjust accordingly and choose to revert to WPO and prepare Bataan to withstand a lengthy siege. Sadly this did not take place and supplies were moved northward to support a defense along the Lingayen Gulf beaches where most expected an enemy landing to take place. The garrison's quartermaster officer asked if he could position a large cache of supplies in Bataan but MacArthur specifically ordered him not to do so.

Over the next few weeks, the PA and U.S. Army forces prepared for an amphibious attack. General Jonathan Wainwright commanded a large portion of the defenders along the Lingayen Gulf while MacArthur retained control over much of the rest along with his armored units near Manila. Finally, on December 18, U.S. military intelligence warned the garrison that a large enemy flotilla was heading toward Luzon and on December 22, they arrived carrying General Masaharu Homma and

43,000 men of his Fourteenth Imperial Japanese Army.[4] They began landing along the beaches of Lingayen Gulf, but high seas precluded the landing of most tanks and heavy artillery. Thus, the stage was set for an impressive victory for the defenders: MacArthur commanded a significantly larger force with more than 80,000 men in the area supported by more than 100 tanks and 75 self-propelled guns.

Instead what developed was a rout of the U.S.-Philippine force. Wainwright asked that the armored battalions be released from the reserve and sent to the beachheads, but the request was denied by MacArthur. The unsupported PA infantry divisions fell back from contact with the Japanese with many Filipinos throwing away their weapons and returning to their homes. The U.S. Army's 26th Cavalry Regiment made a brave stand somewhat inland at the town of Rosario, but MacArthur continued to hold back his reserves. After fierce fighting, elements of the U.S. Army garrison were forced to retreat. For reasons still not clearly understood, MacArthur reported back to Washington that the enemy had landed 80,000 men, that he had only 40,000 on Luzon and he subsequently ordered a retreat to Bataan.

The withdrawal took place in generally good order and the American M-3 tanks were employed to delay the advancing Japanese. However, while most of the defending forces were able to reach Bataan, the great bulk of food, medicine, ammunition, and other supplies were left behind to be captured by the enemy.[5] After concluding the retreat, the garrison was immediately placed on half rations, which was soon cut to one quarter rations of approximately 1,000 calories per day. The men quickly began to lose weight and suffer from tropical diseases.

MacArthur ensconced himself on Corregidor Island and spent most of his time there in the fortified Malinta Tunnel. While he had access to fast PT boats, which could deliver him quickly across the short distance to Bataan at night, he only chose to visit his forces there once in the next ten weeks of the siege. Instead of surveying the defensive lines, he focused his attention on sending messages back to the United States in which he trumpeted his glorious defense and demanded the U.S. Navy sortie from Hawaii to deliver supplies and reinforcements to the garrison.

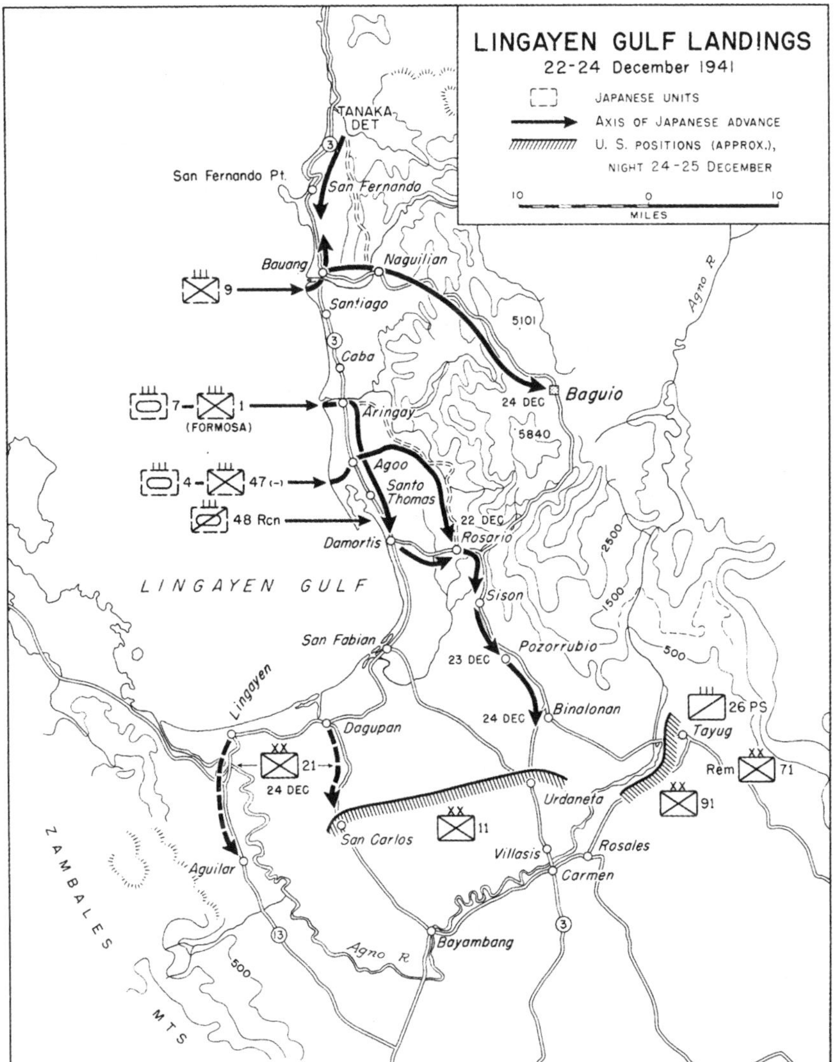

The Japanese invasion overwhelms MacArthur's forces along the Lingaten Gulf.

U.S. ARMY CENTER OF MILITARY HISTORY

He also railed against the Germany First strategy implemented by FDR and argued that the most important battle of the war was for control of the Philippines. However, only a few American submarines dared the Japanese blockade to supply limited amounts of ammunition and medicine to the besieged. As the men of the U.S.-Philippine force slowly starved and weakened over the first two months of 1942, they were forced to withdraw southward into increasingly compressed siege lines.

As the situation on Bataan deteriorated, President Roosevelt decided that the death or capture of General MacArthur would hand too great a propaganda victory to the Japanese. He ordered MacArthur to flee and on the night of March 11 the general and his staff successfully slipped away on a small flotilla of PT boats. Ten days later he arrived in South Australia and made his famous pronouncement, "I have come through and I will return."

Back on Luzon, Wainwright had taken over and informed Washington that he had in excess of 100,000 men under his command of which more than 20,000 were U.S. military personnel. General Marshall was shocked and replied that the size of the defending force was, "greatly in excess of what we understood was there."[6] However, the garrison was no longer able to fight effectively after suffering months of disease and inadequate nutrition. The Japanese force renewed the attack and forced the defenders of Bataan to capitulate in early April and those on Corregidor to follow suit on May 6. It was the largest surrender of an American-led military force in history. While not an excuse for the war crimes that followed, the Japanese were surprised by the number of prisoners that suddenly fell into their care and were not prepared to transport such a large mass of wounded and malnourished men to POW camps around Manila. The result was the tragedy of the Bataan Death March in which thousands died of violence, maltreatment, and starvation.

The garrison had held out for a bit more than four months from the invasion of the Japanese landing force in contrast to WPO, which had called for resistance to persist for upwards of six months. The prewar plan had not counted on U.S. forces being augmented by large numbers of reinforcements equipped with armor, aircraft, and artillery and joined by tens of thousands of Filipino troops. That such a large number of men were forced onto starvation rations when food and other supplies were available for stockpiling on Bataan was a shocking error that likely led to a much earlier surrender. While it is unlikely that the garrison could have held out long enough to receive relief, a lengthier defense would have tied down Japanese forces and acted as a massive boost to American morale.

Of course, Luzon was not the only place where the U.S., British, and Dutch forces performed poorly across the Pacific early in the fighting. Everywhere the Japanese attacked the Allies had been defeated and forced to capitulate or retreat. Many in Washington, London, and Canberra expected Hawaii, India, and Australia to be invaded by the enemy and the outlook was bleak. However, despite the reverses of the first six months of the war in the Pacific, the Allies were beginning to recover, rush reinforcements to the front lines, and prepare to blunt the Japanese advance.

Recovery

The reaction of the three major combatants in the South Pacific (Australia, the United States, and Japan) to the conquest of the Philippines was significant. Despite national rage at Japan for its surprise attack on Pearl Harbor, the FDR Administration held fast to its strategy that Germany needed to be defeated first. However, while decision makers in the War Department and the Joint Chiefs of Staff wished to remain on the defensive in the Pacific and were willing to temporarily sacrifice the Philippines, Guam, Wake, and the Netherlands East Indies, they decided that the WPO defensive line running Alaska–Hawaii–Panama should be pushed out to maintain the communications link between Hawaii and Australia. Such a strategy of protecting the Southwest Pacific was heartily appreciated in Australia where there was great fear that the Japanese would soon be landing on their shores before the bulk of its fighting formations could return from thousands of miles away where they were fighting the Germans and Italians in the deserts of North Africa.

Despite a history of close support of Britain, the government in Canberra made clear that it had no choice but to place the security of its own nation first. There was concern that Churchill and his Cabinet would always elevate the defense of England above that of Australia, and so the latter nation chose to place itself under the protection of the United States. At the end of 1941 the Australian prime minister, John Curtin, wrote in an open letter that, "We refuse to accept the dictum that the Pacific struggle may be treated as a subordinate segment of the general conflict . . . Without any inhibitions of any kind, I make it quite clear that Australia looks to America, free of any pangs as to our traditional links or kinship with the United Kingdom . . . we shall exert all our energies towards the shaping of a plan, with the United States as its keystone, which will give to our country some confidence of being able to hold out until the tide of battle swings."[7]

Britain did not want all of Australia's veteran divisions repatriated from the fighting taking place in North Africa and was willing to acquiesce to the United States taking the lead in the South Pacific. Thus, Washington agreed to send a senior American military leader to Canberra to take command of the region and that several green U.S. Army units would be rushed to the area so as to assure the Australians of their defense. After MacArthur completed his escape from the Philippines, he was awarded the Congressional Medal of Honor in a decision designed to cast a defeat as a defensive victory and boost public morale in both America and Australia. The general was also appointed the commander of the Southwest Pacific Area (SWPA), which included Australia, Papua New Guinea, most of the Dutch East Indies, and, of course, the Philippines.

MacArthur was initially upset that he had few men under his command in SWPA and complained bitterly to Washington demanding reinforcement. Arriving convoys soon improved the situation. Twenty thousand U.S. soldiers had arrived in Melbourne in late February where they were organized as the Americal Division and sent to garrison the French island territory of New Caledonia, which lay across the supply line to Australia. The U.S. 41st Infantry Division arrived down under in early April 1942, the 32nd Division followed the following month, and the 1st Marine Division was shipped to New Zealand and Samoa. Several U.S. Army Air Force squadrons also deployed to the region. Most importantly, the veteran Australian 6th and 7th Divisions returned from the Middle East between March and August. In addition, several new

Australian army and militia units had been formed and were in various stages of training.

As discussed in the previous chapter, "victory disease" convinced the Japanese to launch Operations MO and FS, which called for the conquest of New Guinea, the Solomons, Fiji, Samoa, and New Caledonia so as to cut Australia off from U.S. aid coming from Hawaii. When the Japanese launched an expeditionary force from Rabaul on New Britain Island to seize the first two targets—Tulagi in the Solomon Islands and the Australian base of Port Moresby on the south shore of Papua New Guinea—the U.S. Pacific Fleet was lying in wait. Ultra signals intelligence had begun to break the IJN codes, provided advance notice of the sailing of the Japanese convoy, and Nimitz sent a strong force to intercept it. In the resulting Battle of Coral Sea, both sides suffered losses and the amphibious force heading for Port Moresby was forced to turn back. A month later, Ultra again proved its worth when it allowed Nimitz to ambush a more powerful Japanese force steaming to Midway.

The loss of much of its carrier force off Midway should have convinced Tokyo to conform to its prewar plan to fortify the perimeter of its newly won Pacific empire and fight an attritional campaign from prepared positions. However the sting of defeat off Midway overwhelmed more rational decision making and the Japanese refused to cede the strategic initiative. They landed a large force at Buna on the north shore of Papua New Guinea and began to build an airbase there as well as continuing work on additional ones on the Solomon Islands of Tulagi and Guadalcanal. Nimitz remained aggressive and the U.S. Navy landed the 1st Marine Division on Guadalcanal. This touched off six months of attritional air, land, and sea battles that resulted in a strategic American victory.

In Australia, MacArthur had been instructed to hold Papua New Guinea and began to move reinforcements to the area. He was initially convinced by his intelligence officers that the Japanese planned only to build an airbase at Buna but was soon surprised when a large enemy force began to push along the Kokoda Track, which winds its way south over the jungle-clad Owen Stanley Mountains to Port Moresby. Initially the Japanese easily pushed back the Australian militia units in their way, but the enemy advance was slowed in desperate fighting as reinforcements arrived overland from Port Moresby to dig in along the steep mountainsides.

While the outcome hung in the balance along the Kokoda and on Guadalcanal, the Allies registered their first clear land victory of World War II in the Pacific. Japanese reconnaissance discovered that SWPA forces were building airstrips at Milne Bay on the far eastern tip of New Guinea to protect Port Moresby and launch bombing raids on the enemy forces at Rabaul. The IJN prepared to land and seize this new base for its own use. However, Allied signals intelligence again deciphered enemy intentions and warned MacArthur of the looming threat.

The Milne Bay garrison of a few battalions of militia troops was quickly reinforced by the veteran 18th Infantry Brigade of the Australian 7th Division recently returned from fighting in North Africa. In addition two Royal Australian Air Force squadrons of P-40s arrived at the newly built landing strips and U.S. General George Kenney of the rapidly strengthening Fifth Air Force prepared to attack enemy shipping heading for the area. The Japanese were unaware of these reinforcements and put ashore only about a battalion of Special Naval Landing Force troops on August 25. Assisted by two light tanks, the enemy initially pushed back the Australian militia in their path. However, the tanks bogged down in deep mud, and resistance stiffened as the 18th Brigade entered the battle. The Japanese landed reinforcements but were forced to retreat in heavy fighting and were eventually withdrawn by ship by September 7, suffering close to 1,000 casualties. While a small victory, it was one that gave the Australians a major boost in morale that they could indeed defeat the enemy.

At the same time that the Japanese were being repulsed at Milne Bay, they were steadily advancing along the Kokoda Track, outflanking and overwhelming the Australian defenders. The IJA regiments descending down the south side of the mountain spine of Papua got as far as Ioribaiwa Ridge by September 13. Only 20 miles from the coast, they could see the lights of Port Moresby and the Coral Sea beyond. However, veteran Australian formations recently returning from the Middle East had been deployed to the front and put up an increasingly effective defense.

As the Australians retreated, their supply lines steadily shortened while at the same time the Japanese found it increasingly difficult to transport food and ammunition by foot across the steep, muddy trail winding over the Owen Stanleys. Allied aircraft were also increasingly active over the battlefield dropping supplies to their comrades on the ground while strafing Japanese columns and bombing dug-in positions.

Would the Australians have been able to stop the Japanese from seizing Port Moresby and taking control of Papua? We will never know for sure as Imperial General Headquarters decided that its military capability in the region did not allow for two continuous offensives and Guadalcanal was given priority. The Japanese were ordered to retreat back north along the Kokoda Track followed by the Australians in pursuit. Despite suffering from malnutrition and tropical diseases and being desperately short of supplies, the Japanese put up a spirited defense and the Australians were unable to push to the northern end of the Kokoda Trail until the middle of November.

Green troops of the U.S. 32nd Infantry Division were also deployed north to New Guinea and by the middle of November the enemy force was slowly compressed into a fortified perimeter stretching along the north coast of Papua between the villages of Buna and Gona. While the Japanese had decided to concentrate their efforts on taking Guadalcanal, more than 10,000 men of various units were dug in along well-constructed lines of fortification. This put the Allied forces, attacking out of inland malarial swamps, at a distinct disadvantage. With Nimitz's forces gaining the upper hand in Guadalcanal, MacArthur demanded a rapid victory in Papua. However, the initial assault on the Buna-Gona line was a failure and many men of the 32nd Division abandoned their weapons and retreated from the front. Veteran Australian troops also made slow headway advancing against the Japanese positions, which forced the attackers into concentrated interlocking fields of fire.

MacArthur summoned recently arrived U.S. Army Lieutenant General Robert Eichelberger to his headquarters in Brisbane, told him to take command of American forces at the front, and ordered him to take Buna or not come back alive.[8] Eichelberger arrived at the front and relieved General Edwin Harding of the 32nd Division. The men

Papua New Guinea and New Britain Island. WIKIMEDIA

were suffering from disease and lacking many of the most basic supplies needed for fighting in the sodden jungle from artillery down to oil to keep their rifles from rusting. Eichelberger briefly halted the offensive, brought up supplies, and ordered in an additional regiment from the 41st Division. Fresh Australian forces were also rotated to the front so that eventually the Japanese were outnumbered more than two to one. While this was taking place, Allied airpower was coming to dominate the skies over the battlefield, landing supplies at a landing strip carved out of the jungle, and interdicting any surface ships attempting to bring reinforcements to the defenders.

By early December the attackers began to make headway and, on December 8, Gona was taken by the Australians. Then on December 14, a small force of M3 tanks, secretly transported to the front by Eichelberger, spearheaded an attack by a mixed force of Americans and Australians, which made progress and occupied most of Buna Village. Over the rest of the month, several remaining Japanese fortified lines were relentlessly reduced and overrun. However it was not until late January that enemy resistance collapsed: A few Japanese fled west but most fought at their posts until killed. MacArthur had won a major victory, but one that came at significant cost. Overall Allied casualties were significantly greater than those suffered by the smaller American force fighting on Guadalcanal, which defeated a larger enemy force than that deployed around Buna.

The Battles for Buna-Gona and Guadalcanal concluded in early 1943 and represented a major combined victory for the United States: It seized the strategic initiative for the remainder of the war in the Pacific, the threat to the supply line to Australia was eliminated, and the Japanese lost large numbers of men, ships, and equipment that they could not quickly replace. The FDR Administration was now safely able to focus its primary attention on the Atlantic and defeating Germany while considering how and when to attack the weakened Japanese perimeter.

Causes of Defeat

Like all the other twentieth-century defeats suffered by the United States, the surrender of Bataan and Corregidor took place far from America's strategic core where victory was not essential to the nation's existence. In fact, the defeat on Luzon is the only one in this book that was planned for in advance in Washington. However, the size and scope of the defeat was significantly larger than it needed to be and its import greater than many acknowledge. The U.S. military knew for more than a decade that the Philippines could not be defended successfully in a conflict with Japan. Prewar planning called for a garrison to hold the colony and retreat to Bataan in case of an enemy invasion and hold out for upwards of six months. This force was sized to be large enough to deter any local rebellion but small enough to sacrifice in a war with Japan. As the Philippines were generally quiescent in the 1930s, a force of around 10,000 men was maintained on the islands.

Reinforcement of the U.S. Army garrison increased dramatically in 1941 after MacArthur was appointed to lead all forces in the Philippines and his promise that he could mount a successful defense of the colony.[9] As previously mentioned, large shipments of men, aircraft, artillery, and armor arrived and were deployed prior to the Japanese attack on Pearl Harbor. In the resulting campaign more than 20,000 Americans and 100,000 Filipino soldiers were killed or captured with the great bulk of these losses taking place within three months after the launch of hostilities. A potentially even greater negative was the loss of all the garrison's equipment that was desperately needed elsewhere by the United States.

The proximate cause of the defeat after the start of hostilities was the Philippines' uncomfortably close location to Japanese military bases in the region but in excess of 7,000 miles from the U.S. West Coast. The ability to reinforce the colony during a conflict in the face of concerted enemy air and sea interdiction efforts meant that the garrison would have to make do with what it had for a lengthy period of time before it could expect any relief to arrive. This is what drove the thinking behind prewar planning for U.S. forces in Luzon to retreat to a well-supplied bastion on Bataan and hold out for as long as possible to deny the use of Manila Bay to the Japanese. However, what took place after hostilities broke out was a series of three defeats: (1) the loss of air assets on December 8, 1941, (2) a failure to properly contest the enemy landing at the end of that month, and (3) the oversight of not properly provisioning Bataan, which accelerated the surrender of the defending garrison.

On paper, the large size of the PA made MacArthur's scheme of forward defense along the coastline potentially feasible. The divisions of the PA were not equipped to defeat a combined-arms amphibious invasion on their own, but stiffened with support from the armor, artillery, air support, and local naval squadron of the U.S. garrison, there was a strong argument that a major victory could have been won against the first wave of a Japanese landing force. Much depended upon the Filipinos of the PA being well trained and willing to stand and fight and MacArthur represented to Washington that this was indeed the case. Unfortunately, this did not turn out to be true. Both the Filipino conscripts and the U.S. Army garrison were insufficiently prepared and remained on a peacetime regimen despite repeated warnings of imminent hostilities coming from the FDR Administration.

After the events of December 8, it was clear that the defenders had lost air superiority over Luzon in general, and the likely landing beaches along the Lingayen Gulf in particular. In the weeks that followed, Japanese aircraft continued to degrade remaining U.S. Army Air Force assets. The loss of protective aircover and a devasting bombing raid on the naval base at Cavite on December 10 led to the withdrawal of the U.S. Navy's Asiatic Squadron to Java. This reduction in the strength of Philippine defenses along with the severe losses suffered at Pearl Harbor should have convinced MacArthur and his superiors in Washington to change plans and prepare Bataan and Corregidor to withstand a lengthy siege. Sadly, this did not take place. Instead the bulk of the defenders were positioned near the Lingayen Gulf and waited for the arrival of the Japanese invaders.

Even without control of the air and the sea, MacArthur was still well positioned when the main Japanese landing began on December 22. The defenders knew the territory involved intimately, had significant superiority in men, artillery, and armor on the initial day of the landing, and had access to a well-developed all-weather road network to rush forces to the decisive point of combat. However, MacArthur chose not to deploy his forces most likely to achieve a victory. Arguably his best offensive fighting formations, the 4th Marine Regiment and 192nd and 194th Tank Battalions, were not ordered to the enemy beachhead where they could have helped inflict a stinging defeat on the Japanese. The unsupported PA 11th and 71st Divisions in the area were unable to put up a strong resistance, and the invaders streamed inland and completed landing their heavy equipment.

MacArthur reluctantly ordered a retreat to Bataan, and for the next several days his men pulled back in good order toward the peninsula. Frantic efforts were made to rectify the dearth of supplies on Bataan but these were hindered by MacArthur's refusal to seize the contents of civilian warehouses on the Luzon Plain. In addition, he declared Manila to be an "open city" on December 26 to preserve it from enemy air bombardment but this also precluded moving stores from there to his defensive citadel across the bay. While these decisions were made for the most moral of reasons to protect the Filipino civilian populace, they significantly hampered the stockpiling of supplies on Bataan and MacArthur's men immediately began paying the price.

Of course, once the defenders were penned in behind siege lines with insufficient supplies, an early surrender of the garrison was all but inevitable. However, MacArthur still had one last chance to achieve at least a short-term victory. The Japanese were surprised that they were able to capture Manila and bottle up the garrison so quickly. This led them to shift large components of the invasion force farther south to assist in the conquest of the Netherlands East Indies. Men, aircraft, and artillery were all shipped off Luzon even as the outnumbered invaders had to deploy contingents to multiple garrison points while still maintaining the siege. Fighting in the jungle environment of Bataan was taxing on the besiegers as well and tropical diseases, wounds, and exhaustion took their toll. By late February the besieging forces were reduced to only around 3,000 effective troops who could man the front line.[10]

MacArthur believed he could break out and seize Manila if he chose to mount a sortie and go over to the attack. To take the offensive held risks, but his men were in great need of food and other supplies and much of what they needed was ripe for the taking on the other side of the front lines from the Japanese. Had the garrison been able to break out toward Manila, the local population would undoubtedly have shared what food, clothing, and other essentials it could spare. In the end, MacArthur chose not to attempt a breakout due to a belief that he would soon have to retreat back into Bataan.[11] Thus, rather than take the initiative, the defenders waited in their trenches and starved.

In a final analysis, there were several reasons the defeat was so calamitous. An axiom of military theory is to never reinforce failure. Yet, the FDR Administration was convinced by MacArthur to ship significant quantities of scarce reinforcements and equipment to an exposed colony that military planners knew could not be held against the might of the Japanese Empire. Rather than deter an attack, the arrival of offensive weapons such as B-17 long-range bombers, which could interdict maritime sea lanes, ensured that the Japanese would need to seize the Philippines at the beginning of any war. MacArthur may have been the greatest advocate of a more robust defense of Luzon and overpromised regarding the abilities of the men under his command, but his superiors in Washington deserve their share of the blame for supplying him with reinforcements and equipment, sure to be lost in the early days of the war.

MacArthur was also not the only senior western military leader who dramatically underestimated the abilities of the Japanese armed forces. However, in contrast to those in charge at Pearl Harbor, he had concrete advance warning that his command was under threat of imminent air attack yet most of his modern aircraft were destroyed on the ground to the great consternation of senior officials in Washington.[12] As in many other defeats suffered by the United States over its history, an inability to consider what an enemy could do rather than what one wants him to do directly resulted in failure.

After the loss of control of the air over Luzon, and the withdrawal of the surface ships of the Navy's Asiatic Squadron, an active defense on the beaches in Luzon became much less likely to succeed. However, it seems that MacArthur and his superiors failed to seriously consider a reversion to WPO and prepare for a long siege in Bataan. Even so, that the Japanese chose to land as expected along the Lingayen Gulf on a day with high seas offered the U.S.-led force a serendipitous opportunity to inflict a stinging defeat on the enemy. However, rather than surging the best offensive forces to the enemy beachhead, the landing was opposed by some of the defenders' weakest formations. Thus, the effort to contain the Japanese landing was a failure and MacArthur was soon forced to order a retreat to Bataan.

Lastly, the great error of the campaign is that Bataan was not sufficiently supplied for a siege. This oversight was the result of first underestimating the enemy, secondly refusing to modify the plan of a forward defense after a major deterioration of facts on the ground, and then elevating the needs of the Philippine civilian population over the mission of properly stockpiling the garrison's defensive citadel. Of course, civilian supplies were seized by the Japanese, so failing to move them to Bataan did nothing but aid the enemy.

Causes of Victory

Just as there were several causes of defeat on Luzon, there were multiple factors that assisted MacArthur in recovering and achieving his victory at Buna-Gona in early 1943. First and foremost was the error of the

Japanese in succumbing to strategic overreach and choosing to push into Papua and the Solomons in 1942. This effort was staged from the far end of an already extended supply line and pushed past the perimeter the Japanese had planned to entrench in their prewar planning. Severing the sea communications between Australia and Hawaii was in no way essential to Tokyo's war aims and there were no important supplies of raw materials in this sector of the Southwest Pacific that the Japanese needed themselves or wished to deny to the Allies. Rather than husband their resources in well-prepared defenses around their great naval base at Rabaul on New Britain and wait to counterattack any American offensive efforts in the area, the Japanese experienced a significant diminution of their military power in unnecessary attritional engagements. In the end, the loss of more than 40,000 front-line troops, forty major warships, and several hundred aircraft attempting to take Papua and the Solomons significantly weakened the ability of the Japanese to hold their planned perimeter.[13]

Next, MacArthur was greatly assisted by the professionalism, experience, and grit of the Australian military forces, which he came to command. The Australians were generally competently well led by experienced officers, from their commander-in-chief, General Thomas Blamey, on down. Their relatively untrained militiamen could not stand toe to toe with Japanese front-line troops, but performed well as a screening force and invariably inflicted casualties before retiring in relatively good order. Veteran Australian units returning from combat in the Mediterranean Theater repeatedly proved their competency and were arguably the best infantry units fighting on the Allied side in 1942. With the bulk of the American ground effort directed to fighting on Guadalcanal in the Solomons, MacArthur would never have been able to achieve victory in Papua in 1942–1943 without his Australian allies.

Finally, even though it represented only a fraction of the total output, U.S. military force surged into the Southwest Pacific Area as the war progressed. In no area was this growth more impressive than in the area of airpower. When Major General George Kenney was placed in command of SWPA's budding U.S. Fifth Air Force in the spring of 1942, it had only eighty-five serviceable aircraft. By early 1943 this number had surged to more than 1,000 mostly new modern aircraft flown by increasingly skilled pilots.[14] U.S. ground forces, the 41st and 32nd Divisions, while green and unsteady early in the fighting, soon came to improve in effectiveness as the counteroffensive gathered pace. Lastly, signals intelligence became ever more able to penetrate Japanese cipher codes and began to inform American leaders as to enemy dispositions and intentions. Thus, MacArthur increasingly gained an upper hand in the campaign from improvements both qualitative and quantitative in the forces under his command.

Impact of Defeat

The United States suffered several immediate impacts from the defeat of the Philippine garrison. The loss of a large American-led field army amid a rash of early reverses at the hands of the Japanese was a great blow to civilian morale, increased pressure for FDR to allocate a greater share of limited military power to the Pacific, and helped feed a sense of panic, especially along the U.S. West Coast. There are multiple reasons one can argue that the scale and scope of the defeat in the Philippines lengthened the war.

First, had a decision been made to maintain only a "sacrificial" garrison in Luzon in 1941, upwards of 10,000 U.S. soldiers and marines, a hundred of the nation's most advanced tanks and fighter planes, and three squadrons of B-17s would not have been deployed to such an exposed position. These forces would have been of great assistance in the desperate fighting for Guadalcanal or elsewhere around the world in 1942 when the U.S. military was massively outnumbered in a global two-front war.

Second, had MacArthur been successful in his plan to defeat a Japanese landing along Lingayen Gulf, the conflict in the Pacific could have progressed much differently and ended sooner. Executing an amphibious operation along a hostile shore is extremely complex, and almost everything needs to go according to plan. Indeed, events on the morning of December 22, 1941, when the main Japanese landing took place set the stage for a great defensive victory. High seas limited the ability of the invaders to land their armor and artillery and would have interfered with efforts to provide effective ship to shore bombardment. MacArthur's forces were properly positioned in the area, had a two to one advantage in manpower, and could bring decisive armor and artillery to the beachhead. The result should have been high losses among the IJA's Fourteenth Army along the shoreline and even a potential repulse of the invasion. In such a counterfactual scenario, Allied morale would have received a huge boost, and the garrison of Luzon would have retained strategic flexibility into 1942.

Of course, had the December 22 invasion been defeated along the Lingayen Gulf shoreline, the Japanese would have assembled additional forces to return and overwhelm MacArthur's force. However, this would have taken time that could have been used to rectify the earlier deficiency of not properly preparing Bataan to withstand a lengthy siege. Had the garrison been able to hold out for additional months before surrendering, until after the Battle of Midway, for example, the Allied counteroffensive across the Pacific would have likely started closer to Tokyo. This could have resulted in an earlier capture of the Marianas Islands from which the devastating B-29 bombing raids on Japan were launched.

Finally, had MacArthur been able to achieve a major victory along the Lingayen Gulf, or properly prepared Bataan to withstand a long siege, he likely would have remained in the Philippines past his historic escape on March 11, 1942. In such a scenario, he could have been killed or captured in the fighting or in a later escape attempt to pass through a tightening Japanese blockade. Had he not made it to Australia prior to the Battle of Midway to make his famous "I shall return" pronouncement, it is unclear if the Joint Chiefs would have approved the lengthy advance across the north coast of New Guinea that MacArthur demanded. With the blunting of the Japanese offensive, SWPA could have been safely relegated to a backwater of the war with the primary effort directed to the U.S. drive across the Central Pacific under Admiral Nimitz. In such a scenario, the Marianas likely would have been taken by American forces earlier than in the historical record and prepared to launch B-29 bombing of Japan up to six months earlier than actually took place. The Philippines might have been bypassed by the U.S. advance had the war progressed in this manner, sparing Manila the great destruction it suffered in early 1945, with the offensive instead focused on landings on Formosa, Iwo Jima, and Okinawa.

Impact of Victory

The twin victories at Guadalcanal and Buna-Gona ended Japanese hopes to execute Operation FS and extend their empire's perimeter. The Battles of Midway and Coral Sea may have eliminated the immediate threat to Hawaii and Australia, but the attritional battles in the Solomons and Papua ensured that the strategic initiative passed to the Allies in the Pacific. However, while mostly forgotten in the United States, the victory at Buna-Gona had significant impacts on our nation's history.

The campaign in the jungles and swamps along the northeast coast of New Guinea in late 1942 to early 1943 was hard fought and could have ended in the Australians and Americans being forced to pull back south and regroup due to tenuous supply lines and rampant tropical disease that sapped their strength. The Allies would have taken Papua eventually, but delay would have had critical consequences. MacArthur was quite worried about such an eventuality and believed he would be relieved from his post if this took place. A failure to take Buna and Gona, seen as another defeat after the loss of the Philippines, could have been used by FDR to force the sixty-two-year-old general to leave the U.S. Army with the hope that such a poor battlefield record would work against him were he to run for the presidency.

With POA forces holding Guadalcanal, and the Japanese base at Rabaul being brought under regular air attack, the communication links between Hawaii and Australia were secure and Buna and Gona lost much of their strategic importance. The Americans were ready to go on the offensive and Nimitz and King were most interested in following through on prewar plans to conduct a Navy-led push across the Central Pacific toward the Marianas. In contrast, MacArthur urged an offensive focused on Army forces moving along the northern coast of New Guinea as a critical preliminary move prior to a reconquest of the Philippines. Of course, this plan required a significantly longer route to Tokyo. A significant delay in the conquest of Buna-Gona in January 1943 would have allowed the Central Pacific offensive to move forward with SWPA forces increasingly left behind as the front lines moved closer to Japan.

Historically, it was only the January capture of Buna-Gona, utilization of Ultra intelligence, and surging American reinforcements that allowed MacArthur to leapfrog his forces toward the western end of New Guinea by the summer of 1944. This positioning allowed him to argue, when he met with FDR in Honolulu in July of that year, that he was in striking distance of Mindanao and should be given the resources to invade the Philippines. Had SWPA forces been stymied in front of the Japanese coastal bastions stretching from Buna to Gona and their advance delayed while Nimitz's forces advanced through the Gilberts, the Marshalls, and then retook the Marianas in June 1944, it is likely that the Central Pacific advance would have taken the lead and the next target would have been Formosa, Iwo Jima, or Okinawa rather than the Philippines. MacArthur threatened to resign his post if he were forced into a secondary role in the Pacific and it is likely that he would have followed through on this threat.

Such a change in the historical record due to a failure to achieve victory at Buna-Gona in early 1943 would have meant that the Philippines might not have been liberated until the end of World War II. This would have spared Manila from the massive destruction it suffered in 1945 along with the deaths of a hundred thousand Filipinos. In such a scenario, a different leader than MacArthur would have become the commander of the occupation army in Tokyo. This means a different man would have then been placed in charge of the UN force authorized in 1950 to resist the Communist invasion of South Korea. As will be seen in Chapter 8, such a change in history might have allowed the United States to avoid one of the most embarrassing defeats in its long military history. Thus, while the Battle of Buna-Gona may have not been particularly strategic in and of itself, the consequences of the Australian-American victory there were significant not only for World War II, but for the Cold War that followed.

Chapter Seven

Black Thursday over Schweinfurt to Bombing the "Big B"

Background of Defeat

While limited U.S. forces blunted the Japanese advance in the Pacific and won the victories of Midway, Guadalcanal, and Buna-Gona, the main focus of America's war effort was directed at defeating Germany. As leaked by the isolationist *Chicago Tribune* newspaper just a few days before the attack on Pearl Harbor, in the event of a two-front war, the FDR Administration planned to remain primarily on the defensive against the Japanese while building a multimillion-man army to surge across the Atlantic, invade Europe, and march on Berlin. To achieve this goal, the U.S. economy would be refocused on arms production, its young men inducted into the military, and consumer goods output dramatically decreased.

Senior officers in the U.S. Army Air Force (USAAF), commanded by General Henry "Hap" Arnold, believed that such a bloody invasion of the European continent could be avoided through a strategic bombing campaign that would cripple the enemy economy and force a surrender. A massive heavy bomber force, engaged in precision daylight attacks operating from Britain, would destroy key industrial bottlenecks across Germany, Italy, and their occupied territories forcing the Axis war machine to grind to a halt. Military aviation theorists in the 1920s and 1930s predicted that such a campaign could achieve victory. Over time they came to believe that a fast armored bomber flying at high altitude would be all but invulnerable and could get through to its target regardless of defensive measures taken.[1] Now the United States would have an opportunity to put these ideas into action primarily through the use of B-17 Flying Fortress and B-24 Liberator heavy bombers as well as B-25 Mitchell and B-26 Marauder medium bombers.

In the years since the war began in Europe, Britain's Royal Air Force (RAF) had learned the hard way that squadrons of bombers attempting to strike targets over Germany during daylight suffered unsustainable losses from ground fire and fighter aircraft attack. To make matters worse, cloud cover prevailed over much of northern Europe for long stretches of the year and made precision attacks all but impossible. RAF Bomber Command's Air Marshal Arthur Harris focused on night missions in which losses per attack were lower. He sent his planes out to hit large targets in "area bombing" of German cities in an attempt to reduce that nation's economic output, break enemy morale, and "de-house" its citizenry. After U.S. entry into the war, Harris and many of his compatriots did not believe their new military allies would have any more success with daylight raids, but they eagerly assisted the USAAF and provided a network of airbases constructed primarily in the East Anglia region of England.

USAAF General Ira Eaker arrived to oversee the buildup of American forces. Over the two years that he was in charge of the organization, which was soon named the Eighth Air Force, he was consistently hounded by General Arnold to take greater risks with his men and aircraft and increase the number and size of the attacks on the enemy. Eaker was in full agreement with other American officers in the "Bomber Mafia" that strategic precision bombing attacks could force an enemy to surrender due to the destruction of transportation, energy generation, fuel refining, and manufacturing targets. While USAAF prewar planning allowed that fighter escort would be desirable, it was believed that such small craft could not possibly have the necessary range to fly to targets deep inside Germany and still retain the speed and maneuverability required to challenge short-range enemy fighters successfully. Thus, it was envisioned that well-armed bombers, especially B-17s, flying in tight defensive "combat box" formations so as to create interlocking fields of machine-gun fire, would perform the war-ending missions alone.

The first heavy bomber mission flown by the Eighth Air Force took place on August 17, 1942, with twelve planes attacking railway yards in France. In contrast to this minor initial effort, the RAF had recently staged Operation Millennium with 1,000 (mostly medium) bombers striking the German city of Cologne over the night of May 30/31. Fifteen thousand buildings were destroyed, the urban center was burned out, thousands of casualties were suffered on the ground, and 45,000 people were left homeless at a cost of forty-three RAF aircraft. The mission was viewed as a great success and RAF Bomber Command believed that continuing to target the major population centers of the enemy would soon force a collapse in German morale. Unfortunately, Hitler and his people were unmoved by such damage and death. As with the British earlier in the war when they stolidly carried on in the face of heavy attacks from the air, the bombing of the cities of the Third Reich seemed only to strengthen German citizens' collective urge to continue the fight.

Harris and his peers tried to get the USAAF to agree to join in night bombing missions. However, Americans such as Arnold and Eaker believed that attacks on civilian housing in cities were immoral, and no better than "terror bombing." They also had a great deal of confidence that their top secret and very expensive Norden Bombsight would allow for great precision in hitting targets. It was believed that this invention would allow bombardiers to drop a bomb into a pickle barrel from 20,000 feet. While the postwar United States Strategic Bombing Survey (USSBS) showed that claims of such accuracy were dramatically overestimated, and that the Norden Bombsight produced little in the way of improved performance, this was not known at the time.[2] In addition, the United States had not suffered through the German bombing "blitz" of Britain's major urban areas earlier in the war and lacked an emotional desire to inflict revenge. After multiple meetings, Harris and Eaker agreed to disagree and that with Eighth Air Force daylight strikes complementing RAF night missions, German defenses would be worn down as the nation was "bombed around the clock."

USAAF strength grew rapidly with four Bomb Groups consisting of thirty-six to forty-eight aircraft making up a Bomb Wing. While the air offensive over Europe was exceedingly expensive in terms of aircraft and men, it was seen as critically important in that it would do damage to the enemy's military and economic output. It also had significant political benefits. Most importantly, as the British were extremely wary of joining a cross-Channel invasion, bombing missions in 1942 represented the only way to directly attack Hitler's war machine. In addition, the USSR was engaged in a titanic struggle in the East, and Stalin wanted to know the Allies were making real efforts to win the war and not simply willing to fight to the last Red Army soldier.

The combined British and American bomber attacks drew large numbers of German men, planes, and military equipment away from the Eastern Front. General Eaker pointed out that, "in 1943 there were more than a million Germans standing at the anti-aircraft and fighter defenses on the West Wall to defend against them. And another million Germans were fire wardens of engaged in bomb damage repair."[3] This reallocation of resources, which weakened enemy forces on the front lines, was particularly true for the men manning the vaunted 8.8cm *flugabwehrkanone* or "*flak*" gun. Known as the "acht-acht" (or "88" by the Americans), these accurate artillery pieces fired a high-velocity, large-caliber explosive round, which brought down thousands of aircraft during the war. They were also used in a field artillery role and had great success as an antitank weapon. Forcing thousands of these guns and their crews to redeploy back to Germany saved the lives of innumerable Soviets fighting on the Eastern Front.

Eighth Air Force B-17 missions rapidly increased in tempo and size though the total number of aircraft involved was still significantly lower than what the British could deploy to the effort. Over six months through early 1943, the Americans primarily engaged in attacks on U-boat pens, airfields, and railroad depots located in Belgium, northern France, and the Netherlands that were within the range of escorting fighter squadrons. Bombing U-boat bases was not a "strategic" target but rather a defensive one. However, the Germans had the upper hand in late 1942 through early 1943 in the Battle of the Atlantic and were threatening to starve the British of critical industrial imports. Thus, the Eighth Air Force was ordered to direct a considerable number of missions to knocking out U-boat bases on the occupied French west coast, and later, submarine construction yards in Germany. These early raids were generally unsuccessful as the boats were housed in giant concrete pens that proved impervious to American bombs. However, a small number of four-engine bombers turned over to maritime patrol duties were later instrumental in winning the Battle of the Atlantic. As historian Martin Middlebrook concluded, "The historical judgement must be that, in the offensive against U-boats, those who were responsible for the allocation of resources had erred gravely by backing the strategic bomber campaign at the expense of the maritime air forces."[4]

The result of these relatively short-range missions was that only forty-six planes were lost out of 1,369 sorties, which yielded what USAAF planners believed was an acceptable casualty rate of 3.4 percent.[5] To a great extent the relatively small number of bombers shot down was due to the fact that they were generally escorted to and from the target by RAF Spitfire and USAAF P-47 Thunderbolt fighters. The latter planes had the range to make it almost to the German border before turning back (later, with drop tanks they could fly a short distance into Germany) and protected the B-17s from enemy fighter aircraft. In addition, the U.S. bombers were very robust and could often return to base even after taking serious hits from antiaircraft shells or Luftwaffe (the German air force) machine-gun fire. As one Eighth Air Force pilot explained, "It is here that the ability of the B-17 to absorb such terrific battle damage and still fly is apparent. The plane can be cut and slashed almost to pieces by enemy fire and bring its crew home. It is the brilliant interlocking of its main structural members that keeps the B-17 flying."[6]

The number of bombers that were able to limp back to base damaged after missions was almost always a multiple (sometimes as much as 10X) of those shot down, and this reduced somewhat the casualty rate suffered by the crews who flew the aircraft.[7] An example of this was a raid of 252 B-17s that attacked targets in the Low Countries on October 3, 1943. Seventy-five of the planes were damaged but all 252 returned to England.[8] As U.S. industry ramped up production (astoundingly, more than 12,000 B-17s and 18,000 B-24s were built by the end of 1945), the supply of trained men to fly the bombers was often the constraining input for the Eighth Air Force in 1943 and the first half of 1944.

The lack of deep penetration raids into Germany by the USAAF concerned the British who still wished to have their allies join the RAF in the nighttime campaign of area bombing. At the Casablanca Conference in January 1943, Prime Minister Winston Churchill worked to convince President Roosevelt to make this change. However, General Eaker met privately with Churchill and convinced him of the value of continuing to bomb the Germans on an "around the clock" basis for the time being. Due to pressure to show results, the USAAF expanded its area of operations and on some missions increasingly sent its bombers beyond the range of fighter escort to hit locations in Germany. Targets included aircraft factories, U-boat construction yards, and naval bases.

However, these raids were only to the periphery of that nation so that the Luftwaffe had little time to mass large attacks on the American bombers during the short periods when they were without fighter escort. There were two major reasons the Eighth Air Force did not engage in deep penetration attacks, both of which grew out of the U.S. invasion of the French colonies of Morocco and Algeria in November 1942. First, 200 of the first long-range American fighter, the P-38 Lightning, which could fly 1,000 miles when equipped with an auxiliary drop tank, arrived in England in the summer of 1942. However, these planes, all of the Eighth Air Force's B-24s, and a large number of its B-17s were redeployed to North Africa after the U.S. landings there to support operations in the Mediterranean. This eliminated Eaker's ability to send raids into Germany with accompanying fighter escort. In addition, the Eighth Air Force was left with fewer bombers available to assemble into large, self-supporting formations when flying on missions.

Eaker and his staff were coming to accept that they needed long-range escort fighters. In a January 16, 1943, report to explain the lack of deep penetration raids of the enemy homeland he noted, "we have no fighters with sufficient range to accompany our bombers into Germany. We have had three groups equipped with such long-range fighters, but before they were trained they were taken from us, assigned to the Twelfth Air Force and dispatched to Africa."[9] For this reason, over the next six months Eaker primarily directed his bombers to operate within, or only short distances beyond, escort cover.

During this period, the Eighth Air Force flew 5,958 sorties with 217 bombers lost in action for a casualty rate of 3.6 percent.[10] While many crewmen were able to parachute out of their planes before they crashed, even if they survived, almost all became POWs and their services were lost to the war effort just as surely as if they had been killed. Nevertheless, the USAAF believed this rate of attrition was acceptable for several reasons: (1) Men were asked to fly twenty-five missions to complete a tour of duty and a loss rate under 4 percent gave them at least a statistical possibility of making it home alive rather than being killed in action or shot down and taken prisoner. One of the first crews to achieve this goal, flying the B-17 *Memphis Belle*, returned to the United States in June 1943 and toured the nation in the aircraft in a public relations campaign to raise war bonds. (2) Flights of new aircraft arriving in England were more than enough to make up losses of aircraft in the first half of 1943. (3) The number of newly trained crew and service staff was also growing by this point in the war and these men were integrated into squadrons at a pace that maintained some level of unit cohesion.

While Eaker and his staff realized that losses would climb rapidly with long-range daylight bombing missions without fighter escort, the American commander was under increasing pressure from Arnold to show results, and the B-17s began to be sent on riskier operations. For example, on April 17, the Eighth Air Force launched its largest mission to date when 115 B-17s targeted the Focke-Wulf aircraft factories in Bremen, Germany. Coordinated waves of enemy Fw 190 fighters relentlessly attacked the lead combat wing and 15 U.S. planes were shot down. Another B-17 was lost to antiaircraft fire and an additional thirty-nine were damaged but were able to return to base. While significant damage was done to the target and three Fw 190s were shot down, this 14 percent attrition rate was certainly not sustainable.[11] After two weeks of recovery time, seventy-eight B-17s from the same four groups attacked the U-boat base at the French Atlantic port of Saint-Nazaire. Due to poor weather, only twenty-nine aircraft were able to drop bombs on the target and of these seven were shot down, the rest were damaged, and two had to be scrapped upon their return.[12] Obviously, the Eighth Air Force could not maintain its tempo of operations while suffering such high loss rates. Worse was to come.

The Defeat

On June 14, 1943, the U.S. and British Joint Chiefs issued the Pointblank Directive, which ordered both the RAF and the USAAF to focus their bombing missions on destroying the Luftwaffe so as to gain air superiority over northern France for the Allied invasion planned for mid-1944. Primary targets were the Germans' small number of fighter aircraft factories, ball-bearing plants, and oil refineries. With General Arnold constantly pushing for more aggressive raids, Eaker coordinated a "Blitz Week" with the RAF, which kicked off on July 25. Over six days, ten major German targets were bombed by the Eighth Air Force though losses were quite high with eighty-seven bombers lost yielding a 6.4 percent casualty rate for the B-17s dispatched on the missions.[13]

Operation Tidal Wave, the plan to hit Ploesti, came next. The target was a complex of heavily defended petroleum refineries near Romania's oil fields that produced upwards of 30 percent of Germany's supply. Putting it out of commission was seen as essential to create shortages of fuel in occupied Europe. The USAAF chose to use B-24s for this mission as their longer operating range meant these bombers could make it from captured bases in Libya to Ploesti and back. However, the trade-off was that compared to the B-17, these bombers were slower, flew at a lower altitude, and were significantly less robust. Five Bomb Groups of the Ninth Air Force (three of which were on loan from the Eighth) consisting of 178 B-24s with total crew in excess of 1,700 men took off on the mission early on the morning of August 1, 1943.

One hundred sixty-two planes made it to the target and bombed the refineries. The strike caused significant damage and the USAAF estimated the Ploesti refineries would experience a 40 percent reduction of output. However, bomber losses were extensive: Fifty-four were shot down, another fifty-five were damaged, many severely, and 532 crewmen were killed or captured.[14] This 33 percent loss rate in percentage terms was the costliest American bombing mission of World War II. Unfortunately, repairs to the refineries were rapid, and by September, production was higher than before the raid. While the Allies very much wanted to put the Romanian refineries out of operation, losses in Operation Tidal

Wave were so severe that no additional missions were flown against the target for several months.

Back in England, even after the failure of the raid on Ploesti and the losses of Blitz Week, the Eighth Air Force planned an even larger and more audacious deep penetration attack. As the number of operational B-17s with trained crews now allowed for a raid with 400 bombers, two targets were chosen to be hit the same day. The first was the Messerschmitt Bf 109 aircraft plant in the southern German city of Regensburg. The second was the concentration of ball-bearing factories around Schweinfurt 100 miles to the northwest. The output of these plants was critical to several industries including the production of aircraft. The B-17s conducting the Regensburg attack would strike first and hopefully draw off most of the Luftwaffe's fighter defenses before the bombers continued south and landed in American-occupied Algeria. They would be followed by the force targeting Schweinfurt. One hundred B-26s would also fly a diversionary attack to strike the enemy fighter airfields at Poix and Abbeville in France. At the same time, the B-24s in Africa that had survived the mission to Ploesti would bomb the Messerschmitt aircraft plant at Wiener Neustadt in Austria.

While successfully bombing these targets would be a major step in fulfilling the Pointblank Directive, enemy defenses were significant. Large numbers of fighter aircraft had been withdrawn from the Eastern Front and the Luftwaffe had close to 1,000 fighters available for daytime interception duty in the West. Radar gave early warning of incoming flights of B-17s and helped the Germans direct planes to intercept them.[15] The enemy fighters were deployed in depth and would take off progressively from their bases as the Americans drew closer. P-47s equipped with auxiliary fuel "drop" tanks (which could be jettisoned to improve performance in dogfighting) were able to accompany the bombers over the Low Countries and into the western borderlands of Germany. As the American fighters were forced to turn back due to range limitations, the Luftwaffe would attack the B-17s relentlessly as they flew deeper into Germany. Then, while the bombers flew through antiaircraft fire over their target, the enemy pilots would land, rearm, and refuel, before taking off to shoot down more American planes on their return flight until they were once again under the cover of escorts. This situation led the bomber crews to make the gloomy joke that, "they were escorted all the way."[16]

Tactics had also improved as the German fighters increasingly attacked the bombers from head-on at high speed before diving steeply at the last minute. This limited the number of machine guns the B-17s could fire at the enemy as the heaviest defensive firepower was concentrated in the rear arcs of the big planes. The bombers also were less well armored in the front, and hits to their cockpits could incapacitate control instruments, or the pilots themselves. Finally, the high closing speed of this tactic limited the time the German aircraft were at risk of being hit.

The Luftwaffe had also begun to utilize heavy, two-engine fighters such as the Bf 110 and the Me 410 to attack the American bombers. These *Zerstörer* ("destroyer") aircraft were slower and more heavily armed and armored than the lighter, single-engined fighters. While they were primarily used in a night fighter role against RAF raids, they were often employed during daylight to finish off damaged American B-17s. Also, after July 1943, many carried rockets mounted in launch tubes under their wings. While inaccurate, these missiles could be fired from safely outside the range of the defensive armament of a formation of bombers, and were often quite lethal when they detonated against, or close, to any aircraft.[17]

Poor weather in the north delayed the attacks from England, but on August 14, sixty-five B-24s from the Ninth Air Force (and those on loan from the Eighth) took off from Libya and flew through heavy cloud to strike Wiener-Neustadt. Surprisingly, and perhaps due to the weather, they encountered only light resistance and did significant damage to new aircraft on the ground as well as the assembly factories. Single-engine fighter production there dropped from 270 in July to 184 in August, and was still only 218 in October. The Germans, in a costly effort across the nation, began to dismantle and disperse many of their aircraft factories so that they were more difficult to find and attack from the air.[18]

Now it was the turn of the American fliers in England. The weather remained poor in the north, but finally, on August 17, 146 B-17s took off in heavy fog to strike Regensburg. Though 230 additional B-17s were supposed to follow closely behind, low visibility delayed their launch and negated the hoped-for respite from enemy fighters that would have been attracted to the planes heading for Regensburg. As the two American bomber forces left their escorting fighters behind, they were set upon by swarms of German attackers. Over the course of the mission, the enemy launched 470 enemy single-engine fighter sorties and seventy twin-engine ones against the B-17s.[19]

Despite this fierce opposition, the Americans pushed on and hit their targets. The Messerschmitt factory was seriously damaged and output fell significantly the next month. However, German production of fighter aircraft there was soon higher than it was before the raid. In contrast, bombing accuracy over Schweinfurt was relatively poor. While the production of ball-bearings from the plants was also reduced for a time, prepared reserve inventories of these critical inputs were tapped so that enemy industrial production was not impacted. The American B-17 crews also claimed they shot down 288 Luftwaffe planes with another eighty-one "probables." In fact the Germans lost only twenty-one planes on the day.[20]

Enemy defenses, especially Luftwaffe fighters, took a grim toll on the Americans and sixty of the B-17s failed to return to an Allied base. This represented a loss rate of 16 percent of those dispatched on the missions. Of those that made it back to a runway, 172 were damaged, eleven so badly that they had to be scrapped. In addition, five Allied fighters were also shot down protecting the bombers closer to England. Losses suffered in just this one day were approximately equal to the total casualties recorded by the Eighth Air Force in its first six months of operations. While the Luftwaffe was taking a beating in the air and on the ground, the USAAF was suffering losses that quickly eroded morale and unit cohesion. As Professor Ronald Schaffer concluded in his book, *Wings of Judgment*, "The double mission cost the Eighth Air Force over 550 crewmen killed or captured, leaving it crippled for weeks, emotionally and physically. The worst part was the fact that the fortresses had not damaged the ball-bearing factories enough. The B-17s would have to return to Schweinfurt."[21]

Albert Speer, the extremely effective German minister of armaments and war production, was alarmed. He had warned Hitler as early as September 1942 that the ball-bearing plants at Schweinfurt along with the tank production center at Friedrichstafen were the two most critical

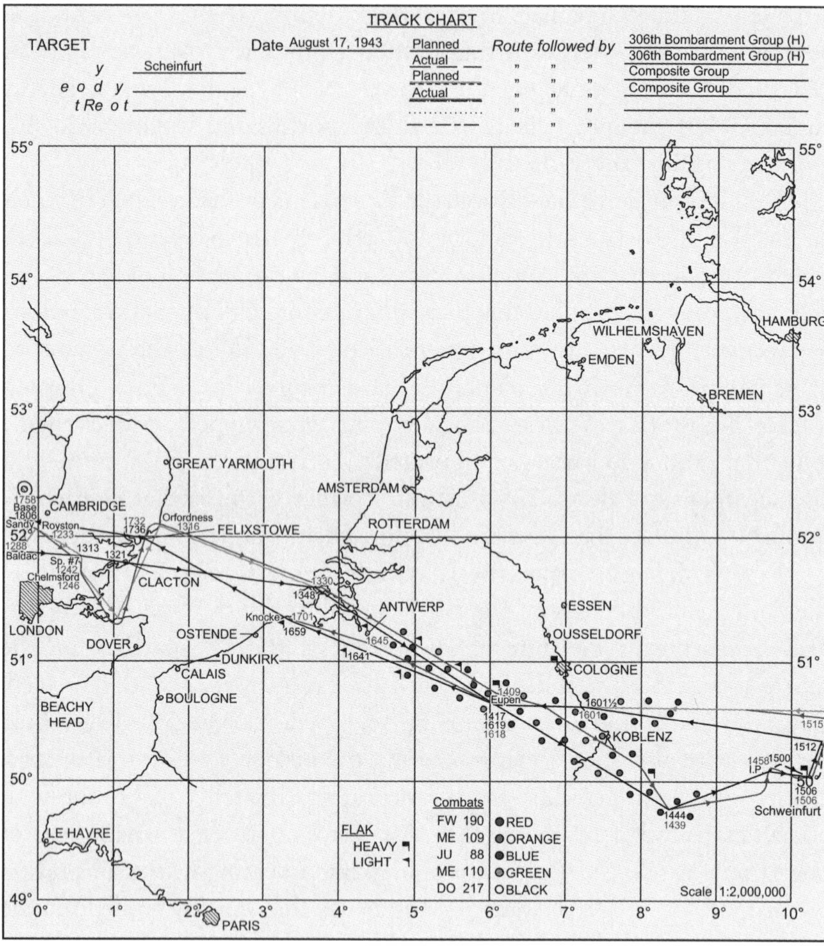

Route taken by the Eighth Air Force to bomb Schweinfurt in August 1943
WAR DEPARTMENT, ARMY AIR FORCE

industrial nodes of the Nazi war effort.[22] He wondered why the Allies had chosen so many different bombing targets—U-boat pens, city centers, aircraft factories, railyards, oil production facilities, etc.—instead of focusing on shutting down one vital bottleneck in the Axis war economy. Finally it was Schweinfurt's turn, but Speer was thankful that the USAAF had sent so many bombers to Regensburg as ball-bearing output was "only" reduced by 40 percent immediately after the raid. Still, he referred to the attack as the first strategic raid carried out by the Americans. Speer expected imminent follow-up attacks on Schweinfurt, but they did not come. As repairs took place, reserve stocks of ball-bearings were run down and production was often shipped from the factories each day in backpacks.[23]

Eaker and his staff were desperate for long-range fighters equipped with external drop tanks that would allow them to escort USAAF bombers on the deepest of penetration missions. The losses recently suffered were viewed as unsustainable and unless results improved, there was worry that the strategic bombing campaign would be deemphasized with resources shifted to other weapon systems.[24] The Flying Fortress was an extremely complex plane with each costing around $250,000. For the price of one of these bombers, the United States could produce five P-51 Mustang fighters or a similar number of M4 Sherman tanks.[25] The B-17 was also manned by a highly trained crew of ten men and additionally each aircraft required an extensive ground staff including mechanics, ordnance loaders, and other specialists to maintain a steady pace of operations. The need to reduce bomber loss rates through obtaining fighters that could protect them and reduce operating losses was becoming imperative as the mid-1944 invasion of France approached.

After the August 17 raids, General Arnold traveled to England to review the condition of the Eighth Air Force. He agreed that long-range fighters were more urgently needed for the Eighth Air Force than for supporting the Allied armies that were in the process of invading Italy. Arnold wrote back to Washington: "Believe it would be a great mistake to divert P-38s from U.K. to North Africa at this time. The battle for complete destruction of German Air Force is approaching most critical stage. Eighth Air Force must be built up rapidly—more rapidly than planned—to administer a knockout blow while they are groping for any respite they can get."[26] However, getting these fighters off the assembly line and to the front would take time. In addition, the P-38 was having only moderate success escorting bombers in the Mediterranean Theater. Doctrine at the time insisted that the fighters stay with the bomber formations they were escorting. This gave the Germans an advantage as squadrons of enemy Bf 109s and Fw 190s would approach at a higher altitude and attack from above.

Over the next two weeks, Eighth Air Force planes were sent on raids over northern France and the Low Countries within the operating envelope of escorting fighters. Losses were relatively low, and the B-17 force grew in size as additional aircraft and crews arrived in East Anglia. A raid was then staged by 338 B-17s on aircraft and weapons factories in the southwestern German city of Stuttgart on September 6. Heavy clouds forced many bombers to turn back, and the targets were obscured by the overcast. The Luftwaffe attacked the U.S. planes relentlessly, and even some Ju 87 "Stukas" dropped bombs on the B-17s from above. Losses were again heavy with 330 crew casualties, forty-five U.S. bombers lost, and more than 110 damaged of which ten would never fly again.[27] The Eighth Air Force returned to shorter-range missions for the rest of the month.

By October 4, Eaker, under increasing pressure to degrade the Luftwaffe, launched 323 B-17s to attack the VDM non-ferrous metal factory in Frankfurt along with other industrial targets in the Saar region. These targets were not that far outside the range of fighter escorts, which reduced the time they were under attack by enemy fighters. Only twelve B-17s were shot down, but 137 returned damaged, seventeen beyond repair. Later that night, more than 400 RAF bombers returned to destroy much of the city center. This was followed up over the next week with costly B-17 attacks on aviation and rail targets in Anklam, Munster, and Bremen.

Finally, the Eighth Air Force mounted a follow-up mission to destroy the ball-bearing factories at Schweinfurt, which had been almost completely repaired from the previous bombing raid in August. On Thursday, October 14, 320 B-17s took off on the mission. The Luftwaffe was waiting, and as with the previous attempt on this target, resistance was fierce. Of the sixty bombers that did not return, fifty-eight were shot down by fighters. In addition, 145 B-17s were damaged, seven to an extent that they had to be scrapped. Bombing accuracy was quite good, and the American crews claimed that in intense air combat, around 300 enemy fighters had been destroyed or damaged. Eaker and his staff calculated that if these estimates of losses to the Luftwaffe were only exaggerated by a factor of three, and one hundred fighters had been destroyed, the day still represented a victory for the USAAF.[28] This was because, by that point in the war, the Germans could not replace planes and trained crews as quickly as the Americans. In fact, on just the one day of the raid, the Eighth Air Force received ninety-three fresh crews and it was expected that 250–300 new bombers would arrive along with additional crews over the course of October.[29]

While the American public was shocked by the loss of sixty bombers and 600 airmen in one day, General Arnold heralded the mission as a great victory and released an upbeat statement regarding the mission: "This attack on Schweinfurt was not merely a spectacular air raid. It was an engagement between large armies—a major campaign. In a period of a few hours we invaded German-held Europe to a depth of 500 miles, sacked and crippled one of her most vital enterprises. We did it in daylight and we did it with precision, aiming our explosives with the care and accuracy of a marksman firing a rifle at a bull's eye."[30] Ball-bearing production at Schweinfurt was reduced temporarily by 67 percent in the attack, and the Germans were forced to begin a costly effort to disperse production of this critical industrial input.[31]

Nevertheless, October 1943 was the month with the highest casualty rate for the Eighth Air Force with 163 B-17s lost.[32] The air battle over Schweinfurt was a final straw for USAAF unescorted strategic bombing operations with the mission coming to be known as "Black Thursday." Squadron cohesion and morale could not be maintained in the face of such an elevated turnover of personnel. As Roger Freeman, one of the preeminent historians of the campaign, described the aftermath: "The loss incurred on October 14th amounted to more than double the 10% of force figure that Eighth Air Force considered prohibitive to operations. Morale at bomber bases was at a low ebb and little wonder when the Fortress crews were currently incurring a casualty rate higher than any other branch of the US Forces. Even with the undeniable good bombing results achieved on many occasions the price was becoming too high to pay . . . So far as the Eighth was concerned, the USAAF's self-defensive bomber formation doctrine was dead . . . The future of the daylight strategic bomber had come very much to depend on the presence of the long range escort fighter."[33] The casualties suffered in this second raid, along with the brutal losses of the prior two months, marked an end of deep penetration missions beyond the range of escorting fighters for the rest of 1943.

Recovery

Winning the war in the air and defeating the Luftwaffe in time for the 1944 invasion of France was going to take the adoption of new doctrines, equipment, and personnel. Luckily the United States was able to supply all three rapidly. First of all, the prodigious output of the American economy was being brought to bear against the Axis in all facets of the war and in few areas as dramatically as in the area of aircraft. Despite the rising losses suffered in bombing missions launched from English and Mediterranean bases, USAAF strength began to soar at the end of 1943 as can be seen from the following graph:

USAAF Aircraft Inventory—European Theater of Operations[34]

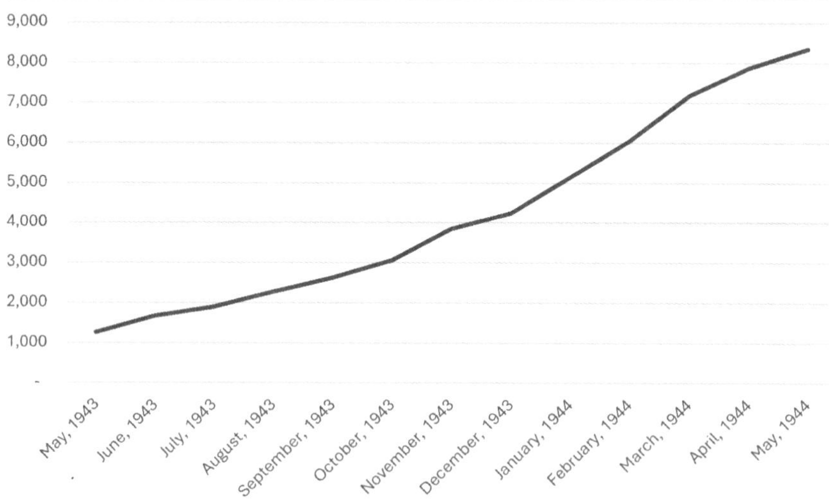

Trained crew also rose at a rapid rate. The Eighth Air Force was joined by two Heavy Bombing Groups per month in July, August, and September 1943.[35] Five more were added by the end of the year. By late January 1944, individual missions with over 500 heavy bombers (mostly B-17s with smaller numbers of B-24s) had become commonplace—a doubling in strength compared to those of just a few months earlier.

As the year wore on, the USAAF was able to launch raids in excess of 1,000 heavy bombers escorted by several hundred fighters. Such massive individual operations sent upwards of 15,000 airmen over Germany at a time to drop over two and a half million tons of high explosives a day on their targets.

U.S. Generals Arnold, Spaatz, Eaker, and others had begun the war believing strongly that long-range fighters were not required to defeat Germany in a strategic bombing offensive. However, they did react to the reality of their bombers suffering unsustainable losses when overwhelmed by Luftwaffe planes uncontested by American escort craft. They pushed for more and better fighters to be produced and shipped to England to join the Eighth Air Force. Most importantly, Arnold realized the potential of the P-51B Mustang and the USAAF began ordering them in late 1942. This was a superb aircraft that proved to be extremely well suited to the escort role due to its speed and maneuverability as well as ability (when equipped with drop tanks) to fly 1,200 miles and escort bombers anywhere in Germany. By late 1943, large numbers of P-38s, and later, P-51s, began to arrive at Eighth Air Force bases in England.

The USAAF had also begun receiving its first bombers equipped with H2X radar, which had been pioneered by the British. This technology allowed heavy bombers to target general areas when cloud cover made visual spotting of individual structures impossible. H2X produced a rough map of the terrain below and could distinguish water, land, and built-up urban areas. A pathfinder aircraft equipped with this radar operated in the lead of an attack formation on overcast days. When over the target, this plane would fire a red flare and then drop its bombs along with a smoke marker. The remainder of the B-17s would then immediately drop their ordnance as well.

These three factors—more bombers, more escorts, and radar—were all apparent in the November 3 attack on the port area of Wilhelmshaven, Germany. The reduction in operations in the previous weeks had allowed the Eighth Air Force to absorb new planes and crews and in the largest mission of the war to date, 438 B-17s and 117 B-24s were dispatched. As the target was only just over the Dutch border, P-47 fighters were able to provide penetration and then withdrawal escort for most of the mission and an astounding 333 were assigned to that role. The 55th Fighter Group operating longer-range P-38s had also become operational and forty-five would travel all the way to the target and back with the bombers. There were whoops of joy from B-17 crewmen when they received the news.[36] Only seven bombers were lost that day along with a couple more damaged planes that had to be scrapped after returning to base.

The radar-directed bombing of Wilhelmshaven was by no means a precision attack, and all planes in a combat box dropping their ordnance simultaneously meant that many explosives fell outside of the port and detonated in residential areas of the city. However, this technique increased the odds that at least some bombs hit the target. In addition, having the heavies fly at altitude over a layer of overcast provided some protection to the Americans from both ground fire and German fighters, and this resulted in a lower loss rate. The practice became common, and during the cloudy winter of 1943–1944, the Eighth Air Force bombed by radar on 90 percent of its missions. This was a major change in doctrine away from the USAAF insistence that it could "drop a bomb into a pickle barrel" from miles in the sky. According to historian Donald Miller, "Radar bombing was actually a form of area bombing. Precision was impossible. This was a clear break with Air Force creed, but the alternative—not bombing at all in bad weather—was unacceptable to air commanders committed to crushing the enemy. Throughout the war, there were only two factors that greatly accelerated the rate of American strategic bombing operations: tremendously increased production of bombers and crews, and widespread employment of H2X."[37]

Another major change in USAAF doctrine was due to new men in the command structure: General Carl Spaatz was named the head of the newly established U.S. Strategic Air Forces in Europe, and General James Doolittle, already famous for his daring raid on Tokyo, took over command of the Eighth Air Force on January 6, 1944. Eaker was reassigned to lead the Mediterranean Allied Air Forces that included the U.S. Twelfth and Fifteenth Air Forces as well as the British Desert Air Force. While technically a promotion, Eaker believed he was being relieved due to failure and took the news hard. The inability of USAAF bombers to knock Germany out of the war was certainly not his fault. He was only finally getting the numbers of B-17s and B-24s necessary to offset losses when he was transferred. Eaker was also not provided with fighters with sufficient range to provide escort service deep into Germany, and had been forced to divert a large number of missions to non-strategic targets such as U-boat pens.

Doolittle wasted little time insisting on a more aggressive posture in his drive to achieve the Pointblank Directive and drive the Luftwaffe out of the sky in time for the cross-Channel invasion. On one of the first days in his new role, he visited General William Kepner who had recently taken over command of the Eighth's fighters. Doolittle noticed a sign hanging on the wall that read, "The first duty of the Eighth Air Force fighters is to bring the bombers back alive." He ordered the message be ripped down and replaced with a new one: "The first duty of Eighth Air Force fighters is to destroy German fighters."

Previously, doctrine had been that fighters would escort the bombers, defend them when attacked, and fly with them back to base. To maintain their place in the formation, the fast P-47s had to weave and limit their speed so as to stay with the B-17s and B-24s. However, after he took command in England, Doolittle ordered his fighters to range ahead of the bomber groups to seek out, find, and shoot down Luftwaffe planes. The escorts were soon ranging up to 50 miles ahead to hunt down the enemy. The crews of the B-17s and B-24s did not like this change at first, but as the number of enemy fighters destroyed rose dramatically, opposition soon faded away. Doolittle later wrote in his memoirs, "As far as I'm concerned, this was the most important and far-reaching military decision I made during the war." He also admitted, "it was also the most controversial."[38]

The P-38s of the 55th Fighter Group were soon joined in early December 1943 by the 354th Fighter Group, which was the first U.S. unit to fly the P-51B Mustang equipped with the high-performance Rolls-Royce Merlin engine. As previously mentioned, these aircraft had the range to travel with the B-17s to targets anywhere in Germany and the performance that made them a match for the best the Luftwaffe could put in the sky. The 352nd and 359th Fighter Groups soon gave up their P-47s for P-51s while the 20th Fighter Group with P-38s also became operational in December 1943.

Finally, by the start of 1944, the USAAF had the aircraft, crew, technology, and tactics it needed to gain air superiority over Western Europe.

Victory

The American bombing effort over Europe entered the final six months before D-Day with its doctrine completely flipped on its head. Rather than the B-17 being seen as an invulnerable aircraft able to bring an enemy economy to its knees through precision air attacks, General Spaatz was now using the big planes as bait. They were sent on area bombing missions over Germany to hit targets the Luftwaffe would be forced to defend. When the enemy Bf 109s and Fw 190s arrived in the skies to do battle, they were set upon by swarms of U.S. fighters.

During the first six weeks of 1944, ever larger raids were sent out to bomb targets in far western Germany as the Eighth Air Force incorporated more heavy bomber squadrons and long-range fighters into their formations. For example, on January 30, almost 600 B-17s and 150 B-24s escorted by more than 600 fighters struck industrial and transportation targets in the cities of Braunschweig and Hannover losing only twenty bombers and four fighters while claiming that upwards of one hundred German planes were shot down and another fifty damaged. Such missions were in preparation for Operation Argument, later known as "Big Week," which was to begin in late February.

This new plan envisioned a maximum effort by both Allies' bomber forces, consisting of a week of continuous raids to target German aviation and ball-bearing factories. The Luftwaffe would either have to allow the destruction of its industrial base, or send up its fighters to defend these targets and have its strength degraded through attrition. On February 20, 1,003 bombers (80 percent of which were B-17s) escorted by more than 800 fighters struck multiple aircraft production factories in Germany. U.S. losses were low and scores of enemy planes were destroyed. The next day, more than 1,400 American bombers from both the Eighth and Fifteenth Air Force (the latter based in Italy) hit industrial targets across the Third Reich. The RAF also launched major efforts against similar targets during the week in a deviation from its campaign to destroy German cities and "dehouse" the enemy's population. The following days saw continuing heavy attacks on the infrastructure of the Luftwaffe including raids on Schweinfurt and Regensburg.

The Eighth Air Force was overtaking RAF Bomber Command in size and was coming to dominate the skies over Western Europe.[39] During Big Week, the USAAF launched 4,000 heavy bomber sorties, and dropped 18,000 tons of munitions on eighteen enemy aircraft plants and two ball-bearing factory complexes. Casualties were high with the loss of 226 bombers, twenty-six fighters, and 2,000 American crewmen against 262 Luftwaffe fighters shot down.[40] Enemy losses were highest among the *Zerstörer* squadrons as these heavy fighters were less maneuverable and were easy prey for P-38s and P-51s. This was important to the Allies as such enemy planes were able to carry more ordnance in a fighter-bomber capacity and could potentially do more damage to a cross-Channel invasion fleet. As impacting enemy fighter strength was now the primary concern of top commanders of the USAAF, Operation Argument was a clear success.

The average German pilot was already less well trained than his American opponent, and the death of 14 percent of its pilot force committed during Big Week was a shock to the Luftwaffe. It also made the relative flying performance in the air between the two sides even worse. In addition, the raids took a significant toll on German aircraft production, temporarily cutting it in half.[41] Importantly in this attritional campaign, surging arrivals of American aircraft and pilots in England meant that Eighth Air Force losses could be quickly replaced. In contrast, the Germans were hard pressed to stop the slide in the number of active aircraft and the quality of its pilots as losses continued on the Eastern Front in the USSR, in Italy, and over Germany itself.

With the conclusion of Big Week, the Luftwaffe seemed to be starting to conserve its planes and pull them back into Germany due to the painful losses it had suffered. In response, Spaatz and Doolittle decided that, in addition to bombing aviation industry targets, they would also order attacks on the city of Berlin. Not only was this a center of the Nazi economy, it was expected that the enemy air force would have no choice

ESCORT FIGHTER RANGE

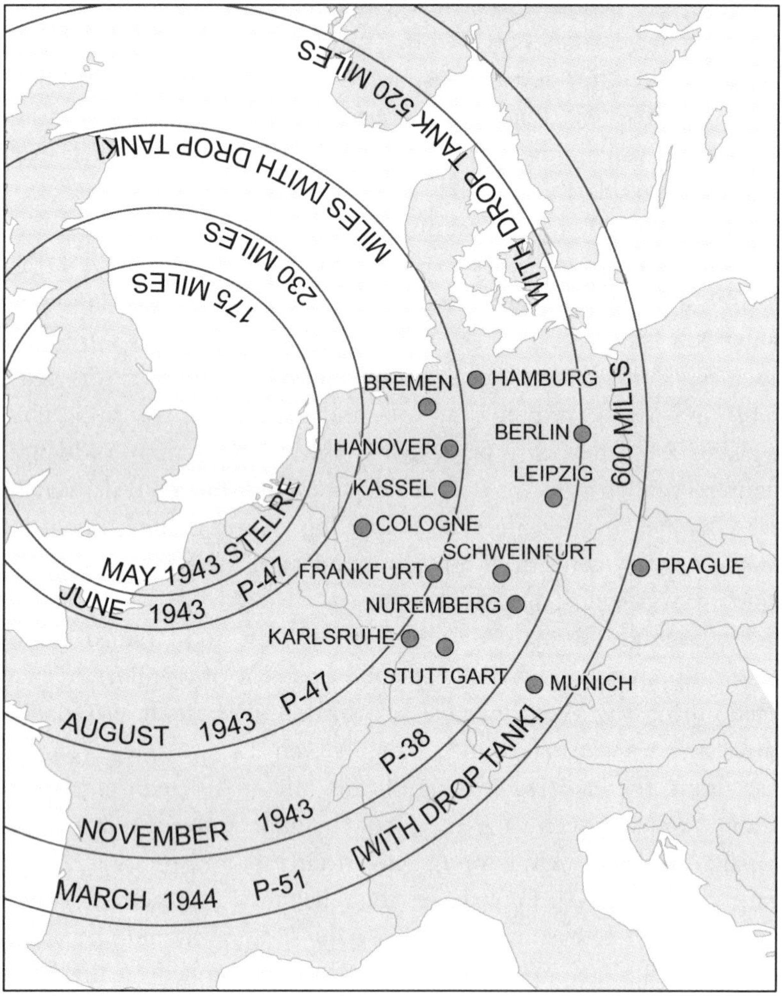

US ARMY AIR FORCE

but to rise to oppose such raids on the capital. Over the course of three weeks in March, on March 4, 6, 8, 9, and 22, five separate missions were flown over the "Big B."[42]

These raids were huge and brutal attritional operations that overwhelmed the defenders. For example, the mission on March 8 dispatched 620 heavy bombers and almost 900 fighters (of which 174 were P-51s).

Eighteen B-17s and B-24s were lost along with eight escorts. The gunners in the heavy bombers, who usually reported wildly high numbers, claimed eighty enemy fighters destroyed or probably destroyed. However, the fighter pilots, whose claims were usually much more accurate with their kills confirmed through gun camera film, reported seventy-nine Luftwaffe planes shot down with another eight probables. When the Eighth Air Force returned to Berlin on March 22 with a mission consisting of 657 bombers and 817 escorts (of which 196 were P-51s), few enemy fighters rose to challenge them. The Germans were being worn down and driven from the sky, and the USAAF was clearly winning the campaign to gain air supremacy over Western Europe.

Over the next two months, American planes increasingly came to dominate the airspace over Europe from Normandy to Berlin. Spaatz shifted the emphasis of bomber missions to the German petroleum and synthetic fuel (produced through the hydrogenation of coal) industries. As Albert Speer wrote of the spring of 1944, "I shall never forget the date May 12, four days later. On that day the technological war was decided. Until then we had managed to produce approximately as many weapons as the armed forces needed, in spite of their considerable losses. But with the attack of nine hundred and thirty-five daylight bombers of the American Eighth Air Force upon several fuel plants in central and eastern Germany, a new era in the air war began. It meant the end of German armaments production."[43]

By the time the D-Day invasion was launched, the Luftwaffe was all but absent from the battle space above Normandy and the German war machine was increasingly constrained by a lack of parts, ammunition, and fuel.[44] While the Nazis were remarkably successful in dispersing industrial production to small and hidden sites, in the great clash of populations and economic production of World War II, the Allies were increasingly ascendant and on the path to ultimate victory. The USAAF and its strategic bombing force could claim that it had been a critical factor in this success.

Causes of Defeat

There were several reasons that the bombers of the Eighth Air Force were blown out of the sky in the summer of 1943. In retrospect, the most obvious is that the upper echelon of the USAAF accepted the assertions of many military aviation theorists that the "bomber would always get through," and that fighter escort was unnecessary. They also believed that a relentless bombing campaign could force an enemy to surrender or at least impair his economy to such an extent that resistance on the ground would crumble. When these theories were confronted with the reality in the skies above Europe, they were shown to be incorrect.

Many USAAF generals, including General Arnold, were convinced that enemy fighters would rarely be able to find and successfully shoot down large numbers of attacking American bombers. Thus, there was no need to send escorting fighter craft along on the mission. Even if somehow such planes could be built that had the range to stay with a bomber force, they would not have the performance characteristics to battle effectively against shorter-range interceptors that might be encountered. Sadly, for thousands of men of the Eighth Air Force, this turned out to be false. Even the extremely robust B-17 with heavy defensive armament was vulnerable to the well-engineered Luftwaffe fighter planes that rose to challenge them.

There had been those in the USAAF who opposed the Bomber Mafia prior to World War II. However, men such as Claire Chennault who championed the role of the fighter aircraft to intercept bombers, or George Kenney, a proponent of close air support, were generally ignored, passed over for promotion, or even forced into early retirement. The result was a USAAF that entered the war with excellent long-range heavy bombers, but no long-range fighter aircraft designed to escort them. It took two years until this error could be rectified.

Next, there was the ongoing, almost schizophrenic, inability of the USAAF to focus on one particular type of enemy target. Much of this was due to outside pressures. For example, in late 1942, senior officers of the Eighth Air Force wanted to focus on strategic targets, but they were ordered to attack U-boat bases. This was effectively just an expensive way to get American airmen killed. More than 2,000 heavy bomber sorties were flown against submarine bases on the French coast October 1942–October 1943 in which 119 bombers and nearly 1,200 crewmen were lost. The bombing attacks did little damage to the massive concrete U-boat pens the Germans had built and had a negligible impact on the

Battle of the Atlantic.[45] In addition, the meeting of Churchill and FDR with their military staffs in Casablanca in 1943 resulted in orders to the air forces that they should destroy a large range of German targets including: submarine pens, fighter aircraft production plants, rail transportation nodes, and fuel refineries.

While the USAAF had developed a short list of specific types of military/industrial targets it wanted to destroy in Europe, it ended up hitting a large range instead. Some of this was due to a lack of flying range from escorting fighters in 1943 that made it inadvisable to focus on one industry with critical choke points far into the east or south of Germany. Another was the large number of days in northern Europe where clouds obscured primary targets and forced the bombers to divert to secondary ones. Lastly, over the course of the war, the Eighth Air Force was ordered to fly "non-strategic" missions to drop supplies to French resistance fighters, as well as bomb U-boat pens, bridges, railyards, civilian areas of city centers, and on one occasion, the Panzer Lehr Division dug in near Saint-Lo in France. In the end, the incredibly detailed and authoritative *Mighty Eighth War Diary* includes forty-eight different types of objectives that were bombed ranging from "Highway Bridge" to "Coastal Battery" to "Water Viaduct."[46]

After the war, Albert Speer expressed his amazement to Allied interrogators that bombing attacks were not staged against the same economic choke points on a regular basis to reduce output, negate repairs, and disrupt production of critical German military armament inputs.[47] Damage done by raids was often severe to specific targets, but the Nazis were then given breathing space to restore operations and disperse equipment so as to bring production back up to previous levels, or even improve upon them. Speer made it clear that regular and repeated attacks on the small number of ball-bearing plants or synthetic oil refineries would have led to a much earlier end to the war.

Finally, and perhaps most importantly was USAAF's inability to coordinate with the British RAF, which dramatically undermined the effectiveness of the strategic bombing campaign and represented a major failure for the Allied war effort. Had RAF Bomber Command been convinced to engage in daylight precision attacks on northern

France, the Low Countries, and northwestern Germany in 1943 through early 1944—areas then within the envelope of effective fighter escort—enemy military power would have been reduced and greater attrition would have been imposed on the Luftwaffe much earlier in the war. Another alternative is that after the British started using H2S ground-mapping radar in January 1943 they could have stopped targeting city centers and focused on hitting economic and military targets in Germany at night. Such a change would also have done much more damage to the enemy's war effort.

Either change—daylight missions within the escort umbrella or nighttime attacks on specific military/economic targets—would have yielded a similar rate of bomber losses for the RAF to what occurred historically. After all, due to Luftwaffe opposition, antiaircraft fire, flight accidents in the dark, and the like, RAF Bomber Command suffered a 5 percent casualty rate from its night missions in the period November 1943 to March 1944.[48] General Harris resisted a pause in his attacks on cities and had to be directly ordered to target specific industry installations during Operation Argument. The surprising result was that RAF crews turned out to be just as effective as their USAAF colleagues in "precision" bombing.

The reason the United States needed to redirect the RAF's bombing focus was for the same reason the Luftwaffe's blitz in 1940 failed: Terror attacks to kill enemy civilians and destroy their homes failed to force an enemy nation to surrender. The RAF's night campaign of attacking city centers did little to injure the German economy or weaken the Wehrmacht's ability to oppose the critical D-Day landings.[49] The postwar USSBS analysis concluded that, "The city attacks of the RAF prior to the autumn of 1944, did not substantially affect the course of German war production. German war production as a whole continued to increase. This in itself is not conclusive, but the Survey has made detailed analysis of the course of production and trade in 10 German cities that were attacked during this period and has made more general analyses in others. These show that while production received a moderate setback after a raid, it recovered substantially within a relatively few weeks. As a rule the industrial plants were located around the perimeter of German cities and characteristically these were relatively undamaged."[50]

Thus, the RAF night bombing campaign did little to reduce enemy military strength and certainly failed to break the enemy's morale to fight in the critical period prior to the D-Day landings. In fact, the effort may have actually stiffened the resolve of the enemy population to carry on the fight. It was only in late 1944 that RAF night raids became so large that rising tonnage of bomb loads transported to the target area and "spill-overs" from aircraft that dropped their ordnance early or late caused significant damage to the German steel industry and electric power generation that had a real impact to speed the end of the war.[51] However, in late 1943, more than a year of British bombings of city centers had failed to impact the ability of the Germans to fight the war, yet the Americans did little to force a change in strategy by their allies. Yes, the Eighth Air Force suffered large casualties when it staged deep penetration strikes, but its overall loss rate was similar to the RAF's, and at least it could point to the destruction of specific German targets that had military significance while also imposing attritional losses on the Luftwaffe.

In addition to the failure of the RAF Bomber Command to give up on its ineffective campaign of nighttime attacks on German civilians and their homes, RAF Fighter Command also refused to coordinate its actions with the USAAF. In early 1943, Eaker asked the RAF to consider configuring some of its Spitfire fighters for long-range escort duty and having them fly alongside his B-17s over Germany on daytime missions. This clearly was technically possible as the Spitfire PR Mark IV model had been in service since 1940 and was used for long-range photoreconnaissance. Unfortunately, the British refused the request and claimed it was not possible. The USAAF later shipped two Spitfires to Ohio where they were modified and their range was extended to such an extent that they were able to fly back across the Atlantic to England in early 1945.[52] Of course, by that point, they were no longer needed as the Luftwaffe had been mostly driven from the skies.

A second request was made at a higher level after the Pointblank Directive was issued. Arnold asked his counterpart at the RAF, Chief of Air Staff Charles Portal, to allocate more of his fighters to escort Eighth

Air Force missions. Arnold especially wanted to gain control of the P-51 Mustangs that had already been provided to the RAF in 1942 (embarrassingly, these aircraft were built in the United States by the North American Aviation company from 1940 onwards to fulfill British orders, but the USAAF failed to purchase them due to a belief that it would have no need for a long-range fighter). Portal was only willing to part with a small number of his planes and the discussion became acrimonious. General Arnold made it quite clear in caustic entries in his diaries that he questioned the motives of the British and their resolve.[53] The USAAF commander then succeeded in having all American fighter production for the next few months directed to the Eighth Air Force in England.

Of course Arnold and Eaker did not have the ability to order General Harris to stop his nighttime city bombing campaign or General Portal to assign his fighters to escort duties, but such a change could have been engineered at the highest levels. By the middle of 1943, the United States was becoming the dominant partner in the alliance, supplying huge inputs to the British war effort via Lend-Lease aid, and an American general was to be supreme commander of Allied Expeditionary Forces. Certainly, the leverage was there to force a change at the RAF. That this did not take place likely lengthened the war and resulted in tens of thousands of unnecessary deaths both in the air over Europe and in the raging infernos that engulfed scores of German cities.

Causes of Victory

Luck plays a great part in every war and whether a fighting force is victorious or defeated. In the case of the USAAF's bombing campaign over Europe, it was saved by the fluke that its mission was changed in the middle of the war and its earlier errors were overcome due to the strength of the U.S. economy. Arnold, Spaatz, Eaker, and other leaders of the American air war wished to have their organization become an independent military branch. They believed the best way to achieve this increase in status was to demonstrate the power of the bomber to force the collapse of an enemy's capacity to wage a modern armed conflict. By the middle of 1943 it had become clear that the USAAF did not have the doctrine, the technology, or the right planes to accomplish this mission.

Then, in June the Combined Joint Chiefs of Staff of the U.S. and British militaries issued the Pointblank Directive. The USAAF's new mission was to destroy the Luftwaffe's fighter force in the air, on the ground, or in the factory. There was great concern that if the German air force was not significantly degraded prior to the planned cross-Channel invasion scheduled for late May 1944, enemy planes would do great damage to the ships of the amphibious force bunched up along the Normandy coast. Rather than attempting to shut down the entire enemy economy, the USAAF now had a much more discrete task and upwards of a year to do it.

Eaker and his staff began to focus their heavy bombers on attacking airfields, air depots, and aircraft industry targets. The hope was that enemy planes could be destroyed on the ground, or would be forced to defend such targets and be worn down in an attritional fight in the air. However, as the Eighth Air Force sent missions farther into Germany, the Luftwaffe increasingly pulled its fighters back away from England to defend in depth and focus its attacks on heavy bombers while avoiding Allied escort fighters when possible. Thus, the B-17s encountered enemy fighters primarily when the big bombers had no escorts or when the Allied fighters were low on fuel and could not engage in lengthy dogfights. This resulted in unsustainable loss rates for the USAAF, only minor damage being done to the Luftwaffe in the skies, and reduced bomb loads being dropped on aircraft industry targets on the ground.

The Pointblank Directive was partially achieved as the Luftwaffe had pulled the bulk of its fighter aircraft out of northern France and the Low Countries. As long as the USAAF continued to fly missions over Germany and hit critical industrial targets there, the bulk of the enemy's fighters in the West were likely to remain away from the Channel coast. The Eighth Air Force also transferred its medium bombers to a new Ninth Air Force in October headed by General Lewis Brereton. This new command had the mission of flying tactical sorties to support the upcoming cross-Channel invasion and it immediately began bombing airfields and transportation nodes in the areas from which the Luftwaffe had withdrawn. The Ninth grew rapidly and by May 1944 it was composed of 5,000 aircraft and 200,000 personnel, a total larger than that of the Eighth Air Force at the time.

However, the Allied Combined Chiefs of Staff did not just want the Luftwaffe bottled up temporarily in Germany. They demanded it be driven from the skies so it would have no ability to redeploy to France to contest the cross-Channel landings. To accomplish this mission, the Eighth Air Force needed a way to fly bombing missions on the generally overcast days that prevailed over Germany during the winter, escort fighters to protect the heavy bombers, and more planes and crews to replace losses suffered in the attritional campaign. Luckily, the surging output of the U.S. war economy was able to supply all these needs.

As already noted, new radar systems installed in a small number of bombers allowed these pathfinder aircraft to lead combat box formations over the general area of a target before initiating a coordinated drop of all ordnance. This was a major deviation from precision bombing practice with Eaker and his staff describing it as "bombing through overcast." The men in the planes often referred to it as "blind bombing." Regardless of the nomenclature this tactic (1) allowed for missions against strategic targets to be flown on days when visual sighting was not possible, (2) resulted in similarly effective damage to enemy installations on the ground, especially with the number of bombers in each mission increasing as the Eighth Air Force expanded dramatically in size, and (3) forced the Luftwaffe to fly more days per month, often in poor weather, against rising numbers of escorting fighters. The result for the enemy was a rapid increase in both combat and operational losses.

The newly arriving long-range fighters, rather than having to remain with the bombers, were let loose to range ahead of and seek out concentrations of German interceptor craft. Enemy pilots, which had been ordered for months to avoid U.S. fighters and focus on attacking bombers, had lost some of their "edge" and were increasingly outmatched by P-38s and P-51s that were flown by men who increasingly had more total flight time and combat experience than their Luftwaffe opponents.

A relentless pace of missions reached a climax with Operation Argument, in which the German air force was struck repeatedly both in the sky and on the ground. Follow-up missions the next month on the enemy capital of Berlin forced the Luftwaffe to engage in unequal battles with American fighters until the German planes were driven from the sky. While the Luftwaffe staged a modest recovery later in the war, the goal of Pointblank was achieved and the Allies enjoyed almost complete air supremacy over Normandy when it launched the D-Day invasion. The USAAF did not achieve its goal of devastating German military output through strategic bombing in 1942 and 1943, though its attacks on industry began to cause increasingly painful shortages of fuel, ammunition, and synthetic rubber in the second half of 1944. However, by this point, several other factors were weighing on the enemy's ability to wage war such as casualties suffered at the front, the defection of allies, and the relentless pressure of the Red Army advancing in the East and that of the Anglo-Americans in the West. However, success in defeating the Luftwaffe and achieving command of the skies remains a significant victory for U.S. airpower.

Impact of Defeat

The failures in 1943 of the RAF and the USAAF to coordinate their strategic bombing efforts, along with the Americans' inability to stage deep penetration missions over Germany in the absence of catastrophic loss of aircraft, was clearly a major defeat suffered by the Allies in World War II. Not only were thousands of crewmen lost, the cost of the aircraft was enormous as was the infrastructure that allowed those planes to fly a relentless series of missions over Germany. To understand the impact of this failure, one can question what would have happened had the United States chosen to build more tanks and fighters rather than heavy bombers in 1942 and 1943.

The M4 Sherman was certainly not the best medium tank fielded in the war. That designation goes to the Soviet T-34 or the Panzer IV, but the American product was rugged, cheap, and adaptable. For approximately every fifty B-17s the USAAF did without, the U.S. Army could have used the savings to upgrade an infantry division to an armored one. Of the ninety-one army divisions America fielded in World War II, only sixteen were armored and sixty-eight were infantry. What could the United States have done with 500–600 fewer heavy bombers and an additional ten armored divisions in Europe? Possibilities include knocking Italy out of the war sooner, breaking out of the Normandy beachhead earlier, and ending the war in Europe prior to what occurred historically.

The same question can be asked regarding the construction of fewer heavy bombers and more fighters that could be used in both air superiority or ground attack fighter-bomber roles. For twenty fewer B-17s, the USAAF could have purchased the one hundred P-51s required to fill out a Fighter Group. Thus, by forgoing 400 heavy bombers, the United States operated twenty additional Fighter Groups with an impressive 2,000 additional long-range Mustangs in England prior to D-Day. Such a force, ranging over Germany, strafing airfields, engaging in dogfights, and even bombing aviation plants from low altitude could have potentially done just as much damage to the Luftwaffe as occurred historically while also providing the flexibility to add additional close air support to ground forces after they landed in France. The result of such a changed resource allocation could have been that the USAAF gained air superiority over Europe sooner, and Allied armies were able to advance more quickly.

This is not to say that there was no role for the heavy bomber in World War II or that there was no need for an Eighth Air Force equipped with such craft to fly missions over Europe. However, the returns the United States gained from building, manning, and arming such an enormous fleet of B-17s and B-24s in the conflict are dubious. A better allocation of resources could have led to the achievement of the goals of the Pointblank Directive sooner while also giving the D-Day invasion a bigger punch. There is no way to know for sure if the war in Europe would have ended sooner if the United States had allocated a larger focus to building military equipment such as tanks and fighters, but the evidence leans in that direction.

In summary, the USAAF suffered a strategic and bloody defeat over Germany in the latter half of 1943. However, it later regained the upper hand through a combination of new technology, surging American military output, rapid crew training, and changes in tactics that were better suited to the task at hand. At least the fight was over the enemy's skies and not our own, or even those of Britain. While painful, the losses suffered in both men and equipment were also ones that could be replaced over time and had little impact on the ability of the Allies to stage their all-important invasion of France in the middle of 1944.

Impact of Victory

The success the Eighth Air Force achieved in the first half of 1944 was significant to the course of World War II. Not only was the Luftwaffe defeated so that Allied air superiority was achieved prior to D-Day, but bombing attacks on targets in the heartland of Germany were a boost to American morale and helped maintain the relationship with the USSR, whose people had to shoulder the burden of the greatest share of fighting and dying to defeat the Nazis. To understand the importance of the victory, we need to consider what would have happened had it not taken place.

Assume for a moment that the adoption of H2X had not been rolled out in time for the Eighth Air Force to fly more missions throughout the overcast period prevailing during much of the European winter over Germany. Or that sufficient long-range P-38s and P-51s had not been delivered in time for Operation Argument. Or finally, that there was no change in tactics that led to fighters ranging ahead of the bomber formations to break up enemy plane concentrations over target areas. Or that all three of these things did not come to pass—what would have been the impact? The likely result compared to what took place historically would have been the Luftwaffe suffering reduced losses in the skies over Germany, inflicting even worse damage on the USAAF heavy bomber force, and still maintaining a significant level of potential attacking strength to sortie to the English Channel on D-Day. In such a scenario, would the Allied invasion have gone forward and would it have been successful on June 6, 1944? The answer to the first question is most likely an affirmative. The second is somewhat more difficult to determine.

The main reason the landings would still have taken place in the presence of Luftwaffe opposition is that the Allies had a massive number of aircraft to deploy for the operation. Their mission was to perform combat air patrol over the amphibious naval force and beachheads while also striking airfields and transportation nodes near the landing beaches. The overall commander, General Dwight Eisenhower, wanted air supremacy, but he was under great pressure to act. Knowing he had thousands of ground-based fighters to provide combat air patrol and that his armada contained many British and U.S. ships (destroyers, cruisers, battleships, aircraft carriers) bristling with antiaircraft guns, and operating their own planes, it is highly likely he would have ordered the operation to proceed even in the face of expected attack from the sky.

Had a large force of German aircraft attempted to challenge the invasion force on, or soon after D-Day, it would have been intercepted by a mass of short-range fighter aircraft operating out of fields in southern England and aircraft carriers offshore. The RAF and USAAF flew more than 14,000 sorties of all types supporting the amphibious landings. Had they been opposed by the Luftwaffe, losses in the air would have been suffered on both sides, and it is highly likely that the Germans would have been overwhelmed by the massive quantitative (and increasingly qualitative) advantages of the Allied air armada operating over the beachheads. The real question becomes how much damage would have been imposed on the invasion armies by enemy aircraft bombing and strafing and to what extent would interdiction efforts against German forces rushing toward the beachhead have been inhibited. A scenario certainly could have unfolded where the Allied beachhead was smaller, the buildup of forces partially disrupted, and enemy counterattacks stronger than what took place historically.

Nevertheless, had the Luftwaffe not been defeated by the USAAF over Germany in the first half of 1944, the Allied invasion of Normandy would still have had a very high chance of being a success. Even if the landings achieved a smaller lodgment along the coast than what actually occurred and the Germans were able to place it under greater pressure through counterattacks, the enemy position in the West would have been undermined quickly. This is because Operation Dragoon, an amphibious assault on southern France on August 15, 1944, put the entire U.S. Sixth Army Group ashore against limited Nazi opposition. Historically, the enemy defense of Normandy was in the process of collapsing by that date. However, if stronger Luftwaffe opposition had allowed the Germans to pen the Allied armies along the northern French coast, the Sixth Army Group in the south would have advanced northward to potentially cut off enemy supply lines. Thus, had more enemy planes challenged the D-Day landings, British and American losses would probably have been higher, and the breakout might have taken longer. However, with huge armies marching on Germany from the east, the west, and the south, it is highly likely that the war would have ended similarly to what occurred historically and in a similar timeframe.

Another question that must be asked is if the victory in the skies above Germany was worth it? The Allied invasion is very likely to have gone forward and succeeded even in the face of Luftwaffe opposition. Through the rest of the conflict, as Soviet, U.S., British, French, and Polish ground forces closed in on Berlin, the USSBS concluded that strategic bombing was only one of the factors that led to German defeat and it is difficult to quantify how much sooner the war ended in Europe due to American efforts in this aerial campaign. So did the U.S. military derive reasonable gains when measured against the costs involved in flying thousands of B-17s and B-24s over the Third Reich from 1943 to 1945?

The Eighth Air Force was an organization that suffered brutal casualties. Of 350,000 men who served in its ranks, over 26,000 were killed for a 7.4 percent fatality rate.[54] However, these losses were almost entirely drawn from the 210,000 men who were in flight crews, so the loss rate for this subset was even higher at 12.4 percent. In addition, another 21,000 of these men were shot down and became POWs. These fatality figures are dramatically higher than those suffered in the war by the Navy (0.41 percent), or the Army (2.25 percent). Even the Marines "only" had a fatality rate of 3.29 percent fighting so many brutal Pacific island battles against the Japanese.[55] In fact, the Eighth Air Force had more men killed in action than the entire Marine Corps whose ranks were a quarter of a million larger in the conflict.

In conclusion, the defeat of the Luftwaffe by the USAAF (with some begrudging assistance from the RAF) in 1944 was an important step in the winning of World War II. However, it was a victory that was paid for in a great deal of American blood, and arguably had a cost greater than it was worth. The failure of the USAAF to achieve its aims in the strategic bombing war should have been a warning that there were indeed limits to airpower utilizing conventional munitions. Unfortunately the U.S. military did not take this lesson to heart, as will be seen in the next two chapters.

Chapter Eight

From the Double Defeat on the Chongchon to the Recovery of Seoul

Background of Defeat

This chapter covers what is arguably the most shocking defeat in U.S. military history. Many of the clashes of arms depicted in this book where American forces suffered a reverse occurred when the enemy force had superior numbers. In others, the opponent had a qualitative advantage such as command of the sea, a higher level of professionalism and training, and technological superiority of weapon systems. However, in late 1950 in northern Korea, a Chinese army attacked a larger, better equipped U.S.-led force that held a massive advantage in armor, artillery, airpower, and naval strength. Nevertheless, the determined and resourceful Chinese achieved a decisive victory that triggered the longest retreat in U.S. military history.

This campaign took place during what was supposed to be the successful conclusion of a war that had broken out in June 1950 when the Korean People's Army (KPA) of the Communist government in North Korea attacked and overwhelmed the Republic of Korea (ROK) military of the American-supported state in the South. President Harry Truman chose to oppose this aggression and General Douglas MacArthur, overseeing the occupation forces in Japan, was placed in command of the effort to push back the Communist invaders. Elements of the Eighth Army were rushed across the narrow sea distance to Korea and pushed into the fight. Due to poor training, a lack of equipment including a dearth of antitank weapons, and being dramatically outnumbered, the Americans were routed by the KPA.[1] However, as reinforcements poured into Korea an armed perimeter was established around the southern port of Pusan by early August. (The English spelling of the city was changed to "Busan" in the year 2000.) The United States–led UN force began to degrade the increasingly outnumbered KPA with airstrikes on its extended supply lines.

MacArthur then achieved the greatest victory of his career with the risky amphibious landing at the port of Inchon adjacent to the ROK capital city of Seoul. The KPA position was unhinged and its men began a headlong flight back to North Korea with hundreds of thousands of UN soldiers in hot pursuit. Truman wished to end the war quickly without antagonizing the Soviets or the communist Peoples' Republic of China (PRC). However, he accepted MacArthur's advice and ordered the UN command to advance into North Korea and destroy the KPA. The president did take the precaution of having the Joint Chiefs of Staff (JCS) order that only ROK divisions be used in the provinces along the borders with the PRC and USSR, and ensure that U.S. airstrikes did not accidentally hit targets in those larger communist nations.

As the elements of the 400,000-man UN force crossed over the border into North Korea, the PRC's dictatorial government run by Mao Zedong began to issue ever-more aggressive statements that it would soon have to enter the conflict.[2] The Chinese Communists saw themselves as heirs to their nation's traditional zone of regional power in Asia, which included the Korean peninsula. In addition, the Japanese had invaded China via Korea and Formosa (now Taiwan) in the 1930s in a brutal war that led to the deaths of millions. With the United States now invading North Korea and supporting the opposition Chinese Nationalist Kuomintang Party (KMT) in Formosa, Mao and other senior members of his government were concerned that history was repeating itself. To forestall an attack on China, the PRC leaders decided they must stage an offensive so that this next war would take place on foreign rather than

Chinese soil. Lacking a navy to attack Formosa, Mao was left with the option of ordering preparations for a military intervention in Korea.

The Chinese realized that their backward military would be at a disadvantage against an American-led force that controlled the air and the seas and was equipped with heavy field artillery and tanks. However, Mao and his generals believed they could win as:

1. They had fought successfully from 1927 to 1949 against opponents who had air superiority (the Japanese and the KMT).
2. They believed they could bring larger forces to bear at the point of attack.
3. The Chinese would be only focused on one front while the United States had major military commitments in Europe and elsewhere around the globe.
4. The UN force would be operating at the end of long supply lines that stretched back all the way across the Pacific to the American West Coast.
5. The United States would not use atomic weapons, as doing so would inflame world opinion.
6. A fight against an opponent with superior firepower could be won if the Chinese avoided frontal attacks and engaged in infiltration tactics designed to outflank UN forces and cut supply lines.[3]

The Truman Administration became increasingly alarmed by the bellicose warnings being issued by the Chinese Communists. MacArthur had rebuffed several invitations from the president to visit him in the United States in previous years due to the general being "too busy" but Truman now decided he needed to meet with his field commander in person. MacArthur claimed he did not have time to travel to San Francisco or even Honolulu so a compromise was made to hold a conference on tiny Wake Island in the middle of the Pacific. When the two men met there on October 15, 1950, Truman asked how much concern should he have regarding Chinese threats that they would intervene in the war. MacArthur's reply was as follows:

> *Very little. Had they interfered in the first or second months it would have been decisive. We are no longer fearful of their intervention. We no longer stand hat in hand. The Chinese have 300,000 men in Manchuria. Of these probably not more than 100–115,000 are distributed along the Yalu River. Only 50–60,000 could be gotten across the Yalu River. They have no Air Force. Now that we have bases for our Air Force in Korea if the Chinese tried to get down to Pyongyang there would be the greatest slaughter.*[4]

However, despite these assurances, while MacArthur was speaking, Mao had already given his orders to intervene. Chinese troops commanded by General Peng Dehuai, designated the People's Volunteer Army (PVA), began crossing into North Korea during the night of October 16. Soon four full field armies had crossed the Yalu.[5] Moving only during the hours of darkness and hiding in wooded areas during the day, PVA forces remained undetected by U.S. Air Force reconnaissance flights and, as the Chinese possessed few field radios, there was little signals intelligence for the Americans to intercept. Mao's forces took up positions in the rugged mountains in the far north of Korea and readied themselves to attack the advancing UN army. They did not have to wait long.

THE DEFEAT

After the conference on Wake Island, MacArthur prepared for a final drive to complete the conquest of North Korea and end the war. We know that he wished to be the Republican Party's nominee for president in 1952 and likely hoped that a final victory in Korea would propel him to the White House. In the west of the peninsula, the Eighth Army was commanded by General Walton Walker, a pugnacious former corps commander in General George Patton's Third Army in World War II. By late October 1950, his forces had reached the Chongchon River, which flows roughly parallel and about 30 miles south of the Yalu River that forms the border with the PRC. In the east, pushing up the coast on the other side of the mountain range spine of Korea, the smaller X Corps was commanded by MacArthur's chief of staff, General Ned Almond. MacArthur thought it would be a simple matter of advancing to the Yalu, defeating the 50,000 or so remaining KPA soldiers in the area, uniting the two Koreas, and bringing the conflict to a successful close.

However, the Eighth Army was low on supplies and its advance was only still possible due to an emergency airlift that provided the force with a minimal reserve of fuel and ammunition. Possibly due to this, and a desire to quickly reach the Yalu, MacArthur issued new orders to his field commanders on October 17: U.S. units would join ROK troops in the final advance. The JCS in Washington immediately objected and asked why their clear instructions to only deploy South Korean forces in the region along the Chinese border had been ignored. MacArthur replied that sending U.S. troops forward was a matter of military necessity, that his orders gave him the latitude to do so, and that he had cleared this change with President Truman at Wake Island.[6] Despite existing transcripts of that meeting not mentioning this subject, the JCS abdicated its responsibility and allowed the advance to continue.

As the UN command moved north of the Chongchon, units were increasingly separated from each other as they advanced along roads running along the floors of valleys that wound toward the border. This would not have been a problem had the opponent only been remnants of the KPA. However, still undetected, Chinese troops had positioned themselves on the high ground dominating these routes. Eighth Army forces first encountered PVA troops on October 25 in steep terrain east of the town of Onjong, about halfway between the Chongchon and the Yalu. The ROK II Corps was ambushed, suffered large losses of men and equipment, and retreated southward in disarray. This exposed the center of the Eighth Army, which the Chinese immediately attacked on its right flank.

In the resulting Battle of Unsan, three PVA divisions enveloped the U.S. 1st Cavalry Division and an ROK regiment. The UN forces were defeated and the cavalrymen were routed and forced back with heavy casualties. General Walker ordered a general retreat of his army to the south bank of the Chongchon on November 3, and PVA pursuit was slowed by American air and artillery strikes. Nevertheless, elements of the U.S. 24th Division were also subsequently defeated and forced back when attacked on the night of November 4. The Chinese were finally stopped over the next two days from reaching the Chongchon by a spirited stand made by the 27th British Commonwealth Brigade. In the east, X Corps also came under attack by three PVA divisions but was not as badly mauled as the Eighth Army. Mao was elated with the initial successes, but his "volunteers" were running low on food and ammunition. General Peng ordered an end to what the Chinese call the First Phase Offensive and the PVA broke contact and retreated back north into the mountains.[7]

MacArthur at first refused to believe that his forces were being attacked by anything more than the remnants of the KPA. Even after both the Eighth Army and X Corps captured Chinese soldiers who willingly related to which divisions and armies they belonged, the general informed the JCS on November 4 that only a small number of Chinese had slipped over the Yalu to join the fighting.[8] However, by November 6, MacArthur's cables from his headquarters in Tokyo took on a much more urgent tone and reported, "men and material in large forces are pouring across all bridges over the Yalu from Manchuria . . . This movement threatens the ultimate destruction of the forces under my command."[9]

As the PVA pulled back and the fighting died out, the British and some in Washington suggested that UN forces pull back to the narrow "neck" of Korea leaving the far north as a buffer zone. If such a line had been held, the vast majority of the peninsula's citizens, arable land, and industry would then have remained under control of the ROK government, leaving the Communists only the sparely populated mountainous region along the Chinese border. MacArthur disagreed vehemently with this proposed policy and argued it to be dangerous appeasement. As quiet prevailed along the front line, he once again became optimistic, convinced himself that the Chinese had not intervened in significant numbers, and that they had returned to the far side of the border. On November 9, MacArthur cabled the JCS:

> *I plan to launch my attack for this purpose on or about November 15th with the mission of driving to the border and securing all of*

> *North Korea. Any program short of this would completely destroy the morale of my forces and the psychological consequences would be inestimable. It would condemn us to an indefinite retention of our military forces along difficult defense lines in North Korea and would unquestionably arouse such resentment among the South Koreans that their forces would collapse or might even turn against us . . . To give up any portion of North Korea to the aggression of the Chinese Communists would be the greatest defeat of the free world in recent times. Indeed to yield to so immoral a proposition would bankrupt our leadership and influence in Asia and render untenable our position both politically and militarily.*[10]

There was great unease among the military and political establishment in Washington regarding the proposed strategy, but the general's standing was so great after the victory at Inchon that few spoke up against the renewal of the offensive. Military intelligence in Tokyo also revealed a large buildup of Chinese troops in northern Korea but this was dismissed by MacArthur. Thus, on November 24, MacArthur flew to Anju on the southern bank of the Chongchon to personally launch what became known as the "Home by Christmas Offensive." In sub-zero temperatures of the Korean winter, UN forces all along the front began to advance toward the Yalu. They did not get far.

MacArthur and Almond (in his joint role of chief of staff of the UN force and commander of X Corps) both expected an easy victory. In contrast, General Walker had reservations. He worried that the Chinese were massing for attack and had his staff draw up plans for a retreat. General Oliver Smith, commanding the 1st Marine Division in the east, had similar concerns, made sure his men took high points above valley roads, and set up a forward airfield where supplies could be landed and wounded evacuated. This slow pace triggered rebukes from Almond who urged a rapid advance. At one point the X Corps commander told a group of U.S. Army officers at the front, "The enemy who is delaying you for the moment is nothing more than remnants of Chinese divisions fleeing north. . . . We're still attacking and we're going all the way to the Yalu. Don't let a bunch of Chinese laundrymen stop you."[11]

Mao had already decided to defend the terrain north of the Chongchon. He expected MacArthur to send only reconnaissance units back into the area but hoped for a general advance. The Chinese leader had earlier radioed orders to his field commanders, "If resistance is on a small scale, the Volunteers will surely annihilate the enemy; but if it is heavy, withdraw and suck the enemy into a trap. Then the enemy can be destroyed by our main forces."[12] Unfortunately for the UN forces, they marched right into one of the largest ambushes in world history.

The PVA's Second Phase Offensive began on the night of November 25. Again ROK forces on the Eighth Army's right flank were overrun. Many units were surrounded and wiped out while others were able to break through a series of roadblocks set up in their rear. The U.S. 2nd Infantry Division and a brigade of Turks were hit next and routed with the American formation suffering 20 percent casualties and losing much of its heavy equipment. Walker put his plans for a phased retreat into action but "bug-out fever" took hold and soon most of the Eighth Army was fleeing southward as fast as it could travel over the North's poor road network.

In the east, X Corps also came under severe attack. Again, PVA units not only engaged in frontal and flank attacks, but Chinese soldiers hiked off-road to establish roadblocks in the American rear, which cut off supplies and unnerved the men at the front. The U.S. 7th Infantry Division and the 1st Marine Division around the Chosin Reservoir were surrounded, under heavy attack, and suffering significant casualties. Their only chance to avoid complete destruction was a fighting retreat in brutal winter weather in an attempt to break out of the trap in which they found themselves.

To the west, UN forces utilized their motorized transport to retreat faster than the PVA could pursue on foot. For a short time in early December, the Eighth Army held at the North Korean capital of Pyongyang on the Taedong River. Walker decided that he needed to pull his UN force back further as it was demoralized, it was unable to stop a Chinese advance on the eastern flank, several units were too damaged to fight effectively, and there were reports of enemy roadblocks being set up to the south. On December 5, Pyongyang was abandoned, hundreds of thousands of Korean refugees fled south before the bridges across

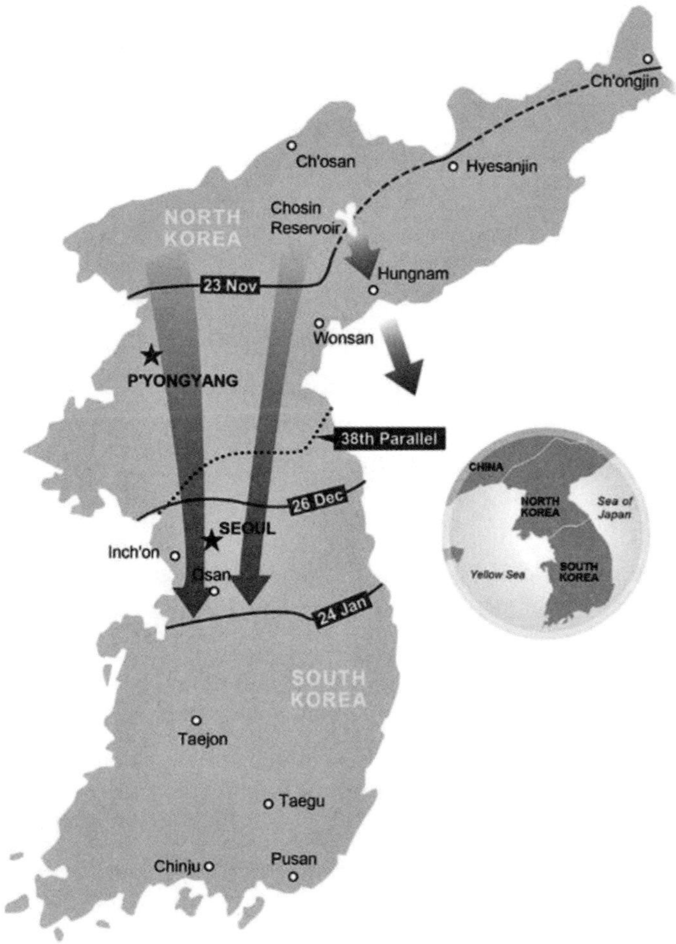

The Chinese intervention and the rout of the UN command.
U.S. ARMY SPECIAL OPERATIONS FORCES

the Taedong were blown, and much of the city burned along with huge stocks of supplies and weapons that could not be loaded onto rail cars or trucks in time. By Christmas, the Eighth Army had withdrawn most of the way back to the old border between the two Koreas.

On the other side of the mountains in the west, the 1st Marine Division led the remnants of X Corps in a courageous fighting retreat from the Chosin Reservoir to the coastal port city of Hungnam by

December 11. Over the course of the next two weeks a defensive perimeter was maintained while the UN forces and 100,000 civilians were evacuated by the U.S. Navy to Pusan. As at Pyongyang, large depots of supplies were destroyed and much of Hungnam was razed and left burning. Elements of X Corps were soon rushed by land to the front line and integrated into the Eighth Army.

The withdrawal from North Korea represented the longest retreat in U.S. military history. Casualties were heavy and morale was shattered in many units. To cap off the string of bad news, General Walker was killed in a jeep crash on December 23, and the UN force was suddenly left without its experienced field commander. As the PVA advanced south toward Seoul, the defeat of the American-led UN force in Korea had clearly become a strategic disaster.

Recovery

MacArthur communicated to Washington that he was hopelessly outnumbered and outclassed by the Chinese invaders. He pleaded with the JCS to send him U.S. reinforcements and KMT soldiers from Formosa, along with atomic weapons under his tactical control that would be dropped on both northern Korea and across the border in Manchuria. MacArthur argued that without these resources the UN military force should be evacuated from Korea or it would be wiped out. In addition, he urged that the war be expanded, Chinese cities should be bombed and its ports blockaded.[13]

These requests were denied as Truman and the majority of the members of the JCS were opposed to such an enlargement of the conflict or a withdrawal from the peninsula. In light of the PVA intervention, the president adjusted his war aims to that of securing the old borders of the ROK and giving up on reuniting the peninsula under a non-communist government. He wished to contain the conflict to Korea so as to reserve American and Allied strength for countering the Soviet Union in Europe. In addition, while Truman did threaten the use of atomic weapons in a press conference, Mao was correct that the United States was unlikely to use them unless its own territory or that of a core ally was at risk. MacArthur scoffed at this set of policies and believed it reeked of "defeatism" and a "lack of will to win."[14] One of his favorite sayings was "There is no substitute for victory," and he did not accept that his nation would be willing to accept anything less than a complete triumph in a regional conflict even if achieving it triggered a nuclear World War III.

Luckily, the key to a victory with conventional arms on the Korean peninsula was already at hand. The new commander of the Eighth Army, General Matthew Ridgway, arrived in Tokyo on Christmas Day. An airborne divisional and then corps commander in Europe in World War II, he was used to being aggressive and finding a way to achieve a mission with limited resources. Despite all signs pointing to doom for the UN force in Korea, Ridgway was upbeat when he met with MacArthur, the theater commander. Surprisingly, the newly arrived general asked for and received permission to go on the offensive if conditions were favorable.

Despite the brutal double defeat of the UN command north of the Chongchon, the situation was not nearly so dire as the lengthy subsequent retreat implied. Despite an impression conveyed by the American press of Chinese engaging in unrelenting "human wave" attacks overwhelming defensive lines, the UN force was actually larger than that of the PVA and its KPA allies. At the start of the Second Phase Offensive, MacArthur had more than 550,000 men under his command. The largest components were 224,000 ROK troops, 178,000 U.S. ground forces, 75,000 U.S. naval personnel, and 55,000 from the Air Force.[15] In contrast, Mao had committed slightly more than 300,000 men of the Ninth and Thirteenth Army Groups assisted by around 100,000 remaining members of the KPA (though many of the latter were engaged as guerrillas well south of the main battle lines).[16] The UN advantage in numbers only grew over the course of December as the PVA suffered more casualties due to both combat wounds and frostbite injuries as the front line moved south.

In addition to this quantitative advantage, the American-led force also held significant qualitative superiorities. While a small number of modern MiG-15s with North Korean markings flown by Soviet pilots had made their appearance over the far north of Korea by the end of 1950, hundreds of U.S. aircraft dominated the skies over the battlefield. Along the coasts, the U.S. Navy was unchallenged. On land, the UN force was mostly mechanized compared to the PVA, which was propelled by foot and supplied by pack animals. The Chinese were also massively outgunned, with only light artillery and no armored vehicles. In contrast the UN force had several hundred tanks (primarily Shermans, Pattons, and Pershings) and a similar number of heavy artillery pieces (105mm and 155mm howitzers). Also, as the Eighth Army retreated, its lines of supply from the ports of Inchon and Pusan compressed. This was in stark contrast to those of the PVA that became ever more stretched and increasingly degraded by interdiction attacks from U.S. aircraft and artillery.

Ridgway's first order of business was to instill an aggressive sense of mission into the demoralized Eighth Army ranks. He replaced overly cautious and defensive-minded commanders and insisted the remainder spend more time near the front lines. He demanded active patrolling to find and maintain contact with the enemy and expected plans to be drawn up to go on the offensive. To the men in the ranks, Ridgway became known as "old iron tits" due to the live grenade and the metal first aid kit he wore on the front straps of his uniform. Such accoutrement were not just for show: As commander of the XVIII Airborne Corps in March of 1945, the general had jumped into Germany with his troops and was wounded in the shoulder by an enemy grenade. Ridgway's bearing, demand for aggressive action, and even his "iron tits" made it clear that the Eighth Army was in Korea to fight and win.

Of course the PVA gave the UN force little time to recover. Despite his forces being low on supplies and worn down from a month of fighting and advancing hundreds of miles on foot in sub-zero temperatures, Mao launched his Third Phase Offensive on December 31, 1950. He hoped to crack the Eighth Army's defensive line, push into South Korea, and potentially force the United States to evacuate the peninsula. PVA forces once again initially struck ROK forces and forced the 1st, 2nd, 5th, and 6th ROK Infantry Divisions to retreat. As the Chinese advanced, they crossed the 38th Parallel, which had divided the two Koreas and threatened to pin the Eighth Army around Seoul. On January 3, Ridgway gave the order to abandon the capital city and withdraw to "Line D" a bit more than 20 miles farther south.

Despite the UN force giving up ground, the PVA and KPA suffered significantly greater casualties. They were also exhausted and low on supplies. After only a week of fighting, the advance was called off after the capture of Seoul. Mao accepted his generals' advice and ordered a halt for two to three months while his forces rested and were resupplied in preparation for a decisive offensive to Pusan in the spring.

While Ridgway was not pleased with the performance of individual units in the retreat, he had come to believe that his force could hold against the Chinese. On January 3 he cabled Army Chief of Staff General J. Lawton Collins, "We shall be in for some difficult days but I am completely confident of the ability of the Eighth Army to accomplish every mission assigned."[17] A week later he followed this up with, "The power is here. The strength and means we have—short perhaps of Soviet military intervention."[18]

In contrast, MacArthur remained pessimistic. He believed that without significant reinforcements and the initiation of a bombing campaign against China, the Eighth Army would be destroyed if it attempted to hold its ground in Korea. On January 10, he reported to Washington that his troops were tired out, and the morale of his force of "insufficient strength" was poor. He continued, "Under these conditions in the absence of overriding political considerations the command should be withdrawn from the Peninsula just as rapidly as it is tactically feasible to do so . . . As I have pointed out before, under the extraordinary limitations and conditions imposed upon the command in Korea, its military position in Korea is untenable, but it can hold for any length of time up to its complete destruction, if overriding political considerations so dictate."[19]

Clearly only one of these two U.S. generals was correct. Either the UN force was strong enough to hold in Korea or it was too weak and would be defeated. The Chinese were about to find out the answer.

Victory

In retrospect the successful American shift to offensive victories in the first half of 1951 is one of the most impressive in U.S. military history. After other strategic defeats, the nation had tapped its large industrial base and population reserves to reinforce the armies at the front. In contrast, Ridgway received little in the way of new fighting units and had to find a way to stop the PVA advance with what he had on hand. He later related that he took inspiration from methods the Germans used to hold their front line to the west of Moscow as winter descended in 1941 and the Soviets launched a massive offensive. Immediately after arriving in Korea he determined the change in tactics required to stop and then push back the Chinese:

> *I knew well enough that our forces were too thin to man a solid line across the peninsula, yet I saw no reason why these could not be mutually supporting, division-to-division and corps-to-corps. Our howitzers had a range of several miles, so that in many cases each unit could support the next to a considerable extent, and the units on the flanks, particularly, could tie in together well enough to offer each other some artillery support when it was needed . . . [O]ur armor was far superior now and we had control of the air. We lacked the manpower to halt the night attacks. But by buttoning up tight, unit by unit, at night and counterattacking strongly with armor and infantry teams, during the day, we had an excellent opportunity to deal out severe punishment to the hostile forces that had advanced through the gaps in our line.*[20]

Ridgway began to implement his counteroffensive on January 15 with a mission designed primarily to find enemy concentrations and destroy them while also seizing defendable territory. The movement kicked off with a reconnaissance in force by the 25th Division to probe toward the city of Suwon. Known as Operation Wolfhound, this limited advance was quite successful and inflicted more than 1,000 casualties on the enemy in return for only a handful suffered by the Americans. A series of subsequent probes pushed the front line northward. The resting PVA armies were clearly not expecting the UN forces to go on the offensive and Ridgway took advantage of this when he launched a general advance with Operation Thunderbolt on January 25. The Eighth Army methodically moved north to retake the port of Inchon, Kimpo airport, and the banks of the Han River across from Seoul in the west. In the east, the advance took Wonju and Hoengsong. This triggered a response from the PVA and culminated in the Battle of the Twin Tunnels in which a U.S. regiment and a French battalion, assisted by artillery and airpower, defeated an entire enemy division and inflicted dramatically higher casualties.

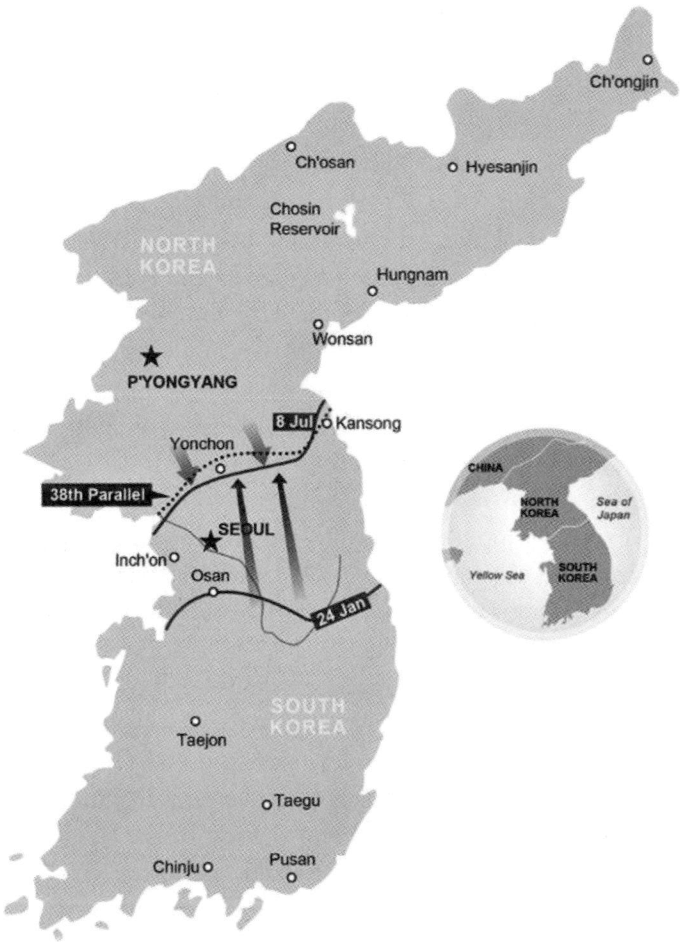

Ridgway's counteroffensive drives back the Chinese.
U.S. ARMY SPECIAL OPERATIONS FORCES

Despite being overextended and worn down, the Chinese attempted to regain the initiative in the east with the Fourth Phase Campaign, which was defeated at the Battle of Chipyong-ni over February 13–15. U.S. troop morale rose on the back of this victory, and Ridgway kept up the pressure with the launch of Operation Killer on February 20. While this name caused some consternation in Washington when it was proposed due to how it would be received by the press, the general kept the designation, which clearly communicated the objective to the men of the Eighth Army. The offensive took territory to the east of Seoul, while killing upwards of 8,000 PVA and NPA troops, which was an order of magnitude greater than UN losses.[21]

Next came the decisive Operation Ripper in early March, which pushed across the Han River, retook Seoul, and forced the Communists to retreat northward all along the front line back toward the 38th Parallel. Once again casualties were much higher on the PVA side, primarily inflicted by artillery and airstrikes. The UN force continued to make incremental advances over the next month, but intelligence detected large reinforcements moving into the area and the Chinese preparing to launch a major spring offensive. This Fifth Phase Offensive, utilizing 700,000 of the PVA and more than 100,000 KPA, began on April 22. For the first time in the war, Mao was able to equip his forces with heavy Soviet equipment including long-range artillery, multiple rocket launchers, and four regiments of T-34 tanks. The PVA gained ground and pushed the front line south but was unable to recapture Seoul while suffering tens of thousands of casualties, which was multiples of that incurred by the UN forces.[22] As the Chinese armies became exhausted, they were counterattacked in late May and lost all the territory they had gained. It was the last significant attempt by the PVA to eject the UN force from Korea. Both sides constructed progressively complex entrenchments and the front lines became increasingly static for the rest of the conflict.

This great recovery on the battlefield orchestrated by General Ridgway is barely remembered today in the United States. This despite the fact that in a short period of time the Eighth Army shifted from abject defeat and likely evacuation from Korea to a hard-won advance. Ridgway does not even make the list in a Gallup poll conducted in America in 2000 of the greatest military leaders in our history.[23] There are likely several reasons for this. Few of MacArthur's field commanders became household names as the "American Caesar" dominated the limelight wherever he went. In addition, the Eighth Army counterattack took place against the backdrop of MacArthur's increasingly dramatic public feud with Truman regarding the direction of foreign policy. The general wanted a victory in Korea at almost any price. The president wanted to avoid starting World War III. MacArthur was fired in April 1951 after he intentionally sabotaged Truman's plan to end the war with a ceasefire proposal. The resulting political fight in Washington first swung in the general's favor, but the president ultimately prevailed after MacArthur was repudiated by senior military leaders such as Generals Omar Bradley, George Marshall, and Hoyt Vandenberg. Finally, Ridgway's success is not celebrated and barely remembered today. While the defeat of the PVA and recovery of Seoul were indeed great victories, the Korean War did not end in the sort of decisive triumph the U.S. public had become accustomed to with the peninsula remaining divided to this day.

Causes of Defeat

The double defeat of the UN force in its two attempts to advance north to the Yalu River was one of the most shocking military victories in history. A relatively untrained army, in many ways less well equipped than a comparably sized force fighting on the Western Front in World War I, handily defeated a larger, battle-hardened coalition employing the most advanced World War II weaponry designed by the world's premier technological power. It is arguably the most embarrassing defeat in American military history and thus one we tend to try to forget or even lie about so as to distort the actual events that occurred.

Some great battlefield events are due to luck: a search plane that somehow misses spotting an enemy fleet, a general's orders wrapped in a few cigars that fall out of a horseman's saddlebag, etc. However, the events in far northern Korea at the end of 1950 had nothing to do with luck. The defeat was caused as much by poor leadership on the U.S. side as brilliant strategic and tactical execution by the Chinese. Much of the blame can be placed on the shoulders of General MacArthur. As in Luzon in 1941, he willfully refused to consider what a potential enemy could do and rather focused on what he wanted it to do despite repeated threats of an imminent attack issued by that potential enemy. MacArthur compounded this error by actively dividing his force, ordering disparate columns to advance northward along the floors of narrow valleys, and failed to send smaller units ahead to reconnoiter. As UN detachments moved north, they could not support each other and had only one route for potential retreat. That a seasoned general would commit such a series of errors is surprising. That he repeated them twice in rapid succession is difficult to fathom.

While Mao's generals organized the PVA to intervene in Korea, they knew that their forces were in no way properly prepared to fight the Americans. First of all, there was reasonable concern regarding how the Chinese could stand and fight the UN juggernaut pushing north for the Yalu. Mao's soldiers had never had to confront the sort of firepower the Eighth Army possessed, some had only limited experience in battle, and a significant percentage had been part of KMT nationalist units only a couple of years previously before they chose to surrender and change sides in the Chinese Civil War.

Supplying the force was a major problem as well. Approximately a third of the men who marched south of the Yalu did not even have rifles and were armed only with grenades. Their assignment was to sneak up close enough to enemy positions, throw their munitions, and then pick up weapons from fallen comrades after the battle commenced. The PVA had no armor in 1950 and what little artillery it had was composed of guns that could be carried by a man or on a horse's back. There were no trucks or aircraft to bring ammunition and food supplies to the front. Everything had to be transported by foot through the snow-clad mountains. While the PVA had a small number of modern Soviet weapons, most of what it brought to the battlefield was surplus Japanese and American gear captured at the end of World War II or the Chinese Civil War. Stalin had promised to provide significant Soviet air support over Korea to the intervention forces, but backed out of this commitment at the last moment. Instead his air force primarily limited its operations to the skies over China itself while beginning to transfer a small number of modern aircraft to the PRC.

Thus, not only would the PVA be outnumbered, its divisions entering northern Korea in late 1950 had significantly less firepower than a similar unit conducting operations in France in World War I: The Chinese had fewer rifles and artillery guns along with a dearth of wheeled transport and longer supply lines. In contrast, MacArthur's mechanized force possessed more than a thousand tanks, hundreds of heavy artillery guns, and overhead support from a fleet of B-29s and F-80 jet fighter-bombers. How could the Chinese successfully defeat such a technologically advanced foe?

The PRC began with ideological preparation of its men for the necessity of the intervention south of the Yalu, spreading slogans and instilling in them the importance of halting the "imperialist" Americans in Korea before they could invade China. The men also engaged in drills to deal with attack from the sky and practiced night movements that would hide them from American aircraft. Veterans of World War II who had worked with U.S. forces in Burma and China were brought in to lecture ground units on the American mindset and doctrine of warfare.

The PVA planned to engage in tactics designed to minimize the UN force's superiority in firepower:

1. The "volunteers" would only travel at night and sleep under cover and remain motionless during daylight hours so as to remain undetected by U.S. reconnaissance flights.
2. The lack of mechanized mobility would be turned into an asset by forcing the PVA units to move off the roads in the rugged terrain of northern Korea. As the UN forces were tied to their wheeled transport, this ceded the high ground to an opponent willing to climb and carry their weapons and supplies.
3. Once near to the front line, Chinese units would attempt to advance undetected after nightfall and, whenever possible, infiltrate or flow along the flanks of UN positions.
4. PVA forces would attempt to advance quietly to within grenade-throwing range. Not only would this allow a large number of Mao's soldiers who did not have rifles to join in the attack, but would also preclude U.S. and ROK commanders calling in artillery and air strikes or risk hitting their own men. Due to the imbalance in firepower and range of weapon systems, compact groups of fifty to one hundred PVA soldiers would rush the final remaining yards to close with UN forces and attempt to defeat them in short-range or even hand-to-hand fighting.

5. These tactics of short night advances would also mitigate the PVA's lack of radio communication to direct forces across the battlefield. Instead, such close-quarters attacks could be coordinated with traditional and inexpensive communications mediums such as horns, gongs, and small drums.
6. In addition to frontal and flanking attacks, Chinese units would also attempt to infiltrate behind UN lines whenever possible to set up roadblocks to the rear. Thinking they were surrounded, MacArthur's troops would be unnerved, and the flow of supplies to the front could be interdicted so as to quickly mitigate the firepower disadvantage of the more lightly armed PVA.

When the PVA launched its first two offensives in November and December 1951, they were uniformly successful all along the front line. These night movement and attack tactics shocked and surprised the UN forces. Chinese troops infiltrating into Eighth Army front lines to engage in hand-to-hand combat sparked the incorrect assessment that the PVA was a "horde" and employing "human-wave" attacks. Of course this was incorrect and in many ways was the opposite of the actual Chinese tactics that were so successful.

How could such a "primitive" force as the PVA best the vaunted U.S. military so effectively? Part of the reason is surely due to the differences in the tactics employed by Mao's men. Many officers in the Eighth Army and X Corps had recent experience in defeating the German and Japanese military in World War II. However, these two enemies had generally fought on the defensive in 1944–1945 and while usually possessing less firepower, had utilized similar weapon systems as American forces including heavy machine guns, artillery, and tanks. While the Germans were ruthless in mounting counterattacks after giving ground, their battle doctrine was generally very different from the night infiltration attacks employed by the PVA. The Japanese did engage in "banzai" charges at night against U.S. positions; however, these were often head-on attacks or simply the final act of a spent defensive force after the majority of its meticulously prepared and interlocking field-of-fire fortifications had been reduced and overrun. The KPA, trained by the Soviets, which had recently been bested by the UN coalition, also had a similar doctrine of attack that was not dominated by nighttime operations and utilized artillery and armor.

A fair explanation of the defeat of the U.S.-led army in northern Korea is multifaceted but can best be summed up as a combination of poor planning, underestimation of the enemy, and risky deployment of forces on the UN side, which was the exact opposite of the excellent preparation, choice of tactics, and patience employed by the PVA.

Causes of Victory

Ridgway was yet another in the long line of American military leaders who have somehow arrived on the scene at just the right moment after a blistering defeat. Occasionally, a U.S. commander has been able to recover from a reverse on the battlefield, adopt new tactics, and win. More often, a replacement has been required to embrace change and achieve victory. From Greene to Grant to Nimitz to Doolittle, American history is replete with examples of a commander with the right training and temperament taking over at the front to turn the tide after strategic defeats.

In none of these instances was it solely the decisions of the commander on the ground that resulted in an American victory, but Ridgway's character and training contained some specific elements that made him particularly well suited for the job of stabilizing the line in Korea. Most important was his background in leading airborne formations. Such leaders are inherently those who are mentally prepared to be flexible and win with what they have on hand: Units dropped into combat are necessarily lightly equipped, forced to deal with rapidly evolving tactical situations, and likely to confront a larger enemy force that must be overcome to achieve a set of mission goals.

The front line in Korea of 1951 that Ridgway took over was certainly a chaotic situation as the U.S. forces dominating the UN coalition had been beaten back by a new enemy utilizing novel tactics. The theater commander (MacArthur) reported to Washington that the morale of his men was broken and the options he offered were either utilizing atomic weapons, or preparing for an evacuation from the peninsula. In contrast, Ridgway looked for a way to win with what he already had on the ground. He quickly realized that the suite of tactics required for victory rested on a foundation of getting the Eighth Army back onto the offensive and making effective use of the dramatically greater firepower possessed by the UN forces. Specifically he decided that:

1. While every infiltration effort by the PVA could not be defeated, it was imperative to build a solid defensive front and have his units "button up tight" to maintain their integrity during the hours of darkness. Heavy counterattacks could then be mounted using the combined arms of infantry, armor, artillery, and airpower during daylight.
2. If the enemy could leave the roads and make difficult climbs to rugged high ground, so could the U.S. and ROK troops. UN forces would also engage in active patrolling to find and fix PVA and KPA formations so as to call in the overwhelming firepower needed to destroy them.
3. While Chinese manpower committed to the war was certainly significant, it was not inexhaustible and only maintained along a tenuous line of supply. Maintaining contact with the PVA so it could be forced to fight in the open when challenged in daylight hours represented an opportunity to inflict dramatically lopsided casualties on the enemy through the use of heavy artillery and airpower over the battlefield.
4. Taking ground in and of itself was not the object but rather inflicting outsized attritional losses on the enemy. The Eighth Army also needed to be willing to retreat when necessary to defendable lines of terrain. Subsequent advances would only take place when, "it might facilitate destruction of enemy forces and the protection of our own."[24] Even in these situations, the front would be pushed northward only as far as the next position that could be turned into a solid defensive line.

To execute on these tactics, Ridgway believed it was imperative to reinvigorate the morale and fighting spirit of soldiers in the UN command fighting through that terrible winter in Korea. While all successful military leaders need to mentally prepare their ranks for combat, there is a particular challenge of motivating men to jump out of a perfectly good airplane into enemy fire. As a former airborne commander, Ridgway was particularly well attuned to managing the outlook of the men who served under him. His bearing, frequent visits to the front, forced changes in command staff, demand for active patrolling, and requirement that formations prepare to take the offensive all paid off quickly. A proclamation was released across the front explaining to U.S. soldiers exactly why they were fighting in Korea and how the democratic way of life in America was at stake. The general also placed a premium on improving the logistical flow of supplies getting to the front and, when possible, rotating units off the line to refit and rest before returning to the fight.

Morale also improved as units moved from passive defense to hiking to seize high ground and close with the enemy. As Ridgway later put it, "What I told the field commanders was that their infantry ancestors would roll over in their graves could they see how road-bound the army was, how often it forgot to seize the high ground along its route, how it failed to seek and maintain contact in its front, how little it knows of the terrain and how seldom it took advantage of it, how reluctant it was to get off its bloody wheels and put shoe leather to the earth, to get into the hills and among the scrub and meet the enemy where he lived."[25]

While Ridgway took his army over to the offensive, he also accepted the political imperative from his superiors that the war remain contained to Korea and not spread to the rest of Asia. He did not focus on driving the Chinese out of the peninsula, but rather the limited goal of restoring the territorial integrity of South Korea and wearing down the Communists' ability to continue the fighting. Attempting to win only a partial victory was anathema to MacArthur, but critical and realistic in the early days of the Cold War when America's allies in Europe were still recovering from World War II and unable to provide much support to any attempt to contain a Red Army advance westward from the USSR.

Of course, more than seventy years after Ridgway's arrival, a large U.S. military force is still required along the 38th Parallel to support its ROK allies. While not the sort of complete victory the U.S. public had come to demand after a century of dictating the terms that concluded wars against the nation's enemies (Mexico, the Confederacy, Spain, Germany, Japan), the conclusion of the Korean War was still a strategic victory for American foreign policy. South Korea has recovered from the conflict to become a prosperous, successful, and dynamic democracy. The Cold War was successfully waged until the USSR finally imploded. While some questioned the wisdom of the decision, the cessation of the fighting in Korea eventually created the conditions under which the United States invited China to open its economy and begin trading with the West. This unleashed massive economic growth that has greatly benefited the living standards of both nations.

Impact of Defeat

The double defeat of the UN force along the Chongchon had major impacts on the postwar world that emerged from World War II that reverberate to this day. Most obviously, Mao's intervention in the conflict heated up the Cold War and made the ideological, economic, and military competition between the western democracies on one side and the USSR and its allies on the other that much more bitter. While friction between the anti-communist United States and Mao's newly established PRC government was inevitable, the massive bloodshed that took place in Korea from 1950 to 1953 hardened opinions on both sides for a generation. Such a reaction was inevitable as America suffered more than 150,000 casualties in the war, and many western sources believe Chinese casualties approached a catastrophic total of one million men killed, or wounded.[26] Soviet support for both the KPA and the PVA only increased the belief among many in the United States that the Communist bloc was a monolithic force bent on world domination.

Of course, the Korean people suffered the most from the late-1950 defeat of the UN coalition force. Hundreds of thousands of Koreans died in the extended conflict and much of the nation's infrastructure was reduced to rubble in the fighting that continued for another three bloody years. Had the Chinese not intervened, or had the UN army been able to blunt the PVA's offensives, civilian casualties would have been much lower and the destruction caused by the war would have been dramatically lessened. The Republic of Korea that emerged in the absence of a successful Chinese intervention would be a significantly larger, wealthier nation than the one we know today. Conversely in such a scenario, a commensurately smaller number of inmates would be living in grinding poverty in the North under the totalitarian rule of Kim Jong Un.

Further afield, Mao's decision to send his forces south of the Yalu also catalyzed fighting in other parts of Asia over the next two decades. While reverberations of the 1950 PVA offensive did not directly cause the Second Indochina War (1955–1975), it is likely that it made both U.S. direct intervention there and China's support to Hanoi more likely to take place. Similarly, civil wars in a great arc stretching across Southeast Asia from Laos to Cambodia, through Thailand, Malaysia, and Indonesia up to the Philippines were that much more violent due to PRC support of local communist insurgencies and American military aid to anti-communist regimes in those same nations. Millions died in these internal conflicts stoked by the mutual suspicion and implacable hatred the United States and China had for each other over a quarter of a century.

The Chinese victory in northern Korea in late 1950 also likely denied MacArthur the presidency. In a scenario where the PVA did not intervene, or the UN coalition successfully dug in along the neck of Korea in late November 1950, MacArthur would have been able to make a triumphant return to the United States. In such a scenario it is very likely that he would have been the one to end twenty years of Democratic control of the White House in the election of 1952 instead of Dwight Eisenhower. After all, even after MacArthur's terrible defeat by the Chinese and public feud with the Truman Administration, he still returned to a nation where he was greeted by massive enthusiastic crowds from San Francisco to Chicago to New York.

It is worth noting that the general had expressed interest and received significant support in becoming president as the GOP candidate in both 1944 and 1948. MacArthur's popularity was so great in the lead-up to the latter election that Truman feared that MacArthur would return from Japan and easily win the presidency. Truman's fears were so significant that he took the unprecedented step of meeting privately with Eisenhower (then the president of Columbia University) prior to the 1948 election and offered to serve once again as vice president if the World War II hero would be willing to run for the Democratic nomination at the top of the ticket.[27] Ike refused the offer, leaving the unpopular Truman to fend for himself in an uphill campaign. MacArthur believed he would be chosen by popular acclaim and elected to run for the presidency from his occupation headquarters in Japan. It was a decision that doomed his candidacy. New York governor Thomas Dewey won the GOP nomination, but then lost to Truman in the general election in one of the great upsets of U.S. political election history.

In a scenario where he was unsullied by a defeat by the Chinese and the subsequent public feud with Truman that led to his relief, MacArthur would likely have been the most popular man in America. With his retirement from the Army and return to the United States, a collection of Republican grandees led by Senator Henry Cabot Lodge would not have felt the need to organize a "Draft Eisenhower" movement, the strength of which convinced Ike to formally become a candidate. Dramatic differences in temperament between the two generals would have surely resulted in a MacArthur Administration that had dissimilar impacts on world history than the one presided over by Eisenhower. Consider just one example:

Historically, in 1954 when PRC-backed Viet Minh communist insurgents were tightening the siege of the French base at Dien Bien Phu in northern Vietnam, the U.S. ally begged Washington to send its B-29s in the Philippines on bombing missions to reduce pressure on the garrison. America was already financing upwards of 80 percent of the French war effort, and Secretary of State John Foster Dulles was in favor of intervening and even considered the use of tactical atomic weapons. President Eisenhower came under great pressure to act, but in the end chose not to do so. The Viet Minh scored a strategic victory at Dien Bien Phu, which led to French withdrawal and the partition of Vietnam.

A President MacArthur would have likely authorized airstrikes to support France in 1954. The general often argued that Asia was more important to America's future than Europe. In addition, after the defeat of his abandoned garrison in Bataan, he likely would have had sympathy for the French soldiers surrounded at Dien Bien Phu. While MacArthur historically warned against deploying American troops for use in a land war on the Asian mainland, he was a strong advocate of using American airpower, and even atomic weapons there to push back Chinese-supported communist movements in the region. Viet Minh forces were exhausted and close to mutiny by the end of the siege of Dien Bien Phu. Thus, it is logical to assume that the French garrison would have been saved had the United States sent squadrons of B-29s to drop tons of conventional munitions on Communist artillery and infantry positions in the area.[28] This certainly would have been the case if a President MacArthur deployed atomic weapons there. While a French victory at Dien Bien Phu might not have kept Ho Chi Minh from taking over northern Vietnam indefinitely, it certainly would have pushed back the founding in 1954 of the Democratic Republic of Vietnam with its capital in Hanoi and the later military struggle over South Vietnam that lasted until 1975.

Impact of Victory

While few remember the remarkable military recovery of U.S. arms in Korea in early 1951, it was truly of great significance in the second half of the twentieth century. Consider that in the absence of Ridgway finding a way to stabilize the UN line and lead a counterattack that regained Seoul, there would have been significant impacts down through history. If American troops had not found a way to halt their retreat south toward Pusan, would Truman have decided to follow through on his public threat to employ atomic bombs to halt the Chinese advance? Or, if not, would MacArthur's advice have been taken to evacuate Korea and pull back to Japan? Such a scenario would surely have weighed on America's psyche and had an impact on subsequent decision making: Would Washington's leaders have become more bellicose through the rest of the Cold War or more hesitant to deploy U.S. troops? Would containment have to be scrapped as a policy, and what would have been the impact of such a change? While barely remembered today, Ridgway's victory in Korea was a major hinge point in history.

Chapter Nine

Losing The War but Perhaps Winning the Fight: Vietnam, Afghanistan, and Iraq

Background of Defeats

The end of the fighting in Korea left many Americans unhappy and disgruntled. The intervention of the Chinese into the conflict at the end of 1950 was concurrent with the percentage of Americans disapproving of President Truman's performance rising above 50. It remained there for the rest of his term and contributed to his choice not to run for reelection in 1952.[1] It was only after Eisenhower entered office that an armistice was signed that locked the front line in place and solidified the partition of Korea that remains in place to this day. Americans asked themselves how it could be that their nation had failed to "win" a war? It also began a complex new era in U.S. military history in which it has (1) won the major battles, but (2) often suffered what appeared to be strategic defeats fighting insurgencies, (3) even as these conflicts took place against the backdrop of even larger struggles in which America has prevailed.

In the decades that followed the great victory of World War II, the verdict on success or failure of U.S. arms has become less clear. America's most violent clash of the Cold War in Vietnam ended in failure. However, the "dominos" of the strategic nations composing East Asia's first island chain did not fall and it was the USSR that eventually collapsed, handing the United States a comprehensive victory. Then, in a new conflict, the "Global War on Terror," Afghanistan was conquered at a shockingly low cost and Osama bin Laden subsequently killed.

However, Kabul is once again controlled by the Taliban and Al-Qaeda operates openly there. Saddam Hussein was ejected from Kuwait and later deposed and executed, but we withdrew from a fragile Iraq only to have to return to defeat ISIS. The result of this recent history is the emergence of two divergent narratives regarding the American military: Many view it as an inexorable juggernaut that has relentlessly overwhelmed one opponent after another across its history through sheer size of population and industrial might.[2] Others believe that image is badly outdated and that the armed services of the nation have become a colossus with feet of clay: unable to avoid scandal, communicate truthfully to the citizens of the country, and incapable of defeating even technologically backward foes. This mindset can be summed up with columnist Brent Stephens's recent conclusion in the *New York Times* that, "in the last 50 years, the United States has gotten good at losing wars."[3] The full story is that neither narrative is truly accurate.

Certainly the image of the United States as an overwhelming hegemonic military power is misplaced. The painful catalogue of defeats chronicled in this book is a testament to that fact. Our military started out as a decided underdog on the world stage in 1776, and the original thirteen colonies represented a relatively inconsequential territory possessing a small population located far from the centers of world power. It was only through hard fighting, determined patriotism, luck, and the assistance of allies that these scrappy British outposts in the New World were able to break away to become a separate nation. Over the following century, there were many critical military junctures when the goal of achieving continental hegemony as imagined in the doctrine of manifest destiny could have been extinguished. After dramatic defeats, the question of whether the United States would prevail in both the War of 1812 and the Civil War was in serious doubt. It took remarkable battlefield recoveries to ensure that the nation would become one unified polity stretching from sea to shining sea, as well as from Lake Superior to the Rio Grande. It was only eighty years later, at the conclusion of two world wars, that one could truly say that Washington had become the capital of a true superpower. However, even then, there always remained peer or near-peer nations that could militarily oppose America's will across great swaths of the world's geography.

Similarly, it is a false narrative to claim that before 1950 we were invincible, but after that date the United States suddenly forgot how to win wars. After all, our country failed in many attempts to impose "regime change" or engage in "nation building" enforced at the point of a gun before the advent of the Pax Americana era and the adventures in Vietnam, Iraq, and Afghanistan. Consider the many U.S. interventions over the course of the twentieth century that failed to establish stable regimes in Latin American states such as Nicaragua, Haiti, Honduras, the Dominican Republic, and, most importantly, Cuba. Further afield, U.S. troops joined with several other powers in marching on Beijing to suppress the Boxer Rebellion in 1899. While this expedition temporarily yielded a Chinese government that acceded to western demands, the Qing Dynasty collapsed soon after and pitched the empire into violence and the unstable rule of rival warlords. Another multinational intervention to support the "Whites" in the Russian Civil War saw thousands of American troops land at the ports of Archangel and Vladivostok in 1918. This action is today almost completely forgotten. While such efforts left behind dead Americans and regimes suspicious of Washington's intentions, no great price was paid for failure.

In this context, the inability to create stable democracies in Vietnam, Iraq, and Afghanistan fit more neatly into the scope of U.S. military history: Our military has been defeated in many battles, and even in several smaller wars, but has always reacted and recovered to win when victory was strategically necessary for America's geopolitical interests. Even when the political will to win has waned on the home front, the military has repeatedly displayed its ability to react and recover so as to gain an upper hand on the battlefield. This flexibility has led to a stabilization of the tactical situation and allowed elected leaders the opportunity to withdraw at a time, and in a way of their own choosing.

In addition, those who bemoan that we have become a nation that is "good at losing" need to consider how much the nation chose to spend in the pursuit of victory. As the following graph indicates, to "win" big wars the nation has needed to significantly ramp up its military expenditure as a percent of GDP. In the case of the fighting in Vietnam, Iraq, and Afghanistan, the United States decided against gearing up for a large conflict and making the economic sacrifices that were deemed necessary to prevail in the Civil War, World War I, and World War II. Perhaps, in war, as in many other things, you get what you pay for.

US Military Spending as a Percent of GDP[4]

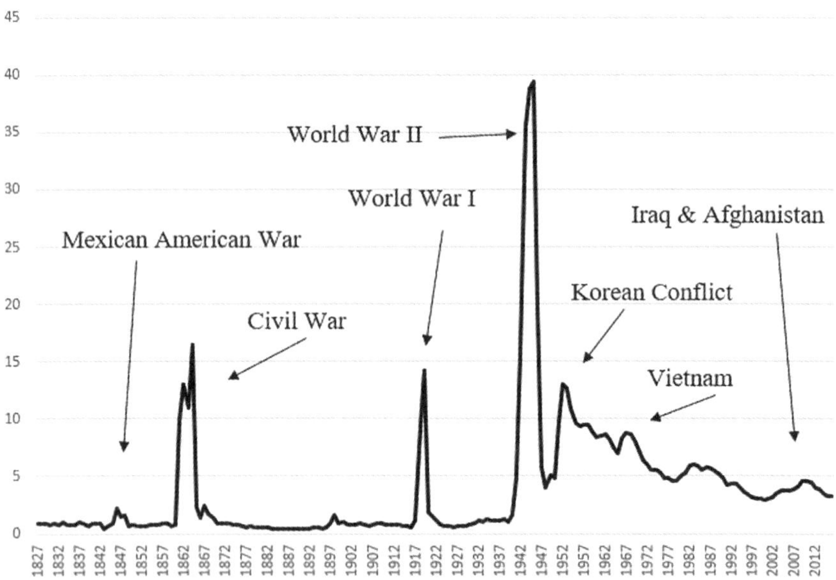

The Savage Wars of Peace by historian Max Boot is an excellent overview of the "salience and centrality of small wars in American foreign policy" that our nation has entered into over its history as we grew from a young nation of upstarts stretched along the eastern coastline of North America into a superpower with truly global reach.[5] In some of these fights we were successful; in others we were not. However, none were truly critical to the nation's future in a way remotely similar to that of the outcomes of the Civil War or World War II. If our armed intervention in Vietnam (officially during the Second Indochina War, 1955–1975) is viewed through such a prism as just one battle in the great confrontation with the Soviet Union and its allies (the Cold War, 1947–1991), our failure in Indochina looks more like a single defeat in a larger conflict that eventually resulted in a dramatic strategic victory. Similarly, failures in Iraq and Afghanistan, while obviously still failures, may also represent short-term defeats in a bigger war in which the United States is prevailing in its core strategic effort.

Prior to 1865, the United States focused its attentions on securing its "manifest destiny" of subjugating Indigenous tribes and pushing out European rivals so as to build a continental empire stretching from the Atlantic to the Pacific and from the Great Lakes to the Gulf of Mexico. After this was achieved, we expanded our foreign policy to ensure that those rival Europeans retained ever less territory and influence across the Western Hemisphere, which the United States claimed as its sphere of political, business, and military interest. By 1917, Washington's foreign policy shifted to an even larger goal of ensuring that no hegemonic power arose on the Eurasian landmass that could potentially threaten the United States across its oceanic moats. To achieve this end, we chose to utilize local allies whenever possible, especially to do most of the necessary fighting and dying. Why, when, and how America intervened in the two world wars looks much more obvious against a backdrop of such geopolitical policy goals.

Looking at American history through this prism and taking this strategic framework into account helps explain Washington's tactical decisions regarding intervening, and then withdrawing from Vietnam, Iraq, and Afghanistan in recent decades. Unpacking this more recent period of U.S. military history places the nation's long record of defeats followed by victories into a proper context.

The Defeat: Vietnam

After its triumph over the Axis powers, the United States was immediately confronted with a new crisis. Germany, Italy, and Japan were defeated, but the USSR had grown tremendously in relative power, was led by a ruthless dictator, and seemed poised to seize hegemony over both Europe and Asia. As Stalin's Iron Curtain descended and a Soviet atomic bomb was detonated, the United States committed itself to a policy of containment and the Cold War began. Any hopes that this conflict would be bloodless was quickly dashed with the outbreak of fighting in Korea.

Against this backdrop, the United States began its support for a non-communist regime in Vietnam, which lasted from 1950 until the fall of Saigon a quarter of a century later. First, Washington supplied the weapons and paid the bill for the French forces fighting to retain control of Indochina against the Communists led by Ho Chi Minh. After the French defeat, Vietnam was partitioned into two nations in 1954 with a Communist regime (the Democratic Republic of Vietnam) in the North with its capital in Hanoi, and a western-backed government in the South (the Republic of Vietnam) based in Saigon. For the next decade, the United States provided assistance and military advisors to the South under the rule of President Ngo Dinh Diem and then the subsequent military junta that assassinated him in 1963. During this period, China and the USSR supported an insurgency that was fought throughout the South by local Viet Cong (VC) communist guerrillas aided by North Vietnamese Army (NVA) units that infiltrated through the nations of Laos and Cambodia via a series of supply networks known as the "Ho Chi Minh Trail."

Initially this was a low-intensity conflict as the Army of the Republic of Vietnam (ARVN) suffered 2,000 killed in 1960 rising to 7,500 in 1964. The size of the U.S. advisor force also grew during this period from 900 to 23,000 though casualties remained quite low.[6] By 1965, the Republic of Vietnam appeared to be teetering due to increasing violence and instability in the wake of the coup against Diem. Congress authorized the administration of President Lyndon Johnson to intervene militarily in the conflict as it saw fit and by the end of 1965 there were more than 180,000 U.S. combat troops in the country. The ARVN also grew rapidly and was equipped with modern American equipment. U.S. allies, such as Australia and the Republic of Korea, deployed significant contingents as well, which eventually totaled more than 60,000 men.[7]

U.S. military actions in Vietnam were justified to the American people on the basis of the "Domino Theory" as enunciated by President Eisenhower in 1954 just a week after the armistice was signed to end the Korean War. This concept, as he described it, was that if Indochina fell to the Communists, geography that was more strategically important to the United States, specifically the Malay Peninsula and the "First Island Chain" of Indonesia, the Philippines, Taiwan, and Japan, would be at risk.[8] Successive administrations continued to argue that the march of communism needed to be stopped or much of East Asia would fall under its control.

As U.S. troop levels increased to 500,000 by 1968, the North Vietnamese responded by surging men and supplies to the South. Casualties soared with both American and ARVN forces suffering over 10,000 killed in action per year after 1966. Communist losses were much higher, but could be replaced due to the North's population of upwards of twenty million who believed in the righteousness of the nationalist ideology to unite Vietnam. Continual shipments of military aid from China and the USSR ensured that the insurgency in the South received a steady supply of weapons and ammunition. As the fighting intensified it also expanded geographically with the United States launching its "Rolling Thunder" aerial bombing campaign against the North in 1965. The Communists reacted by constructing an increasingly sophisticated air defense system that came to include MiG fighters and surface-to-air missiles provided by the USSR. While the U.S. air campaign slowed aid flowing to the South, it did not stop it, and President Johnson chose not to invade North Vietnam due to fears that the Chinese would intervene similarly to what had occurred in Korea earlier in the Cold War.

The turning point in the conflict was the "Tet Offensive" in 1968. This was an attempt by the Communists to shift from guerrilla attacks to conventional battles so as to trigger a mass uprising across South Vietnam. In preparation, upwards of 200,000 additional NVA troops infiltrated south via the Ho Chi Minh Trail.[9] The Communists initially gained surprise when they attacked, but U.S. and ARVN forces recovered and crushed the NVA and VC. Casualties were terribly lopsided against the Communists and in the aftermath of the offensive, leaders in North Vietnam were dejected and believed they had suffered a major defeat.[10] Indeed they had lost militarily, but the result of their effort was a surprising political victory.

The U.S. government had claimed to the American public that it was making headway against the insurgency. Perhaps it was, but the wave of attacks that rippled across South Vietnam starting in January 1968 persuaded many "back home" that the war was unwinnable. The number of Americans opposed to involvement in the conflict, already significant, soared and Lyndon Johnson's approval ratings fell precipitously.[11] By the end of March, he announced that he would not run for reelection. Once again, failure to achieve victory on one battlefield in the greater conflict of the Cold War drove a president out of the White House.

Despite this turn in U.S. public opinion, the military situation in South Vietnam subsequently improved markedly in the next few years. After defeat in the Tet Offensive, the Communists encountered great difficulty rebuilding their network across South Vietnam. The greatest impediment was the Phoenix Program, a joint CIA/military operation that identified and killed tens of thousands of Viet Cong members through infiltration, interrogation, torture, and assassination. While the morality of the program was murky, it was certainly effective and the Communists believed it represented a mortal threat to their struggle to reunify Vietnam.[12] General Creighton Abrams also took over command of U.S. forces in the country in the middle of 1968. He redirected his troops away from focusing on how many guerrillas they could kill to a more traditional counter-insurgency strategy of winning over the "hearts and minds" of the people of South Vietnam. The result was a marked reduction of territory in the South controlled by the Communists, and the conflict increasingly took on aspects of a conventional fight between ARVN forces and infiltrating units of the NVA.

After his election in 1968, President Richard Nixon pursued a strategy of: (1) staged withdrawal of American ground forces, (2) "Vietnamization" of the war by having ARVN units take over the bulk of the fighting, and (3) increasing pressure on North Vietnamese leaders to give up on their goal of seizing the South. U.S. troop levels in the country declined 90 percent from their peak by the middle of 1972 and American casualties dropped commensurately. This reduction in boots on the ground was offset as ARVN total strength continued to grow and soon exceeded one million men. At the same time, a clandestine U.S. Air Force bombing campaign of eastern Cambodia disrupted Communist sanctuaries along the Ho Chi Minh Trail. A separate incursion over the border by ARVN forces did the same in Laos in 1971.

Peace talks began in Paris between the Americans and the North Vietnamese in 1968, but initially progress was negligible. However, Nixon was diplomatically active elsewhere and engaged in a policy of détente with the USSR and then traveled to Beijing to engage in rapprochement with China in early 1972. These events meant that aid to Hanoi from its two patron nations was at risk. In an attempt to force the issue, the North Vietnamese launched the "Easter Offensive" in 1972 with upwards of 300,000 troops backed by heavy artillery and hundreds of Soviet tanks. The goal of the invasion was to trigger a collapse of the Saigon government, or at least gain a better negotiating position in Paris. The ARVN, now fighting mostly on its own, with only air support supplied by the United States, suffered initial reverses but soon staged a counteroffensive. The NVA was forced to cede much of its territorial gains and North Vietnam was bombed relentlessly by the United States in Operations Linebacker and Linebacker II.

Both sides claimed victory as the fighting eased with the NVA having gained about 10 percent of the territory of the Republic of Vietnam. However, the ARVN inflicted much greater casualties on the Communists, and U.S. bombing destroyed significant infrastructure in the North. The relative stalemate on the ground resulted in a breakthrough at the negotiating table and the signing of a peace agreement in Paris in early 1973. The last U.S. combat troops were withdrawn and the North Vietnamese dropped their demand that the South's government in Saigon be replaced by a coalition that included representatives of the Viet Cong. The agreement called for a ceasefire, reunification talks to take place, and the United States being allowed to resupply the ARVN with updated military equipment.

Of course peace did not break out, and fighting continued to flare in contested territory. Two years later in 1975, the NVA launched a conventional invasion of the South. President Gerald Ford appealed to Congress to provide emergency military aid to Saigon. When this request was rejected, he subsequently chose not to provide air support to the ARVN from Navy carriers offshore and U.S. Air Force bases in Thailand. The last president of South Vietnam gave an emotional address to the nation declaring that America had reneged on the promises it had made to its ally. Soon after, Saigon fell to NVA troops amid infamous scenes of a hurried evacuation of the U.S. embassy. America had lost the war.

The Defeat: Afghanistan

With the Tiananmen Square Massacre in 1989 temporarily slowing China's growth, and the formal dissolution of the Soviet Union in 1991, the United States was granted a period when, at least in terms of conventional military power, it had no peer on the global stage. It briefly had to deal with a threat to the international system it had established when Saddam Hussein's Iraq invaded Kuwait. An authoritarian Iraq with its large educated population and vast petroleum reserves allowed to conquer Kuwait represented a potential threat to U.S. interests in the region. Hussein, who had already proven his brutal dictatorial credentials, could be counted on to use the power and wealth of his enlarged realm to build a more advanced military force that would destabilize the Persian Gulf region. The United States had no interest in a stronger Baghdad dominating Saudi Arabia, threatening Israel, and/or reigniting the war against Iran.

In addition, while U.S. imports of oil from the Middle East were relatively small by 1990, this was not the case for major allies and trading partners in Europe and East Asia. Any significant disruption of petroleum flows from the Persian Gulf could easily unhinge the global economy generally, and that of the United States specifically. Thus, the decision was taken by President George H. W. Bush that, "this will not stand, this aggression against Kuwait."[13] The result was the formation of a global coalition, the positioning of a large armed force in Saudi Arabia, and the rapid ejection of Iraq from Kuwait. Hussein remained in power with a diminished military that was still strong enough to act as a counterweight to that of Iran.

For the next decade, the United States had no specific Eurasian hegemonic power to challenge. It viewed both the new Russian Federation and the industrializing PRC warily and attempted to reduce the threat from both by bringing these two nations into the existing international system of free trade between democratic/democratizing states. Russia was accepted into the G7, which for a time became the G8, and China was invited to begin the process of joining the World Trade Organization. Washington presided over a period of relative peace, mostly kept its ground troops out of those conflicts that did take place (the breakup of Yugoslavia, insurgencies in Latin America, the civil wars in southern Africa, etc.), and benefited from the improvement in economic productivity powered by the globalization of trade and rapid expansion of the internet. This all changed dramatically with Al-Qaeda's attacks of September 11, 2001.

Osama bin Laden's movement, based in distant Afghanistan, represented a new type of threat to the U.S. military. Instead of deploying fleets of naval ships or warplanes that could cross the oceans, or even waging insurgencies using guerrilla forces to overthrow small nations in strategic geographies, Al-Qaeda specifically looked to launch asymmetrical terror attacks designed to target America's infrastructure and icons of global strength. This ranged from truck bombs blowing up U.S. embassies in Africa, to a suicide boat attack on the guided missile destroyer USS *Cole,* to the outrageously successful operation by a small group of men with box cutters being able to commandeer commercial jet liners to attack the heart of American power in New York and Washington.

U.S. authorities had previously identified Al-Qaeda as a threat, attacked its facilities with cruise missiles, and placed Osama bin Laden on its Ten Most Wanted list. The movement's expansive ideology/theology, if brought to fruition, would upset the world order by reconstituting a caliphate that stretched from Spain to India controlling much of the globe's energy supplies and a significant percentage of its population. The creation of such a potential hegemonic power in Eurasia was a nightmare scenario for U.S. geopolitical interests. However, in the late 1990s, bin Laden seemed a deadly, but manageable threat. That all changed after the 9/11 attacks, which succeeded primarily due to an abject failure by America's intelligence agencies. Casualties incurred that day were close to 3,000, more than the nation suffered in the attack on Pearl Harbor, and economic losses to the United States were immense.

On September 20, President George W. Bush demanded that the Taliban government of Afghanistan turn over Osama bin Laden or face military attack. More importantly, he declared the start of the "Global War on Terror" (GWOT), which effectively became an effort to (1) degrade and destroy Islamic militant organizations planning to strike against American interests anywhere in the world, and (2) strive to ensure that such groups were unable to gain access to weapons of mass destruction (WMD), be they nuclear, biological, or chemical in nature.[14]

In early October, after the Taliban refused to expel bin Laden, the United States launched a campaign of airstrikes on Afghanistan. Special Forces units arrived to advance with elements of the opposition Northern Alliance on both Osama bin Laden's Al-Qaeda compounds as well as the centers of power of the nation's Taliban government. A Marine Expeditionary Unit and a few other military formations were also deployed. In less than three months, the Taliban was defeated, Al-Qaeda's infrastructure dismantled, and a transitional government installed in the capital of Kabul. It was an impressive military success as the United States had been able to achieve victory in a very short period of time while deploying fewer than 6,000 men on the ground.[15] The major blemish was that bin Laden was able to slip out of the Tora Bora region in the south of Afghanistan and went into hiding in Pakistan.

With a new government in place, the United States could have decided to take its troops and go home. However, there were concerns that the Taliban would soon return to power and senior members of the Bush Administration seemed to willfully ignore that both the British and the Soviet empires had been unable to hold Afghanistan through military means. Many in Washington deluded themselves that the United States could successfully engage in "nation building" in the middle of central Asia in a desperately poor and fractious mountainous territory with a large and rapidly growing Islamic population. Thus began a needless war of extremely dubious strategic significance lasting two decades that cost in excess of $2 trillion and resulted in the death of more than 6,000 American military personnel and contractors.[16]

In many ways, the conflict in Afghanistan mirrored the earlier U.S. experience in South Vietnam: At first, only a small number of American troops were required to stabilize the situation and shipments of arms and money helped to build an Indigenous fighting force to support the new central government. However, the insurgency strengthened over time, casualties rose, and the number of American troops in the country grew. While U.S. forces could defeat local Taliban concentrations to seize and hold almost any position they wanted in Afghanistan, the insurgents remained able to recruit, train, and resupply in relative safety over the border in Pakistan.

The U.S. public, increasingly unsure as to why they were fighting a costly and potentially unwinnable war to support a corrupt regime in a geography of uncertain strategic significance, slowly began to lose faith.[17] In 2010, General David Petraeus was installed as the commander of U.S. forces in Afghanistan after successfully overseeing a "surge" of American forces in Iraq (see next section). A similar strategy was then utilized in Afghanistan that stabilized the situation for a time. The United States then rapidly reduced its force in the country utilizing primarily airpower to support local forces. Nevertheless, the insurgency smoldered throughout the next decade. As American interest in the war faded, a peace agreement was signed in Doha between the administration of President Donald Trump and the Taliban in early 2020, which called for a final withdrawal of remaining American military forces and negotiations to take place between the Kabul government and the rebels. While the United States pulled out, the Taliban kept fighting, government resistance collapsed, and the capital fell in late 2021. As in South Vietnam in 1975, a hurried evacuation took place amid scenes of increasing chaos. Once again, the United States had lost a war.

The Defeat: Iraq

With President Bush's 2001 declaration of the GWOT and the rapid, almost painless conquest of Afghanistan, his administration turned its attention to Iraq. There, Saddam Hussein had continued to oppose any efforts to restrain him in gaining weapons of mass destruction. He had already used poison gas against restive members of his own population, and Pakistan's first test of a nuclear weapon in 1998 increased concerns that Iraq would be the next to gain access to "the bomb." Hussein refused to allow UN weapons inspectors into the country in 1997, and the United States made regime change official policy with President Bill Clinton's signing of the Iraq Liberation Act in 1998. At the end of that year the United States and United Kingdom launched a four-day aerial bombing campaign designed to degrade Hussein's ability to manufacture and use weapons of mass destruction.

Whether or not the U.S. intelligence community and senior members of the Bush Administration actually believed that Iraq was in the process of acquiring WMD remains uncertain, but what is clear is that preparations for a military overthrow of the government of that Middle Eastern nation proceeded in earnest.[18] A coalition led by American forces invaded Iraq in late March 2003 and rapidly overran the country. Baghdad fell to U.S. forces, Hussein and his sons went into hiding, and a Coalition Provisional Authority (CPA) was established to run civil affairs until local elections could be held. On May 1, Bush gave a triumphant speech on the carrier USS *Abraham Lincoln* with a sign reading "Mission Accomplished" behind him. Unfortunately the true struggle was only just beginning.

While the U.S. military brilliantly executed the initial invasion and conquest of Iraq, there were those in its senior ranks who warned that they were going to war with insufficient manpower. In early 2003, Army Chief of Staff General Eric Shinseki testified to a Senate committee that an occupation force of several hundred thousand American soldiers would be required to succeed in rebuilding a stable nation after overthrowing Saddam Hussein's government. This was more troops than the U.S. military could spare, and multiples of the 120,000–160,000 planned for by administration leaders who wanted to move forward with the invasion. As a result, senior members of the Defense Department publicly disputed the accuracy of Shinseki's warning and the general's influence at the White House waned in the remaining months until his retirement. While U.S. military leaders were confident they had enough men to invade Iraq successfully, worries persisted that they were going to war with an insufficient force for the occupation to follow. In the end, General Tommy Franks, in command of U.S. forces in the Middle East, was more than willing to defer to his civilian overseers on strategic matters.[19]

In a relatively short period of time after the capture of Baghdad it became clear that the civilians in charge of building a new government in Iraq were out of their depth. Near the end of World War II, government planners in Washington spent a great deal of time considering how best to pacify and rebuild Germany and Japan after the end of the fighting.[20] In contrast, the CPA, led by diplomat Paul Bremer, made many hasty decisions either against the advice of U.S. military leaders, or often without even consulting them. These included two particularly tragic errors at the very start of Bremer's tenure: He banned members of Saddam Hussein's Ba'ath Party from holding posts in the public sector and he dissolved the Iraqi Army.[21] These pronouncements robbed the new Indigenous military force and government bureaucracy of many of the most effective leaders and technocrats in the nation, which limited the institutions' effectiveness. It also meant that hundreds of thousands of resentful Iraqis, many with organizational or military training and accustomed to holding positions of authority and influence, found themselves unemployed and with few job prospects. These men were primarily Sunni Arabs, a minority group in the country though the one with a preponderance of power under Saddam Hussein. They watched with rising anger as the United States stood up a new government and military that granted greatly increased control to Shia Arabs and Kurds who together represented approximately three quarters of the population.

The occupation forces were soon confronted with a growing insurgency led by Sunni Arabs that targeted American and other coalition forces as well as those who collaborated with the new provisional government. Iraqi Shia, reacting to Sunni attacks on civilians, turned to Iran (whose leaders are also Shia), which wished to destabilize the new regime so as to become the dominant power in the region. Tehran supported and armed Iraqi Shia militias with increasingly sophisticated weapons used to target both American troops as well as the Sunnis. There was not only a rapid rise in guerrilla attacks on U.S. forces but also ethnic cleansing killings of civilians across the nation, especially in ethnically mixed neighborhoods of Baghdad. To make matters even worse, a local offshoot of Al-Qaeda expanded rapidly, terrorized civilians, and attacked both U.S. soldiers and those of the new Iraqi military.

The result was a low-intensity war of car bombs, improvised explosive devices, and firefights that gnawed away at the legitimacy and power of the new Baghdad government and the western soldiers supporting it. In 2003, including the period when the invasion took place, the American military only suffered 488 killed and 2,500 wounded. In 2004–2007 that figure rose to over 800 dead and 6,000 wounded each year.[22] The United States was forced to spend hundreds of billions of additional dollars in Iraq and maintain well over 100,000 men in the nation to keep the shaky government from collapsing.

To regain control of the situation, President Bush authorized a troop surge of more than 20,000 men in 2007. The regional (CENTCOM) commander as well as the ambassador to Iraq were replaced, and, most importantly, General David Petraeus was elevated to command the multinational force in the country. Petraeus had been quite successful overseeing the 101st Airborne Division in the initial months of the occupation in the northern city of Mosul and its environs. While there, he utilized traditional counter-insurgency strategies of billeting his men for lengthy periods among the populace, limiting the use of heavy weapons to suppress insurgents in urban areas, supporting public works efforts, and recruiting local Indigenous leaders and their followers as allies in the rebuilding of the country. Similar strategies were implemented on a greater scale across Iraq in 2007–2008 and the "surge" was successful in pacifying much of the country.

American losses dropped significantly in 2008 and then again in 2009, and President Barack Obama announced that U.S. forces would be withdrawn by 2011 as per an agreement earlier negotiated between the Iraqi government and the Bush Administration. No longer a stable nation run by a brutal dictatorship, Iraq emerged with a weak central government beholden to politicians and militias under the influence, if not the direct control, of Iran. Against this backdrop, an affiliate of Al-Qaeda, Islamic State of Iraq and Syria (ISIS), declared itself the center of a new caliphate and gained strength rapidly in the north of the country and over the border in Syria, which was in the agony of a brutal civil war. After Mosul fell to ISIS in 2014, a few thousand American forces returned, and in conjunction with Iraqi government soldiers and Kurdish militia, took the offensive. By 2016, ISIS had been ejected from Mosul and it was defeated in its remaining territory in Syria by early 2019.

Two decades after the invasion of Iraq, only a small force of American troops remain in the country primarily engaged in advisory and training roles. Clearly, in retrospect, the results of the initial military operation appear to have been failures: (1) WMDs were not seized and destroyed because none were ever found. (2) A stable democratic Iraq was not established. (3) The United States spent upwards of $2 trillion on the conflict. In addition, the major counterweight to Iranian power in the region has been destroyed. As an Iraqi character in Phil Klay's book, *Redeployment*, put it, "You have baked Iraq like a cake and given it to Iran to eat."[23] The result has been the rapid growth of power by Tehran's allies across the Middle East. This change has threatened to destabilize several regional American allies. Once again, the United States had lost a war.

Recovery

After initially being staggered by setbacks suffered fighting guerrilla forces in Vietnam, Afghanistan, and Iraq, the U.S. military repeatedly demonstrated the resilience and ingenuity required to react, recover, and move to gain victory on the battlefield in these conflicts. None of the insurgencies were completely wiped out, but in all three cases, American forces found a way to stabilize the situation on the ground to such an extent, and for a long enough period of time, that elected politicians back in Washington were able to negotiate a successful exit from what had become viewed as a quagmire. This was accomplished through surging additional forces to the region, employing counter-insurgency tactics that won over swaths of the population, weakening the enemy insurgency through the judicial use of force in populated regions, and accepting that guerrilla movements are defeated through political as well as military actions. Efforts such as the Phoenix Program in Vietnam, supporting the "Anbar Awakening" in Iraq, and organizing *arbakai* community-based security networks in Afghanistan were all part of a series of reaction and recovery tactics employed to tamp down insurgent activity.

Reviewing these three interventions, it is clear that the U.S. military was placed in an untenable situation. Each time they were pitted against an enemy that was (1) willing to accept wildly uneven attrition rates that were still not acceptable to the U.S. public and (2) allowed a sanctuary area where American ground forces were not allowed to penetrate. To highlight this first point, in 1946, Ho Chi Minh warned the French, "You can kill ten of my men for every one I kill of yours. But even at those odds, you will lose and I will win."[24] Decades after achieving independence, the Vietnamese government has corroborated casualty totals for 1960–1975 that were quite similar to western estimates: Slightly over one million VC and NVA were killed or went missing and another 450,000 were wounded.[25] This meant that the Vietnamese Communists lost upwards of twenty men for every one American killed in the war. But, of course, 58,000 combat deaths was far too many for a U.S. public that tired of the conflict. An abandoned Republic of Vietnam was subsequently overrun by a conventional invasion from the North.

Similarly lopsided casualty rates were imposed on the Taliban and Iraqi insurgents by the U.S. military, which suffered only a small fraction of men killed in these two latter wars compared to those lost in Vietnam. If American voters are unwilling to support a war where its armed forces, utilizing conventional weapons, can inflict casualty rates ten, twenty, or thirty times that which are suffered, it is difficult to fault the military for failure. In addition, political calculations meant that U.S. ground forces were unable to invade insurgent sanctuaries to disrupt NVA operations in North Vietnam, the Taliban in Pakistan, and Iraqi guerrillas in Iran and Syria. Yes, airpower was often used to strike targets in such sanctuary nations, but as in World War II and the Korean War, we have learned that conventional bombing from the air cannot win a war on its own. After all, U.S. planes dropped more than a million tons of ordnance on North Vietnam alone (similar to the amount of bombs released by the U.S. Army Air Force over Germany in World War II), and still Ho Chi Minh's government refused to cease its armed struggle to reunify with the South.

While the U.S. military has repeatedly shown its ability to inflict massive casualties on guerrilla groups, and suffer relatively low losses in return, these "small" insurgencies continued to smolder. Support for fighting them eroded among the American public, which opposed higher taxes, mass conscription, and a shift to a wartime economy to win as was required in World War II, World War I, and the Civil War. In such a scenario, our battlefield leaders have delivered the best possible result under such problematic circumstances: ask for a temporary surge in forces deployed, engage in major counter-insurgency efforts, and train significant numbers of locally raised soldiers to take over the fight on the front lines. In each of the three cases examined in this chapter—Vietnam, Afghanistan, and Iraq—the U.S. military has been able to engineer a dramatic reduction in American force levels and annual casualties while still ensuring that our client state did not collapse for years. This has offered our elected officials in Washington the time to negotiate an exit strategy and prepare for what comes next. While not a triumph, and arguably a terrible waste of blood and treasure, it still represents a measure of success.

VICTORY AND DEFEAT?

With the fall of Saigon, historians immediately declared that the United States had lost the war.

Or had it only lost a battle?

After all, in the 20 years that America opposed a Communist takeover of Vietnam, much changed in the Cold War, which was always a global rather than a regional conflict. In Europe, nations such as Italy, Turkey, and Greece that looked susceptible to communist takeover were stabilized and joined the NATO military alliance designed to contain the USSR. In East Asia, communist insurgencies outside of Indochina were ruthlessly and successfully suppressed in Thailand, Malaysia, Indonesia, and the Philippines. These nations also experienced significant economic growth and the populations enjoyed rising standards of living as they were tied into trade relationships with the United States. The same was true for South Korea and Japan, which rapidly industrialized in the 1960s and 1970s. To the people of the region, ascension into the Pax Americana system looked increasingly attractive compared to the model of the PRC, which descended into famine and chaos during

Mao's Great Leap Forward and the Cultural Revolution. The allure of the USSR to many across the Pacific Rim also dimmed as Moscow's economic and technological growth stagnated in the 1970s.

Certainly, the U.S. defense of Vietnam ended in a failure, especially for the more than 50,000 Americans who died fighting there. The defeat also created a painful rift among our population and damaged the morale of the military for a decade or more. However, if the U.S. intervention is viewed today as a tactical "spoiling attack" designed to preempt or disrupt a larger offensive by international communism, the effort looks significantly more successful. Was such an operation really necessary to give Thailand, Malaysia, Indonesia, and the Philippines the time they needed so that their governments did not fall to communist dictatorships? We will never know.

What we know for certain is that while we did not win every clash of the Cold War, America clearly prevailed in its global struggle against the USSR. Of course, the policy of containment and the effort to defeat communism was not solely fought with military might as it also had political and economic aspects: It was important to show that democracies practicing free market capitalism could grow faster and provide a better standard of living to its citizens than the results demonstrated by the Soviet Union and its satellites. In that, the United States was extremely successful, but to accomplish this goal it had to ensure that defense expenditures did not grow to such an extent that it crowded out private investment and overtaxed the American economy. This may help explain why military spending as a percent of GDP trended down over the course of the Cold War from 9.6 percent at the height of the fighting in Korea in 1951 to 6.4 percent in 1971, 5.2 percent in 1981, 4.2 percent in 1991, and 3.0 percent in 2001. Winning individual battles of the Cold War was important but not necessarily decisive. In the end, focusing on building an economy that outcompeted that of the USSR was the greater victory that eventually won the conflict.

In addition, the nations Eisenhower identified as being strategically important to the United States along the Pacific Rim never fell to communist insurgents. Instead, they subsequently experienced dramatic economic growth and most developed into robust democracies that remain our military allies. Even in Vietnam, one can reasonably pose the question today if America lost. After all, U.S. Navy ships once again make port calls in Cam Ranh Bay, American tourists frolic on the beach in front of the Four Seasons Hotel in Da Nang, and bilateral trade between the two nations has grown to exceed a quarter of a trillion dollars annually.[26]

Similarly to the conclusion of the Second Indochina War, the United States lost in Afghanistan. But again, what if it was only a battle that was lost? If America's GWOT is truly a war on the use of terror, then we have lost mightily as terror attacks continue to be a scourge across the world. However, if the goal of the GWOT was to ensure that Islamic non-state actors were unable to mount major attacks on significant U.S. infrastructure targets, especially utilizing WMDs, then, to date, it has been a success. Certainly in the wake of 9/11, large numbers of Americans believed that the next devastating Al-Qaeda attack on the homeland was imminent. What would have happened had we declined to invade Afghanistan in late 2001 and Osama bin Laden continued to plot his next move from Kandahar? Many argue today that the costs incurred in this war have been unwarranted, but it is difficult to know compared to uncertain counterfactuals of what has not taken place.

It is too soon to really know the impacts of our defeats in Afghanistan and Iraq. Perhaps they are only two of the many "savage wars of peace," and the reverberations of winning or losing on the United States and the rest of the world is not all that great. After all, had we won in Afghanistan, and the people of that nation somehow created a peaceful mountainous Islamic democracy in the middle of central Asia, what would have been the impact on the globe? Those Americans and Afghans fighting to defeat the Taliban certainly wanted to win, and their sacrifice deserved to have meaning. Certainly, the return to power of the Taliban is an unmitigated disaster for the people of Afghanistan. But to the rest of the world, how much does it matter who rules in Kabul? The most important worry may be that Al-Qaeda is again operating openly in the country and is assuredly planning its next strike. In contrast, while Iraq no longer seems to be a state on the cusp of producing WMDs, which could be handed off to terror groups, the costs America imposed on its military and, even worse, on the people of Iraq make it appear that our adventure into the heart of Baghdad was a terrible disaster. Certainly the erosion of our strategic position in the Middle East two decades later seems significant and the rising power of Iran is of great concern. However, perhaps it is still too soon to know if we lost the war, or just a battle.

As with the Cold War, the GWOT is a struggle not only to win individual clashes of arms, but to outcompete an opponent. The concern after 9/11 was that (1) a terrorist attack on the United States utilizing WMDs could fatally damage our economy and way of life, and (2) the formation of a large, unified Islamic caliphate would potentially come to command a GDP that could threaten the United States militarily on the global stage. Of course the primary need was to ensure that no additional significant attacks struck the American homeland. Secondarily, a reduction of the relative economic power of the Middle and Near East vis-à-vis North America, Western Europe, and the Pacific Rim was also a desired outcome.

To date these goals have been accomplished: In the last twenty years, while American military spending as a percent of GDP has been held at a relatively low level, a technological revolution has supported rapid productivity growth in the United States and its major trading partners. Over the same period, construction of ever-larger renewable energy projects along with advances in hydrocarbon extraction techniques (fracking and horizontal drilling) have reduced the market power of petroleum-producing nations across the Middle East. The relative importance of the region has clearly declined over the last quarter of a century and the U.S. military has been able to "pivot" much of its attention to containing China in the Pacific. The GWOT may be far from over, and many terrible mistakes have been made by the United States since 9/11/2001, but it is undeniable that America has accomplished much of what it set out to achieve in the conflict.

Conclusion

The United States of America is a nation shaped by war. It was born on the battlefield, grew through conquest, and for a time, emerged as the world's sole superpower. However, through these clashes of arms the country has repeatedly suffered embarrassing defeats. What has set the United States apart is its ability to rapidly react, recover, and then move on to victory over multiple centuries, continents, and prevailing military technologies. The more important the fight, the more likely America has found a way to win.

What factors have led to such a consistent ability to effect a reversal of fortune? Each of the first eight chapters of this book focused on one strategic defeat by this nation followed by a major triumph. The most common shared attribute in the reaction and recovery has been a change in tactics employed against America's enemies. These ranged markedly from conflict to conflict. General Washington realized that his rebel force needed to stop not defending coastal positions and instead retreat until smaller British detachments could be defeated in detail. Lincoln learned that he needed to press his generals to fight and wear down the Confederacy through attrition. Spaatz and Doolittle sent their bombers out as bait on area bombing missions while fighters ranged ahead hunting the Luftwaffe. Ridgway ordered his men to entrench and hold at night, advance during the day, and when the Chinese were found, call in devastating artillery bombardments and airstrikes.

While the new tactics utilized differed over time, the main point is that American leaders were either (1) willing to change tactics after a defeat, or (2) replaced with new commanders who adapted to win. Often a replacement at the top was deemed necessary if only to achieve a "fresh start" with the men at the front and the public back home. It is possible that commanders such as Gates, Husband, and Eaker could have found a way to achieve victory, but most historians applaud that their spots were taken by Greene, Nimitz, and Doolittle. The nation has repeatedly found the right man at the right time to lead at the front and find a way to win.

Next, in almost all cases, U.S. defeats were caused by a failure to appreciate the capabilities of opposing armed forces. Too many times, especially in the fragile peace before the outbreak of hostilities, American military leaders focused on what they wanted a potential enemy to do rather than what they could do. Making this cardinal error led to great defeats at New York, Charleston, Pearl Harbor, Luzon, and along the Chongchon. Luckily, after being thrown back on the battlefield, taking on a clear-eyed understanding of enemy capabilities has been a hallmark of the American military. This has allowed for a focus on an opposition's actual weaknesses, which could be targeted and exploited. If U.S. commanders had not been willing to accept a new mindset regarding the strengths of opposing forces, victories at Trenton, Midway, or over Berlin would have been much less likely.

One would imagine, given the nation's history of joining coalitions in war, that U.S. defeats were often turned into victories due to a combination of improved coordination with allies and utilization of America's great economic and manpower strength. Two examples of this are the partnership with the Australians and arrival of new U.S. units, which led to victory in Papua New Guinea, and to a lesser extent RAF Bomber Command joining a strengthened USAAF at the start of Operation Argument. However, the truth is that this only took place on a couple of occasions after a significant American defeat. It is likely that a history of the United States being willing to fight alongside such a large number of other nations has precluded more setbacks and resulted in faster victories. We should keep this in mind in the future as we consider that since 1776, U.S. defeats followed by recoveries on the battlefield have more often taken place when we have been fighting alone.

While the nation has been lucky enough to bounce back from military defeat repeatedly, it obviously makes sense to learn from past mistakes so as to avoid such setbacks in the future. So what lessons can be gleaned from the nation's great string of defeats suffered over the last two and a half centuries? Here are a few thoughts:

1. Too many times training and preparation have been lackluster prior to a military clash. The United States paid dearly for this at the outbreak of the War of 1812, the Civil War, World War II, and the Korean War. Defeats early in those conflicts could have been avoided if American forces began them better prepared for the challenge at hand. How could the United States have concentrated so much military power on Oahu but not operated proper reconnaissance flights to protect the island? After all, the U.S. Navy had been wargaming an aircraft carrier strike on Pearl Harbor for more than a decade. Similarly, how could generals preparing for a clash with the armored might of the Red Army have thrown poorly trained troops bereft of antitank weapons into battle in 1950 to fight a North Korean force equipped with Soviet weapon systems including T-34s? The nation must make sure that its men and women in uniform are properly prepared and correctly equipped when called on to fight in the future.
2. Our military and political leaders have also failed many times relying on doctrine and belief that did not stand the first test of battle. Vigorous debate must be encouraged so as to consider our own weaknesses and those of our weapon systems in a rapidly changing technological environment. Consider the following questions and in what ways might we be making similar errors today: How is it that American leaders convinced themselves in 1812 that conquering Canada would take little more than a bit of marching? Or that only limited forces would be required to suppress a rebellion of the white men of the Confederacy who were threatened with a loss of social status and their largest concentration of investment capital? Why did the United States first claim that the southern half of the Korean Peninsula was not important strategically, but then suddenly declare it must be defended when the Communists invaded from the north? As a people, we must demand that our political and

military leaders enunciate a clear vision regarding where, when, and why we will fight.

3. A similar focus needs to be placed on the more in-depth questions regarding the prosecution of war in the realm of operations and tactics. The nation has gone into multiple wars holding tight to ideas that simply were not true. American generals in the Revolutionary War repeatedly ignored the obvious amphibious power of the British Royal Navy and believed they could safely entrench themselves on peninsulas, or even islands, to hold urban territory. Similarly, time and again, Patriot leaders chose to order amateur militiamen to stand in dressed ranks and trade musket fire with professional Redcoats and Hessian mercenaries. The result was very often a defeat for U.S. forces. Such errors in thinking have cropped up repeatedly from the days of sail right through the era of the strategic bomber. The airplane was still a new device available in limited numbers in 1941, yet somehow our military convinced itself that such untested devices could be used to quickly force one of the largest, most technologically advanced nations in the world to sue for peace. What beliefs do our military men and women hold today that are quickly becoming outdated in a world of rapid technological change? This is a question that must be asked again and again on a regular basis as the answer will change over time.

4. A major lesson from this book is the need to have the right leaders running the fight or suffering a major defeat is all but inevitable. In the eighteenth and nineteenth centuries, the United States often had generals in the field who were political appointees rather than competent military leaders. The nation paid a severe price for making this error. In the twentieth century, generals who were less than excellent were regularly relieved and placed in posts more suited to their abilities. Thomas Ricks's excellent *The Generals* describes how such a system produced a more effective fighting force with a better likelihood of achieving victory.[1] Ricks has also shown how relief of battlefield leaders has become increasingly rare since 1950 and has contributed to American defeats. If the

nation wishes to improve its chances of achieving initial success in war, reinstituting such a regime where mediocre generals are quickly replaced is imperative.

Over the last sixty years, the United States has waged three lengthy wars, in Vietnam, Afghanistan, and Iraq, with a military budget as a percent of GDP that was historically low compared to what we allocated to wage the Civil War, the two world wars, or even the Korean War. Of course, our political and military leaders thought these would be "savage wars of peace": short and quick, or small and relatively painless. They "sold" them as such to the American people, and it was only later, as the conflicts took on the attributes of a quagmire that they became lengthy fights. There should be no surprise that public support to continue such missions indefinitely waned over time. While we may have been victorious in the overarching struggle of the Cold War, and appear to have won the Global War on Terror, our leaders did a disservice to the men and women who served in Vietnam, Afghanistan, and Iraq. They told these troops, and the rest of America, that they were engaged in a do-or-die struggle that had to be won. In fact, the truth was that we were willing to withdraw and abandon our local allies to an uncertain fate when we tired of the fight. How can we avoid suffering defeats in the future even if the nation is still able to win the overarching war?

1. We need to accept that winning a conflict will often be extremely challenging if the economy is not placed on a war footing. Is it better for the country to make a maximum effort and achieve victory quickly or accept a lengthier, cheaper conflict with a less certain outcome? The answer is very dependent upon the individual circumstances but honest talk from our leaders and an open discussion among America's citizens is much more likely to result in the clarity of purpose that will lead to more favorable results. In addition, asking a small minority of Americans to sacrifice in wartime while demanding nothing from the vast majority of the nation's citizens is a recipe for diminished morale among our military forces and a lack of engagement and support from the electorate.

2. Picking our allies carefully is of paramount importance. What made us believe that the people of Afghanistan would fight for a less religious, more inclusive state? Why did we think the men of South Vietnam were willing to risk making the ultimate sacrifice to preserve their historic nation in a partitioned state? Such hard questions should be asked before we commit to placing our own "boots on the ground." Some allies are the right ones to support: The Australians battled the New Guinea jungle, tropical disease, and the Japanese to protect their homeland in a brutal war of attrition. Along the Pusan Perimeter the South Koreans rallied to their flag and proved that they were ready to fight and die to resist a communist invasion from the North. The people of Israel have shown monumental courage, ingenuity, and resilience in their fight to retain control of their historic homeland. To date they have asked only for aid and diplomatic support from the United States. The Ukrainians have proven themselves willing to suffer grievous losses to hold back the Russian attempts to overrun their country. When President Zelenskyy was offered evacuation in 2022 at a time that Kyiv's occupation looked inevitable, he famously exclaimed, "I don't need a ride, I need ammunition." In a dangerous, multi-polar world, these are the sort of allies America needs. Other "front-line" nations in Eastern Europe threatened by Russian aggression have been preparing to fight. Poland now spends close to 4 percent of GDP on defense, is working to double the size of its armed forces to 300,000 members, and is buying significant numbers of advanced weapon systems including 1,000 cost-effective South Korean K2 tanks, most of which will be produced locally under contract. It also held a parliamentary election in late 2023 in which 74 percent of eligible voters participated and resulted in a peaceful transition of power. This is an example of the sort of nation we should be willing to support, and perhaps even fight alongside in conflicts of import for U.S. foreign policy.

3. We can have a military prepared to fight peer and near-peer opponents, or one designed for large counter-insurgency missions. Ask-

ing the armed forces to be ready for both will likely yield a force well prepared for neither. One sort of war requires very different equipment and training compared to the other. After more than a decade focusing on fighting guerrillas in Afghanistan and Iraq, the U.S. military "pivoted" to training to fight a conventional conflict, with China being the most likely potential adversary. If, in the future, our political leaders commit our military to another large nation-building, counter-insurgency sort of mission, it behooves them to be open with the American people. Waging such a conflict is likely to be expensive in both blood and treasure and preclude adequate preparation for other missions.

4. Finally, we need to consider if an intervention is really the best answer when confronted with a choice regarding whether, or how to join a fight. Increasingly, our leaders have relied less on diplomacy and more upon our armed forces to achieve foreign policy goals. A danger of such reliance on the military was pointed out by the author and strategist Edward Luttwak when he introduced the term "post-heroic warfare" in a *Foreign Affairs* article in 1995.[2] As populations age in developed western nations, and families have fewer children, aversion to casualties has grown. Thus, we turn against conflict more quickly even when losses are lower. After all, total combined U.S. military casualties in both Afghanistan and Iraq were only a small fraction (12 percent) of those suffered in Vietnam yet public support for these two more recent interventions declined over a similar timeframe.[3] Luttwak advises that the nation consider smaller-footprint, more focused interventions to achieve lesser gains rather than decisive military victories that may, in any event, prove elusive.

To conclude this study, it is remarkable how often in its relatively short history the United States has quickly reacted and recovered from strategic military defeat to achieve victory. This repeated ability to bounce back from a loss on the battlefield should be included in any honest discussion regarding the American way of war. It also helps explain the great success of American foreign policy as we moved from a small set of coastal colonies to the world's preeminent superpower. After achieving this august status, it has become clear in more recent decades that being the "world's policeman" is a tough job. The result is that the United States has been confronted by a much more difficult set of military decisions since 1950.

Fighting to throw off the yoke of a tyrannical king in 1776 seemed as just a cause to the members of the Continental Congress then as it does to Americans today. Similarly, most of us believe that wars to end slavery and preserve the Union, or defeat Nazi Germany, or halt the Communists from overrunning Asia were morally correct missions. While we may wish the United States can avoid war in the future, this is likely a forlorn hope. Perhaps, at least, we can be lucky enough to fight in righteous causes where we find a way to win.

Notes

Introduction

1. "D-Day: FDR and Churchill's 'Mighty Endeavor,'" Franklin D. Roosevelt Presidential Library and Museum, https://www.fdrlibrary.org/mighty-endeavor, accessed 6/3/24.

2. World Bank data, https://www.macrotrends.net/global-metrics/countries/usa/canada/military-spending-defense-budget, accessed 6/3/24.

3. George and Meredith Friedman, *The Future of War: Power, Technology and American World Dominance in the Twenty-First Century* (New York: St. Martin's Griffin, 1998); Ralph Peters, *Never Quit the Fight* (Mechanicsburg, PA: Stackpole Books, 2006); P. W. Singer, *Wired for War* (New York: Penguin, 2009).

4. See for example, Tara Copp, "Ukraine Pulls U.S.-Provided Abrams Tanks from the Front Lines Over Drone Threats," Associated Press, 4/26/24, https://www.npr.org/2024/04/26/1247403968/ukraine-pulls-abrams-tanks-from-front-lines-russia-drone-threats#:~:text=Hourly%20News-,Ukraine%20pulls%20U.S.%2Dprovided%20Abrams%20tanks%20from%20front%20lines%20over,difficult%20for%20them%20to%20operate, accessed 6/4/24, and "Explainer: The 'Kamikaze' Drones Iran Used to Attack Israel," Radio Free Europe/Radio Liberty, 4/14/24, https://www.rferl.org/a/iran-shahed-drones-israel-attack/32904882.html, accessed 6/4/24.

Chapter 1: From the Battle of Long Island to the Counterattack at Trenton and Princeton

1. David Hackett Fischer, *Washington's Crossing* (New York: Oxford University Press, 2004), 75.

2. Fischer, *Washington's Crossing*, 75.

3. Fischer, *Washington's Crossing*, 76.

4. Fischer, *Washington's Crossing*, 77–78.

5. See "From John Adams to George Washington, 1/6/1776," https://founders.archives.gov/documents/Adams/06-03-02-0200, last accessed 11/14/23.

6. Richard Stewart, ed., *American Military History, Volume 1* (Washington, DC: Center of Military History, U.S. Army, 2009), 64.

7. See "To George Washington from Major General Charles Lee, 1/5/1776 & 2/19/1776," https://founders.archives.gov/?q=Correspondent%3A%22Lee%2C%20Charles%22%20Correspondent%3A%22Washington%2C%20George%22&s=1111311111&r=2 and https://founders.archives.gov/documents/Washington/03-03-02-0242, last accessed 1/8/25.

8. See "From George Washington to John Hancock, 7/10/1776," https://founders.archives.gov/documents/Washington/03-05-02-0188#:~:text=I%20am%20now%20to%20acknowledge,hand%20with%20their%20Important%20Inclosures.&text=It%20is%20with%20great%20pleasure,to%20form%20the%20flying%20camp, last accessed 11/14/23.

9. Sir George Otto Trevelyan, *The American Revolution, Part 1* (New York: Longmans, Green and Co., 1915), 317.

10. Fischer, *Washington's Crossing*, 70–71.

11. See "To George Washington from Major General Charles Lee, 2/29/1776," https://founders.archives.gov/?q=Correspondent%3A%22Lee%2C%20Charles%22%20Correspondent%3A%22Washington%2C%20George%22&s=1111311111&r=15, last accessed 1/8/25.

12. Barnet Schecter, *The Battle for New York* (New York: Walker and Company, 2002), 104.

13. Stewart, *American Military History, Volume 1*, 66.

14. Schecter, *Battle for New York*, 154–56.

15. Edwin Burrows, *Forgotten Patriots: The Untold Story of American Prisoners During the American Revolution* (New York: Basic Books, 2008), 62–64.

16. National Constitution Center, "How Thomas Paine's Other Pamphlet Saved the Revolution," December 19, 2022, https://constitutioncenter.org/blog/how-thomas-paines-other-pamphlet-saved-the-revolution, last accessed 11/19/23.

17. John Ferling, *Almost a Miracle* (New York: Oxford University Press, 2007), 168.

18. National Archives, "From George Washington to Major General Charles Lee, 12/1/1776," https://founders.archives.gov/documents/Washington/03-07-02-0180, last accessed 11/20/23.

19. Ferling, *Almost a Miracle*, 172.

20. Fischer, *Washington's Crossing*, Appendix R, 412.

21. Fischer, *Washington's Crossing*, 313.

22. To George Washington from Major General Charles Lee, 2/19/1776," https://founders.archives.gov/documents/Washington/03-03-02-0242.

23. For example, McCullough in *1776*, 195, or Forrest McDonald, "George Washington: Indispensable Man," *Imaginative Conservative*, 2/21/22, https://theimaginativeconservative.org/2022/02/george-washington-indispensable-man-forrest-mcdonald.html, or Mark Edward Lender, "The 'Indispensable Man': Would the Revolution Have Succeeded without George Washington?," https://www.mountvernon.org/george-washington/the-revolutionary-war/was-washington-the-indispensable-man/would-the-revolution-have-succeeded-without-george-washington./, accessed 8/13/24.

24. "From Major General Lafayette to George Washington, 12/30/1777," https://founders.archives.gov/documents/Washington/03-13-02-0063.

Chapter 2: The Fall of Savannah and Charles Town to the Battle of Guilford Courthouse

1. Charles Town changed its name to Charleston in 1783 with the conclusion of the Revolutionary War. See https://www.charleston-sc.gov/2010/History#:~:text=It%20

is%20the%20oldest%20and%20largest%20city%20in%20South%20Carolina.&text=present%20location%20on%20Oyster%20Point,Charleston%E2%80%93Summerville%20Metropolitan%20Statistical%20Area, last accessed 1/1/24.

2. Thomas Fleming, "The Enigma of General Howe," *American Heritage,* February 1964, https://www.americanheritage.com/enigma-general-howe#:~:text=Had%20Sir%20William%20Howe%20fortified,he%20was%20sure%20of%20Victory, last accessed 1/16/24.

3. George Billias, ed., *George Washington's Opponents* (New York: William Morrow & Co, 1968), 83.

4. Ferling, *Almost a Miracle*, 268–69, 473.

5. See University of Maryland Baltimore County: https://userpages.umbc.edu/~bouton/History407/SlaveStats.htm, last accessed 1/22/24.

6. Ibid.

7. George Livermore, "An Historical Research Respecting the Opinions of the Founders of the Republic on Negroes as Slaves, as Citizens, and as Soldiers," *Proceedings of the Massachusetts Historical Society, Volume 6*, Annual Meeting 1862–1863 (Boston: John Wilson & Son, 1863), 218.

8. Ferling, *Almost a Miracle*, 416–17.

9. Archibald Campbell to Lord Carlisle, 1/18/79, The History of Parliament, https://www.historyofparliamentonline.org/volume/1754-1790/member/campbell-archibald-1739-91, last accessed 1/12/24.

10. David Wilson, *The Southern Strategy* (Columbia: University of South Carolina Press, 2005), 194.

11. Billias, *George Washington's Opponents*, 85.

12. Wilson, *Southern Strategy*, 218.

13. Wilson, *Southern Strategy*, 206.

14. Wilson, *Southern Strategy*, 222.

15. Francis Vinton Greene, *The Revolutionary War and the Military Policy of the United States* (New York: Charles Scribner's Sons, 1911), 210–11.

16. Ferling, *Almost a Miracle*, 451–55.

17. Ferling, *Almost a Miracle*, 451–52.

18. John Buchanan, *The Road to Guilford Courthouse* (Hoboken, NJ: Wiley, 1997), 153–60; also see Jim Stempel, *American Hannibal* (Tucson, AZ: Penmore Press, 2018), Chapter 1.

19. Ferling, *Almost a Miracle*, 441.

20. Ferling, *Almost a Miracle*, 441–42.

21. John Pancake, *This Destructive War* (Tuscaloosa: University of Alabama Press, 1985), 107.

22. Pancake, *This Destructive War*, 107.

23. John Shafroth, "The Strategy of the Yorktown Campaign, 1781," *Proceedings*, Vol. 57/6/340, U.S. Naval Institute, June 1931.

24. Randall Jones, "The Overmountain Men and the Battle of Kings Mountain," ncpedia.org, https://www.ncpedia.org/anchor/overmountain-men-and-battle#:~:text=From%20Gilbert%20Town%2C%20an%20aggravated,country%20with%20fire%20and%20sword.%E2%80%9D, last accessed 1/8/24.

25. National Park Service website, https://www.nps.gov/guco/learn/historyculture/index.htm, last accessed 1/9/24.
26. Ferling, *Almost a Miracle*, 363.
27. Gerald Carbone, *Nathanael Greene* (New York: Palgrave MacMillan, 2008), 143–44.
28. American Battlefield Trust, https://www.battlefields.org/learn/primary-sources/we-fight-get-beat-and-fight-again-nathanael-greene-george-washington-1781, last accessed 1/7/24.
29. Carbone, *Nathanael Greene*, 153.
30. William Johnson, *Sketches of the Life and Correspondence of Nathanael Greene, Volume 1* (Charleston, SC: A. E. Miller, 1822), 346–47.
31. Ferling, *Almost a Miracle*, 479–80.
32. Billias, *George Washington's Opponents*, 210.
33. Andrew Waters, "To the End of the World: Cornwallis Pursues Morgan to the Catawba," *Journal of the American Revolution*, 5/23/19, https://allthingsliberty.com/2019/05/to-the-end-of-the-world-cornwallis-pursues-morgan-to-the-catawba/, last accessed 1/10/24.
34. Ferling, *Almost a Miracle*, 494.
35. Carbone, *Nathanael Greene*, 182.
36. Carbone, *Nathanael Greene*, 182.
37. Terry Golway, *Washington's General: Nathanael Greene and the Triumph of the American Revolution* (New York: Henry Holt & Company, 2006), 263–64.
38. John Ferling, "The Troubled Relationship Between Clinton and Cornwallis and Their 'War' After the War," *Journal of the American Revolution*, 7/15/21, https://allthingsliberty.com/2021/07/the-troubled-relationship-between-clinton-and-cornwallis-and-their-war-after-the-war/, last accessed 1/12/24.
39. Richard Henry Lee to Sam Adams, April 1781, Lee Family Digital Archive, https://leefamilyarchive.org/family-papers/letters/letters-1700-1800/9-family-papers/986-richard-henry-lee-to-sam-adams-1781-april-1, last accessed 1/12/24.
40. Ferling, *Almost a Miracle*, 519.
41. Ferling, *Almost a Miracle*, 468–75.

Chapter 3: From the Failed Invasion of Canada to the Battles of Lake Erie and the Thames

1. *Bicentennial Edition: Historical Statistics of the United States, Colonial Times to 1970*, Part 1, Chapter A, 8, census.gov, https://www.census.gov/library/publications/1975/compendia/hist_stats_colonial-1970.html, last accessed 1/22/24, and University of Maryland Baltimore County, https://userpages.umbc.edu/~bouton/History407/SlaveStats.htm, last accessed 1/22/24.
2. USS *Constitution* Museum website, "War of 1812 Overview," https://ussconstitutionmuseum.org/major-events/war-of-1812-overview/#:~:text=Under%20the%20authority%20of%20the,ships%20between%201803%20and%201812, last accessed 8/13/24.
3. Walter Borneman, *1812: The War That Forged a Nation* (New York: HarperCollins, 2004), 57.

4. Thomas Jefferson to William Duane, 8/4/1812, National Park Service website, https://www.nps.gov/articles/a-mere-matter-of-marching.htm, last accessed 1/23/24.

5. Stewart, *American Military History, Volume 1*, 132–34.

6. UK Ministry of Defense Freedom of Information Act release dated 4/28/17, Reference FOI2017/04440, 4, see also The Napoleon Series Archive, https://www.napoleon-series.org/research/abstract/population/population/britain/c_population1.html, last accessed 1/25/24.

7. Peter Cozzens, *Tecumseh and the Prophet: The Shawnee Brothers Who Defied a Nation* (New York: Alfred Knopf, 2020), 312–13.

8. American Battlefield Trust website, "William Hull: Proclamation," https://www.battlefields.org/learn/primary-sources/william-hull-proclamation, last accessed 1/23/24.

9. Ferdinand Brock Tupper, *The Life and Correspondence of Major-General Sir Isaac Brock* (London: Simpkin, Marshall & Co., 1846), 246.

10. Borneman, *1812: The War That Forged a Nation*, 72–75.

11. Borneman, *1812: The War That Forged a Nation*, 100–101.

12. John Trowbridge, "'Doomed to Their Fate': Kentuckians at Dudley's Defeat, 5 May 1813," *Kentucky Ancestors*, Genealogical Quarterly of the Kentucky Historical Society, Vol. 40, no. 3 (2005), 154–55.

13. Denys Knoll, "Battle of Lake Erie: Building the Fleet in the Wilderness," Naval History and Heritage Command, https://www.history.navy.mil/research/library/online-reading-room/title-list-alphabetically/b/battle-of-lake-erie-building-the-fleet-in-the-wilderness.html, last accessed 1/30/24.

14. Theodore Roosevelt, *The Naval War of 1812* (New York: G.P. Putnam's Sons, 1883), 260–61.

15. Roosevelt, *Naval War of 1812*, 272.

16. Cozzens, *Tecumseh and the Prophet*, 409.

17. Borneman, *1812: The War that Forged a Nation*, 178–79.

Chapter 4: The Rout at First Bull Run to the Critical Victory at Antietam

1. "Fast Facts," U.S. Census Bureau website, https://www.census.gov/history/www/through_the_decades/fast_facts/, accessed 5/23/24.

2. George Davis et al., Board of Publishers, *The War of the Rebellion* (Washington, DC: Government Printing Office, 1897).

3. John Chambers II, ed., *The Oxford Companion to American Military History* (New York: Oxford University Press, 1999), 849.

4. See Samuel W. Mitcham Jr., *It Wasn't About Slavery: Exposing the Great Lie of the Civil War* (Washington, DC: Regnery, 2020).

5. Sidney Blumenthal, "Nikki Haley's Comment on the US Civil War Was No Gaffe," *The Guardian*, January 1, 2024, https://www.theguardian.com/commentisfree/2024/jan/01/nikki-haleys-comment-on-the-us-civil-war-was-no-gaffe#:~:text=%E2%80%9CI%20think%20the%20cause%20of,do%2C%E2%80%9D%20Haley%20began%20haltingly, accessed 5/23/24.

6. The Emancipation Proclamation (1863), U.S. National Archives website, https://www.archives.gov/milestone-documents/emancipation-proclamation, accessed 4/6/24.

7. John McCormick and Shannon Najimabadi, "Nikki Haley Says 'Of Course' Civil War Was About Slavery, Following Criticism," *Wall Street Journal*, December 28, 2023, https://www.wsj.com/politics/elections/nikki-haley-comes-under-criticism-for-failing-to-mention-slavery-as-cause-of-civil-war-6dce6dd1, accessed 3/21/24.

8. James McPherson, *Battle Cry of Freedom* (New York: Oxford University Press, 1988), 332.

9. Alexis de Tocqueville, *Democracy in America* (Chicago: University of Chicago Press, 2002), 331–32.

10. Donald Stoker, *The Grand Design: Strategy and the U.S. Civil War* (New York: Oxford University Press, 2010), 23–24.

11. Bruce Catton, *The American Heritage New History of the Civil War* (New York: Penguin Books, 1996), 69.

12. Catton, *New History of the Civil War*, 63, 102.

13. Stoker, *Grand Design*, 38.

14. McPherson, *Battle Cry of Freedom*, 336.

15. Justin Stanage, communicated by Dr. Donald B. Marty, "The Rifle-Musket vs. the Smoothbore Musket, a Comparison of Effectiveness of the Two Types of Weapons Primarily at Short Ranges," Indiana University Department of History, https://scholarworks.iu.edu/journals/index.php/iusburj/article/download/19841/25918/43984, accessed 3/22/24.

16. John Erath, "Union Success in the Civil War and Lessons for Strategic Leaders," *Joint Force Quarterly* 77, National Defense University Press, April 2015, https://ndupress.ndu.edu/JFQ/Joint-Force-Quarterly-77/Article/581883/union-success-in-the-civil-war-and-lessons-for-strategic-leaders/, accessed 3/27/24.

17. Stoker, *Grand Design*, 42.

18. Tracey McIntire, "'We Bury Our Dead'—The Effects of Civil War Artillery," National Museum of Civil War Medicine, June 8, 2022, https://www.civilwarmed.org/effects-of-artillery/, accessed 3/22/24.

19. Catton, *New History of the Civil War*, 78.

20. McPherson, *Battle Cry of Freedom*, 342.

21. Shelby Foote, *The Civil War, A Narrative, Vol. 1* (New York: Vintage, 1986), 80–81.

22. Mark Greenbaum, "Lincoln's Do-Nothing Generals," *New York Times*, November 27, 2011, https://archive.nytimes.com/opinionator.blogs.nytimes.com/2011/11/27/lincolns-do-nothing-generals/, accessed 3/27/24.

23. Mike Barhorst, "A Brief Overview of the US Navy in the Civil War," Civil War Living History, http://sidneycivilwar.org/articles/a-brief-overview-of-the-us-navy-in-the-civil-war/#:~:text=By%20Christmas%201861%2C%20the%20number,had%20become%20the%20world's%20largest, accessed 3/27/24.

24. McPherson, *Battle Cry of Freedom*, 360.

25. National Museum of the U.S. Army website, https://www.thenmusa.org/biographies/george-b-mcclellan/#:~:text=He%20frequently%20clashed%20with%20Lincoln,for%20a%20time.%E2%80%9D%20Despite%20his, accessed 3/28/24.

26. James McPherson, *Tried By War* (New York: Penguin, 2008), 113.

27. Stoker, *Grand Design*, 30.

28. "General George B. McClellan to President Abraham Lincoln, on the Peninsula Campaign," July 7, 1862, East Tennessee State University website, https://faculty.etsu.edu/history/documents/mcclellan.htm, accessed 4/1/2024.

29. Abraham Lincoln letter to Horace Greeley published in the *Daily National Intelligencer*, August 22, 1862, Library of Congress, https://www.loc.gov/resource/mal.4233400/?st=text, accessed 4/1/24.

30. "An Invitation to Battle: Special Orders 191," National Park Service website, https://www.nps.gov/mono/learn/historyculture/an-invitation-to-battle.htm#xiv, accessed 3/31/24.

31. D. Scott Hartwig, *I Dread the Thought of the Place: The Battle of Antietam and the End of the Maryland Campaign* (Baltimore: Johns Hopkins University Press, 2023), 818–25.

32. Foote, *Civil War, A Narrative, Vol. 1*, 703–4.

33. Stoker, *Grand Design*, 30.

34. Richard Stewart, gen. ed., *The United States Army and the Forging of a Nation, 1775–1917, Vol. 1* (Washington, DC: Center of Military History, U.S. Army, 2009), 203 (Office of the Chief of Military History, U.S. Army, 190).

35. McPherson, *Battle Cry of Freedom*, 339.

36. James McPherson, *Crossroads of Freedom: Antietam* (New York: Oxford University Press, 2002), 155.

37. U.S. House of Representatives, 38th Congress (1863–1865), https://history.house.gov/Congressional-Overview/Profiles/38th/, accessed 4/6/24.

38. Robert Gammage, "British Opposition to the Annexation of Texas, 1841–1845," Sam Houston State University, 1965, https://shsu-ir.tdl.org/items/202ce33c-9f0f-437f-bf9f-222e62f38e0b, accessed 7/8/24.

Chapter 5: Disaster at Pearl Harbor to Victory at Midway

1. U.S. Census Bureau History: Battle of the Little Bighorn, https://www.census.gov/history/www/homepage_archive/2016/june_2016.html, accessed 4/14/24.

2. Mark Harrison, ed., *The Economics of World War II: Six Great Powers in International Comparison* (Cambridge: Cambridge University Press, 1998), 21, 23. Conversion of 1990 US dollars to 2024 U.S. dollars using the CPI inflation calculator found at www.in2013dollars.com/us/inflation/1990?amount=1, accessed 12/17/24.

3. Federal Reserve Bank of St. Louis unemployment rate data series, https://fred.stlouisfed.org/series/M0892BUSM156SNBR, accessed 4/15/24.

4. John Keegan, *The Price of Admiralty* (New York: Penguin, 1988), 196.

5. Fumimaro Konoe, *Memoirs of Prince Fumimaro Konoe* (San Francisco: Pacific Atrocities Education, 2020), 30.

6. Soviet Pacific Fleet data is for June 1941 from J. Rohwer and M. S. Monakov, *Stalin's Ocean-Going Fleet: Soviet Naval Strategy and Shipbuilding Programmes, 1935–1953* (London: Frank Cass Publishers, 2001), 138, and does not include thirty-seven small submarines. Other naval strengths data is for September 1941 from John Keegan, ed., *HarperCollins Atlas of the Second World War* (Ann Arbor: Borders Press, 1999), 67.

7. H. F. D. Davis, "Building Major Combatant Ships in World War II," *Proceedings*, May 1947, U.S. Naval Institute, https://www.usni.org/magazines/proceedings/1947/may/building-major-combatant-ships-world-war-ii, accessed 4/15/24.

8. Willem Remmelink, ed., *The Operations of the Navy in the Dutch East Indies and the Bay of Bengal: Compiled by the War History Office of the National Defense College of Japan* (Leiden, Netherlands: Leiden University Press, 2018), 10.

9. Christopher O'Connor, "A Japanese Connection," *Naval History Magazine*, U.S. Naval Institute, December 2016, https://www.usni.org/magazines/naval-history-magazine/2016/december/taranto-pearl-harbor-connection, accessed 4/18/24.

10. Gordon Price, *At Dawn We Slept* (New York: Penguin Books, 1981), 16. The full quotation can be found at BrainyQuote.com, https://www.brainyquote.com/quotes/isoroku_yamamoto_833448, accessed 4/18/24.

11. IJN carriers in 1941 were the *Hosho, Kaga, Akagi, Hiryu, Soryu, Ryujo, Shokaku, Zuikaku, Shoho,* and *Zuiho.* At that time the British navy had twelve carriers and the United States had eight. See *Naval Encyclopedia* entry "Imperial Japanese Navy WW2," https://naval-encyclopedia.com/ww2/imperial-japanese-navy-ww2.php?amp=1, accessed 4/15/24.

12. "Brig. Gen. William 'Billy' Mitchell," National Museum of the United States Air Force, https://www.nationalmuseum.af.mil/Visit/Museum-Exhibits/Fact-Sheets/Display/Article/196418/brig-gen-william-billy-mitchell/, accessed 5/23/24.

13. David Reimers, "Blueprints for Destruction," *Naval History Magazine*, U.S. Naval Institute, August 2018, https://www.usni.org/magazines/naval-history-magazine/2018/august/blueprints-destruction, accessed 4/19/24.

14. "U.S. Navy Exercise Simulated Pearl Harbor Attack 18 Months Before It Happened," National Museum of World War II Aviation, June 15, 2021, https://www.worldwariiaviation.org/u-s-navy-exercise-simulated-pearl-harbor-attack-18-months-before-it-happened, accessed 4/19/24.

15. "U.S. Navy Exercise Simulated Pearl Harbor Attack."

16. "Italy War Fleet Quit Taranto Base," *New York Times*, November 26, 1940, https://timesmachine.nytimes.com/timesmachine/1940/11/26/113119942.html, accessed 4/19/24.

17. Price, *At Dawn We Slept*, 38–39.

18. Price, *At Dawn We Slept*, 133.

19. William Bartsch, *December 8, 1941: MacArthur's Pearl Harbor* (College Station: Texas A&M University Press, 2003), Appendix C.

20. Price, *At Dawn We Slept*, 72–73.

21. Price, *At Dawn We Slept*, 125–26.

22. Price, *At Dawn We Slept*, 315–19.

23. See "Pearl Harbor Warnings, 27 November and 3 December 1941," George Mason University, https://olli.gmu.edu/docstore/700docs/0901-703-PEARL%20HARBOR%20WARNINGS.pdf, accessed 4/17/24.

24. "Pearl Harbor Warnings."

25. Mark Skinner Watson, *Chief of Staff: Prewar Plans and Preparations* (Washington, DC: Center of Military History, U.S. Army, 1991), 474. Also see, Samuel Cox, "H-001-1/2021: Pearl Harbor, 7 December 1941," *The Sextant,* 12/23/21, Naval History and Heritage Command, https://usnhistory.navylive.dodlive.mil/H-Gram-Series/Article-View/Article/2883072/h-001-12021-pearl-harbor-7-december-1941/, accessed 4/21/24.

26. Richard Frank, "The Three Missed Tactical Warnings That Could Have Made a Difference at Pearl Harbor," National World War II Museum website, https://www

.nationalww2museum.org/war/articles/pearl-harbor-missed-tactical-warnings, accessed 4/23/24.

27. "Japanese Midget Submarine: Sunk Dec 7, 1941—Found Aug, 2002," Hawai'i Undersea Research Laboratory, University of Hawai'i, https://www.soest.hawaii.edu/HURL/midget.php, accessed 4/21/24.

28. Frank, "Three Missed Tactical Warnings."

29. Price, *At Dawn We Slept*, 501–2.

30. "Kermit Tyler: A Call That Would Live in Infamy," The National World War II Museum, https://www.nationalww2museum.org/war/articles/kermit-tyler-call-would-live-infamy, accessed 4/21/24.

31. "Remembering Pearl Harbor, A Pearl Harbor Fact Sheet," National World War II Museum, https://www.census.gov/history/pdf/pearl-harbor-fact-sheet-1.pdf, accessed 4/22/24.

32. "Remembering Pearl Harbor."

33. National Museum of the Pacific War, https://www.pacificwarmuseum.org/about/admiral-nimitz, accessed 5/5/24.

34. Pete Mecca, "A Veteran's Story: The Japanese Failed Miserably," *Clayton News Daily*, 12/7/2018, https://www.news-daily.com/news/a-veteran-s-story-the-japanese-failed-miserably/article_59b501c1-a344-53a1-9c19-331733426522.html#:~:text=A%20young%20helmsman%20asked%20Nimitz,was%20taking%20care%20of%20America, accessed 5/15/24.

35. NavSource Naval History, https://www.navsource.org/Naval/usf01.htm, accessed 5/16/24.

36. *Early Raids in the Pacific Ocean, February 1 to March 10, 1942* (Washington, DC: Office of Naval Intelligence, U.S. Navy, 1943).

37. John Wukowitz, "Pearl Harbor Payback," Warfare History Network, https://warfarehistorynetwork.com/article/pearl-harbor-payback/, accessed 5/21/24.

38. Keegan, *Price of Admiralty*, 212.

39. Ernest King and Walter Muir Whitehill, *Fleet Admiral King* (New York: W.W. Norton, 1952). See chapter 31, "The Shift to the Offensive-Defensive in the Pacific."

40. Samuel Eliot Morison, *The Two-Ocean War* (Boston: Little, Brown & Co., 1963), 143.

41. Walter Borneman, *The Admirals* (New York: Back Bay Books, 2012), 252–54.

42. Borneman, *Admirals*.

43. "U.S. Destroyer Sunk, 44 of 120 Crew Rescued; President Sees No Change in Foreign Policy; Germans Gain in Drive Southwest of Moscow," *New York Times*, November 1, 1941, https://timesmachine.nytimes.com/timesmachine/1941/11/01/99323416.html?pageNumber=1, accessed 5/19/24.

44. "Polling and Pearl Harbor," 12/1/16, Roper Center for Public Opinion Research, https://ropercenter.cornell.edu/blog/polling-and-pearl-harbor, accessed 5/19/24, and "How Did Public Opinion About Entering World War II Change Between 1939 and 1941?," U.S. Holocaust Memorial Museum, https://exhibitions.ushmm.org/americans-and-the-holocaust/us-public-opinion-world-war-II-1939-1941, accessed 5/19/24.

Chapter 6: The Fall of Luzon to the Siege of Buna-Gona

1. Louis Morton, *The Fall of the Philippines* (Washington, DC: U.S. Army Center of Military History, 1953), 35.

2. David DuBois, "Admiral Thomas C. Hart and the Demise of the Asiatic Fleet 1941–1942," East Tennessee State University School of Graduate Studies, M.A. thesis, 2014, 27, https://dc.etsu.edu/etd/2331/, accessed 5/18/24.

3. Alan Schom, *The Eagle and the Rising Sun* (New York: W.W. Norton & Co., 2004), 205.

4. Morton, *Fall of the Philippines*, 129–33.

5. Gerhard Weinberg, *A World at Arms: A Global History of World War II* (Cambridge: Cambridge University Press, 2005), 314.

6. Radio Marshall to Wainwright, 3/26/42, quoted from Morton, *Fall of the Philippines*, 401.

7. John Curtin, "The Task Ahead," *The Herald*, 12/27/41, The John Curtin Ministerial Library, http://john.curtin.edu.au/pmportal/text/00468.html, last accessed 12/16/21.

8. Robert Eichelberger, *Our Jungle Road to Tokyo* (Scranton, PA: Arcadia Press, 2017, original printing 1950), 26.

9. Morton, *Fall of the Philippines,* 381–91.

10. Morton, *Fall of the Philippines*, 412–13.

11. William Manchester, *American Caesar* (Boston, MA: Little Brown & Co., 1978), 237.

12. See Forrest Pogue, *George Marshall Ordeal and Hope: 1939–1942* (New York: Viking Adult, 1966), 234; John T. Correll, "Disaster in the Philippines," https://www.airforcemag.com/article/disaster-in-the-philippines/, accessed 12/7/21; and Stephen Budiansky, *Battle of Wits: The Complete Story of Codebreaking in World War II* (New York: Simon & Schuster, 2000), 10.

13. Weinberg, *World At Arms*, 341, 343–44.

14. Edward Drea, *MacArthur's Ultra* (Lawrence: University of Kansas Press, 1991), 59.

Chapter 7: Black Thursday over Schweinfurt to Bombing the "Big B"

1. See for example, Ross Hall, "Inter-War Airpower Theory and World War II," *E-International Relations*, 6/28/11, accessed 6/24/24, or John Correll, "Targeting the Luftwaffe," *Air & Space Forces Magazine*, 1/30/18, https://www.airandspaceforces.com/article/targeting-the-luftwaffe/, accessed 6/24/24.

2. *The United States Strategic Bombing Surveys*, Summary Report (Maxwell Air Force Base, AL: Air University Press reprint, 1987), 13.

3. John Correll, "Daylight Precision Bombing," *Air & Space Forces Magazine*, October 1, 2008, https://www.airandspaceforces.com/article/1008daylight/#:~:text=However%2C%20he%20said%2C%20%E2%80%9CWhen,engaged%20in%20bomb%20damage%20repair.%E2%80%9D, accessed 6/7/24.

4. Martin Middlebrook, *The Schweinfurt-Regensburg Mission* (New York: Charles Scribner's Sons, 1983), 20–21.

5. Middlebrook, *Schweinfurt-Regensburg Mission*, 18.

6. Wally Hoffman, "We Got Our Feet Wet," Preservation Foundation, www.storyhouse.org/wally6.html, accessed 11/22/21.

7. See Roger Freeman, *Mighty Eighth War Diary* (London: Jane's Publishing Company, 1981), 35–78.

8. Freeman, *Mighty Eighth War Diary*, 121.

9. Thomas Coffey, *Decision Over Schweinfurt* (New York: David McKay Co., 1977), 207–8.

10. Middlebrook, *Schweinfurt-Regensburg Mission*, 18.

11. Freeman, *Mighty Eighth War Diary*, 54. Also see archived data from "The United States Army Air Forces in World War II," https://web.archive.org/web/20090211101806/http://usaaf.net/chron/43/apr43.htm, accessed 6/18/24.

12. Freeman, *Mighty Eighth War Diary*, 56.

13. Middlebrook, *Schweinfurt-Regensburg Mission*, 19.

14. See archived data from "The United States Army Air Forces in World War II," https://web.archive.org/web/20090212182006/http://usaaf.net/chron/43/aug43.htm, accessed 6/19/24.

15. Roger Freeman, *Mighty Eighth War Diary* (New York: Doubleday & Co., 1970), 106.

16. Coffey, *Decision Over Schweinfurt*, 9.

17. Freeman, *Mighty Eighth War Diary*, 81.

18. Wesley Craven, James Cate, eds., *The Army Air Forces in World War II, Volume 2* (Washington, DC: Office of Air Force History, 1983), 484, 684.

19. Middlebrook, *Schweinfurt-Regensburg Mission*, 283.

20. Middlebrook, *Schweinfurt-Regensburg Mission*, 285–86.

21. Ronald Schaffer, *Wings of Judgment* (New York: Oxford University Press, 1985), 66.

22. Albert Speer, *Inside The Third Reich* (New York: Macmillan, 1970), 280.

23. Speer, *Inside the Third Reich*, 284–85.

24. Coffey, *Decision Over Schweinfurt*, 262–63.

25. "B-17 Flying Fortress," Imperial War Museum, https://www.iwm.org.uk/history/b-17-flying-fortress, accessed 8/13/24.

26. Coffey, *Decision Over Schweinfurt*, 264.

27. Freeman, *Mighty Eighth War Diary*, 106.

28. Coffey, *Decision Over Schweinfurt*, 332.

29. Coffey, *Decision Over Schweinfurt*, 332.

30. Coffey, *Decision Over Schweinfurt*, 334.

31. Speer, *Inside the Third Reich*, 286–87.

32. "VIII Bomber Command 119," American Air Museum in Britain, https://www.americanairmuseum.com/archive/mission/viii-bomber-command-119, accessed 6/24/24.

33. Freeman, *Mighty Eighth War Diary*, 79.

34. Wesley Craven, James Cate, Editors, *The Army Air Forces in World War II, Volume 2* (Office of Air Force History, Washington, DC, 1983), 663

35. *Army Air Forces in World War II, Volume 2,* 639.

36. Donald Miller, *Masters of the Air* (New York: Simon & Schuster, 2006), 234.

37. Miller, *Masters of the Air*, 236.

38. Correll, "Targeting the Luftwaffe."

39. "Eighth Air Force History," Eighth Air Force website, https://www.8af.af.mil/About-Us/Fact-Sheets/Display/Article/333794/eighth-air-force-history/, accessed 6/25/24.

40. Arnold Harvey, "The Battle of Britain, in 1940 and 'Big Week' in 1944: A Comparative Perspective," *Air Power History*, Vol. 59, no. 1 (Spring 2012), https://www.jstor.org/stable/26276145#:~:text=14%20Because%20of%20the%20large,both%20campaigns%20was%20to%20weaken, accessed 6/25/24.

41. Freeman, *Mighty Eighth*, 112.

42. Freeman, *Mighty Eighth*, 113, 118.

43. Speer, *Inside the Third Reich*, 346.

44. "The German Response to D-Day," Imperial War Museums website, https://www.iwm.org.uk/history/the-german-response-to-d-day, accessed 6/25/24.

45. Barrett Tillman, "Hard Targets," *Air Force Magazine*, 2/2015, https://www.airandspaceforces.com/PDF/MagazineArchive/Magazine%20Documents/2015/February%202015/0215targets.pdf, accessed 6/27/24.

46. Freeman, *Mighty Eighth War Diary*, 5.

47. Speer, *Inside the Third Reich*, 285.

48. Max Hastings, *RAF Bomber Command* (London: Pan Books, 2021), 334.

49. Everest Riccioni, "Strategic Bombing: Always a Myth," *Proceedings*, November 1996, https://www.usni.org/magazines/proceedings/1996/november/strategic-bombing-always-myth, accessed 6/27/24.

50. *United States Strategic Bombing Surveys*, 13.

51. *United States Strategic Bombing Surveys*, 13.

52. John Huston, ed., *American Airpower Comes of Age, General Henry H. "Hap" Arnold's World War II Diaries, Vol. 2* (Maxwell Air Force Base, AL: Air University Press, 2002), 68.

53. *American Airpower Comes of Age, Vol. 2*, 48–51, 150.

54. "Eighth Air Force History."

55. 398th Bomb Group Memorial Association, https://www.398th.org/History/KIA/index.html, accessed 6/28/24.

Chapter 8: From the Double Defeat on the Chongchon to the Recovery of Seoul

1. James Ellman, *MacArthur Reconsidered* (Essex, CT: Stackpole, 2023), 156–59, 165–69.

2. See Jian Chen, *China's Road to the Korean War* (New York: Columbia University Press, 1996), 164, 169, and Roy Appleman, *South to the Naktong, North to the Yalu* (Washington, DC: Center of Military History, 1992), 608.

3. Chen, *China's Road to the Korean War*, 144–45.

4. Appleman, *South to the Naktong, North to the Yalu*, 760.

5. Chen, *China's Road to the Korean War*, 206–8.

6. Appleman, *South to the Naktong, North to the Yalu*, 670.

7. Shu Guang Zhang, *Mao's Military Romanticism: China and the Korean War, 1950–1953* (Lawrence: University of Kansas Press, 1995), 105–6.

8. Harry Truman, *Years of Trial and Hope* (New York, Doubleday & Co., 1956), 373.

9. James Schnabel, *Policy and Direction: The First Year* (Washington, DC, Center of Military History, 1992), 243.

10. "The Commander in Chief, Far East (MacArthur) to the Joint Chiefs of Staff," Office of the Historian, Department of State, November 9, 1950, https://history.state.gov/historicaldocuments/frus1950v07/d792, accessed 8/13/24.

11. Edward Daily, *MacArthur's X Corps in Korea: Inchon to the Yalu* (Paducah, KY: Turner Publishing, 1950), 83.

12. John Toland, *In Mortal Combat: Korea, 1950–1953* (New York: William Morrow & Co., 1991), 272.

13. Douglas MacArthur, *Reminiscences* (New York: McGraw-Hill, 1964), 376–80.

14. MacArthur, *Reminiscences*, 378.

15. Billy Mossman, *Ebb and Flow* (Washington, DC: Center of Military History, U.S. Army, 1990), 23.

16. Mossman, *Ebb and Flow*, 53–55.

17. Joseph Lawton Collins, *War in Peacetime: The History and Lessons of Korea* (Boston: Houghton Mifflin, 1969), 249.

18. Collins, *War in Peacetime*, 252.

19. "The Commander in Chief, United Nations Command (MacArthur) to the Department of the Army," Office of the Historian, Department of State, January 10, 1951, https://history.state.gov/historicaldocuments/frus1951v07p1/d44, accessed 2/15/23.

20. Matthew Ridgway, *The Korean War* (New York: Doubleday, 1967), 89.

21. Mossman, *Ebb and Flow*, 310.

22. Zhang, *Mao's Military Romanticism*, 152.

23. "Greatest American Military General of All Time? Public Says Patton, Eisenhower and MacArthur," 12/8/2000, https://news.gallup.com/poll/2236/greatest-american-military-general-all-time-public-says-patton.aspx, accessed 2/15/24.

24. Ridgway, *Korean War*, 108.

25. Ridgway, *Korean War*, 88–89.

26. Michael Hickey, "The Korean War: An Overview," BBC website 3/21/11, https://www.bbc.co.uk/history/worldwars/coldwar/korea_hickey_01.shtml, accessed 3/7/24.

27. Rick Bragg, "Truman Wrote of '48 Offer to Eisenhower," *New York Times*, July 11, 2003, https://www.nytimes.com/2003/07/11/us/truman-wrote-of-48-offer-to-eisenhower.html, accessed 8/13/24.

28. Mark Moyar, *Triumph Forsaken: The Vietnam War, 1954–1965* (New York: Cambridge University Press, 2006), 26–29.

Chapter 9: Losing the War but Perhaps Winning the Fight: Vietnam, Afghanistan, and Iraq

1. The American Presidency Project, "Harry S. Truman Public Approval," University of California at Santa Barbara, https://www.presidency.ucsb.edu/statistics/data/harry-s-truman-public-approval, accessed 6/6/24.

2. See for example, "Wanna Fight America? 5 Reasons the U.S. Military Will Make You Dead," *National Interest*, 5/19/19, https://nationalinterest.org/blog/buzz/wanna-fight-america-5-reasons-us-military-will-make-you-dead-58422, accessed 6/10/24.

3. Bret Stephens, "Do We Still Understand How Wars Are Won?," *New York Times*, 5/28/24, https://www.nytimes.com/2024/05/28/opinion/israel-ukraine-war-us.html, accessed 6/10/24.

4. See Barnum et. al. *Global Military Spending Dataset*: chrome-extension://efaidnbmnnnibpcajpcglclefindmkaj/http://cfariss.com/documents/milex_determinants_appendix_JCR_01242024.pdf (2024); and Our World in Data: https://ourworldindata.org/grapher/military-spending-as-a-share-of-gdp-gmsd

5. Max Boot, *The Savage Wars of Peace* (New York: Basic Books, 2002), xiii.

6. Jeffrey J. Clarke, *United States Army in Vietnam: Advice and Support: The Final Years, 1965–1973* (Washington, DC: Center of Military History, U.S. Army, 1988), 275, and http://www.archives.gov/research/military/vietnam-war/casualty-statistics.html, accessed 6/9/24.

7. American War Library website, https://www.americanwarlibrary.com/vietnam/vwatl.htm, accessed 6/10/24.

8. Transcript of News Conference of 4/7/54 by President Eisenhower, Office of the Historian, Department of State, https://history.state.gov/historicaldocuments/frus1952-54v13p1/d716, accessed 6/10/24.

9. Edward Doyle, Samuel Lipsman, and Terrence Maitland, *The North* (Boston: Boston Publishing, 1986), 46.

10. Stanley Karnow, *Vietnam* (New York: Penguin Books, 1983), 544–55.

11. Lydia Saad, "Gallup Vault: Hawks vs. Doves on Vietnam," 5/24/16, Gallup website, https://news.gallup.com/vault/191828/gallup-vault-hawks-doves-vietnam.aspx, accessed 6/10/24.

12. Karnow, *Vietnam*, 602.

13. Remarks by President Bush, 8/5/90, Margaret Thatcher Foundation website, https://www.margaretthatcher.org/document/110704, accessed 6/10/24.

14. "Global War on Terror," George W. Bush Presidential Library, https://www.georgewbushlibrary.gov/research/topic-guides/global-war-terror#:~:text=On%20September%2020%2C%202001%2C%20President,it%20does%20not%20end%20there, accessed 8/13/24.

15. Carter Malkasian, *The American War in Afghanistan: A History* (New York: Oxford University Press, 2021), 70.

16. "Human and Budgetary Costs to Date of the U.S. War in Afghanistan, 2001–2022," Watson Institute, Brown University, https://watson.brown.edu/costsofwar/figures/2021/human-and-budgetary-costs-date-us-war-afghanistan-2001-2022, accessed 6/11/24.

17. "More Americans Now View Afghanistan War as a Mistake," 2/19/24, Gallup website, https://news.gallup.com/poll/167471/americans-view-afghanistan-war-mistake.aspx, accessed 6/12/24.

18. Glenn Kessler, "The Iraq War and WMDs: An Intelligence Failure or White House Spin?", *Washington Post*, 3/22/19, https://www.washingtonpost.com/politics/2019/03/22/iraq-war-wmds-an-intelligence-failure-or-white-house-spin/, accessed 6/12/24.

19. Thomas Ricks, *The Generals* (New York: Penguin, 2013), 396.

20. See for example, Michael Beschloss, *The Conquerors* (New York: Simon & Schuster, 2003) and Michael Schaller, *The American Occupation of Japan* (New York: Oxford University Press, 1985).

21. Thomas Ricks, *Fiasco* (New York: Penguin Press, 2006), 154–65.

22. Defense Casualty Analysis System, Operation Iraqi Freedom (OIF), https://dcas.dmdc.osd.mil/dcas/app/conflictCasualties/oif/byMonth, accessed 6/12/24.

23. Phil Klay, *Redeployment* (New York: Penguin Press, 2014), 85.

24. James Lindsay, "The Vietnam War in Forty Quotes," Council on Foreign Relations, 4/30/15, https://www.cfr.org/blog/vietnam-war-forty-quotes, accessed 6/13/24.

25. Mark Moyar, *Triumph Regained* (New York: Encounter Books, 2022), note 121 in index to chapter 17.

26. Hanh Nguyen, "US-Vietnam Trade Ties: Challenge Ahead," *Journal of Indo-Pacific Affairs*, 3/29/23, https://www.airuniversity.af.edu/JIPA/Display/Article/3344116/usvietnam-trade-ties-challenge-ahead/, accessed 6/10/24.

Conclusion

1. See Ricks, *Generals*.

2. Edward Luttwak, "Toward Post-Heroic Warfare," *Foreign Affairs*, May-June 1995, 109–22.

3. Lance Lambert, "The Coronavirus Has Now Killed More Americans Than Every War Since the Start of the Korean War Combined," *Fortune*, June 10, 2020, https://fortune.com/2020/06/10/coronavirus-deaths-us-covid-19-killed-more-americans-korean-war-vietnam-iraq-persian-gulf-combined-how-many-died/, accessed 7/3/2024.

Bibliography

Adams, John, to George Washington, January 6, 1776. Founders Online, National Archives. https://founders.archives.gov/documents/Adams/06-03-02-0200. Accessed November 14, 2023.

American Battlefield Trust. "'We Fight Get Beat and Fight Again': Nathanael Greene to George Washington, 1781." https://www.battlefields.org/learn/primary-sources/we-fight-get-beat-and-fight-again-nathanael-greene-george-washington-1781. Accessed January 7, 2024.

American Battlefield Trust. "William Hull: Proclamation." https://www.battlefields.org/learn/primary-sources/william-hull-proclamation. Accessed January 24, 2024.

The American Presidency Project. "Harry S. Truman Public Approval." University of California at Santa Barbara. https://www.presidency.ucsb.edu/statistics/data/harry-s-truman-public-approval. Accessed June 6, 2024.

American War Library. "Vietnam War Allied Troop Levels 1960–73." https://www.americanwarlibrary.com/vietnam/vwatl.htm. Accessed June 10, 2024.

Appleman, Roy E. *South to the Naktong, North to the Yalu*. Washington, DC: Center of Military History, 1992.

Barhorst, Mike. "A Brief Overview of the US Navy in the Civil War." Civil War Living History. http://sidneycivilwar.org/articles/a-brief-overview-of-the-us-navy-in-the-civil-war/#:~:text=By%20Christmas%201861%2C%20the%20number,had%20become%20the%20world's%20largest. Accessed March 27, 2024.

Bartsch, William H. *December 8, 1941: MacArthur's Pearl Harbor*. College Station: Texas A&M University Press, 2003. Appendix C.

Beschloss, Michael R. *The Conquerors: Roosevelt, Truman, and the Destruction of Hitler's Germany, 1941–1945*. New York: Simon & Schuster, 2003.

Billias, George, ed. *George Washington's Opponents*. New York: William Morrow & Co., 1968.

Blumenthal, Sidney. "Nikki Haley's Comment on the US Civil War Was No Gaffe." *The Guardian*, January 1, 2024. https://www.theguardian.com/commentisfree/2024/jan/01/nikki-haleys-comment-on-the-us-civil-war-was-no-gaffe#:~:text=%E2%80%9CI%20think%20the%20cause%20of,do%2C%E2%80%9D%20Haley%20began%20haltingly. Accessed May 23, 2024.

Boot, Max. *The Savage Wars of Peace: Small Wars and the Rise of American Power*. New York: Basic Books, 2002.

Borneman, Walter R. *1812: The War That Forged a Nation*. New York: HarperCollins, 2004.

Borneman, Walter R. *The Admirals: Nimitz, Halsey, Leahy, and King—the Five-Star Admirals Who Won the War at Sea*. New York: Back Bay Books, 2012.

Bragg, Rick. "Truman Wrote of '48 Offer to Eisenhower." *New York Times*, July 11, 2003. https://www.nytimes.com/2003/07/11/us/truman-wrote-of-48-offer-to-eisenhower.html. Accessed August 13, 2024.

Buchanan, John. *The Road to Guilford Courthouse: The American Revolution in the Carolinas*. Hoboken, NJ: Wiley, 1997.

Budiansky, Stephen. *Battle of Wits: The Complete Story of Codebreaking in World War II*. New York: Simon & Schuster, 2000.

Burrows, Edwin. *Forgotten Patriots: The Untold Story of American Prisoners During the American Revolution*. New York: Basic Books, 2008.

"Campbell, Archibald (1739–91), of Inverneil, Argyll." History of Parliament Online. https://www.historyofparliamentonline.org/volume/1754-1790/member/campbell-archibald-1739-91. Accessed August 13, 2024.

Carbone, Gerald. *Nathanael Greene: A Biography of the American Revolution*. New York: Palgrave Macmillan, 2008.

Catton, Bruce. *The American Heritage New History of the Civil War*. New York: Penguin Books, 1996.

Chambers, John Whiteclay II, ed. *The Oxford Companion to American Military History*. New York: Oxford University Press, 1999.

Chen, Jian. *China's Road to the Korean War: The Making of the Sino-American Confrontation*. New York: Columbia University Press, 1994.

City of Charleston. "History." https://www.charleston-sc.gov/2010/History. Accessed January 1, 2024.

Clarke, Jeffrey J. *United States Army in Vietnam: Advice and Support: The Final Years, 1965–1973*. Washington, DC: Center of Military History, U.S. Army, 1988.

Coffey, Thomas M. *Decision Over Schweinfurt*. New York: David McKay Co., 1977.

Collins, Joseph Lawton. *War in Peacetime: The History and Lessons of Korea*. Boston: Houghton Mifflin, 1969.

"The Commander in Chief, Far East (MacArthur) to the Joint Chiefs of Staff." November 8, 1950. In *Foreign Relations of the United States, 1950, Korea,* Volume VII. Office of the Historian, Department of State. https://history.state.gov/historicaldocuments/frus1950v07/d792. Accessed August 13, 2024.

"The Commander in Chief, United Nations Command (MacArthur) to the Department of the Army." January 10, 1951. In *Foreign Relations of the United States, 1951, Korea,* Volume VII, Part 1. Office of the Historian, Department of State. https://history.state.gov/historicaldocuments/frus1951v07p1/d44. Accessed February 15, 2023.

Copp, Tara, Associated Press. "Ukraine Pulls U.S.-Provided Abrams Tanks from the Front Lines Over Drone Threats." NPR.org, April 26, 2024. https://www.npr.org/2024/04/26/1247403968/ukraine-pulls-abrams-tanks-from-front-lines-russia-drone-threats#:~:text=Hourly%20News-,Ukraine%20pulls%20U.S.%2Dprovided%20Abrams%20tanks%20from%20front%20lines%20over,difficult%20for%20them%20to%20operate[1]. Accessed June 4, 2024.

Correll, John, "Disaster in the Philippines." *Air & Space Forces Magazine*. https://www.airforcemag.com/article/disaster-in-the-philippines. Accessed December 7, 2021.

Correll, John. "Targeting the Luftwaffe." *Air & Space Forces Magazine*. January 30, 2018. https://www.airandspaceforces.com/article/targeting-the-luftwaffe/. Accessed June 24, 2024.

Correll, John. "Daylight Precision Bombing." *Air & Space Forces Magazine*. October 1, 2008. https://www.airandspaceforces.com/article/1008daylight/#:~:text=However%2C%20he%20said%2C%20%E2%80%9CWhen,engaged%20in%20bomb%20damage%20repair.%E2%80%9D. Accessed June 7, 2024.

Cox, Samuel. "H-001-1/2021: Pearl Harbor, 7 December 1941." *The Sextant*. Naval History and Heritage Command, December 23, 2021. https://usnhistory.navylive.dodlive.mil/H-Gram-Series/Article-View/Article/2883072/h-001-12021-pearl-harbor-7-december. Accessed April 21, 2024.

Cozzens, Peter. *Tecumseh and the Prophet: The Shawnee Brothers Who Defied a Nation*. New York: Alfred A. Knopf, 2020.

Craven, Wesley, and James Cate, eds. *The Army Air Forces in World War II. Vol. 2, Europe: Torch to Pointblank, August 1942 to December 1943*. Washington, DC: Office of Air Force History, 1983.

Curtin, John. "The Task Ahead." *The Herald*, December 27, 1941. The John Curtin Ministerial Library. http://john.curtin.edu.au/pmportal/text/00468.html. Accessed December 16, 2021.

Daily, Edward. *MacArthur's X Corps in Korea: Inchon to the Yalu*. Paducah, KY: Turner Publishing, 1950.

Davis, George B., Leslie J. Perry, Joseph W. Kirkley et al., eds. *The War of the Rebellion: A Compilation of the Official Records of the Union and Confederate Armies*. Washington, DC: Government Printing Office, 1897.

Davis, H. F. D. "Building Major Combatant Ships in World War II." *Proceedings*, May 1947. U.S. Naval Institute. https://www.usni.org/magazines/proceedings/1947/may/building-major-combatant-ships-world-war-ii. Accessed April 15, 2024.

"D-Day: FDR and Churchill's 'Mighty Endeavor.'" FDR Presidential Library & Museum. https://www.fdrlibrary.org/mighty-endeavor. Accessed 6/3/24.

de Tocqueville, Alexis. *Democracy in America*. Translated by Harvey C. Mansfield and Delba Winthrop. Chicago: University of Chicago Press, 2002.

Defense Casualty Analysis System. "Operation Iraqi Freedom (OIF) Casualty Summary by Month." https://dcas.dmdc.osd.mil/dcas/app/conflictCasualties/oif/byMonth. Accessed June 12, 2024.

Doyle, Edward, Samuel Lipsman, and Terrence Maitland. *The North*. Boston: Boston Publishing Company, 1986.

Drea, Edward. *MacArthur's ULTRA: Codebreaking and the War against Japan, 1942–1945*. Lawrence: University of Kansas Press, 1991.

DuBois, David. "Admiral Thomas C. Hart and the Demise of the Asiatic Fleet 1941–1942." Master's thesis, East Tennessee State University School of Graduate Studies, 2014. https://dc.etsu.edu/etd/2331. Accessed May 18, 2024.

Eichelberger, Robert. *Our Jungle Road to Tokyo*. Scranton, PA: Arcadia Press, 2017 (originally published 1950).

"Eighth Air Force History." Eighth Air Force. https://www.8af.af.mil/About-Us/Fact-Sheets/Display/Article/333794/eighth-air-force-history/. Accessed June 25, 2024.

Ellman, James. *MacArthur Reconsidered: General Douglas MacArthur as a Wartime Commander*. Essex, CT: Stackpole, 2023.

Erath, John. "Union Success in the Civil War and Lessons for Strategic Leaders." *Joint Force Quarterly* 77 (April 2015). National Defense University Press. https://ndupress.ndu.edu/JFQ/Joint-Force-Quarterly-77/Article/581883/union-success-in-the-civil-war-and-lessons-for-strategic-leaders/. Accessed March 27, 2024.

Ferling, John. *Almost a Miracle: The American Victory in the War of Independence*. New York: Oxford University Press, 2007.

Ferling, John. "The Troubled Relationship Between Clinton and Cornwallis and Their 'War' After the War." *Journal of the American Revolution*, July 15, 2021. https://allthingsliberty.com/2021/07/the-troubled-relationship-between-clinton-and-cornwallis-and-their-war-after-the-war/. Accessed January 12, 2024.

Fischer, David Hackett. *Washington's Crossing*. New York: Oxford University Press, 2004.

Fleming, Thomas. "The Enigma of General Howe." *American Heritage*, February 1964. https://www.americanheritage.com/enigma-general-howe. Accessed January 16, 2024.

Foote, Shelby. *The Civil War: A Narrative, Vol. 1: Fort Sumter to Perryville*. New York: Vintage, 1986.

Frank, Richard. "The Three Missed Tactical Warnings That Could Have Made a Difference at Pearl Harbor." National World War II Museum. https://www.nationalww2museum.org/war/articles/pearl-harbor-missed-tactical-warnings. Accessed April 23, 2024.

Freeman, Roger. *Mighty Eighth War Diary*. London: Jane's Publishing Company, 1981.

Friedman, George, and Meredith Friedman. *The Future of War: Power, Technology and American World Dominance in the Twenty-First Century*. New York: St. Martin's Griffin, 1998.

Gallup. "Greatest American Military General of All Time? Public Says Patton, Eisenhower and MacArthur." https://news.gallup.com/poll/2236/greatest-american-military-general-all-time-public-says-patton.aspx. Accessed February 15, 2024.

Gallup. "More Americans Now View Afghanistan War as a Mistake." February 19, 2024. https://news.gallup.com/poll/167471/americans-view-afghanistan-war-mistake.aspx. Accessed June 12, 2024.

Gammage, Robert. "British Opposition to the Annexation of Texas, 1841–1845." Sam Houston State University, 1965. https://shsu-ir.tdl.org/items/202ce33c-9f0f-437f-bf9f-222e62f38e0b. Accessed July 8, 2024.

George Mason University. "Pearl Harbor Warnings, 27 November and 3 December 1941." https://olli.gmu.edu/docstore/700docs/0901-703-PEARL%20HARBOR%20WARNINGS.pdf. Accessed April 17, 2024.

George W. Bush Presidential Library and Museum. "Global War on Terror." https://www.georgewbushlibrary.gov/research/topic-guides/global-war-terror. Accessed August 13, 2024.

Golway, Terry. *Washington's General: Nathanael Greene and the Triumph of the American Revolution*. New York: Henry Holt & Company, 2006.

Greenbaum, Mark. "Lincoln's Do-Nothing Generals." *New York Times*, November 27, 2011. https://archive.nytimes.com/opinionator.blogs.nytimes.com/2011/11/27/lincolns-do-nothing-generals/. Accessed March 27, 2024.

Greene, Francis Vinton. *The Revolutionary War and the Military Policy of the United States*. New York: Charles Scribner's Sons, 1911.

Hall, Ross. "Inter-War Airpower Theory and World War II." *E-International Relations*, June 28, 2011. Accessed June 24, 2024.

Harrison, Mark, ed. *The Economics of World War II: Six Great Powers in International Comparison*. Cambridge: Cambridge University Press, 1998.

Hartwig, D. Scott. *I Dread the Thought of the Place: The Battle of Antietam and the End of the Maryland Campaign*. Baltimore: Johns Hopkins University Press, 2023.

Harvey, Arnold. "The Battle of Britain, in 1940 and 'Big Week' in 1944: A Comparative Perspective." *Air Power History* 59, no. 1 (Spring 2012). https://www.jstor.org/stable/26276145. Accessed June 25, 2024.

Hastings, Max. *RAF Bomber Command*. London: Pan Books, 2021.

Hawai'i Undersea Research Laboratory. "Japanese Midget Submarine: Sunk Dec 7, 1941—Found Aug, 2002." University of Hawai'i. https://www.soest.hawaii.edu/HURL/midget.php. Accessed April 21, 2024.

Hickey, Michael. "The Korean War: An Overview." *BBC History*. Last modified March 21, 2011. https://www.bbc.co.uk/history/worldwars/coldwar/korea_hickey_01.shtml. Accessed March 7, 2024.

Hoffman, Wally. "We Got Our Feet Wet." Preservation Foundation. www.storyhouse.org/wally6.html. Accessed November 22, 2021.

"Human and Budgetary Costs to Date of the U.S. War in Afghanistan, 2001–2022." Watson Institute for International and Public Affairs, Brown University. https://watson.brown.edu/costsofwar/figures/2021/human-and-budgetary-costs-date-us-war-afghanistan-2001-2022. Accessed June 11, 2024.

Huston, John W., ed. *American Airpower Comes of Age: General Henry H. "Hap" Arnold's World War II Diaries*. Vol. 2. Maxwell Air Force Base, AL: Air University Press, 2002.

Imperial War Museums. "B-17 Flying Fortress." https://www.iwm.org.uk/history/b-17-flying-fortress. Accessed August 13, 2024.

Imperial War Museums. "The German Response to D-Day." https://www.iwm.org.uk/history/the-german-response-to-d-day. Accessed June 25, 2024.

"Italy War Fleet Quit Taranto Base." *New York Times*, November 26, 1940. https://timesmachine.nytimes.com/timesmachine/1940/11/26/113119942.html. Accessed April 19, 2024.

Johnson, William. *Sketches of the Life and Correspondence of Nathanael Greene*. Vol. 1. Charleston, SC: A. E. Miller, 1822.

Jones, Randall. "The Overmountain Men and the Battle of Kings Mountain." NCpedia. https://www.ncpedia.org/anchor/overmountain-men-and-battle. Accessed January 8, 2024.

Karnow, Stanley. *Vietnam*. New York: Penguin Books, 1983.

Keegan, John, ed. *HarperCollins Atlas of the Second World War*. Ann Arbor: Border Press, 1999.

Keegan, John. *The Price of Admiralty: The Evolution of Naval Warfare*. New York: Penguin, 1988.

Kessler, Glenn. "The Iraq War and WMDs: An Intelligence Failure or White House Spin?" *Washington Post*, March 22, 2019. https://www.washingtonpost.com/politics/2019/03/22/iraq-war-wmds-an-intelligence-failure-or-white-house-spin/. Accessed June 12, 2024.

King, Ernest J., and Walter Muir Whitehill. *Fleet Admiral King: A Naval Record*. New York: W. W. Norton & Company, 1952.

Klay, Phil. *Redeployment*. New York: Penguin Press, 2014.

Knoll, Denys. "Battle of Lake Erie: Building the Fleet in the Wilderness." *Naval History and Heritage Command*. https://www.history.navy.mil/research/library/online-reading-room/title-list-alphabetically/b/battle-of-lake-erie-building-the-fleet-in-the-wilderness.html. Accessed January 30, 2024.

Konoe, Fumimaro. *Memoirs of Prince Fumimaro Konoe: The Secret Negotiations Between Japan and the United States Before Pearl Harbor*. Jenny Chan and Barbara Halperin, eds. San Francisco: Pacific Atrocities Education, 2020.

Lafayette, Maj. Gen., to George Washington, December 30, 1777. Founders Online, National Archives. https://founders.archives.gov/documents/Washington/03-13-02-0063. Accessed August 13, 2024.

Lambert, Lance. "The Coronavirus Has Now Killed More Americans Than Every War Since the Start of the Korean War Combined." *Fortune*. June 10, 2020. https://fortune.com/2020/06/10/coronoavirus-deaths-us-covid-19-killed-more-americans-korean-war-vietnam-iraq-persian-gulf-combined-how-many-died/. Accessed July 3, 2024.

"Lee, Charles, to George Washington, January 5, 1776." Founders Online, National Archives. https://founders.archives.gov/?q=Correspondent%3A%22Lee%2C%20Charles%22%20Correspondent%3A%22Washington%2C%20George%22&s=1111311111&r=2. Accessed August 13, 2024.

"Lee, Richard Henry, to Sam Adams, April 1781." Lee Family Digital Archive, https://leefamilyarchive.org/family-papers/letters/letters-1700-1800/9-family-papers/986-richard-henry-lee-to-sam-adams-1781-april-1. Accessed January 12, 2024.

Lender, Mark, "The 'Indispensable Man': Would the Revolution Have Succeeded without George Washington?" George Washington's Mount Vernon. https://www.mountvernon.org/george-washington/the-revolutionary-war/was-washington-the-indispensable-man/would-the-revolution-have-succeeded-without-george-washington/. Accessed August 13, 2024.

Lincoln, Abraham, to Horace Greeley. Published in the *Daily National Intelligencer*, August 22, 1862. https://www.loc.gov/resource/mal.4233400/?st=text. Library of Congress. Accessed April 1, 2024.

Lindsay, James. "The Vietnam War in Forty Quotes." Council on Foreign Relations, April 30, 2015. https://www.cfr.org/blog/vietnam-war-forty-quotes. Accessed June 13, 2024.

Livermore, George. "An Historical Research Respecting the Opinions of the Founders of the Republic on Negroes as Slaves, as Citizens, and as Soldiers." *Proceedings of the Massachusetts Historical Society, Volume 6*, Annual Meeting 1862–1863. Boston: John Wilson & Son, 1863.

Luttwak, Edward. "Toward Post-Heroic Warfare." *Foreign Affairs*, May–June 1995, 109-22.

Macrotrends.net. "U.S. Military Spending/Defense Budget 1960–2025." World Bank data. https://www.macrotrends.net/global-metrics/countries/usa/canada/military-spending-defense-budget. Accessed 6/3/24.

MacArthur, Douglas. *Reminiscences*. New York: McGraw-Hill, 1964.

Malkasian, Carter. *The American War in Afghanistan: A History*. New York: Oxford University Press, 2021.

Manchester, William. *American Caesar: Douglass MacArthur 1880–1964*. Boston: Little, Brown & Co., 1978.

McClellan, George B. "General George B. McClellan to President Abraham Lincoln, on the Peninsula Campaign." July 7, 1862. East Tennessee State University. https://faculty.etsu.edu/history/documents/mcclellan.htm. Accessed April 1, 2024.

McCormick, John, and Shannon Najimabadi. "Nikki Haley Says 'Of Course' Civil War Was About Slavery, Following Criticism." *Wall Street Journal*, December 28, 2023. https://www.wsj.com/politics/elections/nikki-haley-comes-under-criticism-for-failing-to-mention-slavery-as-cause-of-civil-war-6dce6dd1. Accessed March 21, 2024.

McCullough, David. *1776*. New York: Simon & Schuster, 2005.

McDonald, Forrest. "George Washington: Indispensable Man." *Imaginative Conservative*, February 21, 2022. https://theimaginativeconservative.org/2022/02/george-washington-indispensable-man-forrest-mcdonald.html.

McIntire, Tracey. "'We Bury Our Dead'—The Effects of Civil War Artillery." National Museum of Civil War Medicine, June 8, 2022. https://www.civilwarmed.org/effects-of-artillery/. Accessed March 22, 2024.

McPherson, James M. *Battle Cry of Freedom: The Civil War Era*. New York: Oxford University Press, 1988.

McPherson, James M. *Crossroads of Freedom: Antietam*. New York: Oxford University Press, 2002.

Mecca, Pete. "A Veteran's Story: The Japanese Failed Miserably." *Clayton News Daily*, December 7, 2018. https://www.news-daily.com/news/a-veteran-s-story-the-japanese-failed-miserably/article_59b501c1-a344-53a1-9c19-331733426522.html. Accessed May 15, 2024.

Middlebrook, Martin. *The Schweinfurt-Regensburg Mission*. New York: Charles Scribner's Sons, 1983.

Mitcham, Samuel W., Jr. *It Wasn't About Slavery: Exposing the Great Lie of the Civil War*. Washington, DC: Regnery Publishing, 2020.

Morison, Samuel Eliot. *The Two-Ocean War: A Short History of the United States Navy in the Second World War*. Boston: Little, Brown & Co., 1963.

Morton, Louis. *The Fall of the Philippines*. Washington, DC: Office of the Chief of Military History, Department of the Army, 1953.

Mossman, Billy C. *Ebb and Flow: November 1950–July 1951.* Washington, DC: Center of Military History, U.S. Army, 1990.

Moyar, Mark. *Triumph Forsaken: The Vietnam War, 1954–1965.* New York: Cambridge University Press, 2006.

Moyar, Mark. *Triumph Regained: The Vietnam War, 1965–1968.* New York: Encounter Books, 2022.

The Napoleon Series Archive. https://www.napoleon-series.org/research/abstract/population/britain/c_population1.html. Accessed January 25, 2024.

National Bureau of Economic Research. "Unemployment Rate for United States [M0892BUSM156SNBR]." NBER Macrohistory Database. https://fred.stlouisfed.org/series/M0892BUSM156SNBR. Accessed April 15, 2024.

National Constitution Center. "How Thomas Paine's Other Pamphlet Saved the Revolution." December 19, 2022. https://constitutioncenter.org/blog/how-thomas-paines-other-pamphlet-saved-the-revolution. Accessed November 19, 2023.

National Museum of the Pacific War. "Admiral Chester W. Nimitz." https://www.pacificwarmuseum.org/about/admiral-nimitz. Accessed May 5, 2024.

National Museum of the United States Air Force. "Brig. Gen. William 'Billy' Mitchell." https://www.nationalmuseum.af.mil/Visit/Museum-Exhibits/Fact-Sheets/Display/Article/196418/brig-gen-william-billy-mitchell/. Accessed May 23, 2024.

National Museum of the United States Army. "George B. McClellan." https://www.thenmusa.org/biographies/george-b-mcclellan/#:~:text=He%20frequently%20clashed%20with%20Lincoln,for%20a%20time.%E2%80%9D%20Despite%20his. Accessed March 28, 2024.

National Museum of World War II Aviation. "U.S. Navy Exercise Simulated Pearl Harbor Attack 18 Months Before It Happened." June 15, 2021. https://www.worldwariiaviation.org/u-s-navy-exercise-simulated-pearl-harbor-attack-18-months-before-it-happened. Accessed April 19, 2024.

National Park Service. "History & Culture—Guilford Courthouse National Military Park." https://www.nps.gov/guco/learn/historyculture/index.htm. Accessed January 9, 2024.

National Park Service. "An Invitation to Battle: Special Orders 191." Monocacy National Battlefield. Last updated May 27, 2020. https://www.nps.gov/mono/learn/historyculture/an-invitation-to-battle.htm#xiv. Accessed March 31, 2024.

National Park Service. "A Mere Matter of Marching: Thomas Jefferson to William Duane, August 4, 1812." https://www.nps.gov/articles/a-mere-matter-of-marching.htm. Accessed January 23, 2024.

National World War II Museum. "Kermit Tyler: A Call That Would Live in Infamy." https://www.nationalww2museum.org/war/articles/kermit-tyler-call-would-live-infamy. Accessed April 21, 2024.

National World War II Museum. "Remembering Pearl Harbor, A Pearl Harbor Fact Sheet." https://www.census.gov/history/pdf/pearl-harbor-fact-sheet-1.pdf. Accessed April 22, 2024.

Naval Encyclopedia. "Imperial Japanese Navy WW2." https://naval-encyclopedia.com/ww2/imperial-japanese-navy-ww2.php?amp=1. Accessed April 15, 2024.

NavSource Naval History. https://www.navsource.org/Naval/usf01.htm. Accessed May 16, 2024.

Nguyen, Hanh. "US-Vietnam Trade Ties: Challenge Ahead." *Journal of the Indo-Pacific Affairs*. March 29, 2023. https://www.airuniversityaf.edu/JIPA/Display/Article/3344116/usvietname-trade-ties-challenge-ahead/. Accessed June 10, 2024.

O'Connor, Christopher. "A Japanese Connection." *Naval History Magazine*, U.S. Naval Institute, December 2016. https://www.usni.org/magazines/naval-history-magazine/2016/december/taranto-pearl-harbor-connection. Accessed April 18, 2024.

Office of Naval Intelligence, U.S. Navy. *Early Raids in the Pacific Ocean, February 1 to March 10, 1942*. Washington, DC, 1943.

"One in Twenty—The 398th's Killed in Action." 398th Bomb Group Memorial Association. https://www.398th.org/History/KIA/index.html. Accessed June 28, 2024.

Pancake, John S. *This Destructive War: The British Campaign in the Carolinas, 1780–1782*. Tuscaloosa: University of Alabama Press, 1985.

Peters, Ralph. *Never Quit the Fight*. Mechanicsburg, PA: Stackpole Books, 2006.

Pogue, Forrest C. *George Marshall: Ordeal and Hope: 1939–1942*. New York: Viking Adult, 1966.

Price, Gordon W. *At Dawn We Slept: The Untold Story of Pearl Harbor*. New York: Penguin Books, 1981.

Radio Free Europe/Radio Liberty. "Explainer: The 'Kamikaze' Drones Iran Used to Attack Israel." April 14, 2024. https://www.rferl.org/a/iran-shahed-drones-israel-attack/32904882.html. Accessed June 4, 2024.

Reimers, David. "Blueprints for Destruction." *Naval History Magazine,* U.S. Naval Institute, August 2018. https://www.usni.org/magazines/naval-history-magazine/2018/august/blueprints-destruction. Accessed April 19, 2024.

"Remarks by President Bush, August 5, 1990." Margaret Thatcher Foundation. https://www.margaretthatcher.org/document/110704. Accessed June 10, 2024.

Remmelink, Willem, ed. *The Operations of the Navy in the Dutch East Indies and the Bay of Bengal: Compiled by the War History Office of the National Defense College of Japan*. Leiden, Netherlands: Leiden University Press, 2018.

Riccioni, Everest. "Strategic Bombing: Always a Myth." *Proceedings*, November 1996. https://www.usni.org/magazines/proceedings/1996/november/strategic-bombing-always-myth. Accessed June 27, 2024.

Ricks, Thomas E. *Fiasco: The American Military Adventure in Iraq*. New York: Penguin Press, 2006.

Ricks, Thomas E. *The Generals: American Military Command from World War II to Today*. New York: Penguin Press, 2012.

Ridgway, Matthew B. *The Korean War*. New York: Doubleday, 1967.

Rohwer, J., and M. S. Monakov. *Stalin's Ocean-Going Fleet: Soviet Naval Strategy and Shipbuilding Programmes, 1935-1953*. London: Frank Cass Publishers, 2001.

Roosevelt, Theodore. *The Naval War of 1812*. New York: G.P. Putnam's Sons, 1883.

Roper Center for Public Opinion Research. "Polling and Pearl Harbor." December 1, 2016. https://ropercenter.cornell.edu/blog/polling-and-pearl-harbor. Accessed May 19, 2024.

Saad, Lydia. "Gallup Vault: Hawks vs. Doves on Vietnam." Gallup, May 24, 2016. https://news.gallup.com/vault/191828/gallup-vault-hawks-doves-vietnam.aspx. Accessed June 10, 2024.

Schaffer, Ronald. *Wings of Judgment: American Bombing in World War II*. New York: Oxford University Press, 1985.

Schaller, Michael. *The American Occupation of Japan: The Origins of the Cold War in Asia*. New York: Oxford University Press, 1985.

Schecter, Barnet. *The Battle for New York: The City at the Heart of the American Revolution*. New York: Walker and Company, 2002.

Schnabel, James F. *Policy and Direction: The First Year*. Washington, DC: Center of Military History, U.S. Army, 1992.

Schom, Alan. *The Eagle and the Rising Sun*. New York: W.W. Norton & Co, 2004.

Shafroth, John. "The Strategy of the Yorktown Campaign, 1781." *Proceedings*, Vol. 57/6/340, U.S. Naval Institute, June 1931. https://www.usni.org/magazines/proceedings/1931/june/strategy-yorktown-campaign-1781. Accessed August 13, 2024.

Singer, P. W. *Wired for War: The Robotics Revolution and Conflict in the Twenty-First Century*. New York: Penguin Press, 2009.

Speer, Albert. *Inside the Third Reich*. New York: Macmillan, 1970.

Stanage, Justin, communicated by Dr. Donald B. Marty. "The Rifle-Musket vs. the Smoothbore Musket, a Comparison of Effectiveness of the Two Types of Weapons Primarily at Short Ranges." Indiana University Department of History. https://scholarworks.iu.edu/journals/index.php/iusburj/article/download/19841/25918/43984. Accessed March 22, 2024.

Stempel, Jim. *American Hannibal: The Extraordinary Account of Revolutionary War Hero Daniel Morgan at the Battle of Cowpens*. Tucson, AZ: Penmore Press, 2018.

Stephens, Bret. "Do We Still Understand How Wars Are Won?" *New York Times*, May 28, 2024. https://www.nytimes.com/2024/05/28/opinion/israel-ukraine-war-us.html. Accessed June 10, 2024.

Stewart, Richard W., ed. *American Military History, Volume 1: The United States Army and the Forging of a Nation, 1775–1917*. Washington, DC: Center of Military History, U.S. Army, 2005.

Stoker, Donald. *The Grand Design: Strategy and the U.S. Civil War*. New York: Oxford University Press, 2010.

Tillman, Barrett. "Hard Targets." *Air Force Magazine*, February 2015. https://www.airandspaceforces.com/PDF/MagazineArchive/Magazine%20Documents/2015/February%202015/0215targets.pdf. Accessed June 27, 2024.

Toland, John. *In Mortal Combat: Korea, 1950–1953*. New York: William Morrow & Co., 1991.

"Transcript of News Conference of April 7, 1954, by President Eisenhower." In *Foreign Relations of the United States, 1952–1954, Indochina*, Volume XIII, Part 1. Office of the Historian, Department of State. https://history.state.gov/historicaldocuments/frus1952-54v13p1/d716. Accessed June 10, 2024.

Trevelyan, Sir George Otto. *The American Revolution, Part 1*. New York: Longmans, Green and Co., 1915.

Trowbridge, John. "'Doomed to Their Fate': Kentuckians at Dudley's Defeat, 5 May 1813." *Kentucky Ancestors: Genealogical Quarterly of the Kentucky Historical Society* 40, no. 3 (2005).

Truman, Harry S. *Years of Trial and Hope*. New York: Doubleday & Co., 1956.

Tupper, Ferdinand Brock. *The Life and Correspondence of Major-General Sir Isaac Brock*. London: Simpkin, Marshall & Co., 1846.

UK Ministry of Defense. Freedom of Information Act Release, Reference FOI2017/04440, April 28, 2017, 4.

U.S. National Archives. The Emancipation Proclamation (1863). https://www.archives.gov/milestone-documents/emancipation-proclamation. Accessed April 6, 2024.

"The United States Army Air Forces in World War II." https://web.archive.org/web/20090211101806/http://usaaf.net/chron/43/apr43.htm. Accessed June 18, 2024.

"The United States Army Air Forces in World War II." https://web.archive.org/web/20090212182006/http://usaaf.net/chron/43/aug43.htm. Accessed June 19, 2024.

University of Maryland Baltimore County. "Slave, Free Black, and White Population, 1780–1830." https://userpages.umbc.edu/~bouton/History407/SlaveStats.htm. Accessed January 22, 2024.

U.S. Census Bureau. "Bicentennial Edition: Historical Statistics of the United States, Colonial Times to 1970." Part 1, Chapter A, 8. https://www.census.gov/library/publications/1975/compendia/hist_stats_colonial-1970.html. Accessed January 22, 2024.

U.S. Census Bureau. "Fast Facts." https://www.census.gov/history/www/through_the_decades/fast_facts/. Accessed May 23, 2024.

U.S. Census Bureau. "U.S. Census Bureau History: Battle of the Little Bighorn." https://www.census.gov/history/www/homepage_archive/2016/june_2016.html. Accessed April 14, 2024.

"U.S. Destroyer Sunk, 44 of 120 Crew Rescued; President Sees No Change in Foreign Policy; Germans Gain in Drive Southwest Of Moscow." *New York Times*, November 1, 1941. https://timesmachine.nytimes.com/timesmachine/1941/11/01/99323416.html?pageNumber=1. Accessed May 19, 2024.

U.S. Holocaust Memorial Museum. "How Did Public Opinion About Entering World War II Change Between 1939 and 1941?" https://exhibitions.ushmm.org/americans-and-the-holocaust/us-public-opinion-world-war-II-1939-1941. Accessed May 19, 2024.

U.S. House of Representatives. "38th Congress (1863–1865)." History, Art & Archives. https://history.house.gov/Congressional-Overview/Profiles/38th/. Accessed April 6, 2024.

U.S. Strategic Bombing Survey. *The United States Strategic Bombing Surveys, Summary Report*. Maxwell Air Force Base, AL: Air University Press, 1987.

USS *Constitution* Museum. "War of 1812 Overview." https://ussconstitutionmuseum.org/major-events/war-of-1812-overview/. Accessed August 13, 2024.

"VIII Bomber Command 119." American Air Museum in Britain. https://www.americanairmuseum.com/archive/mission/viii-bomber-command-119. Accessed June 24, 2024.

"Wanna Fight America? 5 Reasons the U.S. Military Will Make You Dead." *National Interest*, May 19, 2019. https://nationalinterest.org/blog/buzz/wanna-fight-america-5-reasons-us-military-will-make-you-dead-58422[1]. Accessed June 10, 2024.

Washington, George, to John Hancock, July 10, 1776. Founders Online, National Archives. https://founders.archives.gov/documents/Washington/03-05-02-0188. Accessed November 14, 2023.

Washington, George, to Maj. Gen. Charles Lee, December 1, 1776. Founders Online, National Archives. https://founders.archives.gov/documents/Washington/03-07-02-0180. Accessed November 20, 2023.

Waters, Andrew. "To the End of the World: Cornwallis Pursues Morgan to the Catawba." *Journal of the American Revolution*, May 23, 2019. https://allthingsliberty.com/2019/05/to-the-end-of-the-world-cornwallis-pursues-morgan-to-the-catawba/. Accessed January 10, 2024.

Watson, Mark Skinner. *Chief of Staff: Prewar Plans and Preparations*. Washington, DC: Center of Military History, U.S. Army, 1991.

Weinberg, Gerhard L. *A World at Arms: A Global History of World War II*. Cambridge: Cambridge University Press, 2005.

Wilson, David. *The Southern Strategy*. Columbia: University of South Carolina Press, 2005.

Wukovits, John. "Pearl Harbor Payback." Warfare History Network. https://warfarehistorynetwork.com/article/pearl-harbor-payback/. Accessed May 21, 2024.

Zhang, Shu Guang. *Mao's Military Romanticism: China and the Korean War, 1950–1953*. Lawrence: University Press of Kansas, 1995.

Index